CITIES OF GOLD

"By setting out with two companions and six horses to track Coronado's army across a thousand miles of brutal desert and mountain country, from the Mexican border through Arizona into New Mexico, the author was ready to risk his life to try to see with his own eyes, as it were, 'that moment, 450 years ago, when the peoples of the Old World and the New World first encountered each other' along this path, and quickly began the strife-torn redefining of America.

"Throughout the book, Preston intersperses the original reports and memoirs of Coronado's adventure with accounts of his own party's hard progress, making the centuries dissolve into a common first-person, present-tense narrative. And along the way, he records stories of the people and places he encounters, making brief excursions into mining booms and busts, the history of livestock ranching, the impact of barbed wire and windmills, the first mail routes, homesteading, the destruction of Indian nations, current disputes over Forest Service and Bureau of Land Management policies, the role of the environmental movement, and much more.

"A book that is so crammed with flashbacks and digressions could become a labor to read, but this one never loses its momentum. The asides add meaning to the story."

—SMITHSONIAN MAGAZINE

"A torturous and sometimes comical attempt to trace Coronado's 450-year-old footsteps through the deserts and mountains of the American Southwest. . . . A *Blue Highways* on horseback, well worth the trip."

—KIRKUS REVIEWS

"This is popular history in its prime, with some extras thrown in. Not only does the reader get lucid history of people and places, but also an account of the journey with all its foibles. . . . a highly readable if somewhat offbeat narrative of a horseback trek across Arizona and New Mexico. The author's sense of mission and his enlivened style make the book a pleasure to read."

—NEW MEXICO MAGAZINE

"A riveting yarn, with as many turns as a switchback road. While relating an expedition jinxed with interpersonal problems and logistical obstacles, Preston slips in stories of gun battles, cattle drives, homesteading, and native American history and religion. . . . a resolutely intimate portrait of people and places."

—THE CHRISTIAN SCIENCE MONITOR

Also by *Douglas Preston*

The Royal Road: El Camino Real from Mexico City to Santa Fe
Photographs by Christine Preston
Text by Douglas Preston and José Antonio Esquibel

"This engaging book, beautifully illustrated and written, traces the route and history of El Camino Real, the great road north from Mexico City to the distant provincial capital of Santa Fe. The authors and photographer examine this exceptional artery of overland commerce, giving us a remarkable portrait of an unfamiliar but unforgettable slice of our continental history. It will be welcomed by all who seek to know our Hispanic past."
—MARC SIMMONS

192 pages, 86 color photos, 3 maps
Cloth: 0-8263-1935-1   Paper: 0-8263-1936-x

Talking to the Ground: One Family's Journey on Horseback Across the Sacred Land of the Navajo

"A gripping adventure that blends Navajo mysticism, prophecy and the epic story of creation with the day-to-day account of a family's physical struggle across the Southwest's deserts and mountains—and their spiritual struggle to find their place in the world."
—PHOENIX GAZETTE

284 pages, maps, photos   Paper: 0-8263-1740-5

Also of interest

Pueblos, Villages, Forts & Trails: A Guide to New Mexico's Past
David Grant Noble

"Noble has squeezed a huge amount of valuable information into his handy guide to New Mexico's historical places. Travelers will find it an indispensable reference, one that will enhance any tour of the Land of Enchantment."
—MARC SIMMONS

357 pages, maps, photos   Paper: 0-8263-1485-6

A
Journey
Across the
American Southwest

University of New Mexico Press
Albuquerque

CITIES of GOLD

Douglas Preston

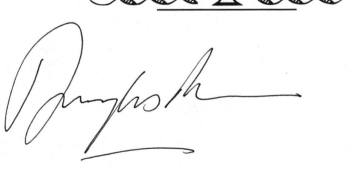

Designed by Nina D'Amario/Levavi & Levavi

Library of Congress Cataloging-in-Publication Data
Preston, Douglas J.
Cities of gold : a journey across the
American Southwest / Douglas Preston.
p.   cm.
Includes bibliographical references (p.   ) and index.
ISBN 0-8263-2086-4 (pbk. : alk. paper)
1. Southwest, New—Description and travel.
2. Southwest, New—History, Local.
3. Coronado, Francisco Vásquez de, 1510–1554.
4. Southwest, New—Discovery and exploration—Spanish.
5. Preston, Douglas J.—Journeys—Southwest, New.
I. Title.
F787.P74   1999
979—dc21   98-54583
CIP

THIS BOOK IS DEDICATED TO MY
BROTHER, DAVID PRESTON, M.D.
IT COMES WITH MY DEEPEST RESPECT,
ADMIRATION, AND LOVE.

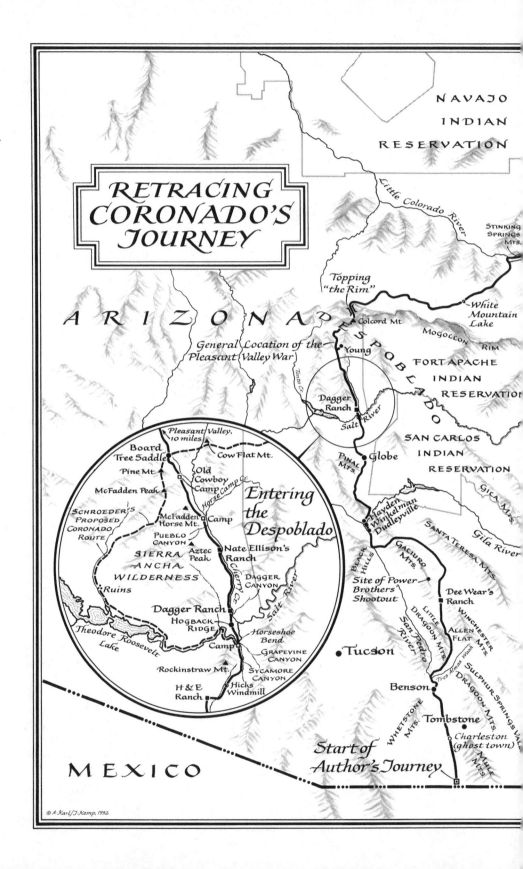

RETRACING CORONADO'S JOURNEY

NAVAJO INDIAN RESERVATION

Little Colorado River

STINKING SPRINGS MTS.

Topping "the Rim"

Colcord Mt.

White Mountain Lake

A R I Z O N A

MOGOLLON RIM

General Location of the Pleasant Valley War

Young

FORT APACHE INDIAN RESERVATION

Tonto Cr.

Dagger Ranch

Salt River

SAN CARLOS INDIAN RESERVATION

Pleasant Valley, 10 miles

Board Tree Saddle

Cow Flat Mt.

Pine Mt.

Old Cowboy Camp

McFadden Peak

Horse Camp Cr.

PINAL MTS.

Globe

GILA MTS.

SCHROEDER'S PROPOSED CORONADO ROUTE

McFadden Horse Mt.

Camp

Entering the Despoblado

Hayden Winkelman Dudleyville

Gila River

SANTA TERESA MTS.

PUEBLO CANYON

SIERRA ANCHA WILDERNESS

Aztec Peak

Nate Ellison's Ranch

Cherry Cr.

DAGGER CANYON

BLACK HILLS

GACIURO MTS.

Site of Power Brothers Shootout

Dee Wear's Ranch

WINCHESTER MTS.

Ruins

Salt River

Dagger Ranch

HOGBACK RIDGE

Camp

Horseshoe Bend

San Pedro River

LITTLE DRAGOON MTS.

ALLEN FLAT

Theodore Roosevelt Lake

Rockinstraw Mt.

GRAPEVINE CANYON

SYCAMORE CANYON

Tucson

SULPHUR SPRINGS VALLEY

H & E Ranch

Hicks Windmill

Tres Almas Wash

DRAGOON MTS.

Benson

WHETSTONE MTS.

Tombstone

MEXICO

Start of Author's Journey

Charleston (ghost town)

MULE MTS.

© A. Karl/J. Kemp, 1992

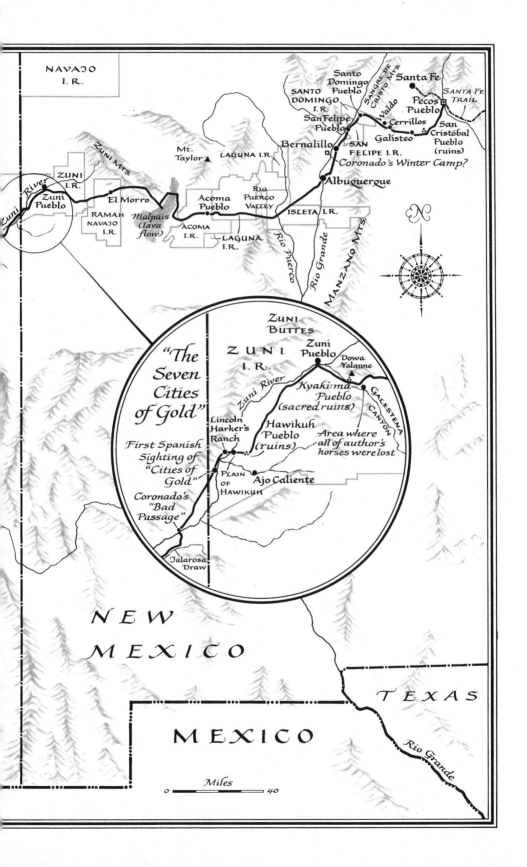

A NOTE TO THE READER

This is a book about a journey, on horseback, across a thousand miles of desert and mountain wilderness in Arizona and New Mexico, following the trail of the first European to explore the American Southwest. It is, ultimately, an attempt to understand that first shocking meeting between Europeans and native Americans in what would become the United States—and the fatal consequences that resulted. For us personally, it would be an elegiac journey through the dying West; for what we saw and experienced will, in a few short years, disappear completely. This is not another story of the winning of the West; it is, rather, a story of loss.

During our journey we ran into many different people: Indians, ranchers, cowpunchers, old prospectors, rattlesnake hunters. Around campfires, in corrals, in hogans, in pickup trucks, these people talked about their lives, about growing up in the Southwest, about finding gold, about losing their ranches, about cattle drives and bronc busting. As they talked, I recorded what they said (with their permission, of course). The stories that are told in this book are transcribed from those tapes, with editing only for clarity and economy. If some vulgar words of language crept into the conversation, I ask pardon, and I assure the reader that I am as shocked, *shocked*, as he or she is by such language. As for those conversations related herein that were not taped, I either took notes or recorded them later from memory, and I believe them to be accurate. In fact, everything in this book is true, or at least I believe it to be true—except that I changed some of the names of people we met, because I didn't want to cause trouble for them back home.

This book is not a comprehensive history of the Southwest. Rather, it is a narrow slice through the bedrock of time, with a slight polishing to bring out the grain. In these pages, the reader will be taken backward and forward in space and time, from the earliest prehistoric Indians to the present day, with many odd and peculiar stops in between. I beg the reader's forgiveness for any jackrabbit starts, sudden stops, and fast turns that may occur as we travel about the centuries. Just hang on and don't worry too much how we're going to get from one place to the next, because I'm not so sure myself.

All this was a long time ago, I remember,
And I would do it again, but set down
This set down
This: were we led all that way for
Birth or Death? There was a Birth, certainly,
We had evidence and no doubt. I had seen birth and death,
But had thought they were different; this Birth was
Hard and bitter agony for us, like Death, our death.
We returned to our places, these Kingdoms,
But no longer at ease here, in the old dispensation,
With an alien people clutching their gods.
I should be glad of another death.
                    —T. S. Eliot, from *The Journey of the Magi*

"When the. . .memory of my tribe shall have become a myth
among the White Men, these shores will swarm with the invisible
dead of my tribe, and when your children's children think
themselves alone in the field, the store, the shop, upon the highway,
or in the silence of the pathless woods, they will not be alone. At
night when the streets of your cities and villages are silent and you
think them deserted, they will throng with the returning hosts that
once filled and still love this beautiful land. The White Man will
never be alone.

"Let him be just and deal kindly with my people, for the dead
are not powerless. Dead, did I say? There is no death, only a
change of worlds."
                    —Seathl, Dwamish chief, 1854

BOOK
ONE

1

When I was growing up, I spent my summers in an old farmhouse on the Maine seacoast. The upstairs bathroom floor had once been covered with linoleum by my grandmother, who thought the old pine boards underneath a sanitary hazard. Imprinted on the linoleum was a giant map of the United States, and by chance the terrain of the bathroom placed the state of New Mexico directly in front of the toilet.

That was how I first heard of New Mexico.

Countless times as a child, I found myself staring at this linoleum state, wondering what sort of place it might be, and if it really was part of America. I imagined myself wandering along nameless roads, the dust rising in curtains, the silvery branches of dead trees trembling in the heat. New Mexico became, in my mind, a strange, empty, mysterious land.

This idea never quite left me. After graduating from college, I took a job in New York City and rented a small apartment on the Upper West Side. After about five years there, I started having a recurring dream. In the dream I woke up in my apartment, got out of bed, and discovered a door that I had never noticed before. The door opened into a large, whitewashed room, with dust motes drifting in banners of

17

light. Through casement windows I could see a landscape of sandstone and yucca, with a line of blue mountains in the distance. The discovery filled me with an inexpressible feeling of joy, as if I had been released from a prison.

Then I really did wake up. There was, of course, no door where I had found one: only a flimsy wall beyond which my neighbors could be heard arguing or listening to the BeeGees. Outside, a siren wailed under a leaden sky as dark figures scurried through the rain toward the subway.

I eventually ended up with a wonderful job, at an outrageously good salary, working for a decent company, with my own office on 57th Street. Things were looking good. I hadn't cooked my own dinner in four years, and like any good yuppie I employed a maid and rented a beachhouse on Long Island in the summer. I thought of myself as a fine, brilliant, successful fellow.

But I kept having the recurring dream. It was a symptom of something, and I began to feel restless and dissatisfied. One day I woke up and, quite unexpectedly, realized that my job was loathsome, my apartment odious, and the city I lived in execrable.

So I quit my job, dropped off my Brooks Brothers suits at the Salvation Army, packed up my car, and moved to Santa Fe, New Mexico. It was the influence of my grandmother's bathroom; it represented something as far removed from my previous life as I could get.

I first had the idea to make the journey that resulted in this book in the spring. I had rented a house with crooked adobe walls in an old part of town. The house sat at the end of a muddy alley flanked by two wrecked cars sunk in chamisa and tumbleweed. An old horse, which apparently did nothing but eat weeds, inhabited the yard next door.

One March evening I walked up to a little hillock behind my house to watch the sun set. The snow had melted away and a scribble of blue flowers had appeared against the red earth. On top of the rise, scattered on the ground around me, I noticed what looked like a few shards of glass glinting in the sun. Disgusted, I reached down to collect them, only to discover that they weren't glass at all, but flakes of obsidian, each chip as thin and precise as a contact lens. Many centuries ago, an Indian had stopped here and deftly flaked out an arrowhead before continuing on his way. It was a perfect little spot to stop for a rest, with a view of the bosque surrounding the Santa Fe

River and out across the plains south of town; an excellent place to search for game or an enemy. Or maybe, to this unknown knapper, it was just a lovely view.

It was a moving, and unsettling, little discovery. In coming to New Mexico, I had unexpectedly felt myself an alien—an immigrant—in my own country, and this lithic scatter reinforced this feeling. I was reminded that we Americans are interlopers on this continent; that we have built our great and towering civilization on the wreckage of a past that we know almost nothing about and can scarcely comprehend. This sprinkling of obsidian, this trash of a distant time, represented something that had once been alive and vibrant, and that had left its ghostly traces all over the Southwest.

Sitting on the hillock, it occurred to me that even after 450 years of occupation, we Americans are still immigrants of sorts; we have not been fully able to make this continent our home—at least not in the sense that "home" is to most peoples. We Americans are a rootless, wandering people, and our living places are fungible: suburban Los Angeles will do as well as the Jersey shore or downtown Cleveland. We cannot even begin to comprehend people—like most American Indian tribes—so rooted to their homes that they would die if removed. In the Southwest I had experienced landscapes so fearfully vast and disorienting that I could not grasp them. These were not landscapes embedded in my genetic heritage, and I felt a stranger in a very strange land indeed.

I began to wonder just what this continent was like when Europeans first arrived—that moment, 450 years ago, when the peoples of the Old World and the New World first encountered each other within the borders of what would become America. I became obsessed with that moment of contact. This was a historical event as shocking and profound as any in the human history of this planet. Unlike the normal ponderous cycles of history, it was a flash in time, a sudden, terrifying instant that left both Europeans and native Americans forever changed. The peoples of two worlds, who had coexisted for twenty thousand or thirty thousand years unaware of each other's existence, were suddenly brought face-to-face. They would attempt to communicate in strange words and mute gestures, and almost immediately would begin killing one another—the first formal engagement between Europeans and Indians on what would become American soil. The battle would last only a few hours, but when it was over the continent—and the world—would have started on a journey that would change it utterly. America was conceived in that moment; and in that same moment another world began to die. That long and bitter journey would end 350 years and 6 months later, on the frozen prairie near Wounded Knee Creek.

There must be, I thought, some way to peel back these layers of history, to rediscover the land and see it as it once was, to understand in a small way what this convulsive moment had been like. In doing so, I felt I would understand finally what it meant to be an American. One could not understand the endpoint without understanding the beginning.

This was when I first had the idea to retrace the route of the Spanish explorer Francisco Vásquez de Coronado. He was the first European to explore the Southwest, coming up from Mexico in 1540 looking for the Seven Cities of Gold. Coronado had been the first to penetrate the deep interior of our continent. I found it extraordinary that eighty years before the Pilgrims landed on Plymouth Rock—and before Shakespeare was even born—a European army had wandered, angry and lost, as far inland as the plains of central Kansas.

The North American continent, locked in slow, immense Stone Age cycles of life, ceremony, and death, was suddenly laid open with one clean stroke. What *was* this country like when white faces first peered over the deserts, when the canyons first echoed with the sound of harquebuses, when the Zuni Indians first saw, approaching from the west, men in armor on horses—a sight so strange that they believed they were seeing the coming of a terrifying new beast?

I wanted to understand what it was that made me an *American*, that quality that bound all of us various immigrants together, and a journey like this seemed a good way to do it. It would be a way to step outside of America while still remaining inside its borders. It still shakes me to the core to think that the very founding of our civilization as well as the standard of living we now enjoy—in fact everything we Americans have—were made possible only through the extinction of hundreds of rich and complex cultures that had evolved on this land across two hundred centuries. What *were* these ancient southwestern civilizations that fell before the Europeans? And was this America we have created worth it?

Can such an outrageous question even be asked?

Most of America has changed so profoundly that in most areas nothing is left of the aboriginal landscape. As I researched the idea of retracing Coronado's journey, however, I made a rather startling discovery: most of the landscapes through which he passed remain almost exactly as they were in 1540. Indeed, the population along most of his route is actually *less* today than it was 450 years ago. Very few changes had occurred in this arid and remote country of mesquite, slickrock, and blue sky.

Thus, by following Coronado's route I would see this landscape unfold almost exactly as it did for the first Europeans. It seemed extraordinary that something like this could still be done in America in the late twentieth century. And by following Coronado's route *beyond* the Seven Cities of Gold to Pecos Pueblo, I would also encounter the direct descendants of the Indians who fought Coronado—those people who witnessed the "discovery" by Europeans of their continent. I wondered what they might have to say about Coronado, the Spanish, and what it means to be an Indian living in America today.

This journey offered the potential for uncovering some kind of truth—metaphysical and historical—about the opening of North America and the subsequent evolution of the Southwest and its people. Where I encountered ranches and towns, I would also see the changes that civilization had wrought. I would have a chance to see how the Southwest had evolved in the four and a half centuries since Coronado swept through.

Thus, I would have a glimpse of the American Southwest at two moments in time. It would be two parallel journeys: Coronado's and my own. The juxtaposition of the two might reveal a deeper understanding of the discovery and conquest of the Southwest.

Coronado's exploration of the Southwest was no trivial piece of work. Indeed, it was the largest expedition of discovery ever launched in the history of the New World—and it may even have been the biggest expedition ever. Among other things, Coronado and his men were the first Europeans to discover the Grand Canyon and the Colorado River, the upper Río Grande, the Pueblo Indians, the Rocky Mountains, the Great Plains, and the Arkansas River. They were the first to bring horses, cattle, and sheep into the Southwest, three animals that would have a profound effect on the development of the region (and also making the expedition the first cattle drive in the American West). Most significantly, they brought a new type of war to the Indians: a war fought with guns and cannon, and a war that didn't obey the ancient rules.

After reading through the Coronado narratives and looking at his probable routes on a map, I realized there was only one practical way to cover this rough and exceedingly remote desert and mountain country. I would have to do it the way he had: on horseback, packing my food, camping in the desert, and finding water and grass where I could. No jeep could possibly cover this ground, and the desert was too hot, and the distances between water and food too great, to do it on foot. By getting off the roads and into the desert, by mingling with the Navajos, Zunis, Acomas, and other Indians, as well as the cowboys and ranchers, by riding through the ruins of the past and the pueblos of the present, I had a chance to slice through the layers of history. No journey by car would ever achieve this. You can't drive up to a Navajo hogan or cowboy bunkhouse in a car and expect anybody to talk to you. But when you arrive on horseback, the Indians and cowboys alike (who still have a deep connection to the horse) will welcome you like family.

I decided to bring along a little shirt-pocket tape recorder. When I sat down in the cowboy bunkhouse or the Navajo hogan, I planned to record what people said; I wanted to ask them about their lives, what it was like growing up in the Southwest, and how things had changed.

No one had ever made a journey like this before. It would be a great adventure. I had visions of sitting around a fire in some vast bowl of the great southwestern desert, swapping stories with my partner and tilting a bottle of Jim Beam to my lips, while the horses, silhouetted against the stars, grazed nearby.

I wouldn't try it alone. I needed a suitable companion. That was when I thought of Walter Nelson.

Walter was my next-door neighbor, the first person I met in Santa Fe. One day, as I was trudging up the lane to my mailbox, I heard a shout and a small man with a red face came swinging out his gate, hand extended. He wore an Australian cowboy hat, cowboy boots with electrician's tape around the left toe, jeans, and a faded workshirt with pearl snap buttons. A red bandanna was tied around his neck and a sheathed knife hung from his belt. Now the truth is I don't precisely remember what he was wearing that day, but I know it was as I described it because he never wore anything else. The only thing he ever changed was the electrician's tape around the boot, since it periodically wore through, letting the sole flap.

Walter was an artist and a photographer. When we met, he was working on a monumental series of paintings which he entitled "Catholicism from Baja Merging with Mayan Tradition from Chiapas,'' called the White Series for short. He worked feverishly from six in the morning until midnight, every day of the week.

All he seemed to eat were beans and rice. He owed money to many people. When his phone service was eventually cut off he would come over to the house (which I shared with my girlfriend) to argue with his creditors. Once every few months he would sell a painting or a portfolio of prints for $5,000 and pay off some of his debts, but he never did catch up. He hadn't filed tax returns for a number of years and finally the IRS came after him.

"I owe the Government," Walter would say darkly. "When the Government wants their money, they *know* how to *git* it."

Walter had once been a successful commercial photographer in Dallas, making a quarter of a million dollars a year doing the Neiman-Marcus catalogs and various annual reports. "I'll never go back to that shit," he often declared after arguing with the electric company over a fifteen-dollar bill. "I'm an Artist."

His house was full of odd things: a bird skeleton picked up in the Australian Outback; the dried eye socket of a hammerhead shark; a cow pelvis from the Texas Panhandle; an old mask from Chihuahua; a half-carved piece of marble; skulls, potsherds, arrowheads, a huge copper cauldron.

Walter became a regular visitor. He'd take a break from his painting around four-thirty and I would hear him shout: "I'm comin' over, git your clothes on." (This latter statement was an allusion to the fact that my girlfriend and I worked at home; Walter had peculiar and no doubt vivid ideas of what we must be doing shut up in the house all day.)

"Let me talk you all out of a little vodka," he'd say, when he came over. Then he would gingerly return to his house balancing a tall glass tumbler brimming with clear liquid.

Later I would hear him, in a fit of exuberance, whooping and singing in his yard. "Doug!" he would cry out. "Git over here and take a look at this!"

The White Series was a powerful work. It was a group of three-dimensional paintings, mostly white, built up with layers of canvas, gravel from anthills, and thick textured paint. At the bottom of each painting was a shelf, on which Walter had placed offerings—shells, calla lilies—made of clay. The White Series was not the kind of art that someone would buy to match the drapes, and the art galleries in Santa

Fe, most of which sold howling coyotes to a middle-brow tourist trade, had no interest in his work.

Walter was my introduction to the Southwest. He disapproved of my working on a computer. It did not fit his conception of what a writer was supposed to be doing.

"What're you doin', sittin' all day in front of that machine?" he would say. "You got to git out and see some *country*."

A real writer, he said, wrote from experience. A real writer drank, fought in bars, and could gut and skin a deer in twenty minutes. A *real* writer would have no use for a computer.

One Saturday morning, Walter banged on my door and said, God-dammit, he was going to show me some country. We climbed into his Blazer and set off for a place he described as the most beautiful in the world. It lay in the canyons north of the little town of Abiquiu, New Mexico.

Walter had once lived in Abiquiu in a cabin with a wood stove and no telephone. He rented the place from a man named Benito. Benito was a *genízaro*, a Hispanicized Navajo who owned a restaurant outside of town. The restaurant had a big sign that said "OPEN" and another that said "CLOSED," the truth being that Benito only fed his friends. We drove up among the rusted piles of machinery that constituted his front yard, and Walter gave a shout. Benito came out on his porch and broke into a slow grin, revealing a pair of yellow teeth. Inside, dozens of stuffed deer heads and mounted antlers were piled on the tables, and the place smelled faintly of corruption and decay.

"Redecorating," Benito said. He had been redecorating for three years.

"I'm showing this Yankee from New York some country," Walter explained.

Benito turned a pair of cloudy eyes on me. "New York," he repeated slowly, as if pronouncing the name of a disease. "New York City?"

"New York City," I said, rather embarrassed.

"You lived there?" he asked.

I confirmed that I had.

"You a long way from home, man," he said.

On the drive out Walter had been telling me about the salubrious effects of Abiquiu air, and now he commanded that I dump the water out of my canteen. "You ain't tasted *water* until you've tasted Abiquiu water," he cried out.

We still hadn't seen country, Walter said. He was going to take me to a place called Copper Canyon. We got back in his car and went past Abiquiu where, without warning, he drove off the road into the chamisa brush. As we drove along it soon became apparent that we were following the bottom of a dry wash. The wash wandered into the mouth of a canyon with steep walls of crossbedded gravels and clay.

After an interminable amount of lurching and pounding along, the canyon widened into an immense bowl rimmed by thousand-foot mesas. The wash split into a dozen dry tributaries coming in from every direction. Walter stopped in a scattering of conical juniper bushes.

Ahead of us stretched a wilderness of erosion: gullied badlands threaded by dry washes, tents of sandstone capped by flat boulders, hills striped red, white, and gray. Here and there a wind-blasted piñon tree—a confusion of dead, corkscrew branches—clung to a rock. In the far distance, tier upon tier of mesas piled up, ending in a distant line of rimrock etched against a blue sky. Everything looked untidy and incomplete, as if the place were only half finished. The smell of unfired clay rose from the earth, and when I bit down I could feel the crunch of grit between my teeth.

Walter hopped out of the Blazer, cupped his hands around his mouth, and let out a yell the likes of which I had never heard before. As the echoes came tumbling back from vast distances, he turned to me with a grin.

"Now you're seein' *country.*"

⬥ ⬥ ⬥

Despite our obvious differences, we became good friends. And we were very different. I came from Boston, and most of the male members of my family had gone to either Harvard or Princeton and the females to Wellesley. Walter came from Wichita Falls, Texas, the tornado capital of the United States, and spelled the word wash, "warsh." I was thirty-two; he was forty-seven. I worried about money and my career and doing the right thing and what other people thought of me; Walter, on the other hand, didn't give a damn about anything but his art and his girlfriend, Robin. He had recently punched out a cop in Dallas who had spoken to him rudely; he drank heavily, swore often, and knew how to frame up a house, plumb, weld, mix cement, and fix cars—all miraculous abilities as far as I was concerned. He had once been a born-again Christian (now lapsed) and had wept at the foot of *penitente* crosses in the remote sand hills of New Mexico.

I decided to invite Walter along on my proposed trip, because he was tough and understood the desert. He didn't look like a quitter. I thought we would make a good team.

He agreed to come along as the trip photographer. We talked to various Coronado scholars and mapped out a route. We would not ride the entire Coronado route, but only the portion across the Southwest from the Mexico-Arizona border to the ruins of Pecos Pueblo, at the gateway to the Great Plains. We soon discovered that his actual route through what would become Arizona was much in dispute, there being several possibilities (see map). Out of a perverse sense of adventure, we decided to take the longest and most difficult, with an additional seventy-five-mile detour along a second possible route. We began mapping it out on large-scale, 1:250,000 topographic maps, and gradually working down to a finer scale.

As the maps got smaller, our apprehension increased.

We ended up with 175 U.S.G.S. topographic maps at a scale of 1:24,000, in which a mile equaled approximately an inch; our actual route was fifty-eight feet long. As we scrutinized map after map—some crowded with dense topographic lines indicating savage mountains, others nearly blank, showing vast, waterless deserts—we began to get a little nervous about our prospects. Most of the time there were no trails whatsoever, and in places water sources were twenty or more miles apart. For one fifty-five-square-mile stretch of eastern Arizona no map even existed.

What concerned us most was the Mogollon Rim country of Arizona and the deserts beyond—what the Spaniards had called the *despoblado,* the howling wilderness. It took Coronado fifteen days to cross the *despoblado,* which consisted of a hundred-mile stretch of mountains culminating in the thousand-foot wall of the Rim itself, and a fifty-mile stretch of harsh desert beyond the Rim. The crossing of Rim country alone nearly killed Coronado and his men, and we wondered whether we would suffer the same fate.

Beyond the Rim, we would enter the southern part of the Colorado Plateau. Here the maps went white, the only markings being an occasional meandering topographic interval. This was harsh desert country, arid, trackless, and frightening.

It was hard to tell just how many ground miles we would have to cover in total, but I figured it at about seven hundred. I estimated we would average about twenty-five miles a day, and that the trip would take us about four weeks.

This is when Walter and I had our first argument.

"Lemme tell you something," Walter said after we'd spent two days poring over the maps, "that ain't no seven hundred miles. As far as ground distance goes, that's easily a thousand. And you're a damned fool if you think this trip is gonna take four weeks."

I thought this a ridiculous exaggeration. I had actually measured the route on the maps, but Walter was highly suspicious. "You can't tell jack looking at these maps," he said. "You gotta git out and see the country."

He wanted to scout out the route by low-flying plane before we left. Neither one of us had been in southern Arizona before, or anywhere along the route. I vehemently protested. I wanted to discover the country as we went along, just as Coronado did, and perhaps deal with some of the same problems he had. I did not want to know what lay over the next hill; that would be cheating.

"And what about water?" Walter said. "How do we know there's gonna be water where it's marked? Some of these maps are thirty years old."

"I want this to be the real thing," I said. "If there's no water then I guess we'll just have to keep riding till we find some."

Walter shook his head. "Jesus Christ, Doug, I don't know about this. I really don't."

I won the argument, and in retrospect we both agreed it was a good thing I did. If either of us had seen the country we were going to be riding through, we never, *ever*, would have attempted it.

The route would take us across nine Indian reservations: eight Pueblo Indian reservations and the Ramah Navajo reservation. I wrote to the governors of the eight pueblos and the president of the Ramah chapter of the Navajo Nation, asking permission. Negotiations continued for many months and at several points became rather delicate; Coronado was not popular with the Pueblo Indian tribes of New Mexico. Walter and I met with the governors and tribal councils of several tribes, explained what we were about, and submitted our routes for inspection, to ensure they were not going to pass over any sacred sites.

We next considered the problem of private land. There was no way we could possibly figure out who owned the land over seven hundred (or a thousand) miles of trail, so we figured we'd simply ride through. If we were caught, Walter would do the talking. I had faith in Walter's rough Texas charm to see us through any tricky situations.

Barbed-wire fences were also going to be a problem. We would have to find gates; if not, we would then have to "lay them down." (Cutting fences was not a healthy option; those who do usually end up dead.) I didn't have any idea how to "lay down" a barbed-wire fence, but Walter assured me he knew all about it.

I also decided, seeing as how I was a greenhorn Yankee from Boston, to hire a wrangler for the horses. Walter knew a bit more about horses than I did, but neither of us had experience in long-distance desert and mountain packing. So I asked around and hired a man I shall call Eusebio Mondragón. He was a fine talker and persuaded me that he was an expert wrangler and horse-packer. In addition to coming along himself, Eusebio would supply three horses, a packsaddle, and two riding saddles. He agreed to do the whole trip for $4,000; if it took longer than five weeks he would earn more on a pro-rata basis. I advanced him $2,750 and agreed to pay him the rest when we got back. We did not discuss what would happen should he be unable, or unwilling, to continue the journey at some point.

Eusebio thought it would be a good idea for me to go riding with him three times a week in the month before the trip. He lived in East Pecos, an old Spanish town in a valley where the Pecos River comes rushing, icy and loud, out of the Sangre de Cristo Mountains. The town wasn't far from our final destination of Pecos Pueblo.

He shared a three-room tarpaper shack with his wife. It sat in the middle of a half acre of hardpacked dirt. The kitchen was the center of life in the house, with a large wood stove for heat and cooking and a single hydrant delivering cold water into a plastic bucket. An outhouse stood on a little hill about twenty yards away. Nearby was a fifteen-foot pile of split piñon and juniper wood that Eusebio had cut, waiting to be sold. A dry wash, littered with burned mattresses, blackened tin cans, engine blocks, and other refuse, ran through some slickrock and junipers in the backyard. The shack looked out over the lush Pecos River Valley to the snow-covered mountains beyond.

A large, machine-made polyester rug depicting the Last Supper in Day-Glo colors dominated one room, and holy pictures hung in the others. Eusebio's saddles and tack, which he kept on racks, took up at least one-third of the tiny kitchen and added the aroma of warm leather and horse sweat to the smell of piñon smoke and roasting tortillas.

We rode in the mornings. Sometimes Eusebio would take me off the trail and into some light brush and steep slopes.

"See?" he would say proudly, pointing to King, the horse I was riding. "He's a good horse, handle this country good. We ain't going through any worse country than this."

"Oh no," I said in my ignorance.

"This is *rough* country," Eusebio said.

It certainly seemed so to me.

Once we came to a draw in the Sangre de Cristo foothills.

"I remember when we come through here after them wild horses. We shag ass, hoo boy! We come down offa that mountain, run 'em like hell!" He showed a row of teeth the color of burnt sienna. There were no more wild horses, Eusebio said. Somebody had shot them all.

He called the horse's breast collar a brassiere and always roared with laughter when I unhitched one.

"You gettin' good practice, boy! You bet!"

At the end of a morning's ride, we sat down at the linoleum table in the center of the kitchen and drank coffee. Often Eusebio's wife served homemade tortillas with beans, mutton, and hot green chiles, with a plate of Wonder Bread. "Watch out for them chiles," Eusebio would say, with a grin of anticipation as I bit into one.

I liked Eusebio's family. His wife, a short, gray-haired woman with a crossed eye, was part Taos Indian and a lovely person. While we sat eating around the kitchen table a procession of family members would pass through—grandchildren, children, cousins, nephews—all part of a complex web of relations.

I think Eusebio told me he was fifty-three. He was short and wiry, with a brown, wrinkled face, in which were set two intense brown eyes within deep, Asiatic lids. The top of his brow, which was almost always covered by his cowboy hat, was shockingly white. His speech was halting and explosive, punctuated with staccato gestures, vigorous noddings of the head, and rapid wrinklings and unwrinklings of his brow. He said he came from an old family that had settled in the Pecos River Valley centuries ago. The tiny Spanish town up the valley from Pecos bore his last name.

While we were planning the trip in his kitchen, Eusebio had asked me whether I was going to bring any drink along.

Sure, I said, why not.

"We don't need that shit," he replied. "That *bad* shit. I know. I used to drink that shit alla time."

Mrs. Mondragón nodded. "It was killing him," she said.

"One day," Eusebio said, "I say to myself, 'I gonna die or I gonna quit.' I start drinking that whiskey, *man* did I drink that whiskey!" Eusebio pounded on his breastbone.

"That's what he said. 'I'm going to die or quit,' " Mrs. Mondragón added.

"I was out on the floor, right there! Lying just like that! Stone cold!" The table rattled and shook under his thumping hands.

"I thought he *was* dead," said Mrs. Mondragón.

"Twenty-five years ago, and that was my last drink. That shit's *bad* stuff, you better believe it. And lemme tell you, it don't mix with horses neither, you bet!"

We decided on a dry trip.

Eusebio made it clear what his duties would be. "I ain't cooking, and I ain't washing up them dishes," he declared. "I don't do camp work. I'm a wrangler."

I also learned that Eusebio had been in prison. During one of our visits Walter once mentioned that he had spent a night in jail (that was after slugging the cop), and when Eusebio heard this he became animated.

"I know about them jails," he said. "When they slip that cold steel over your wrists, man, you *know* it!"

"You were in prison?" I asked.

"You're Goddamn right, State Pen."

"What'd you do?"

Eusebio was suddenly silent, his eyes narrowing.

He also said he had ridden the rails and been a migrant worker in Colorado. But whenever I tried to probe deeper Eusebio got suspicious. "You don't know *nothin'* 'bout me, boy. You ain't getting me in that book," and he wheezed with laughter. "Not me, no way! I ain't goin' in *no* book!"

Another time he mentioned a son in derisive terms. I said I didn't know he had a son.

"I ain't got no son now," he said, his face wrinkling with disgust. He then told a story about how his son had married a bad woman whose family turned the son against him. The son had eventually sued Eusebio for $20,000 for "being a bad father."

I asked Eusebio what that meant, "being a bad father."

"Sum-bitch say I don't raise him right!" Eusebio shouted, stabbing into the air with the blade of his hand.

"But that's ridiculous," I said. "You can't sue someone over that."

"He *sue!* Sum-bitch got a lawyer and sued me!"

The case dragged on for several years, and Eusebio finally settled for $6,000. "I said 'Go ahead, take the money! I don't give a shit! It's just money! *Take* it!' " The table danced under Eusebio's pounding. "I lose *everything.* I had to sell my horses, saddles, everything to pay that sum-bitch. When I'm gone, he's getting *nothing.* I'm rich too, got twenty acres up there," and he swept an arm toward the mountains.

Eusebio was a character, and I thought he would make an interesting companion on the trip. Even more so than Walter, his background and life were utterly different from mine. I also liked the idea that we would have someone of mixed Spanish-Indian descent along. Despite his quirks I knew he was a decent person.

The problem was that he—like us—had absolutely no idea of what he was getting into.

Walter and I disagreed about Eusebio. Walter disliked Eusebio from the beginning and made inquiries. "Dick Pool, down at the Camel Rock Ranch, tells me Eusebio's a Goddamn woodcutter," Walter reported. "What the hell you hire a woodcutter to wrangle us across a desert for?"

I defended Eusebio, saying he owned and bred horses, was a roper, and had caught and broken wild horses in the mountains around Pecos. He had also been, so he said, on long pack trips, which he described in convincing detail. Walter shook his head and went to see a cowboy friend of his, who showed him how to pack, hobble, feed, and doctor horses over hundreds of miles of desert travel. "When your woodcutter craps out," Walter muttered, "we're gonna have to survive on our own."

Things fell into place. A book publisher accepted my proposal and advanced me some money. The *Smithsonian* magazine liked the idea and offered to sponsor the trip. Most of the people we talked to thought it was a terrific idea.

There were a few exceptions. A man we respected—a wilderness guide, fly fisherman, and outdoorsman—was not enthusiastic. He had spent some time in the Mogollon Rim country of Arizona, and when he heard we were going through there he became alarmed. He looked over our maps for a long time and started asking questions. Had we been over the country? (No.) Had we worked with horses before? (No.) How many miles a day did we think we'd average? (I said twenty-five,

Walter said ten.) And how much did we know about the wilderness? (We'd been backpacking many times.) Yes, he said, backpacking on established trails, with plenty of reliable water, for no more than a week at a time, right? (Right.) But not with horses you didn't know, over months of travel across hundreds of miles of savage, mountainous desert, without following trails, and with highly uncertain sources of water, right? (We guessed so.) And with no one knowing where you were, or when you were expected back, right? (We supposed so.) And across nine Indian reservations, no less, where some old Navajo or Apache might just take a potshot at you. (Come on, this is the twentieth century.) Not out there it isn't. And were we going to carry a radio? (No.) What about feed for the horses? (We'd find grazing as we went along.) What about getting through barbed-wire fences? (We'd find gates or lay them down.) And what did we think some crazy old rancher would do when he saw us fiddling with one of his fences? Say howdy?

Finally he looked at us and said, in an unnaturally loud voice:

"Jesus Christ. Either you are totally ignorant, or you are totally crazy."

I said I did not think we were crazy, and that I was a little irritated at his other implication, and that I did not care for the tone of his questions.

We argued for a while and finally we got up to leave.

"Let me leave you with this thought," he said. "There is a fair probability that this trip will actually *kill* you. I'm not kidding: a fair probability."

After hearing this, Walter reiterated his desire that we at least scout out the country a bit before beginning. I once again vetoed it.

The second sour note came from a cowboy in Abiquiu, from whom we were trying to buy a mule named Bud. We went out to a pasture and the cowboy shook a bucket of oats and whistled the mule over. We talked for a while and Walter tried to strike a deal, but the cowboy was awfully fond of the mule and the more we talked about our trip the higher the price got. He shook his head and grinned at every question we asked. "Why, hell," he finally said, "you boys ever seen that southern Arizona desert?" And he chuckled evilly when we said no.

In the end, he refused to sell us the mule, at any price.

We began buying equipment. Although we were not trying to re-create every detail of the Coronado expedition, our equipment did not differ all that much from what Coronado had taken. Long-distance travel by horse over rough country had been perfected by the Spanish, and virtually all of the cowboy's equipment—from saddles to clothing—had evolved from earlier Spanish models.

We would start with six horses: three to pack and three to ride, rotating the packing and riding among the animals.

First there was Whiskey, a shaggy brown gelding with a cold back and wild eye, belonging to Eusebio, who swore up and down that he would buck off any sum-bitch other than himself who had the guts to mount him. Eusebio also brought Socks, a quiet sorrel mare with bandy legs and white socks, and King, a sorrel gelding whom I was to ride.

Walter acquired a handsome, fat, gentle, flabby quarter horse which we named Bobby after my uncle, who had given us money to buy him. (Sorry, Bob, we named the horse before we found out what he was like.) Walter's second horse was an Arabian mare, a hysterical, spooky, hot-blooded horse, which he named Robin in honor of his girlfriend. (Walter will take strong exception to this description of his horse, but I stand by it.)

Walter then went to a horse auction and for $600 bought an ugly, small, bad-tempered bay horse with a roached mane. He was allegedly an "unregistered" quarter horse, but he looked more like an Indian pony than anything else. Walter named the horse Pedernal, after Pedernal Peak, the mountain that Georgia O'Keeffe loved to paint. ("Pedernal" means "flint" in Spanish.) Despite his looks and temper, Pedernal would turn out to be a truly magnificent horse—one in a thousand.

Our equipment consisted of:

Three old-time sawbuck packsaddles, with heavy canvas panniers.
Three riding saddles, including Eusebio's roping saddle, a heavy tooled affair, which I was to use.
Tack, including cotton lead ropes, halters, bridles, and so forth.
Heavy sacks of flour, rice, quinoa (an Inca grain high in protein), lentils, nuts, oatmeal, dried fruits, coffee, sugar, Tang, and powdered milk.
A Wonder Bread bag full of homemade jerked beef, brought by Eusebio; the meat had hung so long under his roof that it had turned white.
Cooking oil and a sack of spices, including a pound of ferociously hot ground red chile.
Six dried Italian salamis.
Burlap gunny sacks, for use as grain bags and which, supposedly, could double as hobbles. (To hobble a horse you tie his front feet together, which allows him to graze free at night but he cannot run away.)

A quart of neat's-foot oil, a leather dressing.

Rolls, scraps, and strings of leather for repairing saddles and tack.

A leather punch, screwdriver, files, pliers, and wrench.

Fencing pliers for laying down, cutting, stapling, and repairing barbed-wire fence.

A small, nasty roll of barbed wire and some fence staples.

An under-and-over 20-gauge shotgun, .22 rifle.

Shotgun shells, bullets, and 20-gauge slugs.

An axe.

A shovel with most of its handle sawed off.

Canteens that would hold up to forty pounds of water.

Canvas water bags that would hold an emergency supply of another forty pounds, and a canvas bucket.

A fifty-pound sack of crimped oats.

Horseshoes, nails, and hammer.

One good compass and one bad compass.

A pair of binoculars.

A complete medical kit for the humans, including a hypodermic needle, glass vials of epinephrine for anaphylactic shock, a snakebite kit, prescription painkillers and antibiotics, and bandages.

A medical chest for the horses, including electrolytes and vitamin supplements, gall salve, antibiotic sprays, "bag balm" antiseptic ointment, pine tar for the hooves, and bandages.

A tiny, blackened, dented backpacking stove.

A liter bottle of white gas.

A tent.

Bedrolls.

Plastic and canvas tarps.

Two bottles of a Dr. Bronner's organic peppermint soap, with dense, strange writing all over the label.

Frypan, stew pot, coffee pot, three tin plates, three tin cups, forks, spoons.

For each of us: two shirts (with snap buttons, so you wouldn't have all your buttons torn off in a disturbance), two pairs of jeans (Wranglers or Levi 501's—all others are frauds), a sweater, heavy jacket, good elkskin gloves, cowboy boots, second pair of shoes, oilskin riding raincoat, three pairs of socks, five pairs of underwear, toothbrush.

Buck knife for each person.

Pair of chaps for each person.

Cowboy hat for each person. (Walter's was from Australia, made from kangaroo fur, lifted from an advertising shoot. Mine was my grandfather's, found in a trunk in Maine, from his days working for the Rockefellers in the Grand Tetons.)

Bandanna for each person, worn around the neck to prevent neckburn.

Walter's photographic equipment. This consisted of a large plastic suitcase
   filled with lenses, film, and other accessories; a specially made set of
   panniers designed by Walter to house his $8,000 Deardorff 8 × 10
   view camera and film holders; rubber bags for sealing the equipment
   while we forded rivers; and much more. The photographic equipment alone (which also included three Nikon cameras) weighed over
   a hundred pounds and took up one packhorse.
A book called *The Packer's Bible,* by Joe Back.
Several books on Indian mythology, brought by Walter, who had visions
   of leisurely evenings reading by the fire.
Notebooks and pens.
Tape recorder, tapes, and batteries.
Five thousand dollars in traveler's checks.

On April 13, 1989, we arrived at the little town of Palominas,
Arizona, on the San Pedro River. We were about three miles north of
the point on the Mexico-Arizona border where many scholars believe
that Coronado entered what would become the United States.

The trip had not begun well. On the drive down, in the parking lot
of a gas station in the town of Truth or Consequences, New Mexico
(the only town I know of that was named after a television show), I had
been leading one of the horses to water when the ugly brute stepped on
my foot and broke my little toe. I heard (or rather felt) a little click and
the thing had swelled up like a Vienna sausage. I was now mincing
around on the game foot, embarrassed, denying vehemently that anything was wrong, and sneaking doses of ibuprofen.

The cowboy who had hauled us and our horses from Santa Fe, a
fellow named Wicks, helped us unload our gear. As soon as Eusebio
was out of earshot, Wicks pulled me and Walter aside. He had talked
to Eusebio on the trip down, he said, and he thought there was something we ought to know.

We asked him what it was.

"That wrangler of yours, he's been trying awful God damn hard to
impress me with his knowledge of horses." He paused. "And you know
what?"

No, what? we asked.

"He don't know *jack shit!*" And he roared and wheezed with laughter, clapping us on the backs and stomping around the trailer.

That said, he shook our hands, got back into his truck, spat a stream
of tobacco juice out the window, popped a beer, and drove off in a cloud
of dust, still laughing.

We stood there by the side of the road, with seven hundred pounds of food, equipment, and tack piled in heaps around us, and six horses milling about.

There was a long, dismaying silence, as the dust slowly settled over everything.

"Well," Walter finally said, "let's get the show on the road."

2

The European discovery of the American Southwest did not begin with Coronado. It began with a bizarre incident that occurred some four years earlier. In March of 1536, four Spanish slave traders, riding along the far northern frontier of Mexico, came across an astonishing sight. A white man, virtually naked, with a mass of tangled hair and a beard that reached to his waist, appeared in the desert crying out in Spanish. With him was a black man, also naked, carrying a gourd rattle, and some Indians. The four horsemen were "dumfounded" by the sight and would not approach.

The white man spoke wildly. Eventually the horsemen came to understand that his name was Alvar Núñez Cabeza de Vaca, and the black was Esteban. Cabeza de Vaca said they had spent the last eight years wandering across the face of the North American continent, from Florida to Mexico.

He was sent to Mexico City to repeat the story to the viceroy of New Spain,* Antonio de Mendoza. The viceroy, recognizing the importance of what Cabeza de Vaca had to say, ordered it recorded.

---

*"New Spain" referred to the Spanish holdings in the New World, which at this time included the Valley of Mexico, parts of Central America, and Peru.

This is the story Alvar Núñez Cabeza de Vaca* told:

He had been treasurer and high sheriff of an expedition to Florida, under the captaincy of a cowardly and incompetent adventurer named Pánfilo de Narváez. The purpose of the expedition was, as usual, the seeking of gold. Five vessels with six hundred men left Spain in June of 1527, and landed near Tampa Bay on the Gulf Coast of Florida in April of 1528. Incessantly inquiring after gold among the local Indians, they soon heard what they wanted to hear and set off for a kingdom called *Apalachen,* which lay to the north, where there was said to be gold.

They left their ships in May of 1528, marching inland. After a hard overland journey they entered Apalachen and discovered, to their dismay, that it was an impoverished village of forty thatched huts, with no gold or riches of any kind.

Narváez's planning for the expedition had been less than adequate, and one of the things he hadn't counted on was the difficulty of finding food in the midst of a wilderness that could barely support its indigenous population, let alone hundreds of hungry Spaniards. After a month in Apalachen, already starving, they retreated to the nearest coast, hoping they could bring their ships around, only to find that it was so shallow and marshy that no ship could approach. Greatly weakened, suffering from malaria and probably dysentery, the Spaniards could do little but camp helplessly along the sandy beaches and eat oysters and, eventually, their horses. By the dozens they began to succumb. "It became clear," Cabeza de Vaca wrote in his report, "that we could leave this terrible land only by dying."

In desperation they built five shallow-draft boats made from horse-hides, with fifty men crammed into each boat. Only four inches of gunwale stood above the water. They started along the Gulf shore, going west, hoping to reach Mexico. Nobody knew the science of navigation or had any idea of the immense distance they had to cover; Narváez, like his countrymen of the time, believed that Mexico was immediately adjacent to Florida. The idea that a continent might lie between the two never occurred to him.

The adventurers journeyed through waist-deep mangrove swamps and along shallow inlets for weeks. The horse-skin water bags began to

---

*Cabeza de Vaca literally means "Head of Cow"; it was an honorary title bestowed on a peasant in 1212, who by marking a pass with a cow's skull had led a Spanish army to victory over the Moors.

rot and burst. A storm held them up for six days on a waterless island, where many of the men drank salt water and died in an agony of convulsions and vomiting. As they passed the mouth of the Mississippi, they were finally able to assuage their desperate thirst by drinking fresh water pushed by the great flow far into the ocean itself, but the current drove them far out to sea.

A few days later Cabeza de Vaca's boat couldn't keep up with Narváez, and so he called out to the captain to throw him a rope so they could travel together. Narváez refused, saying that from now on it was every man for himself. Later, Narváez would row out of sight, never to be seen again.

Cabeza de Vaca's boat and several others drifted aimlessly for days. "By sunset [of the fourth day]," he wrote, "all the people in my barge had fallen over on one another, close to death. Few were any longer conscious."

The waves finally drove some of the boats ashore at a barrier island, now believed to be Galveston Island, Texas. They tried to relaunch the boats but they capsized and were swept out to sea with "the loss of everything we had." Those few who survived, Cabeza de Vaca wrote the viceroy, washed up on the beach, as "naked as they were born . . .look[ing] the very picture of death." They named the place *Malhado,* "Island of Doom."

The Indians of the island, who had appeared friendly at first, seized and enslaved the weakened castaways. After a year on the island only half a dozen or so of the eighty castaways were still living: among them Cabeza de Vaca, the black slave Esteban and his owner, Andrés Dorantes, and another Spaniard named Alonso del Castillo Maldonado. The rest had disappeared or starved to death and some, in the end, had resorted to cannibalism.

The four survivors were taken to the mainland and enslaved by the Indians as bearers. They lived naked, Cabeza de Vaca reported, and shed their skins twice a year "like serpents" from the extremes of sun, heat, and cold. They ate berries, nuts, fish, and prickly pear cactus.

The Indians had other ideas for their captives. Perhaps because of their strangeness, the Indians thought they might have healing powers. "The islanders," Cabeza de Vaca noted dryly, "wanted to make physicians out of us without examination or review of diplomas." The Indians withheld food until they agreed to cooperate. Reluctantly, one Spaniard said a *Paternoster* and *Ave Maria* and made the sign of a cross over some sick Indians. The effect was instantaneous and the Indians were cured on the spot. In gratitude the tribe gave the Spaniards a feast and danced and sang for three days.

After five more years of servitude and healing among the Indians of the Texas coast, the Spaniards escaped, and the four castaways made their way westward.

As they followed the Gulf Coast, still hoping to reach Mexico, the news of their healing powers preceded them. The castaways found themselves hailed as powerful medicine men, as "Children of the Sun." As they wandered westward, they attracted a tremendous following of Indians.

The African, Esteban, came to be held in particularly high esteem. What little information we have about him suggests he was a man of physical strength, handsome, a good talker, fond of fine clothes and jewelry, and attractive to women. He quickly mastered the native languages. Wherever the four men went they drew boisterous crowds of Indians, who pressed about them, pestering them for cures and blessings. Entire towns would decamp and follow them for days. Along the way Esteban picked up a sacred gourd rattle, which he used to very great effect in his cures. The gourd, of a type possibly used by Plains Indian medicine men, was ornamented with two feathers, one red and one white, and decorated with bells and ribbons.

They continued to work their way toward the setting sun, and after another year of wandering struck the Río Grande near present-day El Paso. From there, the little party pushed on to what is now northern Sonora. Here, Cabeza de Vaca recounted to the viceroy, they heard tell of great cities north along the river, and they saw Indians from that area wearing fine woven shawls and turquoises, and carrying "emeralds."

One day, after six thousand miles of wandering, Castillo Maldonado came across an Indian wearing a Spanish belt buckle and horseshoe nail stitched into an amulet around his neck. It was the first sign the Spaniards had seen of European civilization in nearly eight years.

"Casually we inquired what had become of those men" who had given them these things. "They had gone to sea, said the Indians. They had put their lances into the water, got into the water themselves, and finally were seen moving on top of the water into the sunset."

The ragged Spaniards pressed on, and eventually came to a country laid utterly to waste. The few Indians still alive said that parties of Christians had come on horses, taking slaves, burning villages and fields, killing all who resisted. Cabeza de Vaca, who in his years of wandering had come to love the Indians, was deeply shocked. "With heavy hearts," he wrote, "we looked out over the lavishly watered, fertile, and beautiful land, now abandoned and burned and the people thin and weak, scattering and hiding in fright. . . . All along the way we could see the tracks of the Christians and traces of their camps."

Cabeza de Vaca's large Indian escort was terrified. Cabeza de Vaca promised them safety, and they picked up the trail of one party of Spaniards. In March of 1536, they walked out of the desert and into history as the first Europeans (and the first African!) to have crossed America.

Yet the story was not finished. The slave traders plotted to seize Cabeza de Vaca's Indian escort, and when Cabeza de Vaca found out he was enraged. "We got in a hot argument," he wrote. One of the slavers then attempted to drive a wedge between the Indians and Cabeza de Vaca by telling them that he was a Christian just like the Spaniards, and that Cabeza de Vaca and his party were inconsequential, while they were the lords of the land.

"The Indians paid no attention to this," Cabeza de Vaca wrote. "Conferring among themselves, they replied that the Christians lied: We had come from the sunrise, they from the sunset; we healed the sick, they killed the sound; we came naked and barefoot, they clothed, horsed, and lanced; we coveted nothing but gave whatever we were given, while they robbed whomever they found and bestowed nothing on anyone."

The slavers became angry and "arrested" Cabeza de Vaca and his companions, separating them from their Indian allies to prevent them from warning the Indians. They were sent back to "civilization" in chains. As soon as the significance of what they had to say sank in, they were immediately freed, feted, and brought with honor to the viceroy himself in Mexico City.

The viceroy was astonished at this extraordinary tale. There was one detail in particular that intrigued him: this mention of great cities in the north. The viceroy closely questioned Cabeza de Vaca on this point. Cabeza de Vaca explained that they had met four women, elaborately dressed in woven cotton mantas and soft buckskins, wearing beautiful jewelry made of turquoise. They appeared to be highly civilized, and said they came from large cities in the north.

After some thought, the viceroy made Cabeza de Vaca a proposal: would he be willing to lead a reconnaissance party back to the north, to look for these cities?

Cabeza de Vaca declined the honor, as did his other two white companions.

The viceroy then turned to the African, Esteban. The African agreed to lead a scouting party to the cities of the north. The viceroy engaged the services of a French friar from Nice named Marcos, who was in Mexico City, to be the leader of the exploring party.

On March 7, 1539—three years after Esteban had first emerged from the wilderness—he left Mexico with Fray Marcos de Niza and a party of Aztec (Nahuatl) Indian allies. The two made an interesting pair. Fray Marcos went on foot, dressed in the usual rough, gray zaragoza robe* of his order. He carried in his pockets samples of metal to show the Indians: gold, silver, copper, and iron.

Esteban, still carrying his sacred gourd rattle, departed in high style, with two hunting greyhounds at his side. He wore brightly colored clothes and a sweeping cape, with bells around his wrists and ankles that jangled as he walked.

For five months the two men were gone.

Then Fray Marcos returned alone, emaciated but triumphant. His story electrified the New World.

He announced he had discovered "the greatest thing in the world": he had actually gazed upon the first of the fabulous cities Cabeza de Vaca had heard about. There were, in fact, seven of them in a kingdom called Cíbola. Seven cities of great power and wealth. Seven cities of gold.

After leaving Mexico City, Fray Marcos related, they had wandered north with their Indian entourage, not really knowing where they were headed, or, as Marcos put it, going "whither the Holy Spirit led me." Eventually they met Indians who had never seen or heard of Christians. Marcos laid out his samples of metal and the Indians picked out the gold, saying that the people in the great cities to the north had much metal like it. They wore it as jewelry, drank from jugs fashioned from it, and even made blades of it to scrape the sweat off their bodies.

Marcos immediately put Esteban in charge of an advance party of Aztecs and sent him ahead. They agreed that the African would send back with a messenger a small wooden cross if the land was poor; if good, a larger cross; and if "greater and better than New Spain," an even bigger cross.

Four days later, a messenger came staggering into camp under the

---

*Later the Church would allow the Franciscans in New Mexico to wear robes of blue—the color of the Virgin's robe—in recognition of the great danger and hardship the friars faced on this far northern frontier.

weight of a cross as tall as a man. The messenger added that Esteban had heard from local Indians that only thirty days ahead lay the cities, bursting with wealth.

As Marcos hurried on, another and yet another gigantic cross arrived with messages from Esteban, exhorting the friar to hurry, hurry.

Then, some distance from the Seven Cities, an Indian member of the advance party limped into Marcos's camp, "exhibiting great sadness of countenance, his face and body covered with sweat." He had barely escaped with his life from the first of the Seven Cities. Esteban was dead, and his Indian servants killed.

It happened like this, said the messenger: as Esteban traveled, he carried with him the gourd rattle, his companion of years of wandering and healing in the desert. When he approached a town, he would send the gourd ahead with a messenger, as the symbol of his authority.

Thus, when he reached the first of the Seven Cities, Esteban, in his usual fashion, had sent the gourd with a message to the governor of the city. The governor had received it and "at once hurled the gourd to the ground with much wrath," saying that he knew very well what sort of people these were. He said that if they set foot in his city he would "kill them all."

Esteban was not so easily put off. His charisma and charm had always saved him before. He told his Indians that what the governor said was of no importance, and he boasted that when he met the governor he would be received "all the better."

He entered the city. Once inside he was promptly arrested and his arms and trading goods confiscated. The next day—the Indian's story went—Esteban and his Indian servants were set loose on the plain outside the Indian *pueblo,* or village, where the Cíbolans chased them down and filled them with arrows.*

Whatever the reasons behind Esteban's death, it was a grim end to a man who must surely rank as one of the greatest explorers in the history of the New World. Indeed, it is this native of Africa, and not the European Coronado or Fray Marcos, who must be given original credit for the Old World discovery of the Southwest.

On hearing about the massacre of his advance party, Fray Marcos was seized with fear, and his Indian assistants (many of whom were

---

*There are other, more interesting versions of Esteban's death, which we shall explore later.

relatives of the Indians killed) broke into a loud wailing. But, the friar told the viceroy, he wanted to see the wonders of Cíbola for himself, even at the risk of his life. With much persuasion and a wholesale distribution of the friar's trading goods, the Aztec Indians agreed to continue. In several days' travel, they topped a low rise and saw, "situated in a plain, at the base of a round hill," the first of the Seven Cities.

What a glorious sight it was! "Larger than the City of Mexico," it had buildings up to ten stories high. This, his informants told him, was the smallest of the Seven Cities; the largest, not many miles away, had so many houses and people that there was "no end to it."

Fray Marcos had one final responsibility. From his hidden vantage point in a scattering of juniper trees about three miles from the city, he built a little cairn of stones and gathered a few sticks of wood, which he fashioned into a "small and slender" cross. There, 453 years ago, in the desert lands of what would become the United States, no more than a few hundred yards from the present-day border of New Mexico and Arizona, he read the formal proclamation of annexation:

> I declare that I erect this cross and landmark as a sign of possession, in the name of Don Antonio de Mendoza, Viceroy and Governor of New Spain, for the Emperor, our Lord, in accordance with my instructions.

His hushed voice echoed and died among the mesas, wholly unheard by the people whose land he was annexing.

Then the friar turned toward home.

On his way back he was met by the governor of New Galicia, then the northernmost province of Mexico. The governor, a twenty-nine-year-old nobleman named Francisco Vásquez de Coronado, listened to Marcos's story with very deep interest indeed—so much so that he, personally, offered to escort the friar to the viceroy's court.

It would be hard to overestimate the sensation caused by the friar's report. Only a few years had passed since the Spaniards had looted the fabulous wealth of the Incas and the Aztecs; to the north, surely, lay another such empire waiting to be conquered. In the months following Fray Marcos's return, few in New Spain could talk of anything else.

The story had also struck a peculiar nerve in the medieval Spanish psyche. At least since the thirteenth century, there had been legends and rumors of seven lost cities, founded by seven bishops who had fled Portugal in the eighth century during the Arab invasion. There were also tales of seven lost islands, or perhaps seven caves full of gold. It was a story that held as much resonance for the medieval Spanish as the legends of the Holy Grail did for the medieval English. When Fray Marcos came back with a story of the Seven Cities of Cíbola, almost immediately they were transformed into the Seven Cities of Gold.

In all fairness to Fray Marcos, his report (which survives) contains no outright falsehoods. While much is overheated and exaggerated, the friar was very careful to distinguish between hearsay and what he actually saw. The city Marcos saw was three and a half miles distant, built up on the shoulder of a hill, and it could very well have looked "ten stories high." As for it being larger than the City of Mexico, the nascent capital of New Spain in 1539 had a mere thousand inhabitants. Nevertheless, Marcos himself, caught up in the eagerness of his listeners and the excitement of his celebrity, stretched the truth as far as it would go.* But those who repeated Marcos's story felt no such compunction for the truth, and the story grew quite out of control.

Such was the clamor that Viceroy Mendoza himself wanted to lead the conquering expedition, but he was prevailed upon to stay at home. Reluctantly, he awarded the plum job of conquest to his protégé, Francisco Vásquez de Coronado, the man who had first heard Fray Marcos's tale. The expedition would be privately financed, with the emperor taking a 20 percent cut and the rest going to the conquistadors and their backers. The viceroy himself put up 60,000 gold ducats in the endeavor, and Coronado mortgaged his wealthy wife's estates to invest another 50,000.

Recruiting began later that year. Criers beating drums wandered through the plazas and streets of Mexico City, and Franciscan priests recounted their own blown-up versions of Fray Marcos's story from the pulpit. Hundreds signed up.

·   ·   ·

*There are many scholars who believe Fray Marcos never got anywhere near the Seven Cities of Gold; that when he heard about Esteban's death he immediately turned around. This would explain the seemingly inexplicable: why would Fray Marcos tell such lies? I do not subscribe to this theory; a close reading of Marcos's report shows that, in fact, the friar never did lie *outright*—it was exaggeration. The actual lies recorded in the narrative were all told to Fray Marcos by Indian informants, and all about things that Fray Marcos did not see himself. Besides, the exaggeration starts right from the beginning of the narrative, not at the point where he is supposed to have turned around.

One of those young adventurers was a common soldier named Pedro de Castañeda of Náxera, Spain. We know virtually nothing about this man, except that twenty years after the expedition he would pen (in his verbose style) the following:

> I do not blame those inquisitive persons who, perchance with good intentions, have many times troubled me not a little with their requests that I clear up for them some doubts which they have had about different things that have been commonly related concerning the events and occurrences that took place during the expedition to Cíbola, or the New Land. . . .
>
> He who wishes to employ himself thus in writing out the things that happened on the expedition, and the things that were seen in those lands, and the ceremonies and customs of the natives, will have matter enough to test his judgment, and I believe that the result can not fail to be an account which, describing only the truth, will be so remarkable that it will seem incredible. . . .
>
> All this has had a large part. . .in making me wish to give now, although somewhat late, a short general account. . . . Things enough will certainly be found here which are hard to believe. All or the most of these were seen with my own eyes, and the rest is from reliable information obtained by inquiry of the natives themselves. . . .
>
> And now I will proceed to relate all that happened from the beginning.

He then followed with one of the most extraordinary narratives in the history of the Americas. Castañeda was no ordinary observer; as his narrative progresses we find an increasing sympathy for the Indians, and an increasing disgust with his own people. By the time the narrative reaches the pueblos along the Río Grande, the conversion is complete, and Castañeda is openly siding with the Indians against the Spanish. His descriptions of pre-contact native American culture have an acuity of observation and objectivity that would do justice to a modern-day anthropologist. In some places the observations even foreshadow cultural relativity, the monumental idea of twentieth-century anthropology that all cultures are intrinsically equal, with no culture being more "advanced" or better than another.

Others with Coronado would leave a record of the expedition. One of Coronado's captains, Juan Jaramillo, would write a short account, and several of Coronado's reports have also survived, as do some legal documents relating to the expedition. The Spanish were consummate bureaucrats and kept every document in triplicate.

. . .

Castañeda begins by telling us that "they had in this expedition the most brilliant company ever assembled in the Indies to go in search of new lands." It would be the largest expedition ever to explore the New World. No expedition before or since has equaled the size of Coronado's.

The company, however, was hardly "brilliant." Most of the Spanish recruits were indolent, parasitic "gentlemen," second sons left penniless by the laws of inheritance. Since the most degrading thing a Spanish gentleman could do was to work, many of these second sons sailed to the New World, hoping to share in the spoils of conquest and gain estates of their own. Mexico City was full of them, "who, like a cork floating upon water," one Spaniard noted, "went about with nothing to do. . .all importuning the Viceroy to grant them favors, and the citizens of Mexico to feed them at their tables."

So many young men signed up that some citizens of Mexico became alarmed. Rumors and charges circulated that Coronado was doing nothing less than "depopulating" New Spain.

The viceroy felt it serious enough to convene hearings that would answer the charges. Witness after witness stood up and testified that the recruits were men of "no occupation, [who] were bad characters . . .without income, and lazy." Another witness noted that it would be "one of the greatest blessings that had come to this New Spain" if these people departed, as "they were mostly single and dissolute men without anything to do. . .but eat and loaf."

And yet within this sorry group there was a great deal of hope and spirit. These men were young, in their teens and twenties. Few were older than Coronado, who was himself only thirty. Most had grown up in easy circumstances, only to find themselves thrust out into the streets on the death of their fathers. They had not chosen to be born second sons and were wrestling with an untenable situation: gentility without means, along with a strict prohibition against remunerative work and the expectation that, as gentlemen, they would keep a household and stable befitting their station.

With no prospects or backing, they had left their country of birth to see what they could make of themselves in a New World that was vastly farther from Spain than anything we can imagine today. There is no modern equivalent to the absolute isolation and loneliness experienced by the explorers of this era.

And now these men were choosing to go even farther afield, leaving civilization entirely to explore and settle a country about which nothing was known. They might never see the miserable pungent streets of Mexico City again, let alone their homes, parents, and friends back in Spain. These men were adventurous and brave—but also men who had exhausted all their other options. They were not much different from the Anglo pioneers who would settle the Southwest some three hundred years later.

Coronado's orders included two very strict injunctions. First, he was to show the greatest regard for the Aztec Indians who accompanied him on the expedition as wranglers, cowboys, camp assistants, cooks, grooms, servants, and foot soldiers. Even more important, he was to show every consideration, kindness, and forbearance to the Indians of Cíbola and any other settlements they might encounter. There was to be no cruelty, unnecessary warfare, forced labor, or even the taking of food or clothing without compensation. The viceroy's only requirement was that the Indians of Cíbola render obedience to His Majesty the Emperor and to God. How Coronado was to acquire the wealth of the Seven Cities without bloodshed, and what he was to do if the inhabitants refused obeisance, were questions that were not addressed.

⚫ ⟗ ⚫

When Coronado and his army finally departed from Culiacán, the northernmost Spanish outpost in the New World, on April 22, 1540, their ranks had swelled to 250 horsemen, 70 foot soldiers, 1,300 Indians and blacks, 1,000 horses, 500 pack animals, and large herds of sheep, oxen, and cattle. Coronado himself had 23 horses, 3 or 4 suits of horse armor, as well as a gilded suit for himself with helmet and plume. Others brought coats of mail, cuirasses, buckskins, swords, crossbows, harquebuses, and even several small cannon.

Not everyone was Spanish. There were at least two Italians, one Frenchman (besides Fray Marcos), a German bugler, and—of all unlikely people—a Scotsman recorded in the muster roll as "Tomás Blaque."

At Culiacán, Coronado divided the army into two groups. He went ahead with a lightly equipped force of 100 men, with Fray Marcos as guide. The lumbering, witless army and its herds of livestock followed at a much slower pace.

By the time Coronado and his advance party approached what would become the U.S. border, they knew something was wrong. Coronado wrote back to the viceroy that the easy passages, lush pastures, and flowing waters described by the good friar did not correspond to the savage mountains, crack-bottomed arroyos, and thorny scrub through which they found themselves struggling.

"We all marched cheerfully along a very difficult way," he wrote. "This troubled the soldiers not a little because everything the friar described was found to be quite the reverse. . . . The truth is that there are mountains which, however well the trail might be repaired, could not be crossed without great danger that the horses would fall over the cliffs." The sheep lost their hooves in the rocks and went lame. A dozen horses died of exhaustion and starvation, as did several blacks and Indians. What was worse, a scouting party and reports from local Indians indicated that even harsher land lay ahead, that "there was nothing to be found in the country beyond, which continued very rough, entirely uninhabited by people. . . . The whole company felt disturbed by this, that a thing so much praised, and about which the father had said so many things, should be found so very different."

But Coronado tried to keep the spirits of his men up: "When I noticed [that the soldiers were troubled], I tried to encourage them as well as I could, telling them that Your Lordship had always thought that this part of the trip would be a waste of effort, and that we ought to devote our attention to those Seven Cities and the other provinces about which we had information—that these should be the end of our enterprise."

Finally, in May of 1540, Coronado crossed into what would become the United States, probably following the meager flow of the San Pedro River, midway between Nogales and Douglas, Arizona. Here, while they were camped along the river, they met their first Americans: "Some poor Indians came out to see the general," Jaramillo reported, "with presents of little value, with some stalks of roasted maguey and pitahayas."

The European discovery of the Southwest had begun.

3

W
icks, the cowboy, had dropped us off along a paved
road about three miles north of the Mexico-Arizona border.

It was Thursday, April 13, 1989, almost exactly 450 years to the day
since Fray Marcos and Esteban came through, and 449 years since
Coronado had made his *entrada* along this river.

We rode the three miles south to the border. The San Pedro River
flowed out of Mexico under a five-strand barbed-wire fence in a grove
of old cottonwood trees. The river was little more than a braided stream
sliding over a buckskin-colored bed of sand; Arizona, unbeknownst to
us, was edging into its worst drought in half a century. Cicadas roared
in the hot cavern of shade created by the overhanging trees, and beyond
that rose up the humps of barren hills. In the farthest distance we could
see a zigzag of blue mountains. Tumbleweeds had piled up along the
fence, and the border was deserted; the only sign of human activity was
a column of smoke rising from a burning field in Mexico.

Our beginning was not so very different from that of the Spanish.
One chronicler tells us the Spaniards hardly knew how to pack their
horses and lost many loads on the steep rocky trails. We, too, could
barely saddle or pack a horse. They were full of high spirits and
bursting with optimism about their prospects; so were we. Our ignorance of what lay ahead was nearly as profound as theirs.

At the border, Walter and I hopped over the fence and hopped back, making an illegal sortie so that we could say that we started in Mexico. Walter then announced that he wanted to take a formal portrait with his 8 × 10 camera. He waded out into the stream and set the camera on a sandbar. Eusebio and I stood on the bank, while Walter draped a black cape over his head and examined us through the lens. When everything was set, he sloshed toward us, uncoiling a long shutter release.

The photograph that resulted arrived the other day with a stack of others taken on the trip. Walter is his usual scruffy self: beard, burnt face, knobby hands roughened by a lifetime of outdoor labor, scruffy beard. Eusebio stands next to me, short and lean, thumbs hooked into his chaps, Resistol hat tilted back at a rakish angle. I stand in the middle, arms crossed, sporting a crisp new bandanna, starched cowboy shirt, dark glasses, and hat. My stomach is sucked in, my jaw set.

In short, I look like a perfect ass.

We camped a half mile from the border at a cattle tank brimming with cold water, near some broken-down corrals. We went to sleep listening to the trilling, sucking sound of an old Chicago Aermotor windmill cranking in the breeze, like a Rube Goldberg contraption running in high gear.

When Eusebio roused us at 4:45, my bedroll crackled with hoarfrost. The sun rose at six and by 9:50 the temperature was close to 100 degrees, having spent all of forty minutes climbing through the comfort zone. As we saddled up, the cottonwood trees loosed their cotton, which swirled about us like confetti, giving us a nice send-off.

Based on my estimate of twenty to twenty-five miles a day, I figured we would be camping that evening at the old ghost town of Charleston some twenty miles downriver.*

We started down the river, each rider leading one packhorse. Leading a packhorse sounded simple enough: with the reins of your own horse in your left hand, you hold the lead rope to the packhorse in your right. In practice it was like driving two cars at once, and I immediately got into trouble.

We had been watering the horses in the river and, through inattention, I had allowed the lead rope to my packhorse to become wedged up under King's tail. Horses hate the feeling of anything up under their

---

*"Downriver," of course, means north; the San Pedro is one of the few rivers in the United States that flows from south to north.

tail, and so King responded by bucking furiously. Since we were standing in water and the horse had no hard platform to launch from, I managed to ride it out. Eusebio scolded me for my ineptitude and we continued on.

Soon we found ourselves in a thicket of brush and deadfalls. The friendly trail we expected to find along the riverbank did not materialize, and the riverbottom shivered with quicksand and boggy holes.

Figuring that the higher floodplain would be easier, we struggled up a cutbank into a stand of black, dead mesquite. The horses blundered through, breaking branches, and we emerged into an immense field of yellow grass. The grass was as tall as our horses' eyes and the grass dust rose up in hot clouds as we rustled through.

Eusebio began cheerfully cursing his horses in Spanish. Whenever my horse King tried to snatch a mouthful of grass, Eusebio would shout "Keeng! *Cabrón!*" and the poor animal would jerk his head up, ears flattened.

"That sum-bitch listen to *me*," Eusebio would cry out, in an effort to teach me the subtleties of fine horsemanship. "You make him listen to *you!*"

"How?" I asked.

"Whip the sum-bitch! Kick him!"

About ten minutes into the field, the ground suddenly dropped out from beneath me, and King and I tumbled into a yawning, five-foot hole. I could hear Eusebio's hysterical voice echoing faintly from above. The horse had landed on his belly; I jumped off him and he clambered out, frightened but unhurt.

The field, it turned out, was riddled with many such fiendish holes, rendered invisible by the blinding white sun reflecting off the tall grass. We dismounted and began leading our horses, sometimes probing ahead with our feet.

In another ten minutes, Eusebio's cursing suddenly moved up a notch, and we turned around to see him struggling to prop up his packhorse's load, which had slipped sideways. We helped him right it. It seemed strange to me that Eusebio, a professional packer, would suffer this problem when Walter, who had packed his own horses for the first time (as he had been taught), had had no such trouble. I put the thought out of my mind.

Twenty minutes later Eusebio was bellowing again. This time the pack had turned upside down, and all 175 pounds of it was hanging off the horse's belly. The horse stood choking and trembling, while

Eusebio swore and fumbled with a knot that was as hard as an oak burl. Walter, the picture of calm, strode over, whipped out his buck knife, and with a few quick strokes cut the pack off the horse.

Walter rewove the cut ends of the rope, and using a piece of leather from our repair kit, repaired the damage, while Eusebio stood there, hands tucked into his chaps, muttering that it had been some time since he'd packed and that it always takes a while to get back into the swing of things. Walter shot me a dark look while he jerked the lash rope tight around the pack.

We finally emerged from the field, exhausted, and rode down a dirt track toward the town of Palominas, a dozen roofs wedged into the cottonwoods. We camped that night along the river, just outside of town.

In a hard day's riding, we had made all of three miles.

As I lay in my bedroll that night, looking up at an immense pasture of stars, several thoughts ran through my mind. The first was that Eusebio was no more a wrangler than I was a bronc buster. He didn't even know how to pack a horse, let alone wrangle six horses across seven hundred (or, as was suddenly clear, more like a thousand) miles of the worst deserts and mountains in the Southwest.

The second was that the twenty-five-mile-a-day average I had estimated was clearly absurd. Again, Walter had been right, and we'd be lucky to average ten. The journey, instead of taking us four weeks, was going to take longer. Much longer.

It also seemed quite clear to me, in my overheated state, that twice that day I had come within a hairsbreadth of violent death. How many more days would pass before I was finally kicked upside the head? Or bucked into a cactus? Conversely, what would have happened had King broken his leg in that field? The thought chilled me, and I remembered Eusebio's insistence that we bring a gun—not, he had said, for shooting game, but "for the horses." Here it was the first day and I had already broken my toe, with, no doubt, more broken bones to follow.

Suddenly the expedition did not seem like such a great idea. The problem was, we had already spent $8,000 the Smithsonian had advanced us, as well as the money I had been paid by the book publisher—money I could never hope to repay. I wondered when Coronado had started to regret the 50,000 ducats of his wife's money that he had spent.

Close by, Eusebio began to wheeze and sputter in a fitful sleep.

That night, illegal aliens came up the river pursued by the border patrol, and two of Walter's horses broke their hobbles and went galloping off in the dark. I huddled in my bag, pretending to be asleep, while Walter hunted them down. The dogs of Palominas set up a desperate howling all night long.

The next day, April 15th, we rode through Palominas. It was the last town we would see for some time. The only store, a whitewashed building with a crooked porch, was run by a friendly woman named MaryFrances Clinton, whose grandfather, she said, was the first homesteader there. Like many settlers in Arizona, he had come looking for water. Farther north, Mormon farmers had struck an immense artesian aquifer along the river—some of the wells yielding five thousand gallons a minute—and old man Clinton dug a thirty-foot well with a shovel and pickaxe, hoping the hand of God would strike again. His hole got a little wet but no artesian gusher ever erupted; he figured he might as well stay anyway.

The store consisted of two abandoned miner's cabins that had been moved by truck from the Tombstone mines down the river and stuck together. The move had been a major event in the history of the town and MaryFrances, on hearing that I was a writer, hauled out a file of newspaper clippings of the move. We were just getting settled in when Walter clattered through the door, savagely cursing the heat and demanding to know where his soda was. I apologized as Walter hustled me out.

When we were outside, he looked me up and down and began to laugh, his irritation vanishing.

"Jesus, Doug," he said, "with those sunglasses you look like a dern New Yorker on vacation."

For its first thirty-five miles, the San Pedro flows through a wilderness of quicksand, cactus, cutbanks, sudden arroyos, and brutal mesquite. The land belonged to the Bureau of Land Management, the largest landowner in the United States, who had closed most of it to human entry as a riparian study area. We had been given special permission to pass through.

This thirty-five-mile stretch of river would be a proving ground of sorts, our introduction to horses, packing, and overland travel.

Back on our horses, we plunged into the thicket along the river, crossing and recrossing the river as it swung in wide arcs across a broad floodplain. The river created a corridor of green sweet humidity a quarter mile wide; beyond that lay harsh catclaw desert and barren mountains. Due to boggy and shivering sands, each crossing was fraught with danger, and the horses often panicked as their hooves sank into the soft sand—lunging forward to escape, splashing water and mud over everything. What felt firm to a stick or human foot would often turn liquid under the weight of a horse, and we never knew if a crossing would send one of our horses to a boggy grave.

We had been warned about quicksand in the San Pedro. Sometimes, we were told, the sinking horse would be lucky and hit bottom before disappearing completely; then a backhoe could dig the animal out. Sometimes bottom would be deeper, and the horse out of luck. There were, it was said, quite a few horse skeletons standing deep within the treacherous sands of the San Pedro.

We camped that evening at a slow-moving stretch of river, near a bank covered with thick green grass for the horses. A perfectly even row of cottonwoods lined the near bank, and behind that lay the distant blue outline of the Huachuca Mountains. As the air cooled off, the sweet smell of cottonwood catkins filled the air.

As soon as we had unloaded the horses, Walter and I tore off our clothes and waded into the river, whooping and hollering. It was only a few inches deep, but we found we could lie down and roll, letting the water spill over us.

"Git on in here," Walter shouted to Eusebio, but he remained sitting on the bank, frowning and picking at his bleeding gums with a chewed stick.

Later, Eusebio showed me a scar on his back, explaining that it would start running if it got wet.

I asked him how he got it.

"A sum-bitch shot me in Pecos," he said with grim satisfaction.

I asked him why.

"I was walking down a street and a sum-bitch just shot me, is all," he said, and refused to elaborate.

Walter washed his horses, pouring water over their backs with a canvas bucket. Eusebio took me aside.

"Him," he said, jerking his chin in Walter's direction.

"Walter, you mean," I said.

"*Walter.* That *Walter* don't know shit about horses. You wash a horse like that, and his skin will stick to his bones and he'll *die*." He lowered his voice and added, with savage delight: "You wait. You *see*."

After we broke camp the next morning, Walter tried to show me how to pack a horse. Theoretically, it works like this: you first saddle the horse with the packsaddle, called a sawbuck because it has two crossed pieces of wood. Then you hang the two filled panniers on the sawbucks, pile other stuff on top, strap it all down, cover it with a tarp, and then lash the whole load down with a diamond hitch or similar knot.

Packing a horse takes great artistry, along with a powerful set of lungs and an inexhaustible supply of curses. Walter set to work.

His first effort at the hitch failed, and so did a second. He zinged the rope off the pack and started over, his face reddening with anger.

"That Mexican lied to you," he hissed in my ear. "Wicks was right: he don't know *shit* about packing a horse."

"I can see that," I said. I thought it prudent not to mention Eusebio's absurd theory that washing a horse would kill him.

"And did you see him pickin' his teeth back there? All that blood and shit coming out of his mouth?"

I nodded.

"There's something wrong with him. I'm scared to go near the son-of-a-bitch." Walter's voice had risen and I glanced at Eusebio, who was fussing with something at the far end of camp.

"Keep your voice down," I whispered.

"I swear he's got a *disease*," Walter said in a loud voice.

"Shut up, for chrissakes," I said.

"I'll tell you one thing: he ain't drinking out of my canteen."

The hitch fell apart again. Walter turned to me.

"Quit lookin' so close, you're makin' me nervous. Git over there and turn your back."

I obeyed, and I soon heard a grunt of satisfaction. When I turned around the hitch was crisp and tight.

"So what did you do?" I asked.

"I'll be Goddamned if I know," Walter said, and roared with laughter.

From that point on, Walter and I would pack the horses while Eusebio wandered around the camp, pretending to be busy. As our ersatz wrangler continued to refuse to cook, clean dishes, or do camp-work, Walter and I found ourselves having to do everything. This was (although we didn't know it at the time) Eusebio's great gift to us.

As we rode downriver, we passed through landscapes of surreal beauty. The river was like a loud green cave, bursting with humming, clicking, buzzing, and rustling life, beyond which lay a desperately hot desert. In one grove of fat cottonwoods we surprised a colony of great blue herons, which wheeled slowly above our heads. Later we flushed a family of javelina and sent them snorting into a field of tumbleweed. Other images are imprinted in my mind: blood-red arroyos slicing through oceans of green mesquite; barren hills covered with skinny ocotillo; a deer bounding through yellow grass. At one bend in the river Walter went off to take a photograph, and I watched him ride off into a plain of sacaton grass so high his horse was invisible, with him gliding across the field like a phantom.

The strange beauty of the river was more than matched by the difficulty of making our way along it. The heat was brutal, and the endless thickets of mesquite—with their inch-long thorns—tore into us and our horses. Even with our chaps and our heaviest clothing our faces were scored and bloody at the end of the day. We continued to make terrible progress, but our ability to precipitate disaster improved with every turn in the river.

On the afternoon of the third day, as we were crossing a stretch of deep sand, Walter's horse Bobby sank to his belly in exhaustion. We had no choice but to unpack right there and make camp. We had fallen into the habit of naming our camps, and so we called this one Tired Horse Camp.

As the sun set a group of illegal aliens passed by on the far side of the river, moving silently on bare feet, looking neither right nor left. We had been warned never to leave our boots unprotected in the camp at night, for they are highly prized by barefoot illegals.

The sands along the San Pedro were loaded with millions of vicious little burrs, stickers, and goatheads. As soon as the horses were unloaded they gleefully rolled, covering themselves with thorns and burrs, which had to be picked off. Every morning we had to massage our bare hands into the horses' backs, as well as the saddle pads and cinches, thereby locating all the invisible thorns that would gall and ruin a horse.

The extraordinary difficulty of the trail left us dazed. Aside from muttering threats to our horses, we rarely spoke while on the trail; our attention was thoroughly occupied with finding a route through the mesquite and arroyos and with keeping the horses under control. There actually was no trail—merely endless thickets of mesquite, saltbush, wolfberry, catclaw, whitethorn, tarbush, tumbleweeds, willows, and salt cedars.

Our horses were as unready for the experience as we were. Not only was Bobby sinking fast through exhaustion, but Walter's other horse, Robin, was showing alarming signs of sickness. She coughed constantly, and when she grazed the half-chewed grass would spill out of her mouth. While drinking, she sucked water into her mouth only to have it dribble back out her nose. Her eyes were dull and she was in a bad mood, kicking savagely at any horse that came within twenty feet of her.

Walter asked Eusebio to look at Robin, so he opened her mouth and peered inside. After a moment he announced, with dark pleasure, that someone long ago had abused her with a bit, nearly cutting her tongue off, and a huge lump of scar tissue had formed. Walter, he said, shaking his head sadly, had bought a bad horse.

The next morning at Tired Horse Camp, Walter and I climbed a hill behind our encampment. He slung the forty-pound Deardorff over his shoulder and we set off before breakfast, just as a line of translucent pink was forming in the eastern sky.

The hill was a perfect cone, with a sparse covering of blooming creosote bush and catclaw. Here and there an ocotillo sprang up, with a spray of scarlet flowers dangling from the tips of each stalk. As we picked our way up through the rocks and brush, the sun broke through the Mule Mountains, spilling a trembling light over the strange view that was unfolding around us.

For the first time we saw the landscape we had been struggling through. The San Pedro, hidden in a vale of puffy cottonwoods, looked like a vein of malachite twisting through the gray desert. A dozen small mountain ranges rose abruptly from the rolling desert floor, each range with a different shape and character. The Mule Mountains, to the east, stuck up straight and muscled from the plains, the light glinting off their granitic flanks. To the west, the Huachucas, heavily forested, reared up like storm-tossed waves. Other distant ranges were sawtoothed, rounded, and spiked. To the northeast the gray Tombstone Hills covered the ground like a wrinkled blanket. These mountains had no logic or reality; they did not look as if they had been shaped by natural forces. It was one of the most extraordinarily beautiful and otherworldly views I'd ever seen.

The only sign of life was the distant town of Sierra Vista, nestled against the Huachucas some twenty miles away, a faint grid of streets etched into a brown flat.

At the top of the hill I sat down on a rock and began writing in my journal, while Walter went off looking for photographs. A crow glided past on an air current, close enough that I could see his beady eyes swivel around and peer at me before he banked off into space. I finished my entry and lay back against a stone, looking into an empty sky. The color had none of the ultraviolet intensity of the New Mexico sky; it was a pale, hot, salty blue. It was a color that promised raging heat later on.

Walter came over. "It looks," he said quietly, "like the strange landscape of a dream."

● ⊠ ●

The "poor Indians" who brought food to Coronado along the San Pedro, which Jaramillo heard called "the Nexpa," were probably Sobaípuris, a now-extinct tribe of Pima Indians who once farmed, hunted, and harvested wild plants in the San Pedro Valley.

The river that Coronado saw was still in its aboriginal state, somewhat different from the San Pedro of today. The old San Pedro, as described in some early trappers' accounts, was marshy and dammed up by beaver; beyond its banks spread groves of cottonwoods and fields of high sacaton grass. The killing of the beaver and overgrazing by cattle would later cause the river to cut into its bed, draining the marshes and generating a fractal maze of arroyos spreading miles away from the river.

The change in topography would also create an ideal habitat for the mesquite tree. The mesquite tree followed cattle wherever that beast was introduced in the lower elevations in the Southwest. It is a particularly tenacious plant, whose green, feathery crown extends only eight to twenty feet above ground, but whose black roots will penetrate sixty or more feet below, seeking distant moisture. The mesquite has many uses: a member of the pea family, it produces sweet, gummy bean pods which are eaten with delight by livestock; its flowers produce excellent honey; and its branches and roots are rock-hard, making for good fenceposts and fires. Castañeda reported that the Indians of this area make a "bread of the mesquite, like cheese, which keeps good for a whole year." Some Mexican Indians still grind up mesquite beans to make bread and beer. Cabeza de Vaca noted that mesquite beans were considered the greatest delicacy of all among many of the tribes he encountered.

We could not eat or drink the useful mesquite; the beans had not yet formed and, despite coaxing, the horses refused to eat the flowers. A still, baking heat collected in the twilight within the mesquite groves, and as we passed through, the continuous sound of thorns rasping and tearing our packs filled the air, punctuated now and then by an explosion of savage cursing from Eusebio. Nothing, not even our chaps, could stop the thorns. Clusters of them broke off and fell down our shirts, and sometimes entire branches covered with thorns would get hung up in the fork of our saddles or caught in the pack ropes and dragged along. Sometimes we would (as one cowboy put it) "emerge from a thicket with enough wood hanging in the fork of [the] saddle to cook a side of yearling ribs."

Possibly the most difficult of all skills in horsemanship is riding through brush. Cowboys who worked cattle in brush were known as "brush poppers." The great southwestern historian J. Frank Dobie wrote over half a century ago about the skill of the brush hand:

> In running in the brush a man rides not so much on the back of his horse as under and alongside. He just hangs on, dodging limbs as if he were dodging bullets, back, forward, over, under, half the time trusting his horse to course right on this or that side of a bush or a tree. . . . Patches of a brush hand's bandanna hanging on thorns and stobs sometimes mark his trail. . . .
>
> Unseen and unapplauded, the brush hand almost daily exerts as much skill and grit as any rodeo star ever displayed in conquering the most savage outlaw horse. . . . But nobody ever sees the brush popper in action. When he does his most daring and dangerous work he is out of sight down in a thicket. . . .
>
> A brush hand can work on the prairie as well as any prairie-trained cowboy, but a prairie-trained cowboy is as helpless in the bad brush as any tenderfoot. After struggling in the brush, any kind of horseback work on the prairie seems as "soft" to a brush hand as a cushioned rocking chair seems to a leg weary ditch digger.

Like the brush poppers of old, we left our own trail in the mesquite thorns, mostly pieces of plastic torn from the space blanket that covered Walter's camera or pieces of tarp ripped from our packs. As we proceeded, I regularly plucked off ragged pieces of space blanket from the mesquite, which I stuffed in my saddlebags. At the end of the day Walter would stitch the pieces back together for the next day's ride.

None of our horses had seen mesquite before, and they quickly learned to hate it. Sometimes, when they came to the edge of a thicket, they would stop and back up, ears flattening.

But nobody hated the mesquite more than Eusebio, who had never seen anything like it. (The open, sagebrush deserts of northern New Mexico are as different from the cactus-choked deserts of southern Arizona as Korea is from Kansas.) When he wasn't cursing the horses he turned his invective on the plant. "Sum-bitch stickers!" he would cry out, trying to work a cluster of thorns out of his neck. "This Arizona, this is the *sorriest* Goddamn country I ever seen! I ain't never coming back here, you bet, *shit!*"

There was one plant the horses hated more than mesquite, and that was catclaw. Catclaw inhabited the drier hills around the San Pedro, picking up where the mesquite left off. Catclaw is a low, gray, scrubby-looking thing with recurved thorns that grab into and literally tear off chunks of flesh. (For this reason it is sometimes called "wait-a-bit brush" by the cowboys.) Mesquite was bad, but catclaw, being low to the ground and dense, was truly impassable. With persuasion the horses would go through mesquite but they drew the line at catclaw.

It took Coronado two days to ride down the San Pedro; with the mesquite it would take us eight.

⊷ ⚏ ⊶

On April 17th, four days from our start at the border, we decided to give the horses a half-day off. I washed my jeans and draped them over a bush; the heat was so intense that in fifteen minutes they were bone dry and I had to let them cool off in the shade before I could put them on.

This same day I made a mistake that I would regret for the rest of the trip. I left my only cowboy boots in the sun, and they shrank one full size smaller. I pulled and struggled, finally wedging my broken toe into the front. The pain was magnificent. I ate four prescription ibuprofen tablets and then read the back label to learn that I could soon expect severe liver damage. At least, I thought, I didn't break my leg, as one of Coronado's friars did in the first days of the expedition. Somehow, the broken toe made me more determined than ever to finish this trip. Walter, who had broken many bones in his variegated life, had advised me that even a doctor could do nothing with a broken toe, so I made up my mind to live with it.

We set off about three, after the worst heat of the day had passed. Robin was clearly very sick by this time, and Walter decided to walk.

We picked up a dry track that wound through some hills west of the river, and in a few miles the track led us to a couple of sunbeaten trailers and an adobe ruin. A fellow in one of the trailers told us that the nearest vet would be in Tombstone, a day's ride to the northeast.

As we left the town, a long, low, sad-looking hound dog began following us.

"Ya! Go home!" I shouted. He retreated under a bush and, as soon as we were moving again, followed at a safe distance.

"If he wants to come, let him come," said Walter. "Our trip ain't gonna be complete without a dog."

"He belongs to somebody," I said. "Anyway, how the hell are we going to keep a dog alive on this trip?"

"Damn, Doug, where's your sense of adventure? What's a trip without a *dog?*"

We continued on. After several miles, we rounded a bend and came to a bridge across the river. A truck whizzed by.

"A road!" I shouted. Although it had only been four days since seeing a road, I felt elated.

We came into a clearing by the bridge, with a dirt turnaround. Two blue-rinse ladies and their husbands sat in lounge chairs next to a camper, drinking iced tea. As we rode out of the brush they leapt up.

"Oh my," one of the women said, her hand pressed to her bosom.

They were from Illinois, and they offered us iced tea. We had been drinking hot San Pedro water for four days, and laying aside any vestige of manners we demanded glass after glass until at least a gallon had disappeared down our throats and there was none left.

Two women in a car pulled up. They had seen our packhorses and wanted to find out what was going on.

"Let me talk to 'em," Walter said. "I'll get us a vet."

Walter charmed them with a long, colorful story of our adventures, told in his thickest Texas dialect, and he painted a bleak, heartbreaking portrait of our sick horse, Robin.

"If only we could get to a vet," he said. "Otherwise, she'll probably die. . ."

They wished us luck and drove off.

"So much for your charm," I said.

Three minutes later they appeared again, backing up on the road, and one woman threw open the car door. "We were just thinking about that poor horse," she began.

Walter flashed me a grin as he climbed into the car.

While Walter went to Sierra Vista, Eusebio and I set up camp a quarter mile upriver on a sandy flat near some humps of rubble. We had to lay down a barbed-wire fence to get back to the river and scare some cows out of our campground. The theory behind laying down a fence is to get through the barbed wire without cutting it. To lay down a fence, you unstaple the wires from five or ten posts and press the wires to the ground. Then, while you stand on the fence, your partner leads the horses across. When you release the wires they spring back into position, where you can restaple. The process is exceedingly tiresome, and no matter how careful you are it inevitably rips up your clothing and bloodies your hands.

The vet, a big friendly fellow named Gary Thrasher, arrived in a pickup at nine o'clock that night. He pulled up next to the camper.

We led Robin over. He climbed through the fence and examined her by the glare of his headlights.

"Something stuck in her throat," he said.

"What about her tongue?" Walter asked. "Someone told us it'd been cut by a bit."

Thrasher pried open her mouth and dragged out an unwilling tongue.

"Why hell," he said. "That's the smoothest, pinkest damn tongue I ever seen. What fool told you that?"

Walter shot me a very dark look.

Thrasher wrapped a twitch around Robin's nose. "Hold that tight," he said to me, "or she'll go up."

He then gave her a good shot of tranquilizer.

"If she starts toppling over," he said to Walter, "wake her up by hitting her on the nose."

He inserted a thick plastic tube in her right nostril and worked it into her throat. The poor horse's eyes rolled around.

He worked the tube deeper and deeper. "Aha!" he said. "Got it."

He prodded and pushed at the obstruction with the tube. It finally gave way. He shoved more of the tube into her nose, sometimes stopping and putting his ear to the other end.

"Here, listen to this." He passed the end of the tube to me. I heard the faint gurgling of gas.

"That's how you know you've reached the stomach."

He tipped a gallon jug of mineral oil into the tube and drained it. "Don't worry, she'll shit all this out tonight."

He then told us the bad news: Robin would need at least a week's

4

Back in camp, we stoked up the fire against the desert chill. Thrasher had told us that we had finally reached the ghost town of Charleston and were camped in its ruins, near the famous "hanging cottonwood" that was toppled by the river in 1928. It had taken us five days to cover what I had originally estimated we could ride in a day. By this time I had given up even thinking about when our journey might be over.

The profound darkness of the desert night grew upward from the ground, enveloping us in silence. The night was moonless, and the stars like glowing clouds. Here, I thought, once stood Charleston, one of the great boomtowns of the West. So thoroughly had it vanished from the face of the earth that we had camped in the middle of it without even noticing.

Charleston had once been a mill town where much of the ore from the Tombstone mines was crushed, refined, and poured into eighty-pound ingots of silver. A hundred years ago, the stretch of river from Charleston to St. David was lined with roaring towns filled with saloons and whorehouses, and stamp mills hammering ore all night long. All this activity serviced the great mines around Tombstone, with names like the Lucky Cuss, the Tough Nut, the Graveyard, the Grand Central, and the Contention. In 1864, before the silver strike, a census showed that there were three people living along the San Pedro; in 1886, less than ten years after silver was discovered, there were between ten thousand and twenty thousand; in 1989, none. The banks of the San Pedro had returned to a wilderness.

The Tombstone strike, which gave birth to Charleston, was the last great silver strike in Arizona. In 1875, a young prospector named Ed Schieffelin arrived in the territory with a dollar twenty-five cents in his pocket. Two years later he began prospecting in the hills around the San Pedro River, using Fort Huachuca as a base. The area was on a main Chiricahua Apache raiding trail and the soldiers thought he was insane to be wandering around by himself, where the dust he raised could be seen for miles. "All you'll find out there," one of them said to him, "is your tombstone." Schieffelin liked the comment so much that he christened the area he was prospecting Tombstone.

"He was about the queerest specimen of humanity ever seen," one acquaintance wrote, "with long black curly hair that hung several inches below his shoulders. His long untrimmed beard was a mass of unkempt knots and mats. His clothing was worn out and covered with patches of deerskins, corduroy, and flannel, and his old slouch hat, too, was so pieced with rabbit skin that very little of the original felt remained." Schieffelin was a rather typical Western prospector, caring almost nothing for riches; it was the hunt for gold that gave him a thrill. Nobody could dispose of a fortune more efficiently than a lucky prospector.

In the San Pedro Valley Schieffelin found some interesting-looking float (loose rock) and outcropping rock. He brought the rock to Tucson, but mining operators there declared it not even worth assaying. He threw most of it away but kept a few pieces of float, and went to Globe, Arizona, to see his brother Al. Al introduced him to a mine operator named Dick Gird, who assayed a piece of float and came back with astonishing news: it paid $2,000 to the ton in silver, spectacularly rich ore indeed.

The three men formed a partnership, agreeing to divide all profits equally, and secretly made their way to the San Pedro. Because Gird was well known in Globe as a clever miner, several parties of idle prospectors packed their mules and set off after them.

Here, the three Tombstone partners immediately began looking for the mother lode from which the float might have come. They went to the place where Ed had found the float, but it looked so poor that they called it the Graveyard, as that was where Al and Dick "buried their hopes." But Ed insisted on continuing, and not many days later he came across an outcropping that looked unbelievably good: the ore was so rich and soft that he could imprint a half-dollar in it. When Gird assayed the ore, it contained between $12,000 and $15,000 to the ton in silver, with another $1,300 or so in gold. In other words, the ore was nearly 50 percent pure silver.

Gird turned to Ed: "You lucky cuss, you found it." They immediately staked a claim and called it the Lucky Cuss. The slopes around the Lucky Cuss were covered with rich float and ridged with splendid outcroppings of ore. Since the standard claim boundary was 600 by 1,500 feet, it became quite a trick for the prospectors to figure out the dip and course of the ledges, to make sure the claim boundaries encompassed the richest ore bodies. (The Tough Nut Mine was so named because the strike of the ledges was exceptionally difficult to figure out; it was a "tough nut to crack.") They located mine after mine, which Gird surveyed, marked, and filed on.

Rumors spread and the San Pedro was soon crawling with prospectors. Money poured in from New York and Boston to develop the mines. Tombstone, six miles from the river, had no water, so the mills to process the ore were built along the river itself, which was dammed and diverted through massive banks of machinery to run the stamps that pulverized the ore. Towns grew around the mills, of which Charleston was the biggest. It had originally been named Red Dog, but the miners later changed the name to Charleston, after the city in South Carolina. The entire town was owned by one Amos W. Stowe, who filed a homestead claim to 160 acres in 1878 across from the Tombstone Mill and Mining Company's stamp mill. He platted a town site and attracted people by offering free three-year leases. Since many boomtowns in the West lasted barely that length of time, his offer was very popular and the town quickly sprang up.

Charleston, like Tombstone, was a raucous Western town. In fact, during the boom years it had a far worse reputation than Tombstone itself. It is likely that, had the shoot-out at the O.K. Corral not occurred, Charleston—rather than Tombstone—would have gone down in lore as the archetypically violent Western town.

Charleston roared all night long. When the day miners got off their ten-hour shift, all hell broke loose. "The nervous man," one writer commented, "would not have been happy in this setting." Exuberant gunshots were often fired into the air, and music and the shouting of gamblers, vying with the clanging of the stamp mills, went on for most of the night.

Both Charleston and Tombstone were packed with men who had come to strike it rich. "A man," one resident of Tombstone recalled, "might have only a dollar in his pocket, but in his heart he had millions; he could pull from his pockets a number of mining claims, each showing title to 1,500 × 600 feet of untold wealth needing only development to be another Comstock Lode. He could eat on credit, especially at the Chinese restaurants. [Many Chinese had come west to work on the railroads.] Perhaps even trade a location notice for a suit of clothes, especially if the merchant were a newcomer." All day and all night, people could be seen in the streets and saloons, poring over maps, unloading and passing around pieces of rock from their pockets, arguing over assay certificates, or promoting one dubious venture or another. Card playing was the diversion of choice, and no one played without betting. Many people carried guns and an argument could quickly escalate into a shoot-out. Sometimes even the schoolchildren came to school with six-guns strapped around their hips. The first teacher in the one-room Charleston schoolhouse made the children check their guns at the door. One new teacher in Tombstone was so horrified at seeing her students armed that she threw their loaded guns into the wood stove. They immediately started to go off like popcorn.

Life was not easy. Dinner for most miners was coffee, salt pork, and beans. Prospectors spent their days in the ferocious sun, tramping up and down the hills and arroyos, thrashing their way through catclaw and mesquite. Miners spent ten hours underground, six days a week.

Most of the saloons featured "hostesses," whose job it was to get the miners to buy drinks, for which the ladies were paid a commission of two and a half cents per drink. Most of these women also entertained men on the side, in their miserable shacks behind the saloons. Many of the girls died young, usually of pneumonia contracted after their immune systems had been weakened by venereal disease.

Sometimes a successful man, or a man courting one of the few available "decent" single women, would invest in a good suit of clothes. "If the swain felt himself a fair hand with Mr. Colt's pistol," the historian Odie P. Faulk wrote, "he might even purchase a derby hat, which to wear on Allen Street was to court a fight; someone would knock off such a headcovering, and first one and then another would kick it along. . . . If the owner was a dude and took the incident goodnaturedly the crowd usually would chip in to purchase him the regulation soft (cowboy) hat. If, however, he was an old hand and should have known better, then he had to be prepared to fight to defend his choice of headgear."

Charleston, like many frontier mining towns, filled up with men and women who had rather good reasons to vacate more settled areas of the country. These included gamblers, faro dealers, murderers, prostitutes, cattle thieves, and con-men. While most of these early towns had a modicum of law, many of the people who sought to become lawmen were criminals themselves. It was a great convenience for the criminal to get himself elected town marshal, and from this position he could then deputize his cronies. Votes could be bought for whiskey, and crimes could then be committed under perfect cover. It was also a useful way to eliminate competition from other criminals. Virgil Earp of Tombstone, the brother of Wyatt, was a prime example of a crooked marshal; the historical evidence strongly suggests he was a professional stagecoach robber. He, like many others in Charleston and surrounding towns, had been obliged to leave, in haste, places farther east.

Preachers also swarmed over these towns, as there were many souls to be saved. Endicott Peabody, the aristocratic Boston Brahmin, spent a year preaching in Tombstone before returning to Massachusetts and founding Groton School. People noted that a preacher had to have a good strong voice to drown out the cockfights, music, drinking, and swearing that went on of a Sunday morning.

By late 1883 there were 50 mines, 12 steam hoists, 150 stamps at 7 mills, and a half-dozen towns along or near the river.

In 1884, six years into the boom, the inevitable happened: the mines, having reached the depth of five hundred feet, struck the water table. The mine operators, ready for this contingency, moved in huge pumps, which were capable of sucking millions of gallons of water a day out of the mines. As the shafts sank deeper into the earth, the pumps worked harder to draw the water table down. Around this time the two Schieffelin brothers sold out, against Gird's advice; later Gird sold his share for more than twice as much. Gird then went to some trouble to look up the two brothers and divide his extra profit with them, although he hadn't the slightest moral or legal obligation to do so, thus honoring their original handshake agreement that all profits would be divided equally. They were men of rare honor.

Gird got out just in time. The price of silver began declining, and in

1886 the Grand Central Pumphouse burned and the mines began to flood. A few months after that the pumphouse at the Contention Mine burned; sparks from the conflagration set the Contention shaft itself on fire and the flames roared out of the ground like an erupting volcano. With the two biggest pumps dead the mines flooded and mining ceased instantly. The miners lost their jobs, and when they left so did the shopkeepers, preachers, whores, lawyers, rustlers, assayers, faro dealers, bartenders, mule drivers, and drifters. Charleston quickly became a ghost town, and not even a year later nature provided the final blow: an earthquake leveled many of its adobe houses.

In 1889 a reporter passing through Charleston noted that its only inhabitants were a few poor Mexicans scavenging a living among the ruins. Cattle roamed the streets and passing cowboys broke up the wooden roofs for firewood. Even the graveyards were looted, and the bones, scattered by people looking for wedding rings, were soon gnawed up by mice and rats. The mesquite trees came back with a vengeance, sinking their black-fisted roots into cellarholes, breaking apart adobe walls, choking the hardpacked dirt streets—until almost nothing was left.

Ed Schieffelin ended up far too rich to dissipate his fortune, but he found the life of a grandee not to his liking. He soon went off prospecting again with his mules, pick, and shovel, telling his friends he couldn't be happy unless he was digging in the earth looking for riches. He died in the mountains of Oregon in 1896. His body was found in the doorway of a mining cabin; nearby was a sack of ore that was later assayed at $2,000 to the ton.

"It is my wish," Schieffelin's will read, "to be buried in the dress of a prospector, my old pick and canteen with me, on top of the granite hills about three miles westerly from the City of Tombstone, Arizona, and that a monument such as prospectors build when locating a mining claim be built over my grave, and no other slab or monument erected."

"Schieffelin," one writer stated, "was heard to remark that the two most glorious nights of his life had been those when he had slept at the side of his initial discovery in the San Pedro Valley."

In our camp, as we looked about us, all we could see of Charleston were some uneven sections of ground, several piles of rubble, and a few depressions filled with tumbleweeds. If Thrasher hadn't told us that this was Charleston, we would not have noticed anything at all. I snuggled down into my bedroll and watched the great Milky Way of the galactic arm, glowing faintly like breath on a cold night, arching over the San Pedro Valley in amoral splendor. Its permanence made humanity's fleeting, boisterous presence along this river all the more ephemeral. The land was as empty as on the night that Ed Schieffelin had gazed skyward, thinking wild thoughts about the bag of rocks that lay by his side.

5

That night, the hound dog crept up to the fire and made himself comfortable. The next morning Walter and I argued.

"We got to have a dog for this trip," Walter said, and hauled out a sack of dried dog food that he had apparently bought in Sierra Vista, on his trip to get the vet. "We'll just take this along with us, and everything'll be fine. Think what a dog'll do for your story."

"Walter," I said, "we just can't take somebody's dog. He's got a collar on, for chrissakes."

For some reason the idea of taking care of a dog, on top of having to care for the six horses—which in my ignorance I had concluded were the most brutish, loathsome, and cretinous animals in all of God's creation—made me unreasonably angry. I seized the bag, tore it open, and dumped the contents into the sand.

"Okay, okay," Walter said. "No dog then. Jesus."

I could see the hound dog at the edge of the brush, peering at us, looking for a safe moment to creep back to the fire. "Ha!" I shouted again. His sad face dissolved into the shadow.

It was to no avail. As soon as our backs were turned the dog was grunting and rooting in the sand, stuffing himself with the dog food, and as we departed he again followed.

That morning we also acquired a new horse. A pickup truck and trailer arrived, and a woman hopped down and coaxed a white horse out, chattering and talking to it while we came up.

"This is Pepper," she said, and hauled the horse's face around so he was looking at her. "Isn't that right, Pepper?"

The horse, who was munching on a few wisps of straw taken out of the trailer, snickered his lips. He had long yellow teeth and bright black eyes, behind which lurked a devious horse intelligence. He was an Arabian, but not with the sleek, elegant lines typical of the breed. He was coarse and tough-looking, with a flea-bitten-gray coat.

She vigorously shook our hands. "Marilyn McCoy," she said, by way of introduction.

McCoy was one of Arizona's top endurance riders. The week before, we learned, she had ridden a race from El Paso, Texas, to Lordsburg, New Mexico, a distance of 285 miles. It took her five days. Nineteen riders had started, ten had finished. She came in second.

Pepper had once been her star endurance mount. "He used to ride a hundred miles in a day," she said. "But he's retired now, so you aren't allowed to ride him more than thirty-five."

On hearing this both Walter and I laughed. "Yesterday I think we made six miles," I said.

"Well I'll be darned," McCoy said, "you've hardly been *moving*. Gosh, I'd *hate* to be riding with you boys."

Pepper was pulling her away like an unruly dog, straining to reach a tuft of choice grass. After ripping that up he started pulling toward another.

"Oh you *pig*," McCoy said to the horse. "You've been eating all morning."

Endurance riding is similar to other horse races, only the distance covered can be as much as five hundred miles. Most of the rules in endurance competitions are aimed at preventing damage to the horse. Any breed can be entered, and the rider can walk, trot, lope, or gallop, although most endurance riders trot their horses. A horse cannot be ridden for more than a hundred miles in a day. The riders must stop periodically to have their mounts checked by a vet to see that they are not being hurt or overworked, and a horse that is getting overly tired is immediately disqualified. It is forbidden for the winner to get money; nobody wants to see horses ridden to death for a fat purse. McCoy supported her horse habit by getting up at 5:30 every morning to drive a schoolbus.

McCoy's farrier went to work shoeing Pepper while Thrasher, who had arrived at the same time, drew up a document on a paper towel, stating that we were temporarily trading Pepper for Robin and giving a legal description of the two horses including their breeding, brands, and color. Robin would rest at McCoy's place for the next ten days while we rode Pepper; then we would trade back.

She refused to accept anything but reimbursement for her costs. "Oh, don't you all worry about money," she said. "I just want to see you get where you're going." She paused for a moment. "Whenever *that* is."

McCoy had grown up in the lushness of Washington State. "When I first saw the desert," she said, "I felt this feeling, like I'd been released from a green hell. I could never live anywhere else but in the desert."

McCoy lectured us about Pepper. Pepper and McCoy had once gone down in San Pedro quicksand and had barely escaped with their lives. "If he doesn't want to go somewhere, you just better pay attention," she said. "He *knows* this river."

As we were leaving she added: "He's a darling. He's just like a dog; he'll stay right around camp."

We saddled up and headed downstream, Pepper in the lead. We felt that our problems with quicksand were over: Pepper would show us the way. And for a while he did, stopping from time to time to probe the sand ahead with his hoof like a skater testing thin ice. Soon, however, it became apparent that Pepper was also a very nimble horse: he would skitter across a boggy stretch of river that our less experienced horses would start sinking into, with much thrashing and panic. We finally had to ride back into the mesquite.

We stopped for lunch past the ruin of an old mill, under a spreading cottonwood. These ruins would suddenly loom out of the mesquite—a cement platform, a twisted iron girder, a trench, a cut in a hillside—and just as suddenly disappear. We turned the horses loose to graze and began eating lunch.

Suddenly Eusebio was up, hollering and waving his arms. My horse, King, was kneeling, getting ready for a lovely, satisfying roll in the dust. The only problem was that he still had Eusebio's thousand-dollar roping saddle on his back.

"Keeng!" he screamed. "¡Cabrón! Ándale, jodido. ¡Levántate!"

Walter tried to grab Eusebio as he went by. "Dammit, you're spooking the horses!"

"The *chingado* is breaking my saddle! KEENG! ¡*Te convierto en carne para los perros si quiebras mi saddle, jodido!*"

All six horses jerked their heads up and looked at the small, hysterical man running toward them, his chaps flapping and arms gyrating, screeching like a marmot. They did what any self-respecting horses would do and bolted off into the brush. Eusebio redoubled his yelling and continued after them, and soon disappeared in a rising cloud of dust.

There was a short silence.

"Did you see that?" Walter finally said. "That Mexican woodcutter of yours just lost all our horses." He sat on a log and carved a hunk off a stick of dried salami, poked it in his mouth, and began chewing while staring straight ahead.

Not knowing what else to do, I went off following the horses' tracks. In a half mile I met Eusebio riding King back with the rest of the horses in tow. I relieved him of three and we rode back into camp.

"Hey, anyone seen my hat?" Eusebio asked, to no one in particular.

Walter continued to sit on the log, chewing and silent.

We had finally passed the halfway point of our journey down the San Pedro River. As we struggled through the mesquite, I pictured with envy the image of Coronado and his party riding through endless fields of grass, with very few mesquite trees. The smaller party of picked horsemen—without the army's livestock—moved quickly. The narratives indicate that they followed established Indian trails all the way. They strung out along the trail, with Coronado and Fray Marcos at the front with the horsemen; the pack train brought up the rear, guarded by an escort of armed men led by a fierce Spaniard named Juan Gallego.

According to Castañeda, most of the country they traveled through was inhabited, with the exception of the *despoblado*. As they passed through settlements they stopped to inquire about the Seven Cities, and they would often hire local guides to take them on to the next village.

"The women paint their chins and eyes," Castañeda wrote about the inhabitants of lower Arizona, "like the Moorish women of Barbary. They are great sodomites. They drink wine made of the pitahaya, which is the fruit of a great thistle which opens like the pomegranate. The wine makes them stupid. They make a great quantity of preserves from the *tuna* [the fruit of the prickly pear cactus]; they preserve it in a large amount of its sap without other honey. . . . In this country there were also tame eagles, which the chiefs esteem to be something fine."

As they went through, they found the Indians of the country friendly and "in peace." All the Indians agreed, without apparent protest, to swear allegiance to the king of Spain, which Coronado dutifully required as per his instructions.

During this time Coronado followed to the letter his orders to be considerate to the Indians along the trail: the Indians were to be "treated as if they were Spaniards"—that is, as human beings. Even though food was scarce, he charged his men not to take food from them without compensation. One man who stole some roasting ears of corn was severely punished. When they camped near Indian settlements at night, guards were posted to prevent any thefts, mistreatment, or sexual misconduct.

The viceroy had specifically ordered that no Indians—neither the locals nor the Aztec followers from Mexico—could be used as carriers. (This had been a rather infamous Spanish practice.) The poorer Spaniards—those who had only one horse—were obliged to pack their horses and walk, which caused no little grumbling. But soon the men lost all pretensions to gentility.

"As each one," Castañeda wrote, "was obliged to transport his own baggage and all did not know how to fasten the packs, and as the horses started off fat and plump, they had a good deal of difficulty and labor. . . . In the end necessity, which is all powerful, made them skillful, so that one could see many gentlemen become carriers, and anybody who despised work was not considered a man." A great change was taking place in the outlook and experience of these spoiled gentlemen.

The same process occurred to us. I had never worked so hard in my life: we labored sixteen hours every day, from before dawn until well after sunset. In those sixteen hours I barely had time to snatch twenty minutes for jotting notes in my journal. There were no cozy evenings swapping stories around the campfire: as soon as we had wolfed down our dinners we crawled into bed.

Rather belatedly, I realized that exploration is hard physical labor. That, in fact, is what makes exploration what it is: you can come to know the true value of something only by gaining it through unrelenting effort. If we had been dropped down by helicopter in the middle of this river, it wouldn't have been the same place at all. When you travel somewhere by car or plane, you don't really *get* there.

I will now tell you a curious phenomenon. If you were to ask me what I did four days ago, I would be hard pressed to answer. But even as I write this, nine months after the end of the trip, I can close my eyes and see—as if I had recorded it on video—every single step we took, every inch of country, every hill and mountain, every spring we drank at. The heat, the mesquite, the lack of any trail, the quicksand, the foul water, the freezing nights, the endless work—every step of the way had been won only at great cost. I was starting to feel alive in a way I'd never felt before.

April 18th was another day spent blundering, cracking, and chopping our way through mesquite, and when six o'clock rolled around we began looking for a place to camp. We soon spied a lovely apron of sand on the far side of the river, covered with green grass. It was a perfect campsite. Pepper helped us find a crossing.

With much swearing and utterings of dreadful imprecations, Walter and Eusebio doctored the horses' bloody legs with gall salve. Walter then turned Pepper and Bobby loose to graze, and Eusebio turned Socks loose. We staked out the other horses on the forty-foot lash ropes.

I hauled some mesquite limbs out of the scrub, chopped them up, and built a roaring fire to make our usual "cowboy" coffee: a few fistfuls of grounds in a pot of bad water, which we would boil like hell until soupy.

Once the coffee was on and the horses set, there was sometimes a moment for rest, which I used for writing. Walter came over and peered in my face.

"Why," he said, "you're the dirtiest son-of-a-bitch I've ever seen." He roared with laughter and slapped me on the back. "You don't look like a New Yorker anymore. You're startin' to look *good.*"

"You look pretty ripe yourself," I said. In fact, Walter looked positively frightful: the mesquite had scored two deep cuts across his face, one across his nose and the other along his cheek, and his cheekbones were smeared with crusty blood and dirt. A dark, greasy sweat stain was creeping through his hatband and his beard was matted and sprinkled with twigs and bark.

The hound dog rolled about in the river and came shuffling into camp, completely covered with mud and still optimistic about his prospects with us. He walked over to me and laid his nose on my shoe. He gazed up, his eyebrows wrinkling in the most pathetic, hopeful way.

"Oh for chrissakes," I said.

"Let's call him Redbone," said Walter.

"Redbone?" said Eusebio. "What's a redbone? Naw, we call him *El Mujado.*"

"El Moohow?" asked Walter. (In Eusebio's Spanish dialect, the "j" is pronounced like an "h" and the "d" is silent.)

"*Mujado!* Wetback! He a wetback, for sure!" Eusebio wheezed with laughter. "He come from Mexico, that one! Just like we did! We all *mujados* now!"

We called him Redbone Moohow.

Our dinners had consisted of what we had begun to call the Coronado Plan: a pot of rice and beans, with a liberal dose of hot red chile, cooked to a mush. Quite a few doves were calling back and forth across the river, and I suggested to Walter that maybe we could use something to flavor the pot. He unshipped the under-and-over and went off to find dinner.

While he was gone, Eusebio came over.

"I don't like this," he said, nodding toward Pepper.

"What?"

"That Pepper, he wanna go. I been watching him. All the time, he wanna go."

"Go where?"

"He's missing that woman. Look at them ears."

Pepper was gazing far up the river, ears perked.

"Why don't you tie him up?" I asked, not knowing that it is bad form for a horseman to touch somebody else's horses.

Eusebio spat and ground the glob into the sand with his bootheel.

"That guy, what's his name, he don't listen to *nobody.*"

"Walter."

"*Walter.* That *Walter* don't know *shit* 'bout *nothing.*"

I shrugged my shoulders. "Marilyn said he'd stay around camp." It didn't seem likely that the horses would go anywhere, surrounded as they were by mesquite and quicksand, both of which they had shown a great aversion for. We hadn't used hobbles after our experience the first night, when Pedernal and Bobby broke their gunny-sack hobbles and took off. Instead, we had been staking the horses, tying them on long ropes so they could move about and graze at night. A horse can only be staked when the grazing is excellent, which it had been so far.

I could hear in the distance the *thump-thump* of the shotgun.

The sun had begun to set, suffusing the air with a warm glow. An intensity of orange and gold collected in the treetops, and the sky deepened to ultraviolet, the two colors vibrating against each other. The river purled silently over its bed, its surface a rilled confusion of green and blue and gold. The three loose horses grazed at the far end of the sandbar, and the smoke from the crackling fire tumbled upward into the still air. It was such a beautiful scene that I sat, entranced, and soaked it in.

Walter returned with two doves and tossed them at my feet.

"What am I supposed to do with these?" I asked, alarmed. I had never cleaned a bird in my life.

Walter laughed. "Cut off their heads, pluck 'em, gut 'em, and chop off their feet. I'm gonna take a photograph."

When I was finished there were two tiny carcasses left, each about as big as my thumb. It was a disappointment, and I had temporarily lost my appetite.

Walter was setting up his camera at the far end of camp when the light suddenly failed; in the desert, the air is so clear and thin that once the sun sets the atmosphere cannot hold or scatter light and darkness falls instantly. Walter began cursing and muttering. I got a pot of beans and rice boiling on the fire, and tossed in the two birds. Walter came back and squatted by the fire, filling his tin cup with coffee.

"Missed it," he said. "Should've been out photographing instead of shooting birds."

In the sudden twilight, tree frogs began calling, a shrill, human cry that started as a throaty muffled scream and then opened up and died away. They sounded very much like a fat woman being slowly murdered.

During dinner, Walter spooned his piece of bird onto my plate.

"What's this?" I asked. "You don't like my cooking?"

"Don't want it," he said.

"Why not?"

"Just don't want it." There was a short pause, then Walter added: "I'd forgotten what it was like to kill something beautiful."

"I thought you were a hunter," I said.

"Used to be."

"Why'd you quit?"

Walter stared into the fire.

"I once learned something about the value of life," he said quietly, and fell silent.

Darkness flowed around us, and the vast mists of stars reappeared above us. The temperature began its nightly plunge toward freezing. We stood around the embered fire in silence.

Then we heard it: the distant thudding of hooves. We turned, and saw the shapes of the three horses—one white, two dark—suddenly materialize from the blackness, galloping straight at us, legs churning, nostrils flaring smoke in the cold air, ears flattened. It was a fantastic and terrifying sight. I instinctively turned to run.

"Don't move," Walter hissed.

At the last moment the animals divided and peeled past, spraying us with flying clots of dirt and sand. The thunder of their hooves rolled off into silence, a reverberation echoing and dying along the river.

Walter stood transfixed. "Beautiful," he murmured, his voice trembling with emotion. "They were like ghosts, like spirits of the night, like. . ." He gestured mutely into the darkness.

Eusebio went off to get them, cursing, while we listened into the silence, trying to hear what had spooked them.

⊷ ☒ ⊶

When I awoke at five o'clock, Eusebio was already up and I could hear him talking to Walter, the sound of voices rising over a crackling fire. By the time I hauled on my jeans Eusebio had gone upriver on foot, with Walter after him.

The three loose horses had disappeared completely during the night. I started the coffee and a half hour later Walter returned.

"I found their tracks on the far side of the river," he said. "Those sons-of-bitches are *traveling*." He saddled Pedernal, cinched him up tight, and trotted off.

It was only after he left that I realized neither he nor Eusebio had taken any water. It was still dark and freezing at this point.

Since we had been following the river we had not yet had to worry about finding water. We had been drinking the river water, but running it first through a little hand-held pump that was supposed to remove bacteria, parasites, and heavy metals. Since the San Pedro originated in Mexico in an area of mines, open sewers, and poisonous tailing ponds, I dreaded to think what might happen if one of us drank straight from the river.

During the past week we had acquired a healthy respect for the amount of water we needed to consume in this kind of heat. Each of us emptied a four-quart canteen daily, drinking deeply every thirty to forty minutes. Despite these enormous quantities of water, I needed to piss only once a day (if that), and a damn pathetic stream it was. Some incredible mechanism had gone to work in my body, hoarding every drop of moisture.

It was quite alarming just how thirsty one could become in the heat of the desert—so thirsty that sometimes no amount of drinking seemed to quench it. Going without a drink for even two or three hours in that heat would be extremely uncomfortable, and to go for a day would, I believe, have been incapacitating.

In addition to our needs, each horse required ten gallons or more of water per day. Our total requirement, then, was at least 63 gallons a day, or just over a quarter ton of water. I thought to myself: once we leave the river, just where *were* we going to find a quarter ton of water, every day, in the deserts of southern Arizona?

At any rate, the lesson was now clear. There was almost no margin for error. We could never, ever, allow ourselves to run out of water. Ever. (The Spaniards probably had it easier than we would. Coronado, with his Indian guides, almost never had trouble finding water—unless, as happened on a few occasions, his Indian guides deliberately led him astray.)

After Walter left, I went to search for the horses from on high, so I took the binoculars and hiked into some barren hills east of the river. I climbed through several barbed-wire fences, crossed some old railroad tracks, and picked a prominent hill as an observation point.

The sun rose just as I reached the top, throwing a purple light across the valley. The river was mostly hidden by cottonwoods and willows, surrounded by sparse mesquite. I could see Walter far below, appearing and disappearing as he threaded his way through the scrub.

At the very summit of the hill lay a peculiar flat stone, which I sat down on. With the binoculars I scanned the river, waited, and scanned again, hoping to catch sight of the loose horses as they moved into a clearing.

Dropping away from me was the surreal landscape of southern Arizona. The masses of rounded hills, with their light covering of greasewood and catclaw, looked like a crowd of balding men, their scalps visible through a thin fuzz of hair. The country was becoming much hillier, and I could see range upon range of mountains to the north, where we were headed—the beginning of the great *despoblado*.

I thought about our problem. These missing horses were only the culmination of what had become one long, undifferentiated struggle. In nearly a week of travel we had progressed no more than twenty-five miles north. Walter and I still knew next to nothing about what we were doing, and Eusebio had turned into an unwelcome hanger-on, whose primary functions in life appeared to be cursing, spitting, and

whacking his horses. I began seriously to question why I had undertaken this trip in the first place, and I hoped, for a fleeting moment, that
the horses would not be found.

I took comfort in the fact that the Spanish soldiers were probably
even more perturbed at this point than I was. Fray Marcos had been
shown up as an exaggerator; and several of the Indians who had gone
with him had already been "caught in lies." Their animals were exhausted; their food was running low; and they were still hundreds of
miles from their goal. They, unlike me, did not have the luxury of
going back. There was nothing for them in Mexico City or even back
in Spain, as most of them had sunk every penny they had into the
expedition. I wondered what the poor Scotsman, "Tomás Blaque"—
Tom Black (or was it Blake?)—had thought of this ferocious landscape.
Now there was a man who had had good reason to be lonely and
frightened. He was, literally and figuratively, as far away from home as
a human being could get.

No, I told myself, it was harder for Coronado and his men than it
was for us. What was more, the early trappers, mountain men, and
prospectors in this area faced worse situations. The first Anglo-American in this valley, James Pattie, had come up the San Pedro trapping
for beaver in the 1820s. He buried a fortune in skins right along this
very stretch of river, and then the Apaches stampeded his horses. He
had to walk six hundred miles back to Santa Fe. He arrived a scarecrow,
more dead than alive, spent months recuperating, and went back to the
San Pedro to recover his skins, only to find the Apaches had dug them
up and stolen them.

I made a decision sitting on that rock. I would be Goddamned if I
was going to quit. For one thing, I had a superstitious feeling that I was
being tested, and that only stiffened my resolve. Besides, Walter and
Eusebio had been harping on my greenness—hollering at me to loosen
my reins, tighten my reins, shorten up my lead rope, show that Goddamn horse who's boss, do this and not do that. The more they harped,
the more I was determined to outlast those sons-of-bitches. If those
greenhorn Spaniards did it, so could a greenhorn Yankee. The only way
I'd abandon this trip was if they had to remove me from the trail on
a stretcher.

Despite these thoughts, sitting on top of the hill gave me a wonderful
moment of peace. For the next forty-five minutes the temperature
ranged through the comfort zone, and I was alone, with nothing to do,
for the first time in days. I took off my jacket and hat and closed my

eyes, feeling the infrared warmth of the sun. I breathed in the air, faintly redolent of cottonwood and salt cedar. The sky was clear, and the distant mountains slowly turned from pink to blue as the sun climbed in the sky.

I roused myself and stood up with the binoculars, scanning the thornscrub again. Quite unexpectedly I noticed that two Indian petroglyphs had been pecked into the sandstone rock I had been resting on. One was the stick figure of a man with big hands, and the other was a spiral, a prehistoric symbol thought possibly to represent the *sipapu*, the sacred hole where human beings emerged from the Third World into this, the Fourth World.

Long before the coming of the Spanish, then, the San Pedro Valley had been inhabited by prehistoric Indians, in this case the Hohokam. The Hohokam, the Anasazi, and the Mogollon people had built some of the greatest prehistoric civilizations America had ever seen. By the eleventh century, for example, the Anasazi were living in enormous thousand-room structures, some connected by extensive road systems, and their civilization spread over tens of thousands of square miles. During this time they built the fantastic structures at Chaco Canyon. But these great civilizations went into decline, and many of the large pueblos—some inhabited for less than fifty years—were abandoned and the roads no longer used. Was it drought? Warfare? Environmental degradation? Social disintegration? Nobody really knows. But these prehistoric Indians did not disappear; they moved to other areas and eventually evolved into the Pueblo Indians encountered by Coronado. Not death, but a change of worlds.

I traced my finger around the rough indented spiral. Once, many centuries ago, a Hohokam Indian had stopped here and chiseled this sacred figure into the rock. Where was he going? Did he live in the valley? What was the importance of this hill? Was it sacred? In thinking these thoughts, I had a momentary, dislocating sense of time and scale, a fleeting sense of something immense, dignified, and very human. It was a sudden glimpse back into a very different past, a past whose meaning had vanished forever with its makers.

I suddenly knew why I was making this journey.

6

I made my way back to the river. Walter and Eusebio were still gone, so I began to break camp. The temperature rapidly peaked at a hundred degrees and I thought about the two of them out there, drinking poisonous water from the river. Just as I was finishing, Walter returned.

"Did you drink from the river?" I asked.

"Hell no. Gimme that canteen."

With trembling hands he drank the water, spilling it down his shirtfront and over his horse, who flicked his ears with annoyance.

"We got a problem here," he said, after catching his breath. "Those horses aren't following the river. They went into the desert."

"Did you see Eusebio?"

"Saw his tracks. I'm going back out."

I gave Walter a gallon of water, a hundred dollars, and some food. We figured he might be gone for a few days.

Just as he was about to leave, we heard a shout. Eusebio appeared on the far side of the river, riding Pepper bareback and leading the other two horses. He was controlling Pepper with makeshift reins fashioned out of Redbone Moohow's collar.

We whooped as he dismounted. He was in a high state of excitement.

"Aiee! Sum-bitch!*"* he cried out, waving his arms, his face a mass of excited wrinkles.

"Where did you find them?" I asked.

"Find 'em? That sum-bitch was right *there,* waiting!"

"Right where?"

"Where he been unloaded! Sum-bitch went right back, waiting for his owner!"

"You mean where Marilyn unloaded him yesterday morning?"

"That's what I'm telling you! That sum-bitch *know* this river. He shag ass, man, follow 'em back trails. You know it!"

Eusebio then hawked up his finest gob of phlegm yet, a lump as solid as a tumor, which he rocketed into the sand.

"You didn't drink from the river, did you?" I asked.

"Not me! That horse, he knew a spring in the desert. He go right there, straight! Just like that! He *know* this country, boy!"

Redbone Moohow, who had followed Eusebio back to the Charleston bridge, had decided to return home after all, but not before providing one tiny, but essential, gift to our expedition: his collar. I was actually sorry—I had started to like the old dog. Walter was crestfallen.

We saddled and packed the horses, and set off in nearly intolerable heat. We soon came out on a trail, which brought us to a white ranch house under a cool spread of trees.

This was the old headquarters of the Boquillas Ranch, a place once owned by William Randolph Hearst. The convoluted history of land ownership along the San Pedro had prevented this river—with its year-round flow, immense aquifer, and artesian springs—from suffering the same fate as almost all the other rivers in the Southwest: heavy development.

Hearst's parents, George and Phoebe, had acquired one of two old Spanish land grants along the San Pedro in the late nineteenth century. The grant, called the San Juan de las Boquillas y Nogales, was owned by dozens of obscure heirs to the original Spanish grantee, who had been chased out by Apaches in the 1830s. Most of the heirs hadn't ever seen the property and didn't even know they owned it. The Hearsts searched them out and paid them nominal sums to sign quitclaim deeds. Then they successfully sued to clear their title and promptly ran off the Mormon and Mexican farmers who had settled along the river. There had been quite a bit of violence and many of the departing farmers had blown up their irrigation wells and ditches as they left.

The southern part of the river belonged to a second land grant, the

San Rafael del Valle. The nineteenth-century owner of the San Rafael grant was William C. Greene, himself a colorful and violent character. He once gunned a man down in the streets of Tombstone because the fellow had allegedly dynamited one of Greene's dams along the San Pedro; the flooding water had drowned Greene's daughter. Along with the San Rafael grant he assembled an enormous landholding that stretched from the San Pedro deep into Mexico. He discovered immense copper deposits in Cananea, Mexico, at the headwaters of the San Pedro, which he turned into the Cobre Grande mines, at one time the richest copper mines in the world. (It was Greene's bloody suppression of a strike at the Cobre Grande mines that helped trigger the Mexican Revolution of 1911.)

Both the Hearst and Greene landholdings were eventually bought by Tenneco West, Inc., which ran cattle along the river. In 1986 the Bureau of Land Management, in a farsighted move, saved nearly fifty thousand acres along the San Pedro from development by swapping the Boquillas and San Rafael grants with Tenneco for another valuable piece of land the BLM owned near Phoenix. As a result, thirty-five miles of one of the most beautiful—and most developable—rivers in the Southwest was miraculously preserved.

Just before noon we arrived at the ghost town of Fairbank, the last town along the San Pedro to die. It started as a station on the railroad and lay within the railroad right-of-way. It had managed to survive the Tombstone bust, and had hung on until the railroad tracks were shifted farther west. The last resident left in 1967.

All that was left of Fairbank was a crazy, leaning shell of a building with a peeling sign saying "Fairbank Commercial Company." Next to that was the ruin of the old post office, and in a dirt patch stood a pair of abandoned gas pumps. A brand-new prefabricated building—the local BLM office—rose rather incongruously out of the brush. As we tied the horses up at the pumps, a man in a crisp uniform came out.

"We thought you must've ridden through days ago," he said.

"We been detained by the mesquite," Walter said.

The man invited us in to fill up our canteens.

At the door a stream of air conditioning spilled over us, bringing with it the smells of new carpeting, vinyl, ink, and Xerox machines. We shuffled about inside, hats off, feeling dirty and suddenly aware that we stank of horse sweat.

Beyond Fairbank we followed a dirt track through the mesquite, hoping to reach Contention City, another ghost town several miles downriver. The track ended in a wash and we ate lunch at the ruins of the old Grand Central Mill, now a cement retaining wall streaked with rust.

Just beyond the Grand Central Mill, on the far side of the river, a low adobe wall could be seen poking up above the brush. This was the ruin of Quíburi, the *rancheria* of a seventeenth-century Jesuit priest named Eusebio Francisco Kino, and the fortified home of Chief Coro of the Sobaípuri Indians. It was an unremarkable ruin with a remarkable history.

Father Kino was the first European to enter the San Pedro River Valley after Coronado and his ragged army had passed through it on their way back to Mexico in 1542. He was a curious but seminal figure in the history of Arizona. He wasn't Spanish, but a South Tyrolean born in 1645 into a wealthy family named Chino.

He began life as a young man of great learning, an intellectual of the first rank, who studied astronomy, cartography, and mathematics in Austria and Germany. He learned to speak Chinese and joined the Jesuit order, hoping to be sent to work in the ancient civilizations of Cathay.

Instead, the Jesuits assigned him to convert the Indians in the most barbarous hinterlands of New Spain.

In Mexico, he discovered that the word "Chino" was an insulting term that referred to half-breed Mexican peasants, so he changed it to Kino. Padre Kino soon set up a mission seventy-five miles south of the San Pedro River and, in the 1680s, rode north into what would become Arizona. It would be interesting to know what the Sobaípuri first thought when they saw this thin, scruffy white man with a bulbous nose and the broad-brimmed hat of his order emerge from the thorn-scrub.

At this very spot, Kino met a Sobaípuri chief named Coro. The two became friends, although Coro steadfastly refused to convert and remained a pagan for the rest of his life. But the chief had no objection to Kino's proselytizing and allowed Kino to set up *visitas* (preaching stations) and *rancherías* (temporary camps) along the river. Kino established his most prominent *rancheria* here, at Quíburi, where Coro held court. He explored other parts of the Southwest and made two expeditions down the Colorado River. His map of the northern Sonora/ southern Arizona area was so fine that it was the basis of all maps of the region until the nineteenth century.

On many of his visits to the Sobaípuri, Padre Kino would drive herds of longhorn cattle and horses up from Mexico for the Indians, following the same route we had. As a result, Kino is honored as being America's first cowboy in the Cowboy Hall of Fame in Oklahoma City.

Kino was an unlikely cowboy, and he followed a strict vow of poverty by giving away everything he owned to the Indians. He wore hair shirts, mixed his food with bitter herbs to make it as distasteful as possible, and slept on the bare ground with only his horse's stinking saddle blankets for warmth. He built many missions in southern Arizona ranging farther north than this stopping point. Kino's successor once surprised the old priest savagely whipping himself in his church. As he was dying, he insisted on remaining in his primitive bed, his head resting on his saddle.

After his death, many of Kino's longhorns escaped and went wild, roaming along the river and through the surrounding hills. As Apaches began drifting into the valley in increasing numbers they hunted the wild cattle, and by the 1780s had driven the Spanish and the Sobaípuris completely out of the San Pedro Valley.

When the Mormon Battalion of the U.S. Army passed near the site of future Charleston in 1846 while cutting a wagon road to California, the ferocious descendants of Kino's cattle became so enraged at the sight of domestic oxen that the bulls attacked the train en masse. Rifle and six-gun fire wouldn't drive them off and the several wagons were wrecked in the melee. The only human casualty was a soldier, who broke his thumb. This peculiar engagement became known as the Battle of the Bulls.

◦ ⊠ ◦

We lolled about in the shade of the cottonwoods, while Walter covered his face with his hat and snored for fifteen minutes. We were soon riding again, and quite abruptly we found ourselves in the midst of Contention City—or what was left of it.

The name of the town resulted from a quarrel between the Schieffelins and an unscrupulous prospector over a rich silver ledge. The argument was settled by dividing the ledge in two. The Schieffelins, continuing their penchant for humorous names, called their half of the mine the Contention. (The other was named the Grand Central.) These two mines would turn out to be among the richest silver mines in Arizona.

Contention City was even shorter lived than Charleston; its post office opened in 1880 and closed in 1888. It wasn't much to look at, although unlike Charleston you could tell that something had once been here. The stubs of a few deeply rilled adobe walls ran through the mesquite, interspersed with cellar holes and a line of posts going nowhere. On a nearby hill we could see some lumpy ground, the remains (we had been told) of the old graveyard. The wooden tombstones had been broken up for firewood and the graves looted.

A narrow-gauge railroad grade went past the ruins, and we could see, winding along the hills east of town, the remains of the old stagecoach road from Tombstone to Benson. It was now gutted by erosion and choked with catclaw, impassable by even a single horse.

Along this road a few miles north of Contention City, on March 15, 1881, a stagecoach with a Wells-Fargo strongbox containing about $25,000 in silver was attacked by masked bandits. The stage driver, a fellow named Bud Philpot, and a passenger were killed. It was the killing of Bud Philpot that finally brought law and order to the Territory of Arizona. It precipitated the famous shootout at the O.K. Corral in Tombstone between the Wyatt Earp–Doc Holliday gang and the Clanton–McLowry gang. This gunfight, misrepresented in legend and by Hollywood, was nothing more than the culmination of a sordid feud between a group of cattle rustlers headquartered at the Clanton Ranch near Charleston and the three Earp brothers and Holliday, who were almost certainly professional stagecoach robbers.

The shootout at the O.K. Corral, and the revenge killings that came afterward, raised a national outcry. They became a cause célèbre, and the yellow press back east had a wonderful time painting a picture of Arizona as a savage, lawless, bloodthirsty place. President Chester A. Arthur, jumping on the bandwagon, threatened to put Arizona under martial law if, by May 15th, 1882, Arizonans had not ceased "aiding, countenancing, abetting, or taking part in. . .unlawful proceedings." This proclamation infuriated all Arizonans, who felt the president had defamed their territory. To prove their respectability, vigilante groups formed and began stringing up suspected criminals in record numbers. Crooked marshals were run out of towns and many shady characters, who had initially come to Arizona to escape the law, packed their bags and disappeared. Law and order came to Arizona, and Wyatt Earp went to California.

By the time we rode through, the sound and the fury of the Tombstone era had died away. The only sounds we heard, riding through Contention City, were tumbleweeds rustling in a light breeze. Time had erased even the memory of the Old West here.

7

That evening, we camped a few miles beyond Contention City at a scrubby flat where there was grass for the horses. I tied up Pepper, using three half-hitches which I tightened down as hard as I could. Walter was still excited by the vision of the horses galloping by us the night before.

"I got a painting all worked out," he said, taking out his notebook and showing me a sketch. "It'll be called 'Ghost Horses of the Night.'"

While we ate our usual dinner of rice and beans, I asked Eusebio: "What do you think of the trip so far?"

There was a long shaking of the head. "In all my life," he said simply, "this is the hardest riding I ever done."

"Would you have done it if you'd known what it was going to be like?"

"Nope," said Eusebio.

I was awakened in the dark, as usual, by the sound of Eusebio breaking wood for the fire and Walter hooting and yipping like a coyote as he crawled into the bitter cold—his way of waking up. I fished around for my flashlight and checked my watch.

"For chrissakes, it's 12:45," I called out.

"Oh," Walter said, and without another word they both went back to bed.

The next morning Eusebio complained. "We ain't getting up early enough," he said. "We ain't going *nowhere*."

"We're gettin' up too Goddamn early," Walter said. "What's the point of gettin' up if you can't see jack shit?"

Soon, according to our maps, we would pick up a dirt track that led to the tiny Mormon settlement of St. David, which would mark the end of our struggle down the San Pedro.

Later that day we nearly lost Eusebio. He was riding ahead and we heard a sudden commotion and a torrent of Spanish, along with the sound of something large thrashing about in mud. Eusebio and his horses had broken through some crusty, alkali ground near the river and were sinking rapidly in quicksand.

He whipped and hollered, his horses flailing about, sending up a spray of flying clots. After a horrifying moment, when it seemed all was lost, his horses broke free with a loud sucking noise and bounded to the bank, heaving and slick with black mud from their bellies down.

"Aiee!" Eusebio cried. "*¡Ya mero los perdia!*" His hands danced about in the air. "Hoooo, sum-bitch quicksand!"

I rode along the river looking for a crossing farther up. Then I spied the end of a dirt track on the far side, next to a sluice gate. I knew this must be the irrigation ditch we were looking for. We had made it. Without thinking, I moved my horse onto a flat.

An explosion—a shock of flexing muscle—took place underneath me. Like a complete fool, I had ridden onto the same treacherous ground that had nearly sunk Eusebio. Nothing will panic a horse as efficiently as sinking in mud. King threw his head back and lunged forward, only to land again with a sickening flop. He tried to leap, but couldn't break free, and struggled and whinnied in high-pitched terror.

"Aiee! Get off him!" Eusebio shouted.

I instantly complied, landing in the mud and scrambling free of the thrashing animal. Relieved of my weight, he made another lunge and freed himself. He stood on the bank, his eyes rolling in terror, a ropy piece of saliva hanging from the bit.

We had to ride two miles back to find a safe crossing, and then come back up the west side of the river. This time, we were in a mesquite jungle that paled anything we had seen before. I could hardly believe the savagery of it. Adding to our difficulties, every hundred yards or so we would come to a deep arroyo cutting through the red earth, with sheer, thirty-foot banks. Some of these arroyos we had to ride alongside for a mile or more to find a way down, and then ride along the bottom for miles trying to find a way out. At numerous points we had to stop and hack a tunnel through the mesquite with our axe and knives.

Finally we struck a little track, which paralleled a greeny, swift-flowing irrigation ditch. I wanted to get down off my horse and kiss the ground. It had taken four hours to get ourselves up the final hundred feet of river.

As it was getting late we started hunting for a place to camp. We rode down to the river's edge.

There was no grass. In fact, there was no river, just an ugly mud flat covered with an alkaline crust. The entire flow of the San Pedro had been diverted at the sluice gate to irrigate the cotton and alfalfa fields of St. David and Benson.

Walter was disgusted. "Will you look at that? The sons-of-bitches stole the whole river!"

We made camp in the middle of the track, next to a grassy clearing for the horses.

"Where's my gun?" Walter asked, examining his shredded pack. The gun had been tied up in a leather scabbard and lashed to the pack; now there was nothing left but a dangling rope. Somewhere in the mesquite it had been torn off, but the question of going back into that green hell to retrieve it was not raised.

"Mesquite must've et it," Walter concluded with a snort.

That evening a black mood settled over the camp. Coming out of the mesquite hadn't cheered us up at all; rather it had suddenly empha-sized just how much further we had to go. The trip was ten days old, but I could barely seem to remember my former existence.

While silently drinking coffee in the dark the next morning, Walter suddenly said: "Bullshit."

There was a silence.

"This trip is *bullshit*," he said. "What's the point of killing ourselves in this mesquite? I ain't getting any photographs or anything else worth shit out of this trip."

"Well," I said lamely, "it looks like the mesquite is past us."

Walter grunted. "It's taken us ten days to ride thirty-five miles. We got another, what, nine hundred and sixty-five miles to go? And this was supposed to be the easy part. We got mountains and deserts ahead that'll make this look like a picnic. Shit, Doug, I don't know about you but I got a life to live and paintings to paint and a girlfriend back there who's probably right now having a balling good time with some guy."

"You don't really believe that," I said.

"You just can't go off and leave 'em like this, and expect 'em to be waiting for you when you get back. Women need regular loving."

Eusebio broke in. "Don't you be thinking about your woman, or you ain't *never* gonna finish this trip. Man, I *know* what I'm talking about." Eusebio laughed bitterly, and I suddenly realized that he, too, had been struggling with thoughts of his wife and family.

Walter tossed the grounds from his cup into the fire and we silently broke camp.

Knowing that Walter and Eusebio were suffering as I was made me euphoric. They weren't so Goddamn tough after all. I had also come to realize that, if I truly wanted to understand what the discovery of the Southwest had been like, and what it had meant to Coronado and his men, I would have to take the bad with the good. If I really wanted to extract some truth out of this business, I was going to pay for it.

Later that day, we had our first encounter with civilization. We entered the town of St. David, covered with dried mud and stinking of horse sweat, and somebody promptly called the police.

We bought a sack of rolled oats from an elegantly coiffed elderly lady, who came running out of her house in bare feet to greet us. We hit the main road and farther on we rode into a Circle K gas station and convenience store, much to the consternation of everyone there, and bought doughnuts and cold drinks; later we passed a cafe where we put in orders for hamburgers. There I spied a battered telephone.

I called up my girlfriend, Peggy, who was in New York City.

"Jesus, where *are* you?" she asked over the crackling, hissing wire.

"St. David." I had given her a map of our estimated itinerary, which had us going through St. David a week ago, on April 14th. It was now April 21st.

"Oh my God," she said.

I pressed her for news of the world. Abbie Hoffman had killed himself. Lucille Ball had died. A jogger had been gang-raped in Central Park. I listened to her talking about our friends in Santa Fe and New York, and how at dinner last night everyone had toasted our trip and wondered where we were. It was so terribly unreal that I found myself choking with laughter at the absurdity of it.

We ate the greasy hamburgers under the trees and a reporter named Laurie Tipling, from the *San Pedro Valley News-Sun*, came by and took our picture. "If you want," she said, looking us up and down, "you can stop by my place and shower."

We headed out of St. David on a main road, going toward Benson. It started to get late. Traffic roared past us. We passed a motel and trailer park on the outskirts of Benson, and then the police station. There was nowhere to camp. We began to panic.

"What're we going to do?" I asked Walter.

"Let's go to that reporter's house," Walter said. "We'll tie our horses up there and buy them some hay."

"Ride into someone's yard with six horses?" I said. "This is *suburbia* for chrissakes."

Walter turned around in his saddle. "Well, then, let's hear your brilliant idea."

Following Laurie's directions, we rode into an immaculate suburban neighborhood of square bungalows, neat green lawns, and freshly paved streets. We rode close by the houses, looking for her number. Sometimes a curtain would rustle or a door open, and someone would watch us go by with surprise and suspicion.

The odor of civilization—of exhaust, asphalt, and cut grass—lay across the town, a familiar smell made alien by nine days of wilderness. Our first horseback encounter with late-twentieth-century civilization was singularly unpleasant. Not only did we feel out of place—it was, in fact, illegal to be riding a horse in Benson—but we were in more danger here than at any other point on the trip so far. The horses were trembling and ready to spook at the slightest opportunity; the asphalt was, to a shod horse, like glare ice; and the potential of being hit by a car seemed quite high. It was a powerful reminder of how much the frontier had changed.

Walter hollered. "If you think this is bad, wait till we have to ride straight through downtown Albuquerque. That'll be a trip."

That seemed like a very long way off indeed.

Our proposal to turn Laurie's yard into a stable didn't seem to faze her. "I didn't have any plans for tonight anyway," she said.

We turned the horses loose in the tiny fenced yard, where they stood around, pricking up their ears, looking bewildered. Laurie drove me around in her pickup, looking for hay. Everything was closed, so we went to call on a local rancher named Eldon Barney.

Barney answered the door. He pointed us to a shed. "Load yourself up over there. I'll see you in a minute."

We heaved a bale into the back of Laurie's pickup and Barney came walking over. He had a face as wrinkled as a dried apple, hidden in the shade of a crumpled, soiled straw hat.

"How much do I owe you?" I asked.

There was a long silence. "Well," he finally spoke, "tell me what you're up to here."

I launched into a long explanation about the trip. He listened, head cocked, looking at the ground. When I was finished there was another long silence.

Then he looked up. "No charge."

Back at the house, while Walter was taking a shower, I heard Laurie's police radio burst into noise. The dispatcher was putting out an all-points-bulletin on three suspicious men with six horses.

Getting through downtown Benson was tricky, as it was bisected by Interstate 10. The horses became increasingly nervous riding through town. Directly under the Interstate overpass, both of Eusebio's horses finally decided they'd had it with civilization: the hollow roar of traffic over their heads was the last straw. Both of them started bucking at the same time, Socks turned her pack upside down, and Eusebio began screeching unintelligibly. He couldn't dismount so I ran over and cut the pack off Socks.

During the wreck Pedernal had gotten loose and was standing in the middle of the Interstate off-ramp, in front of a stopped Cadillac. The horse was staring, ears cocked, at two elderly people behind the windshield. The big, shiny brown Cadillac seemed to fascinate him, almost as if he recognized what it represented. It was a strange meeting between the respective vehicles of choice of the nineteenth and twentieth centuries.

⊸ ✖ ⊶

Scholars have long argued about exactly where Coronado went in Arizona. The expedition reports contain tantalizing clues about rivers, distances traveled, inhabited vs. uninhabited areas, canyons, mountains, ruins, springs, descriptions of Indians encountered and plants observed. The trick has been for scholars to map these clues onto the actual landscape, to puzzle together a likely route.

The narratives themselves are extremely thin on Coronado's trip through what would become Arizona. It was desperately difficult and disappointing country, and Coronado and his advance party raced through as fast as they could.

Jaramillo's report contained the most detailed information about their trip across Arizona. "We continued down the arroyo [the Nexpa] for two days. Leaving it, we went to the right in two days travel to the foot of the mountains, where we learned it was called Chichilticale.

"Crossing the mountains, we came to a deep and reedy river, where we found water and forage for the horses. From this river back at Nexpa, as I have said, it seems to me that the direction was nearly northeast. From here, I believe that we went in the same direction for three days to a river which we called Saint John, because we reached it on his day. Leaving here, we went to another river, through a somewhat rough country, more toward the north, to a river which we called the Rafts, because we had to cross on these, as the river was rising. It seems to me that we spent two days between one river and the other. . . . From here we went to another river, which we called the Cold river, on account of its water being so, in one day's journey, and from here we went by a pine mountain, where we found, almost at the top of it, a cool spring and streamlet, which was another day's march. In the neighborhood of this stream a Spaniard, who was called Espinosa, died, besides two other persons, on account of poisonous plants which they ate, owing to the great need in which they were."

What are these rivers, these springs, these mountains?

Coronado also describes the country into which we would soon be venturing:

"For a change from our past labors," he wrote back to the viceroy, "we found no grass during the first few days, but a worse way through the mountains and more dangerous passages than we had previously experienced. The horses were so exhausted they could not endure it, and in this last *despoblado* we lost more than previously. The way is bad for at least thirty leagues* or more. But when we covered these thirty leagues we found fresh rivers and grass like that of Castile." Castañeda's narrative talks about pine nuts and sweet acorns in these mountains.

There are just enough clues here to create a scholarly furor.

From these clues, scholars have mapped out a half-dozen possible routes (see map). When we originally planned this trip, we elected to take the westernmost route. But we would make a test: we would follow parts of a second possible route, to see if we could eliminate one or the other. While we had little chance of proving that either route was the right one, we had hopes of perhaps disqualifying one route from consideration. Disproof is always easier than proof.

---

*The "league" used by Coronado was probably the 3.1-mile league.

Pleasant Valley, 10 miles

Board Tree Saddle

Cow Flat Mt.

Pine Mt.

Old Cowboy Camp

McFadden Peak

Horse Camp Cr.

SCHROEDER'S PROPOSED CORONADO ROUTE

McFadden Horse Mt.

Camp

Entering the Despoblado

PUEBLO CANYON

SIERRA ANCHA WILDERNESS

Aztec Peak

Nate Ellison's Ranch

Cherry Cr.

DAGGER CANYON

Ruins

Salt River

Dagger Ranch

HOGBACK RIDGE

Theodore Roosevelt Lake

Horseshoe Bend

Camp

GRAPEVINE CANYON

Rockinstraw Mt.

SYCAMORE CANYON

H & E Ranch

Hicks Windmill

All possible routes converge at the remote Zuni Indian reservation, which has been identified with certainty as the Kingdom of Cíbola, the Seven Cities of Gold. From there Coronado's route to Pecos has been well established.

I bring this up now because two variant routes diverged just north of Benson, at a dry canyon called Tres Alamos Wash. We would leave the San Pedro at this wash and follow one route into the high grassland country of southern Arizona; after following this route for seventy-five miles or so we would cut back to the San Pedro and follow the other route to the Seven Cities of Gold. From there to Pecos, a distance of about three hundred miles, we would be on Coronado's trail with certainty.

North of Benson we followed a dusty road that ran parallel to the San Pedro. We left the river, "going to the right" (as Jaramillo said) up a dirt road along the broad outwash plain of Tres Alamos. We passed a very flat, very dead rattlesnake in the road and came around a bend. A sudden wash of wet, sweet air swept over us and hundreds of acres of alfalfa fields came into view, so green they hurt the eyes. High-powered sprinklers sent hissing jets of water sparkling and arching through the sunlight. The manager of the ranch, a fellow named Robin Davis, welcomed us and let us turn our horses loose in a corral.

He invited us up to the ranch house, which stood on a hill above the fields. His wife, also named Robin, gave us tall glasses of iced tea. She was baking something in the oven that nearly drove me mad with hunger. We sat in front of a plate-glass window and watched the hissing sprinklers rotating in the bright sun.

"They run day and night," Robin said. "When the wind's right, why it's the best Goddamned air conditioning there is."

Most of the ranches in the Southwest are big enough that they are measured not in terms of acreage, but in terms of sections, a section being a square mile, or 640 acres. Robin's ranch, called the Dusty A-7 Ranch, covered several hundred sections of arid, hilly country west of the river, but the grass was so sparse that Davis couldn't run more than six or eight head of cattle per section: about one cow per hundred acres. The alfalfa fields, irrigated by artesian wells along the river, covered one section only, but that one piece of land was able to support nearly two thousand head of cattle. To run that number of cattle on non-irrigated pasture would have required 183,000 acres of land—a powerful example of just how vital water is to the Southwest.

It is hard for anyone who has not lived in the desert to appreciate the importance of water. Water isn't just part of the story of the Southwest, it is the whole story. In the Southwest, controlling a source of water was always more important than acquiring land. Without water, land was worthless; on the other hand, to be in control of the one water source in an area meant, in practice, that you controlled the entire area. A century ago a settler could homestead his 160 acres around a spring, and then run his cattle on fifty thousand acres of empty land around the homestead without fear of competition. The rights to divert water from rivers for irrigation became extremely valuable and were (and still are) hotly disputed.

Only 16 percent of the land in Arizona is privately owned. All the rest is divided up between the federal government (44 percent), the Indians (27 percent), and the state (13 percent). The federal government owns more land in Arizona than in any other state outside of Alaska.

Robin Davis managed the ranch for the Riley West Corporation. He was, I believe, about twenty-six years old, in charge of two million dollars' worth of meat wandering around a piece of land one-fifth the size of Rhode Island.

Davis was a modern cowboy. He represented what the West had become, the new way of life that had evolved in the late twentieth century.

"It used to be any fool could run cattle and make money," he said, "but now it's gotten so damn competitive that a cowboy's gotta have some business sense." He was planning to go to business school and get an MBA.

While the other cowboys went roping on Saturday mornings, Davis played golf. "I'm ropin' all week. Why the hell would I want to go ropin' on my time off?"

When he was younger, Davis was a cowboy on an old-fashioned ranch, where everything was done the traditional way. The cowboys each had a string of horses, and during roundup moved through the ranch, camping as they went along, rounding up each pasture in turn, roping, cutting out cows they wanted to sell, branding, and castrating. A chuck wagon with a cook was hauled around from camp to camp. Each cowboy kept at least three horses in his string, and rotated animals daily. "Some days workin' cattle I'd ride a hundred miles, never see camp in daylight," Davis said.

On one of these roundups he broke his collarbone roping a maverick cow. He continued working off the back of a horse for three days, blood pouring from his nose. Another time he injured a leg and kept on working. When a bump formed months later he went to a doctor, who X-rayed it and told him it had been broken. "You just beat hell out of your body every day. You see these thirty-year-old cowboys, shit, they look like they're fifty. It's ridiculous."

We got ready to leave. He told us to watch out for rattlers; there were quite a few on the ranch.

I asked if he'd ever been bit.

"Yeah," he said. "On a putting green. I felt this tap on my shoe and there was a little old baby rattler hanging with one fang from my toe. Must've stepped on the son-of-a-bitch." And he roared with laughter.

8

The Dusty A-7 Ranch represented the culmination of nearly five hundred years of livestock raising in the New World. The industry that would transform the West started on January 2, 1494, when on Columbus's second voyage to the New World, he anchored off the coast of Hispaniola and proceeded to unload ten mares and twenty-four stallions (along with a herd of cattle) by tossing them overboard and letting them swim ashore. These were the first horses to have set foot in the New World in ten thousand years.

The horse had originally evolved in North America and had migrated to Asia over the Bering Land Bridge. After the Bridge disappeared, horses became extinct in the New World but continued to evolve in the Old.

Now they were returning, and the New World would be forever changed.

It would be impossible to overestimate the impact the horse would have on the conquest and settling of the Americas. More than anything else—more than guns, cannon, armor, technology, manpower, or strategy—the horse was the instrument of conquest. Ironically, the horse would also become the chief instrument of resistance.

Ranching and horse breeding were the first commercial activities conducted in the New World. In the beginning enough stock had to be brought over to create a diverse breeding pool, so by royal decree all the earliest ships coming to the New World were required to carry cattle and horses. Later, the situation was reversed: so many of Spain's best horses were being sent to the New World that their exportation was banned.

It was extremely expensive to ship livestock across the Atlantic. The horses had to be carried in slings, and only the minimum of fodder and water could be brought along. If a ship were becalmed the horses and cattle were promptly thrown overboard. So many horses were thrown overboard in the windless region between 30 and 35 degrees it has been called the Horse Latitudes ever since.

Ranching conditions were so ideal in the New World that horses and cattle ran wild and multiplied far beyond their need. After about 1550 anyone who wanted a horse could have one simply for the trouble of catching and breaking it. Most cattle ranged free and wouldn't even see a human being until it was time for slaughter. It wasn't long before the supply of meat outstripped demand. The grass, at the time, seemed inexhaustible.

Almost as soon as ranches were established, the New World *vaqueros* (cowboys) began modifying their equipment and techniques to adapt to New World conditions. The Western ranch, the Western cowboy, and virtually all the traditional equipment and techniques of American ranching and riding came directly from these early Spanish *vaqueros*, who themselves had adapted the riding style and equipment of the North Africans who had occupied Spain for nearly eight hundred years.

The heavy Spanish war saddle was discarded for the *jineta*, a lighter design that became the basis for the cowboy's stock saddle. The *jineta*, which is actually a whole style of riding, had in its turn been brought from Africa in the eighth century by the Moors; it was the "secret weapon" that won them Spain.* The Spanish soon invented the *lazo*, or lasso, to rope cattle, and the saddlehorn to anchor the rope. Today, when a cowboy wraps the rope around the saddlehorn after roping a calf, he calls it a "dally"; like so many other words it comes from the old Spanish, *da la vuelta*—"to turn around."

The requirements of managing cattle on a very large, unfenced piece of land became the basis for the *vaquero* and the cowboy way of life. Since the herds mingled, cattle had to be branded—that is, marked—to

---

*To ride *a la jineta* was to ride like a Zenate—one of the Berber tribes of North Africa.

indicate ownership. Every year, the herds had to be "rounded up" so the new calves could be roped and branded. The steers going to market had to be "cut" from the herd and sent to the slaughterer, the feedlots, or the railhead. That could be done only by getting them together in a herd and "pushing" or "driving" them where they had to go.

The Spanish, at first, did not believe in castrating the bulls, and it was hell to drive them anywhere. (They derogatorily called a castrated bull a *joto*, meaning "homosexual" or "ball-less one.") One bull had to be trained to lead the herd, and so he would be tied to a horse and dragged around for days until he got the message. The early *vaqueros* rode stallions, preferring them to mares or geldings because they were thought to be stronger. A stallion was judged on the size of its *huevos* and the loudness of its neigh. Later, American cowboys would castrate bulls, turning them into steers (which made them more manageable and their meat more palatable). They would castrate their stallions, too, turning them into geldings. A gelding was calmer and more sensible, and would pay more attention to the rider instead of sniffing around for mares.

As with the cowboy, the *vaquero* never dismounted to do anything except eat, sleep, make love, and relieve himself. He did not have the romantic status that the nineteenth-century cowboy and Mexican *charro* would belatedly gain in the twentieth century: he was considered to be a lowly, illiterate laborer who happened to work off the back of a horse. The *vaquero*, and later the cowboy, developed a peculiar way of life and a peculiar culture.

When we rode through the Southwest, we saw the last dying ember of this old way of life. I had been under the impression that the old cowboy way of life was dead. Actually, we would discover that it still survived in a few rural pockets where the ranches were vast, the land rugged, and the cows few and far between. Southern Arizona was one of those places.

The first great change in ranching was the fence. The fence became a force when land finally started to run out in the latter part of the nineteenth century—when it became obvious that grass was not an infinitely renewable resource. Up to this time fences had been built only to keep livestock *out*; in fact, Spanish law made it the farmer's responsibility to fence his land to protect his crops, not the rancher's responsibility to control his livestock. Custom and the law said "fence out," not "fence in."

But some ranchers in Texas decided that it was no damn good

owning land if your neighbor's cattle were going to be running over it, eating up the grass. Also, many ranchers began livestock breeding programs to improve their herds, something that would be impossible on the open range. When the Southwest was incorporated into the United States, in many places English "herd law" replaced Spanish custom and the burden of segregating and controlling livestock was shifted to the ranchers from the farmers. In New Mexico, however, the "fence-out" law still survives; if your neighbor's bull busts out of his pasture and digs up your flower garden, it's your problem, not his.

"As long as the range was unfenced," writes the historian J. Frank Dobie, "no owner of land or cattle could keep control of his own property. Without fences, no man could keep his own cattle on his own range, to brand and sell the increase; no man could breed up a herd, for all the scrub bulls in the country were free to mingle with his stock; no man could afford to feed his cattle during droughts, for any feed put out would be largely consumed by cattle not his own; nor under such conditions was there much incentive for a cowman to spend money in digging wells, building tanks and making other improvements."

Barbed wire (correctly pronounced "bob wahr") was invented in 1873 by an Illinois farmer named Glidden. At first, cattlemen were deeply suspicious of this Yankee invention, believing it would cut up their livestock. That changed when an entrepreneur named Gates built a big corral in San Antonio, Texas, using barbed wire. He then had twenty-five longhorns driven into the corral, followed by (one story goes) men with torches who charged about trying to frighten the cattle into getting hung up on the wire. The cattle passed the test and Gates got more orders for the wire than he could handle.

Despite Gates's experiment, in the beginning many cattle and horses were dreadfully hurt by barbed wire. The next generation proved to be different; stock that had been raised behind barbed wire learned to respect it.

Despite its convenience (and its low cost), many old-time stockmen and drivers hated barbed wire to their deathbeds. In 1884 one trail-driver wrote:

"In 1874 there was no fencing along the trails to the North, and we had lots of range to graze on. Now there is so much land taken up and fenced in that the trail for the most of the way is little better than a crooked lane, and we have hard times to find enough range to feed on. These fellows from Ohio, Indiana, and other northern and western

states*—the 'bone and sinew of the country,' as the politicians call
them—have made farms, enclosed pastures, and fenced-in water-holes
until you can't rest; and I say, Damn such bone and sinew! They are
the ruin of the country, and have everlastingly, eternally, now and
forever, destroyed the best grazing land in the world. . . . Lord forgive
them for such improvements! I am sick enough to need two doctors, a
druggery, and a mineral spring, when I think of onions and Irish
potatoes growing where mustang ponies should be exercising, and
where four-year-old steers should be getting ripe for market. Fences,
sir, are the curse of the country!"

Soon ranchers came to be as dependent on barbed wire as farmers.
Ranches were soon broken up into pastures, so that grazing, water use,
and breeding could be more carefully managed.

Without a doubt the greatest change we saw in the landscape was the
barbed-wire fence. Nowhere that we rode—not even in the remotest
reaches of the desert where we traveled for days without seeing a single
human being—could we escape barbed wire. We would learn to loathe
it beyond all reason.

Ranching quite literally changed the face of the Southwest. Barbed
wire, had it been invented and introduced ten or twenty years earlier,
might have saved much of the grass of the Southwest. The open range,
for all its romanticism, encouraged—indeed made inevitable—severe
overgrazing. The faster you could increase your herd the better, because if your cattle didn't eat the grass your neighbor's cattle would.
When the range became fenced and the rancher had absolute control
over the land, it made much more sense to avoid overgrazing.

But by the time ranchers cut back their herds, it was too late.
Arroyos—the curse of the West—had already started cutting into the
overgrazed rangeland. In the early 1880s the ranges were still mostly
unfenced and there were more cattle in the West than at any time
before or since. The summers of 1881 through 1883 were dry, and the
great herds of cattle ate the grass right down to dirt. A starving cow or
horse will even pull grass up by the roots. By the summer of 1883 the
grass was dead and the cattle were starving. In late August of 1883,
Krakatoa erupted, spewing billions of tons of dust into the atmosphere.
In the Southwest, twelve thousand miles away, it began to rain. And
it rained, and it rained—all that winter and the following summer.

---

*By "western states" he means, of course, those states that were "western" in the
1870s, states that we would consider midwestern today.

Now, however, there was little grass to hold the soil or spread out the water. The runoff tore across the naked ground, cutting small channels. Each successive rain deepened the channels, until almost every valley and canyon bottom had a small arroyo running through it. Another drought followed by heavy rains occurred in 1886, greatly increasing the damage.

Once an arroyo starts it never stops, and as it cuts deeper it eventually lowers the water table. It also acts as a conduit, shunting away water that previously would have spread out and soaked into the desert floor. Water pans and playas were sliced across and drained.

By the time the herds were cut back, it was too late.

The other great invention that changed ranching was the water well and windmill. There is no romance in well drilling, and as a consequence historians have paid little attention to this change which was equal to barbed wire in importance.

The fence and the windmill went hand in hand. Once the free range was fenced, many natural sources of water were cut off. But the rancher had no more need of natural water; by the end of the nineteenth century a rancher could haul a rig out to some remote waterless portion of the ranch, sink a well, and install a pump operated by a windmill. As long as the wind blew and the water table held up, water would flow.

The Texas cattle baron C. C. Slaughter was one of the first ranchers to put up a windmill.

"Shortly after its erection," one cowboy recalled, "a round-up was held near the well. Colonel Slaughter appeared in his buckboard, drawn by two very fine horses. After the herd was 'worked' and 'shaped up,' everybody went down to the well to drink. The wind was blowing hard, the windmill was racing around, and a thin stream of water was pouring out into a trough. . . . Colonel Slaughter took a drink from the end of the lead pipe, looked up at the revolving mill, and said:

" 'Boys, that there machine is going to revolutionize the cattle business of Texas. The windmill assures water on millions of acres of grass that has heretofore gone to waste.'

"For a minute nobody said anything; but while the Colonel was prophesying, a gangling cowboy whose mouth was considerably wider than his forehead had been guzzling water. He stopped, got a breath of air, then retorted:

" 'That windmill reverlutionize anything! Hell, I can drink water faster than one of them things can ever pump it.'

" 'How long could you keep drinking before the mill got ahead of you?' Colonel Slaughter asked.

" 'Until I starved to death for water.' "

"On any modern ranch nowadays," one cowman said, "one will hear twenty times as much talk about windmills as about ropes, mavericks, broncos, and other things."

These windmills are now a ubiquitous feature on the western landscape, often rising over the horizon in the middle of nowhere, dozens of miles from the nearest house or paved road. Walter, having grown up in Texas, knew all about the mechanics of windmills and knew how to turn them on and off. A rattling, creaking windmill, the sun flashing off its turning vanes, became the most beautiful sight we would ever see in the desert—saving our lives more than once.

In the twentieth century, the pickup truck would cause further changes. Now the cowboy could spend every night in the bunkhouse, load his horse for the day into a trailer, and drive it out to where it was needed. Soon, the "cutting horse" (the highly trained horse used to chase and separate a cow from the rest of the herd) was replaced by fancy corrals, where the cowboy got down on foot to do the chasing and cutting using lanes and gates. Roping went the same way as cutting; a cowboy could chase a calf on foot into a separate pen and brand him there, rather than roping him from the back of a horse in the open range. The trail drive became replaced by the stock trailer.

And on some ranches, the horse has even been replaced by the four-wheeler. Instead of a roundup, some clever ranchers have trained their cattle to come at the sound of a honking horn.

Much of this was happening in southern Arizona at the time we went through. And yet, forces of history and geography in Arizona also conspired to prevent the modernization of some of the ranches.

For one thing, the ranches in Arizona are huge, often several hundred square miles. There may be few roads and many brushy canyons, mountains, and draws. The carrying capacity of the land is so poor that the cattle are spread far apart. The only way to find them is on horseback, riding from camp to camp, spending the night under the stars.

There is also the conservative, cantankerous attitude of the Arizonans themselves. It was the last frontier state in the lower forty-eight, with much of it not even being homesteaded until after 1900. It didn't even become a state until 1912. Rural Arizonans from pioneer stock are not as thrilled by modern management techniques, new breeds, and scientific grazing systems as are folks on the big ranches in Texas, California, or Colorado. The old ways that were handed down are still remembered and practiced.

Thus, in a few isolated pockets in southern Arizona, the real cowboy still exists. He often owns his ranch and works it alone or with his wife and kids, as this is the only way to break even these days. He is his own vet, his own fencebuilder, his own handyman, his own horse trainer. He still rounds up on horseback. He hangs on by the skin of his teeth, and counts it a good year when he breaks even. But every year he gets that much closer to bankruptcy or the temptation to sell out to a big corporation.

That afternoon we started up Tres Alamos Wash, leaving the San Pedro River behind us. Once away from the San Pedro aquifer the mesquite and catclaw immediately thinned out and we could ride freely.

There wasn't a blade of grass anywhere. We finally came to water—a windmill. We would have watered the horses and moved on, but our maps indicated (and Robin confirmed) the next water was many miles up the wash. They would have to spend a night with no feed.

I built a fire and after dark Robin arrived in his pickup with three enormous bloody slabs of beef, which he chunked down on our stack of wood. He'd like to join us, he said, but two of his cowboys had gotten in a fight and he had to return to the ranch. "You know how it is, you git a cowboy from Montana and a cowboy from New Mexico, and you know they do things differently in different places, so right off they're pounding the shit out of each other."

We slapped the steaks down on the coals and pulled them out when they were as heavy and black as a slab of basalt.

That night, Eusebio declared that he wanted to quit.

Arizona, Eusebio said, gesturing furiously in the firelight, was the *sorriest* Goddamn country he'd ever had the misfortune to experience, this was the hardest riding he'd ever done, and when we got to the next road he thought he'd just load up his horses and head back to Pecos.

Walter was delighted and immediately tried to accept Eusebio's resignation, the first time he had ever agreed to anything Eusebio suggested.

I was furious and insisted Eusebio stay.

We talked about it heatedly, Eusebio finally said he'd continue, and we went to bed in a foul temper.

The next morning, April 23rd, Walter and I climbed a hill a mile from camp to watch the sun rise. I was still wearing my long johns from the sack, having been disinclined to change into the cold, greasy, and stiff clothing that I had balled up into a makeshift pillow the night before. Walter carried his Deardorff view camera and I carried my journal.

"Every day you look more like a dirty old prospector," Walter declared.

At the top we caught our breath.

"Maybe you just should've let Eusebio quit," Walter said.

"We can't finish this trip on our own," I said.

"Why not?"

"We don't know anything about horses."

"That's bullshit. We've learned plenty. What the hell is that wood-cutter doing for us anyway? He just sits around pickin' at his teeth."

"Don't forget, he owns three of those horses."

Walter shook his head. "That woodcutter's gonna quit on us any-way. By the time we reach Globe that bastard'll be long gone."

The sun rose, spreading dark green light over the Dragoon Moun-tains, lying in a confused heap to the south of us. Walter set up his camera at the point of the hill, while I sat down and tried to locate the old wagon road used by the Jackass Mail.

The Jackass Mail was the first effort to send mail and provide overland transportation between the goldfields of California and the East. One of the most dangerous and rugged parts of the route went through these same Dragoon Mountains, where the Dragoon Springs station would later become the most notorious along the line.

The Mail ran from San Antonio, Texas, to San Diego. Officially called Route 8076 (so named because of its designation in the original contract) it was nicknamed the Jackass Mail because mules were used instead of horses over the Arizona part of the route.

It never succeeded. Only three decent stage stations were built and for most of the trip passengers had to bed down in the open desert. The trail was rough and it actually took less time for travelers to go to California via the Panama route (taking a boat to Panama, crossing the isthmus, and taking a boat up the west coast).

In 1857, the Jackass Mail's route was taken over by the Butterfield Overland Mail, after John Butterfield was promised an annual subsidy from the U.S. government of $600,000. The opening of the Butterfield Mail marked the first commercial transportation system across the American continent—some 321 years after Cabeza de Vaca and Este-ban made their epic transcontinental journey.

The Mail had two eastern terminals, one in St. Louis and the other in Memphis, and went to San Francisco via El Paso, Tucson, Yuma, San Bernardino, and Los Angeles. Many northerners opposed the line, viewing it a "slaveholders' swindle" because it made a wide, seemingly senseless detour through the slaveholding South. The route had been planned because it could be operated year-round and took advantage of existing trails.

The Butterfield Overland Mail was an extraordinary accomplishment, even more remarkable in some ways than the Pony Express which later helped put it out of business. The route covered 2,700 miles, and passengers were promised passage in 25 days or less. Fortified stations were built at each stopping point, protected by walls and armed men. Over 1,500 horses and mules were stationed along the route to provide fresh changes of animals. As with the Jackass Mail, mules were used on the long, difficult journey across Arizona. Passengers were also transferred to a specially built stagecoach called a Celerity Wagon, designed for rough travel.

It was an unbelievably dangerous business. In the four years of its operation, 168 employees and customers of the Mail met violent death—and yet during this same time the stage arrived late in San Francisco only three times.

The opening of the faster Pony Express in 1860 cut into the Butterfield Mail's postal business, and the outbreak of the Civil War finished it off.

The Dragoon Springs station was in the heart of Chiricahua Apache country, and sleepless travelers often saw the blinking fires of the Apaches in the surrounding mountains. In 1858 Mexican employees of the Mail butchered and robbed three Americans at the station. Later, in 1872, General O. O. Howard ratified a peace treaty with the Apache chief Cochise here.

If traces of the Butterfield Overland Mail could still be found, we could not see them. The morning sun lay over the mountains and as we watched, it imperceptibly invaded the valleys and canyons, flooding them with yellow and violet.

9

＊ ▱ ＊

The horses were weak after a night of no feed, so we redistributed the packs among all six and started up Tres Alamos Wash on foot. Now that the country had opened up, we hoped to make at least twenty miles that day, reaching a distant place marked "Deepwell Ranch" on our maps.

Tres Alamos was a long, grim piece of work. The water in our canteens got so hot that it burned our lips when we tried to drink. Every rusted can and scrap of corrugated tin was riddled with bullet holes. The sun was so bright that it burned all the color out of the landscape, rendering it flat and without detail, as if seen through a screen of smoke.

We finally came to a windmill, cranking and creaking away in a light breeze. After watering the horses, Walter and I stuck our heads in the cool water, and I soaked my shirt and bandanna and put them on wet. The chill sting of water felt wonderful.

After about fifteen miles, the wash spread out and vanished, and we arrived at a rolling, cactus-dotted grasslands called Allan Flat, part of the Deepwell Ranch.

It was starting to get late. We wanted to reach the ranch headquarters before dusk and see if we could get our horses some feed. We came to a dirt track and then to a little house and barn marked "Deepwell Camp" on our map.

We tied our horses up at a fence and a cowboy in bright red long johns stepped out of the bunkhouse, scratching his head. At that moment a bull came snorting and chuffing out of the open barn and went straight for the cowboy. He ducked back inside.

"Aiee!" Eusebio said and we all quickly moved up near the fence. "¡Ese toro se ve medio cabroncito!"

The bull trotted around the yard, spoiling for a fight, tossing his head, throwing off flecks of frothy saliva.

"Hooo," Eusebio said under his breath. "He a mean one! Watch out!"

The bull saw us and waggled his head. Then he spotted an opening in the yard fence and went thudding past us, his eyes rolling maniacally, and ran off down the road.

The cowboy came back out, grinning. "That ol' bull, I don't know why, he jist likes to hang around the yard here."

We asked if we could buy some hay from him. He shook his head. "Ranch is two miles," he said. "Ask there."

We got back on the road, grumbling. The sun was setting and we'd already walked close to twenty miles.

"I'm gonna ride the sum-bitch," Eusebio announced, and climbed on top of the load lashed to his saddle. We all did the same, riding precariously atop the swaying loads as if we were riding camels.

At sunset we came to a large ranch house set on a rise in the middle of the Flat. Behind the house was a fine set of corrals and stables, where a dozen or more muscled quarter horses and sleek thoroughbreds trotted about. They whinnied a greeting to our horses, who whinnied back.

There was no one at the main house, so we went to the cowboy bunkhouses behind the corrals and started knocking on doors. We roused a fellow in a bathrobe with a fat black chaw wedged behind his lower lip. He introduced himself as Dave Hudson. He had an oozing hand the size of a melon.

"We was ropin' some calves," he said, holding up the hand with a grin. "My horse went right when he shoulda gone left." As the roped calf hit the end of the rope, he explained, Hudson's hand had become caught between the rope and the horn when his horse turned toward the calf instead of away from it. Many cowboys have lost their thumbs in this manner; Hudson was lucky.

That evening he came by with a jug of iced tea and a stack of burritos. We had our little primus stove going, boiling coffee, and we all hunched down around it.

Hudson, in contrast to Robin Davis, was a more traditional cowboy. In his youth he had wandered from job to job, working as a cowhand on ranches from Wyoming to Oregon. "As soon as you get a job, you start looking for another," he said. "You jist start getting restless, start thinking the ranch is no damn good anymore, maybe you could find something better up north or farther west. We called it 'workin' up a quit.' That was the way the cowboy life was. Used to be a man was single all his life. Hell, I even went to college, but now I've clean forgotten how to write." He laughed.

There were, he said, very few of what he called the "old-time" ranches left—eastern Oregon, a few remote parts of eastern California, and southern Arizona. That was about it. Corporations and wealthy people from elsewhere had bought up most of the old ranches in the rest of the country. That was even happening here, like the fellow that owned this place. The new ranchers were bringing new ideas with them: special breeds of cattle and better ways to breed them; a new grazing system, developed in Rhodesia; and branch businesses like thoroughbred horses and show cattle. They hired MBAs and tax shelter accountants, lived in distant cities, and reduced the operation of the ranch to thick computer printouts. The local kids had ended up as hired hands on the ranches their fathers used to own.

Hudson made $1,350 per month, plus his house, medical insurance, and the standard cowboy perk: unlimited free beef. He was doing well; most cowboys earned only about $800 a month. The best situation, Hudson said, is when you had an absentee owner. There, you could make $2,500 a month and when you got too old to ride you could set yourself down and give orders.

We rolled out in our bedrolls in the dust next to the corral where we had our horses. That night, I dreamed I was back in Santa Fe, at a trendy party where an Italian, dressed in a raw silk jacket, picked up my girlfriend and took her home. I woke up furious.

The next day we crossed Allan Flat and camped at a place called N-O Spring, which proved to be a cheerful corral full of tall grass. A cranky old bull was sleeping next to the spring, and the horses wouldn't go anywhere near him, so I climbed on a fence and shooed him out. Next to the spring, on the side of the hill, was a one-room adobe ruin where a man had been murdered in 1890.

We ran into the owner of the N-O Ranch, Nan Cambern, who told us that the next ranch we would hit was thirty miles away, and that she didn't think there was a drop of water between here and there, as all the wells were dry. We were boxed in by two mountain ranges and there was no other way to go. We'd have to make a dash for it.

I washed my clothes in the spring and draped them over the corral fence to dry. I lounged around while Walter climbed some hills to photograph the sunset with Eusebio in tow. Later I went up to the roofless ruin near the spring and walked inside, hoping to derive some sort of literary inspiration from the murder scene, but the ruin was as squalid and uninteresting as the murder had been. The nearby spring had created a riot of vegetation and a slick of mud on the hillside. A gray range horse peered at me from behind the vegetation, whinnied, and went trotting off.

When they returned, Eusebio was in an expansive mood. We sat around a crackling fire and ate our usual stew of beans, rice, and three small pieces of dried salami, while Eusebio talked about roping, bronc-busting, and chasing wild horses. "I got a bronc in Moriarty," he bragged. "He's the meanest sum-bitch you ever seen. I'll give you a thousand dollars to ride him. Thousand dollars."

⬤ ⊠ ⬤

That night, I lay awake thinking about the Spanish riding through this country. They would have probably stopped at this spring; it was the only water for miles around, and it lay along the natural pass through the two mountain ranges. My thoughts turned to one member of Coronado's advance guard, Fray Juan de Padilla, who was perhaps one of the most intriguing members of the expedition.

Out of all of Coronado's company, Padilla was the most obsessed with the Seven Cities of Gold. But Padilla had a vision of the Seven Cities that stood in stark contrast to Coronado's: Padilla was convinced they were actually the Seven Cities of Antillia of medieval Spanish legend. Seven Portuguese bishops—so the story went—fled the Moslem invasion of Spain in A.D. 714, and with their congregations sailed off to the west. Each bishop had founded a Christian city, and the cities had grown fabulously wealthy and powerful. Padilla was convinced that these cities lay somewhere north of Mexico, and he fervently hoped that Antillia and Cíbola were one and the same.

Unlike Coronado, Padilla was not interested in the riches of the Seven Cities; after all, as a Franciscan friar he had taken a vow of poverty. Besides, if they were Christian cities—as he believed—then the riches would not be for the looting. Rather, Padilla had a millennial view of what these lost Seven Cities had become: a veritable Kingdom of God on Earth. In the Seven Cities of Antillia, Padilla believed, the Christian ideal had finally become a reality: they were no less than a vision of heaven itself.

The friar had one overwhelming, burning, fanatical desire: to reunite these seven cities with the rest of Christendom.

Padilla was no retiring, dreamy padre. Born in Andalucía in southern Spain, he probably came to the New World with a group of twenty friars in 1529. He became an accomplished soldier and fighter, and distinguished himself in a minor war in northern Mexico. Among Coronado's soldiers he had a fearsome reputation, and he possessed a towering temper, which he turned against blasphemy, idolatry, and immorality wherever he found it.

I wondered what Padilla, wrapped up in his horse blanket, would have been thinking in the dark, restless nights of their journey to Cíbola.

The next morning, while I was lashing down one of the horse's packs, Eusebio grabbed the horse's halter and moved her around, and the horse stepped right on my broken toe, mashing it again. It felt like someone had just taken off my foot with a chain saw.

Anyone who is stepped on by a horse is, by definition, an idiot. But that didn't matter. I hauled off and slugged the poor animal in the neck and called Eusebio a stupid bastard and a number of other things. I pulled off my boot; the toe looked awful, black and swollen like an overfed leech.

Eusebio acted like a gentleman. He stepped back and listened to my outburst without comment; then he gracefully accepted my apologies.

I could no longer wear my cowboy boots at all, so I put on my only other footgear, a pair of canvas hiking shoes that had no heels.*

We rode up N-O Canyon. Just as Nan had said, all the water sources were dry. We finally emerged on a high ridge and ate lunch in a stand of blooming century plants, their fat, blood-colored stalks shooting into

---

*The reason cowboy boots have long heels is to prevent the foot from slipping all the way through the stirrup. One of the most common causes of death among horsemen is being thrown and dragged.

the air like skyrockets. It had been windy and cold, and neither we nor the horses were thirsty.

We pressed on, climbing up and over a series of ridges that lay between two great mountain ranges, the Galiuros and the Winchesters. The trail ended at a place called Deer Tanks (which were dry) and we set off cross-country, up and down rough draws. Finally we came out on a high plateau, and at the very edge we found, at last, water. We were now at six thousand feet, and all cactus and mesquite had vanished, leaving nothing but dry grasslands, dotted here and there with a lone juniper.

A great vista had opened up, very different from the desert we had just come from. The land rolled away from us in great folds the color and texture of chamois. A cold wind pressed across the endless spaces, vibrating the stalks of grass. It was a strange and beautiful country.

Now assured of water, we stopped and Walter carried his camera off to take photographs. I could hear his shouts and whoops echoing among the hills, and later I heard him singing a strange, tuneless song. All I could see was his black speck creeping along a massive ridge.

I sat cross-legged on the ground, which was littered with black, bubbly volcanic rock, and wrote in my journal; when I finished I then sat back and let my mind wander.

Suddenly, without warning, a memory came flooding out of nowhere. It was so strong that my eyesight failed, momentarily obscured by the inner vision, and I felt as if I had been briefly transported through space and time, back to a lake in New Hampshire where I had spent my summers as a child.

I was standing on the Underwater Rock. The Underwater Rock lay about thirty yards offshore, in water that was over your head, but if you reached the rock you could stand on its peak and the water would only be up to your knees. I was waving my arms and shouting at someone on the shore. "Look at me!" I cried. "I'm standing on water! It's magic, magic!"

Then quite suddenly I found myself back on the barren ridge, Eusebio dozing with his cowboy hat pulled over his eyes, three horses tied up around a lone juniper, three others grazing nearby. It was as if my mind, which had been slowly loosening up, had suddenly popped like an ice cube melting in water. It was such a peculiar experience that I wondered for a moment if I hadn't suffered some kind of stroke.

We descended into another canyon along a steep trail covered with loose rock. The canyon was filled with live oaks and the biggest alligator juniper tree I'd ever seen—a massive dead thing with corkscrew branches.

Eusebio, the woodcutter, was impressed. "Shit, man," he said, "I could pull a cord at least out of that sum-bitch, you bet."

We stopped for the night at a deserted corral on top of a place called Bare Ridge, at a spot called the Mesas. The corral was thick with oat grass and had a water tank scummed with algae.

We had reached the highest point in a broad valley between the two mountain ranges. Standing there, looking out into vast open spaces, made me dizzy, like that long dreaming fall before awakening. The wind roared through the corral and rattled away over the immense grasslands, each gust skimming the grass in rolling waves, sending rippling bands of color fleeing into the distance.

For the first time, I had the feeling that Coronado had been through here; I could imagine his group strung out over a mile of the landscape. Coronado and Fray Marcos would be in front, perhaps with several Indian guides; the horsemen would be following, some mounted, some on foot; and in the rear would come the pack string guarded by Gallego and the horse herd tended by Aztec wranglers.

Walter had the same idea. "Coronado came through this pass," he said. "I can feel it in my bones."

Had Coronado stood at this spot, looking out over this sweep of grasslands and mountains, he would have seen precisely the same landscape we now saw. Nothing had happened here in a thousand years.

We turned the horses loose in the pen and they ran free, kicking and bucking and shaking their manes, happy to be rid of their hateful burdens. Someone had hauled an old Airstream trailer out here, along a faint track that wound off into unimaginable distances, but the door and window frames were shattered and the interior smelled of dry rot, so we unrolled our bedrolls in a corner of the corral. Eusebio rigged up a shelter from the wind by tying three tarps together. We found a heap of broken corral posts and started a small fire.

Eusebio was pleased with his shelter, and he kept grinning and saying: "Not bad, eh? You don't feel no wind in here, boy!" Every time a big gust boomed through the camp, Eusebio would say, "That *some* wind, hooo!" and rub his hands, his small eyes gleaming intensely in the firelight. Something about the landscape had filled him with energy. Walter and I, too, felt elated.

That night, I dreamed I was carried aloft like a spark in the roaring wind. I could see our tiny campfire flickering in a bowl of blackness. Beyond the mountains rose a clear, empty sky without moon or stars. I felt terribly far away from everything I knew.

I then found myself in my grandparents' old house in Hingham, Massachusetts. My grandmother had died just five days before the start of our trip, and I had gone almost directly from her memorial service in Boston to the San Pedro River. In the dream, my ninety-year-old grandfather had begun living with a younger woman, a brassy-voiced, orange-haired widow who was clearly after his money. The woman had shown up in the old Hingham house to take my grandfather on a cruise around the world, and everyone in the family was worried that she would marry him in Timbuktu and get her hands on his money. Suddenly my grandmother's ghost, smelling of chamomile soap and oakwood smoke, appeared above the querulous assembly. "So what if she takes his money," my grandmother said, smiling. "Let him have a little fun in his last years. I don't mind."

I awoke in the dark, bewildered, struggling to understand where I was. And then for a long time I listened to the horses snorting and moving about in the night.

⚫ ▬▬ ⚫

The following day, Wednesday, April 26th, we spent the morning in camp to give the horses a rest and a full belly of oat hay. Walter went off to photograph and then, after the sun had risen, wrote a letter to his girlfriend. He wrote feverishly, grunting approvingly at his work, and then carried the sheafs of paper over to me.

"You gotta hear this. This is good."

He began reading with great feeling, the broad Texas diphthongs rolling off his tongue like the slow coppery waters of the Red River itself. I have reproduced it here, from the original, keeping Walter's idiosyncratic orthography.

From the toughest and most unbelievable journey I have ever taken:

Brushing the cob webbs from ones mind—This is what this journey is turning into.—The space, vista's with such awesom grandure, makes one sit in silence, in connection with the creation. Intense winds, heat, calm and coolness—Sun that warms ones body in the early morning dawn, intensifys in lower latitudes to penetrate deep within in latter morning hours. Terrain, from where I now sit "The Messas" over Pine Ridge, between the Winchesters Mts and the Gulures Mt., one holds in silence connection within—rolling yellow grassland messas, with deeply, deeply cut gourges, connecting to distance mountain ranges, near and far, in a 360 degree view. The whispering of the wind caress-

ing the lightly blowing grasses, like natures Messas wind chimes—
Moonlight so intense it makes it hard for one to sleep for long inter-
vals—always causing an anticipation of the coming dawn. Star light
before the moon's rising or after its setting becomes a eternal voyage
into our unknown or our beginning—The physical sences are at alert
constantly, for our horses take continuing awareness—The mesquite
and cat claw at lower elevations on the San Pedro River between Fair
Banks and St. David was like riding through curtains of green and
brown, rouged landscape with tough aroyas, warshes, flat land marsh
like plains with grasses five feet high, hidden holes that a horse if fallen
into would completely disappear. . . .

We are in search of what lies beyond the next, after the next,
mountain range, that is what makes our journey so unique. . .

"So how's that for writing?" Walter hollered. "Whooo, look at this
country! This is what we been busting our asses for!" He danced
around the grassy slope, clutching the leaves of paper, and whooped at
the top of his lungs, a sound that was instantly whisked away by the
wind.

Afterward I walked around the camp, listening to the wind and
gazing over the unending landscape. Walter's letter, for all the idiosyn-
crasies of his style, had moved me. Whatever was happening to me was
also happening to him.

I wandered into the Airstream and found a broken telephone and a
1973 Mesa-Tempe-Chandler phone book. Inside the book I looked up
my last name, and there I found two Richard Prestons and a Roscoe
Preston, the names of my brother and a long-dead dog, respectively. I
stood in the trailer with the wind gusting and banging through the
broken window frames, and began to wonder what I was doing there,
why I had really undertaken this trip. The original reasons—to write
a book, to clear my head, whatever—seemed remote and theoretical. I
couldn't seem to connect my presence in the trailer, in the middle of
nowhere, with anything else in my life. It was as if I had stepped
entirely outside my own existence.

One of the most important landmarks on the road to the Seven Cities
was a "city" made of red earth, which the Spanish heard called "Chichilticale." (The word means "Red House" in the Nahuatl Indian
language, and was probably the name given it by the Aztec servants

with Fray Marcos.) It marked the end of the country settled by Indians, and the beginning of the great *despoblado*—the howling wilderness.

Chichilticale also marked the boundary of two geological zones and two life zones. It stood, Castañeda tells us, at the base of the *cordillera*, or mountains, at the foot of a pass. He also noted that here "the country changes its character again and the spiky vegetation ceases." Thus, the Red House lay somewhere along the margin separating the basin-and-range topography of southern Arizona—with its hot, cactus-choked deserts and mountain islands—and the forested, wet mountain zone of central Arizona, known as the Mogollon Rim. (The word is pronounced "Muggy-on" or "Muggy-own.")

As Coronado and his men pressed onward in the early summer of 1540, they eagerly anticipated this landmark, which would, they hoped, confirm the truth of Fray Marcos's story (which by this time had come under a cloud) and mark the final leg of the journey to Cíbola.

They arrived at Chichilticale in late May. Castañeda described their disappointment. "After the general had crossed the inhabited region and came to Chichilticale, where the *despoblado* begins, and saw nothing favorable, he could not help feeling somewhat downhearted, for, although the reports were very fine about what was ahead, there was nobody who had seen it except the Indians who went with the negro [Esteban], and these had already been caught in some lies. Besides all this, [Coronado] was much affected by seeing that the fame of Chichilticale was summed up in one tumble-down house without any roof, although it appeared to have been a strong place at some former time when it was inhabited, and it was very plain that it had been built by a civilized and warlike race of strangers who had come from a distance."

Castañeda adds later: "Chichilticale is so called because the friars [he means Fray Marcos] found a house at this place which was formerly inhabited by people who separated from Cíbola. It was made of colored or reddish earth. The house was large and appeared to have been a fortress. It must have been destroyed by the people of the district, who are the most barbarous people that have yet been seen. They live in separate *rancherías* [camps] and not in settlements. They live by hunting. The rest of the country is all wilderness, covered with pine forests. There are great quantities of pine nuts. The pines are two to three times as high as a man before they send out branches. There is a sort of oak with sweet acorns, of which they make cakes like sugar plums with dried coriander seeds. It is very sweet, like sugar. Watercress grows in many springs, and there are rosebushes, and pennyroyal, and wild marjoram.

"There are barbels and picones, like those of Spain, in the rivers of this wilderness. Grey lions and leopards were seen."

There are several mysteries hidden in these passages. First, and most important, where exactly *is* Chichilticale? Scholars have argued more over this point than any other relating to Coronado's expedition; if Chichilticale could be identified, it would settle, once and for all, Coronado's route through Arizona.

We do know that Chichilticale lies somewhere in the southernmost foothills of the Mogollon Rim country. Without a doubt the Rim country and the arid deserts beyond it were the *despoblado* of the Spanish. No matter which way Coronado went, he would have had to cross this rough chain of mountains, which extend halfway across Arizona and part of New Mexico.

As the altitude increases at the beginning of Rim country, the landscape does indeed change its character. The "spiky vegetation"—the mesquite, prickly pear, cholla, and saguaro cactus—gives way to the largest ponderosa pine forest in the world. There is little doubt the pine tree described by Castañeda was the ponderosa.

But exactly where along the Mogollon Rim foothills is Chichilticale to be found? There is no shortage of candidates: dozens of large pueblo ruins are scattered throughout central Arizona and New Mexico, many built with reddish earth.

The scholars favoring the middle routes believe it lies at the northern end of the Sulphur Spring Valley, the area we were just entering—possibly a large ruin on the 76 Ranch at the base of the Pinaleño Mountains. The westernmost-route proponents feel it may be one of many large ruins along the Salt River near Roosevelt Lake—perhaps even a complex of ruins that were drowned when the Salt River was dammed. Still others, advocates of an eastern route, place it farther, near the Gila Wilderness and Mogollon Mountains of New Mexico (see map).

⊸ ⊠ ⊶

That afternoon we rode across the rolling hills of the Mesas and into a series of lush valleys, dotted here and there with a copse of oaks. The effect made the landscape look more like an English park than the high Arizona desert. At one point a herd of fifteen or twenty antelope jogged

"The
Seven
Cities
of Gold"

First Spanish
Sighting of
"Cities of
Gold"

Coronado's
"Bad
Passage"

Jalarosa
Draw

ZUNI
BUTTES

Z U N I
I. R.

Zuni
Pueblo

Dowa
Yalanne

Zuni River

Kyaki:ma
Pueblo
(sacred ruins)

GALESTENA
CANYON

Lincoln
Harker's
Ranch

Hawikuh
Pueblo
(ruins)

Area where
all of author's
horses were lost

PLAIN
OF
HAWIKUH

Ajo Caliente

along a ridge and stopped to watch us pass by, their long ears sticking out at attention. We would often see a lone antelope or black-tailed deer zigzagging away from us.

After some miles of riding we rounded a small hill and saw, lying in a bowl of yellow grass, hemmed in by hills, a perfect little ranch. There was a windmill turning briskly in the breeze, the sun flashing off its blades. There was a ranch house buried in the shade of oaks and cottonwoods, corrals and horses, a barn, and a water tank. Beyond the hills the landscape opened to the Sulphur Spring Valley, perhaps twenty miles across, and an ever more distant range of mountains beyond that.

The door was answered by a brisk woman with the bright quick eyes of a mouse and a face wrinkled by years in the sun. The old rancher, a slow-talking, slow-walking fellow named Dee Wear, pressed my hand and we sat down at the kitchen table where I spread out my maps. I told him I had some questions about how we were going to get across the Sulphur Spring Valley to Aravaipa Creek, but I was more interested in meeting the owner of this beautiful little ranch.

While we pored over the maps, Dee's wife, Peggy, asked me if I was interested in relics. I said I was and she brought out a box filled with flaked spear points and arrowheads which she had found in the valley. She tumbled them out of tissue paper into my hands. The knapped blades of flint were light and balanced to the touch, like cool leaves of stone.

Wear told us about a closed-up dude ranch, called the Buckskin, about three miles distant, where he thought we might be able to corral our horses for a day. It was now April 26th: we had been on the trail for thirteen days and our horses badly needed a rest.

The valley, we learned, was first settled by a man named Colonel Henry Clay Hooker. Hooker, one of the great pioneer stockmen in Arizona history, was born on a farm in New Hampshire in 1828. He ran away to the California goldfields in '49, opened a hardware store in Hangtown, California, and became a prosperous merchant. In 1866 a disastrous fire swept away his uninsured house, business, and goods, leaving him nearly penniless with a wife and three children to support.

But Hooker had an idea. Scraping together all his remaining money, he bought five hundred turkeys from the local ranchers, and announced his intention to drive them from Hangtown over the mountains to Carson City, Nevada. Everyone thought it a ridiculous idea and when it came time for him to leave much of the town turned out.

"With the aid of one helper and several trained dogs," an account went, "he headed his strange procession across the mountain tops. . . . As he was coming down the mountains not far from his destination he was suddenly confronted by a precipice too steep to descend and all but impossible to skirt. The dogs so pressed and worried the birds, trying to force them to make the descent, that they finally became desperate and took to the air. Said Colonel Hooker: 'As I saw them take wing and race away through the air I had the most indescribable feeling in my life. I thought, here is good-bye turkeys! My finances were at the last ebb; these turkeys were my whole earthly possession, and they seemed lost.'

"But the case was not so bad as it seemed. In the valley below Hooker, his helper, and his dogs succeeded in rounding up the aerial squadron and steering it once more toward Carson City and Victory."

He sold his turkeys at a spectacular 350 percent profit, and with this money laid the foundations for one of the great cattle fortunes in Arizona Territory.

He started buying cattle in Texas and Mexico and driving them to Arizona, in herds of four thousand at a time, to supply beef to the army and the reservation Apaches. "The clouds of alkali dust rising above the arid plains," an old friend of Hooker's reminisced, "and the tinkle of the mules' bells, mingled with the resonant cracks of the whips, all told that 'Hooker was coming right along.' "

Some of Hooker's men were killed by Chiricahuas on these drives, but Hooker himself was left alone. One time, Hooker was driving a team through the Dragoon Mountains when the Chiricahuas closed in around him. Rather than giving the impression he was afraid by fleeing, he turned his team and drove directly into Cochise's camp. Cochise was impressed by Hooker's bravery and told the cattleman that the reason he hadn't killed him, despite many opportunities to do so, was because Hooker was bringing steers, which the Indians liked to rustle, into the country.

One night in 1872, Hooker camped at a watering place called Oak Grove, in the Sulphur Spring Valley not far from the Buckskin Ranch where we would camp. His cattle stampeded during the night, and the next day the *vaqueros*, following the trail, came across a *cienega* (water seep). Hooker liked the place so much he homesteaded it, calling his ranch the Sierra Bonita, the Pretty Mountains.

Soon Hooker was running cattle over an area that stretched all the way from the San Pedro River and down the valley nearly to the Mexican border—a piece of ground encompassing over eight hundred square miles. It was said that a person would have to ride 180 miles to make a circuit of the ranch. He created and ruled an estate of baronial proportions, and his hospitality and table became famous throughout the territory.

A surviving photograph of Hooker shows a shrewd, weatherbeaten little man, wearing a frock coat and white tie. His chin is tilted upward, giving him the look of a belligerent schoolboy. Hooker was a horse fancier and kept a stable of five hundred American mares with six blooded stallions to breed them. He took great pride in his ability to drive a four-in-hand team (the four sets of reins control the four horses in the team). He drove his carriage with its magnificent trotters every-where, usually at high speeds, and he once raced them down the main street of Tombstone at such a furious pace that he got three speeding tickets in rapid succession. "What I came for was to show off my horses," he declared, "and I have succeeded in doing it." He also kept a fine kennel of greyhounds and wore elegant European clothes.

Hooker controlled his vast holdings by locating, surveying, and filing on all the sources of water he could find in the area. When homesteaders began moving into the valley in the 1880s, Hooker took more extreme measures to enforce his control. He would send a group of Mexicans to visit the homesteader; if that didn't dissuade the man from filing for his 160 acres, then the Mexicans would, as one rancher told me, "put him under the ground." Soon the homesteaders came in such large numbers that Hooker accepted the inevitable, and his vast, extra-legal ranch got broken up. The Sierra Bonita Ranch still exists, but somewhat pared down in size.

Late the next afternoon I went back to the Wear place with my tape recorder, to see if I could get some good stories out of Dee and Peggy. The Wears and I sat around the kitchen table and I asked Dee if he would be willing to be interviewed.

"Sure," he said. "What do you want me to say into that thang?"

Wear told me his grandfather had driven a herd of cattle from Alpine, Texas, and homesteaded up the canyon. In 1912, the year Arizona became a state, Dee's father homesteaded the place we were in now. He started his herd with sixty cows, back in the days when the nearest town, Willcox, called itself the Cattle Capital of the Nation. The railroad went into Willcox in those days, and every year Wear and some of his neighbors would cut the cattle they wanted to sell out of their herds and drive them together to the railhead.

"We'd go to town," Wear said, "with maybe a hundred fifty or two hundred head and five or six owners. It'd take us two and a half days to git to Willcox driving 'em. If we'd go good enough we'd git in there maybe by dark the second day. Lots of times we'd have to hold 'em out of Willcox about five, six miles and go in the next morning. They'd just night herd 'em, you know. Maybe two men could hold 'em—course they'd find a grassy spot where they'd git grazin' and they'd graze until, oh, maybe eight, nine o'clock and then most of 'em lay down and rest."

He added scornfully: "Now they haul 'em. People don't know how to drive cattle any more. Why, they wouldn't even know how to take 'em without a *trailer*."

He paused, and I could hear the faint sounds of the wind in the cottonwoods outside. I asked if they'd ever had a stampede.

"I remember one time," he said, "that's gittin' up in later years, we went in there with three hundred fifty head of mother cows with the calves on 'em. We got in there about a hundred yards of the stock pens where the railroad ran right along, and here come a freight train through there. *Man* it was one of them old engines, a-*whistlin'*, and *blowin'*, and *smokin'*, and makin' a racket. Those cattle, they ran about two miles back up the country. It was excitin', but I'll tell you," he said, raising his voice, "you git in front of 'em they'd just *mow* your horse down."

In the past fifty years, Wear had seen the Old West disappear in the valley. Very few of the old ranchers remained, he said, with the exception of the Sierra Bonita, which was still owned by the Hooker family. Most of the ranches had gone bust—sometimes several times in a row—and had had five or six owners since World War II. Almost all the original families were gone, moved to Tucson or hired themselves out to other ranches or just disappeared.

"Ranching used to be fun," Wear said, "but now you don't git to work cattle like you used to. It's all changed completely. Now," he said with a tone of disgust, "if you want to move a bunch of cattle from here a mile or two you take 'em in *trucks* and drive 'em all the way. It used to be on these big ranches, that Eureka Ranch for instance, when they was down there during roundup it would take maybe fifteen or more cowboys. They'd have a chuck wagon, and they'd just go from one camp to the other, and they'd work the cattle as they'd go and they'd brand and gather what they wanted to sell. On that Eureka place it'd take 'em about three weeks or a month to work it. It's all different now altogether."

"How so?" I asked.

"Most of 'em now work cattle in the corral. You used to have your good cuttin' horses, what they call 'em. You'd have your certain horses to cut cows, you'd git in there and cut out what you wanted, yearlings or whatever.* Now they go in the corral. Some of 'em still use horses in the corral, but a lot of 'em git down on *foot*"—Wear snorted at the idea—"and open gates and run 'em down *this* lane and *that* lane."

I heard Walter banging onto the porch outside.

"Can I come in?" he asked, coming in.

Peggy fetched the pitcher of lemonade and poured him a glass. Walter pulled a chair up at the table.

"You been tellin' him some good stories?" he asked Wear. "That's what he's lookin' for."

"You'll have to ask him," Wear said.

I said he was.

Wear started talking again. "Her folks came here— When did your folks homestead down there in the valley, Peggy?"

"In 1883," Peggy said.

"They actually homesteaded down there before we came here."

Peggy went into the living room and brought back an old brown photograph, mounted on a piece of nicked cardboard. It pictured a large, southern-style house with gabled windows and a porch, sitting rather incongruously in the Arizona prairie. She laid it on the table. She explained that her grandfather had been on the rowing team at Harvard and had developed asthma and "leakage of the heart." The doctor told him to go to a drier country, so he came to Arizona, homesteaded, and built the large house in the photograph. It was modeled after his family's plantation home in Virginia.

"They had lookout windows," Wear said, "and they'd watch for Indians comin' from Cochise Stronghold across Apache Pass. Sometimes they'd be gettin' real close to the house, and part of that time the Apaches got on the warpath and they *sure* did watch 'em through these windows, thinking they might mean business, but the Indians never did bother 'em."

While we had been talking, Peggy had been up roaming around the house, opening drawers. She came back holding a silver six-shooter.

"That's a Colt .45," she said, laying it on the table. "That was owned by one of the big lawmen of this country. It is Mexican silver

---

*Today, cutting has been reduced—like so many other cowboy working skills, such as roping and bronc busting—to a competitive sport done in an arena.

and engraved bone handle, Colt .45, and it was my mother's for her twenty-first birthday.''

"Who owned that?" Dee asked. "Trainer?"

"Bill Trainer."

"That's a beautiful gun," Walter said, picking it up and turning it over in his hands before laying it down again. "Well balanced."

"He was a marshal," Wear said, "been there for years, and he and Peggy's mother was kinda, well. . ." He reached for the gun and slipped it comfortably into his hand, like he was slipping on a glove. "It kicks like a mule," he said.

Walter asked: "Think it killed any people?"

Wear chuckled. "I'm sure it did, that Trainer he lived by the gun. She's been offered a lot of money for that pistol."

There was a long silence. I hefted the gun. It was smooth and very heavy.

I asked Wear if he ever did anything crazy when he was a kid.

"Well," he said, chuckling, "I don't know. . ."

"Dee," Peggy said, "tell him about the time you roped the bear."

"Well now, that was in 1932 or '3."

"You roped a bear?" I asked.

Wear chuckled and there was a momentary silence. He snorted again, cleared his throat, and leaned heavily on his arm. He had been helping his dad round up wild cattle, and they had chased some renegades up a box canyon. So Wear's dad sent some men up into the canyon to flush the cattle out, while Wear and a friend positioned themselves at the opening, ready to rope them as they came out.

"I heard the brush a-crackin' and some fellows hollerin'," Wear said, "and I thought, They're comin' out of there with those wild cattle. I looked over and a black bear is coming right around the hillside towards me. He was right close, so I decided, Well I'll just rope that gentleman. I roped him right quick and that horse kinda stampeded with me and we just went off the hillside there a ways just draggin' that bear. We was running over square boulders draggin' that bear over the top. Well, that old bear he just hung up that rope and started to climb up that rope. I'd have to run and hit a bunch of brush and knock him loose, and my horse would git a little time to breathe before he'd go to climbing up that rope again. And finally I was just gittin' ready to turn him loose—I was about ready because he got within fifteen feet of me. I was hollering for those guys to help me."

Wear was reluctant to cast off the rope from the saddlehorn because a cowboy should never lose his rope.

"I had that little horse, that old black streak-faced horse. He was a good horse, but a course he was so scared of that bear I was having trouble keeping him under control. All I'd do was just loosen my reins and he was gone.

"The others finally showed up and one of them heeled him as you would a cow by roping its hind legs.

"He was so stout that I had my rope on his head and this guy had him by both hind feet, and when he stood up he'd just draw our horses together, he was that stout. And then we'd git him straightened out again and then he'd just pull our horses together and I was gittin' kinda worried there. I didn't know what was gonna happen."

Wear and his friends finally managed to tie the bear up to a tree, muzzling him and putting a harness on his feet so he couldn't claw off the rope.

"I don't know what in the world we coulda done with him, but boy, we was sure gonna have us a *bear.*"

Wear returned with his friends the next day. "There was just a little piece of rope left there, twisted into nothing. And he was gone, that rascal was."

He stopped and chuckled, then cleared his throat.

"I didn't know really why I roped him to start with. It's the kind a thing you do when you're seventeen. You do it before you think about it. But I sure wouldn't want to rope another, I'll tell you that, God *damn!*"

Wear's father had once run a large ranch in the valley, the Eureka Springs Ranch. The ranch had gone broke during the war and the War Finance Board took it over, hiring Wear's father to manage it until they could sell it. The ranch had gone to hell and all the cattle had run wild.

"Dad took two, three men year-round catching those big maverick steers," Wear said. "Sometimes they'd catch 'em seven or eight years old and they'd never been branded."

"Now my dad," Wear said, again looking out the window, "when he took over the Oh-Bar-Oh and managed it they also had a bunch of old outlawed steers on top of the mountains. So he hired some boys to catch those steers. I believe he paid 'em twenty dollars a head to catch those steers. *Man* they got some old, *old* renegades—that's some old, old steers maybe ten or twelve years or older."

"These renegades," said Peggy, "were steers that would get out of the roundup year after year, and they would break out and go to the mountain."

Wear continued. "They brought them renegades down to a flat

pasture over there at the Oh-Bar-Oh." He raised his hand two feet off the table. "Grama grass was that high, but they beat a trail around that fence, and you never did see one of 'em take a bite of that grass. You'd go down there anytime and you'd see those old steers just a-walkin', just a-walkin' *real* slow you know, around that pasture. Those steers *grieve* themselves. See, takin' 'em out of the country they been all their lives and puttin' 'em where they's seein' new things, people and vehicles and all that. . .Well, they just couldn't *stand* it. One by one, those old outlaws died."

Wear was silent, looking out to the grassy hills that marked the border of his ranch. He had spoken with feeling. Something about the sight of those old, grieving, renegade steers had affected him deeply. I felt that he was, in a way, talking about himself.

The afternoon light was pouring in across the valley and in through the windows and the wind had died down. The grass, glowing with golden light, lay like a soft buckskin blanket on the earth.

"Oh I'll tell you," Wear finally said, smoothing a knotted old hand over his hair, "it's all changed. Changed completely."

10

⬥ ⤳ ⬥

There is another mystery buried in Castañeda's passage about Chichilticale. Who were these "most barbarous people" who lived about its ruins? Some scholars have suggested they might have been Apache Indians. From the start of our trip we had been following, in reverse, one of the major Chiricahua Apache plunder routes into Mexico, and we had now just entered the southwestern edge of the ancient Chiricahua homeland. (This in itself suggested that Coronado came this way, since we know the Spanish were following established Indian trails most of the way to Cíbola.)

For the next forty-five miles we would be traveling through aboriginal Chiricahua lands. It was in this area that some of the bitterest battles of the Indian Wars took place. The defeat of the Chiricahuas and their leader, Geronimo, effectively ceded the last chunk of Indian-held land to the United States. Wounded Knee may have been the last battle, but the Indian Wars were over with the defeat of Geronimo.

The Apaches originally migrated to the Southwest from northwestern Canada and Alaska, where Athabascan tribes speaking closely related languages still live today. The Apaches probably began moving into Arizona and New Mexico between A.D. 900 and 1200, although some scholars believe they might have arrived as late as the fifteenth century. Over time the Apaches evolved into different tribes, of which the most distinct were the Navajo.

The Apaches do not call themselves "Apache"; the word is actually Zuni and it means "enemy." The Apache call themselves simply *Diné,* "The People." Conversely, the Apache word for most other tribes and the white man includes the term *ana,* which itself means "enemy." (Even the Navajo word *Anasazi,* whose standard translation is "Ancient Ones," actually means "Enemy Ancient Ones.") The Navajo term for the white man is *Bilagáana,* thought to be a corruption of the Spanish *Americano;* even so, it manages to squeeze in the *ana* term, the enemy label.

These linguistic points sum up the relationship of the Apaches to the rest of the world: the Apaches were the enemy of everyone, and everyone was the enemy of the Apaches. Long before the coming of the Europeans the Apaches lived by raiding and plunder. They warred endlessly with the other tribes of the area—the Pima, Papago (now Tohono O'odham), Zuni, and Comanche—and the different Apache bands often quarreled among themselves. They were remorseless guerrilla fighters, and possibly the most brilliant military strategists of the Indian Wars.

As soon as the Spanish moved into Arizona they came into conflict with the Apaches, particularly the Chiricahuas. At first they tried to Christianize them, but succeeded only in adding many names to the long list of New World Martyrs to the Faith. Father Kino's Sobaípuri Indians were driven out of the San Pedro Valley and nearly exterminated by the Apaches. In the eighteenth century the Spanish attempted to erect a cordon of *presidios* (forts) from the Gulf of California to the Gulf of Mexico to contain the Apaches. That too failed. In the 1770s the Apaches wiped out an entire garrison of Spanish troops along the San Pedro River, and by 1780 New Spain's northern frontier had all but disintegrated: the Apaches held all the strategic passes, river valleys, and water sources. At the close of the eighteenth century the massively fortified *presidio* of Tucson was the only place of any importance in Arizona to remain inhabited by Spanish. Eventually the Apaches became victims of their own success and found themselves having to travel hundreds of miles into Mexico to find settlements to raid.

By the time Mexico achieved its independence from Spain, the war with *Apacheria* had become total. Neither side showed any mercy. Gruesome and creative torture, the mutilation of women and children, rape, the buying and selling of captives, and the burning of victims alive were practiced enthusiastically by both sides.

The Apaches welcomed the arrival of the Americans in the late 1840s. They knew the Americans had defeated the Mexicans in war, and this made the Apaches well-disposed toward them. One mining manager remarked in 1856: "The Apaches have not up to this time given us any trouble; but on the contrary, pass within sight of our herd, going hundreds of miles into Mexico on their forays rather than breaking their [friendship]. . .with the Americans."

This friendship could have lasted a considerable period of time, if not indefinitely. The Americans did not covet the Apache's homelands the way they would covet, for instance, the Black Hills of the Sioux or the woodlands of the Micmac. The Apaches had learned the value of the new international border established by the Gadsden Purchase and were quick to exploit it, raiding into Mexico and retreating back to the United States. It is likely they would have been content to prey on the Mexicans and leave the Americans alone.

It was not to be. In 1861, a dull-witted cavalry lieutenant named Bascom quite needlessly won the hatred of the Chiricahua chief, Cochise, by kidnapping and hanging six of his relatives for a crime they did not commit. Cochise himself barely escaped hanging by slicing a hole in a tent while being interrogated and running a gauntlet of firing troops. Cochise was outraged by the injustice and proceeded to exact a terrible and bloody revenge. He was a formidable enemy. One of the few photographs of him that exist shows an old man with delicate, intellectual, almost effeminate features. He looks into the camera with long thin lips and heavy, supercilious eyes, a man who clearly regarded most others as his inferiors. When it came to warfare, Cochise *was* an intellectual. The *beau geste*, the brave but hopeless stand to the finish, the fight against overwhelming odds—common among the Sioux and Cheyenne—was not the Chiricahua way. Cochise's focus was on strategic and military success. For Cochise and other Apache leaders, negotiation, retreat, prevarication, and even surrender were not dishonorable if tactically useful. The Chiricahua were more than able to match the Americans in the art of lying and breaking treaties.

The casualty figures of the Apache wars confirm the success of their military strategy. Although the exact figures will probably never be worked out by historians, it is probably accurate to say that for every Apache man killed, at least ten white men—and God knows how many Mexicans—died.

Historians have largely failed to recognize the nature of the war with *Apacheria*. It was not, as is usually assumed, a war over land or resources, although these played a role. The ancient Chiricahua homelands are as empty today as they were when Coronado rode through.

It was, rather, a tribal war—between the Apache tribe and the American tribe. Tribal wars are wars of vengeance and honor. The fighting between factions in Lebanon and the war between Protestants and Catholics in Northern Ireland are modern examples of tribal warfare. They do not admit logic, and they are not susceptible to negotiation and compromise. They are wars of annihilation, not aggrandizement. They usually do not end until one side or the other is destroyed.

Not twenty-four hours after the kidnapping and murder of his relatives, Cochise and his band attacked a Butterfield Overland Mail station, killing a man. Later that same day they attacked a wagon train and roasted the captured Mexicans alive on wagon wheels. The two unfortunate Americans on the train were tortured at leisure; the army surgeon who later examined their remains could not tell where one body ended and the other began.

The Americans retaliated and the cycle of killings began.

Shortly thereafter the Civil War broke out, and large numbers of troops were recalled from Arizona. This gave Cochise and his Chiricahuas free rein. They made the most of it, swooping out of their main camp (which the Americans called Cochise Stronghold) and other inaccessible mountain retreats in the Dragoon and Chiricahua mountains, raiding, killing, and plundering.

"Our prosperity has departed," one Tucson newspaper lamented with only a little exaggeration. "The mail is withdrawn; the soldiers are gone, and the garrisons burned to the ground; the miners murdered and the mines abandoned; the stockraisers and farmers have abandoned their crops and herds to the Indians, and the population general have fled, panic struck and naked in search of refuge. From end to end of the territory, except alone in Tucson and its immediate vicinity, there is not a human habitation."

The last sentence of this editorial attests to a universal American belief within Arizona: the Apaches were not human. As in most tribal wars, each side denied the humanity of the other. It is impossible to understand the fury and hatred that Arizonans felt for the Apaches, and vice versa, without understanding this fact.

The close of the Civil War changed things little. The "Apache problem" continued to grow and Washington did nothing. It wasn't until 1871 that the U.S. government finally took action: President Ulysses S. Grant sent several peace missions to the Apaches. They managed to persuade all the major Apache tribes, including the Chiricahuas, to settle on reservations. This was not as difficult as it sounds, since the new reservations largely encompassed the original homelands of the tribes anyway; the Apaches were merely asked to stop raiding in return for receiving food and supplies from the Indian agencies. The reservation established for the Chiricahuas included the Sulphur Spring Valley and the mountain ranges and valleys to the east and south.

Cochise died in 1874. The mourners placed his body on a litter and carried it into Cochise Stronghold, where it was hidden so carefully no white man has ever been able to find it.

In the meantime, problems developed with the agent in charge of the Chiricahuas, a man named Thomas Jeffords. Unlike the other Indian agents in the territory, Jeffords was honest; in fact he was incorruptible. Once a Mississippi riverboat captain, he had come to Arizona to manage one of the segments of the Butterfield Overland Mail. While working for the Mail, Jeffords became annoyed at Cochise's attacks against his wagon trains, so he saddled up his horse and rode alone into the Stronghold to complain to Cochise in person. The old Indian was so impressed by Jeffords's bravery that the two became close friends and eventually, in a traditional Apache ceremony, blood brothers. When Cochise agreed to settle on the reservation, his only condition was that Jeffords be the agent.

Normally, the Indian agent would buy beef, grain, and supplies at grossly inflated prices from crooked contractors. The contractors kicked back money to the agents and everyone was happy—except the Indians, who were getting maggoty beef, moldy grain, rotten manta cloth, and blankets made of coarse buffalo hair. There was little the army could do: the management of the Indian agencies was under civilian control in Washington.

This process of swindling the Indians was part of a much larger swindle being operated by a group known as the Tucson Ring. The Ring was a group of contractors who made a living from supplying the army and the Indians with beef, grain, hay, and supplies. Not only did they cheat the Indians, but they fleeced the army as thoroughly as some of today's military contractors. The process was so lucrative that the Tucson Ring became powerful and rich, controlling the major newspapers of the territory, running lobbyists in Washington, and influencing friends in high places all over the country.

The Tucson Ring had two goals. The first was to keep the Apaches stirred up and on the warpath. This would guarantee a large military presence in the territory and continued business for them. If the Apaches were forced to settle on reservations, then the Tucson Ring wanted to ensure that they would never become self-sufficient, but would be dependent on the agency for their food and supplies.

The Tucson Ring's newspapers whipped up anti-Apache hysteria and even fabricated massacres to rouse and panic the citizenry. They agitated in Washington for the removal of fair-minded army officers. They particularly wanted to undercut Jeffords and induce the Chiricahua to go back on the warpath.

Their lobbying in Washington finally worked. In 1876 the Chiricahua's meat ration was eliminated, and Jeffords had to tell the Apaches that they would have to hunt their own game from now on. This ploy put Jeffords in a tight spot, angered the Indians, and placed armed Chiricahuas into the countryside seeking scarce game, where the temptation to butcher a cow or steal a horse might be too much to resist.

Cochise's son, Taza, who assumed leadership of the Chiricahuas after his father's death, turned out to be a poor leader. When the meat ration was eliminated Taza lost control of a dissident faction of the tribe, which wanted to resume raids in Mexico. A fight ensued and several Indians were killed. A Chiricahua medicine man, Skinya, and a small band of followers then jumped the reservation and made a series of raids in Mexico. On their way back (following the route we had just taken), they attacked a settlement on the San Pedro River, and a few days later killed a settler in the Sulphur Spring Valley.

This was exactly what the Tucson Ring had been hoping for. For some time the Ring's lobbyists in Washington had quietly been working Congress, and as soon as news of the raid broke the reservation was abolished and the Chiricahua homelands confiscated. No distinction was made between the vast majority of the Indians who had stayed on the reservation and the small band of fighters. The Indians were told they were going to be moved to the already crowded San Carlos Agency.

On July 12, 1876, the Chiricahuas were rounded up. Four hundred of them broke away and fled to Mexico, under the leadership of Juh, Nolgee, and a rising young warrior named Goyakla, or "One Who Yawns."

. . .

Goyakla was not strictly a Chiricahua, but a Bedonkohe Apache. He married a Chiricahua woman and, as the Apache are matrilocal, went to live with his wife's tribe. In the 1850s Mexican troops had murdered his mother, wife, and all his children, inducing in Goyakla an almost pathological hatred of Mexicans.

The defining moment of Goyakla's life came soon afterward, when he led a raid into Mexico against the murderers of his family. At the start of battle, for mysterious reasons, one of the Mexicans pointed at Goyakla and called him "Jerome," *Geronimo*. As the battle unfolded, Goyakla killed so many Mexicans in hand-to-hand combat, and fought so furiously—tearing among them, covered with the blood of his victims, slashing and stabbing and firing arrows—that the Mexicans began crying out the name in terror, *Geronimo, Geronimo, Geronimo!*

Goyakla immediately adopted the name Geronimo, liking the way it sounded in the stricken throats of his enemy. His conduct in the battle had been so unusual that the Chiricahuas promptly elected him their war chief. During peacetime he was subject, like any other Apache, to the hereditary chiefs, but when war came he would be in charge.

Geronimo was possibly the greatest Indian military leader of the nineteenth century. In the end, it would take five thousand cavalry troops and five hundred Apache scouts, at a cost of one million dollars, to run Geronimo and his band of nineteen warriors, encumbered with women and children, to earth. During this time he would keep the entire population of the Southwest and northern Mexico in a state of turmoil and panic. In the process Geronimo would not lose a single man.

There are two photographs of Geronimo, taken about twenty years apart, that bracket his life. The first is the famous picture taken in 1884. He is dressed in buckskins and leggings, with a sash around his neck. He kneels, rifle in hand, staring across the years with a maniacal intensity. The second photograph shows Geronimo twenty years later, a prisoner of war at Fort Sill, Oklahoma. He is standing in his watermelon patch, where he often posed for tourists, charging them twenty-five cents a photograph. He is wearing greasy canvas clothing and he cradles a large watermelon in his left arm. His expression is almost beyond my ability to describe: there is no bitterness, no anguish, no fight or hatred left; only the most profound sadness I've ever seen on the face of a human being. He was a man who had witnessed, in a span of twenty-five years, the entire destruction of his people.

. . .

After Juh, Nolgee, and Geronimo fled the reservation in 1876, they retreated to exceedingly remote canyons in the Sierra Madres of northern Mexico. From there they cut a swath of terror on both sides of the mountains and across northern Chihuahua and Sonora. When things got hot in Mexico, Geronimo and his band would dash north to New Mexico, where they would catch some rest and relaxation at the Warm Springs Agency, home to an Apache tribe closely allied with the Chiricahuas. Geronimo had a touch of arthritis and loved to soak in the hot springs there.*

Geronimo spent two short stints on the San Carlos reservation: once when he was captured at Warm Springs, and a second stint in 1884 when he became tired of raiding. But each time conditions were so abysmal, and the depth of corruption of the Indian agents so profound, that he was soon gone. During each stay, however, he observed a great deal about the white man, his military tactics, and his technology.

By the mid-1880s Geronimo and his loose confederation of bands had become a remarkable fighting force. Through raiding, the Chiricahuas had acquired the finest firearms then available—better even than the arms Congress had voted to supply the army. They became highly expert in the use of them. No longer would they have to use the tactics of ambush and retreat because the army had superior firepower. Now they could stand and fight, knowing they could outgun and outshoot any equal force opposing them. They had also learned the value of binoculars and almost every warrior had a pair. Most important, they figured out how the telegraph worked. Instead of merely cutting the wires, they would cleverly splice a small rawhide string across a cut and put them back up. It would then take days of painstaking checking for the army to discover the break and resume communications.

Meanwhile, the army had assigned a new commander for the Department of Arizona, General George Crook. Crook was a hard but honorable man, who was just coming from decisive victories over the Cheyenne and Sioux. Unlike many of his contemporaries, he fought fairly and treated the Indians with dignity. Red Cloud, the great Cheyenne chief, said of him: "He at least never lied to us."

---

*The Warm Springs reservation would also be abolished on flimsy pretexts. It later became the retirement-resort town of Truth or Consequences, named after the television show, and populated by blue-rinse ladies and men with white shoes and chunky turquoise bolo ties.

He was also a great eccentric. His eccentricity was most startling in his appearance, but it found its full expression in his military tactics. His camp dress was a rough canvas suit and a Japanese summer hat. He wore no insignia of any kind, not even his general's star. Unlike most officers he knew how to pack a mule, track, and scout. While on campaign he mingled with his men and ate their food, taking no privileges for himself. On one of these campaigns a packer saw him walking through camp in his faded suit and called him over.

"Say, mister," he said, "do you understand mules?"

"I think I do," Crook replied.

"Have you ever had experience in that line?" the packer asked.

"Well, considerable, here and there," Crook said.

The packer looked him up and down. "Well," he finally said, "I'll give you forty dollars a month and grub to help us in this campaign."

With a perfectly straight face Crook responded, "I am much obliged for the offer, but I already have a job."

The packer was irritated that this shabby man would refuse such a generous offer. "Is that so?" he asked sarcastically. "What is the job?" Crook told him and left the astounded packer among a circle of laughing soldiers.

Crook recognized at once that the corruption of the Indian agents had a great deal to do with the Apaches' raiding and plunder, and he protested to Washington. A grand jury, belatedly convened to examine charges against several corrupt individuals, concluded: "We feel it our duty. . .to express our utter abhorrence of the conduct of. . .that class of reverend peculators who have cursed Arizona as Indian officials, and who have caused more misery and loss of life than all other causes combined." The jury went on to say that "the desolation and bloodshed which have dotted our plains with the graves of murdered victims" were more the responsibility of the Indian agents and contractors than of the Indians themselves—a remarkable conclusion from a jury of white Arizonans.

Such was the depth of corruption that even this scathing report failed to change things. The San Carlos Agency remained practically a concentration camp. "San Carlos," one officer noted, "won unanimously our designation of it as 'Hell's Forty Acres.' . . . Everywhere the naked, hungry, dirty, frightened little Indian children, darting behind bush or into wikiup* at the sight of you. Everywhere the sullen, stolid, hope-

---

*The brush hut of the Apache.

less, suspicious faces of the older Indians challenging you. You felt the challenge in your very marrow—that unspoken challenge to prove yourself anything else other than one more liar and thief, differing but little from the procession of liars and thieves who had preceded you."

Geronimo's last stay at San Carlos ended in May of 1884, when he persuaded some of the other chiefs to join him in a break for Mexico. They cut and spliced the telegraph lines, and by the time the Agency repaired them and wired out news of the escape, the Indians were 120 miles away, having ridden their mounts to death and stolen fresh horses.

The civilian population went into a virtual paroxysm of fear. Across Arizona and southern New Mexico the army was mobilized and all known waterholes staked out. The Tucson Ring exploited the situation, using their newspapers to whip up hysteria with a series of grim editorials and graphic reports. Settlers across the Southwest became so jumpy that some even fabricated a Geronimo sighting to attract a company of cavalry to their area, as a kind of insurance. From reading the newspaper reports, one would have thought that the entire Apache Nation had escaped and were pillaging the country. In fact, only forty-two "bucks" (as one officer called them) had jumped the reservation; the other four hundred Chiricahua, along with thousands of other Apaches, stayed behind.

There was genuine reason to be afraid. The renegades broke up into small bands and raided back and forth across the international border, killing soldiers wherever they found them and swooping down on ranches for cattle and fresh mounts. The raids were surgical in their precision and could happen anywhere, at any time. So high was the tension that a barking dog could throw an entire town into panic. "City is wild tonight with rumors of all kinds," one person wired from Tombstone. "All is excitement and confusion," wrote another from Bisbee.

On the other side of the border the Mexicans were even more frightened; Geronimo still reserved a special hatred for the Mexicans, and his attacks against small Mexican villages were utterly merciless. Mexico and the United States had recently signed a treaty allowing troops of either country to pursue Indians across the border, and when American soldiers entered Mexican towns the inhabitants would run from their homes, crying *"soldados Americanos!"* with delirious excitement.

Geronimo and his loose confederation of chiefs were nearly impossible to track through the rugged mountains of southern Arizona and northern Mexico; certainly no white man, or most Indians, could track them. But Crook had unconventional ideas. First, he replaced his Pima and Papago Indian scouts with other Apaches. While this may seem like a commonsense idea today, at the time it was widely resented and feared because it brought large numbers of armed Apaches off the reservation.

In the past, the cavalry had pursued the Apaches only for short stretches, and that during good weather. Come winter, and heavy snows in the mountains, everyone went back to the fort to wait for spring. Crook reversed all this. He would pursue them relentlessly, day and night, winter and summer. He would give Geronimo no rest.*

This was easier said than done. To give one example, a cavalry troop picked up Geronimo's fresh trail in southern Arizona. The fifty-six-year-old Geronimo and the nineteen warriors in his particular band (along with some forty women and children) led them thousands of miles across northern Mexico, up into New Mexico, and back down to El Paso, Texas, before losing them. The unsuccessful pursuit ruined dozens of fine horses, permanently crippled the famed Indian scout Al Sieber, and induced the officer-in-charge to quit the army for an easier life—ranching.

The skill—and the gall—of the Apaches was not to be believed. Geronimo, although the overall war chief, was not the only brilliant strategist among the Apaches. One band, led by a lesser war chief named Josanie, raided what would have seemed to be the most unlikely target in the Southwest: Fort Apache itself, in the heart of the San Carlos Agency. Josanie correctly surmised that the fort would be more or less undefended. (Who would have thought the Apaches would attack their own reservation?) After wreaking havoc at the fort, Josanie turned his attention to the Indians. He killed twenty White Mountain Apaches, because these latter Indians—traditional enemies of the Chiricahuas—had been supplying scouts for the whites. In a final humiliation, he stole all of the horses belonging to the White Mountain chief. Josanie fled eastward through Aravaipa Canyon, thereby eluding the pursuing cavalry, who assumed he was heading back to Mexico. In the six weeks Josanie and his small band (which also included women, children, and infants) rampaged across the country, they traveled 1,200

---

*One of the first lessons of tracking—one that we learned early—is to get on the trail immediately and stay on it relentlessly until success is achieved.

miles, killed 38 people, stole 250 horses, and destroyed property worth many thousands of dollars. During this time he lost only one warrior.

In all these engagements, the Indians outmaneuvered and outfought the army and its five hundred scouts. But most important, they out-*thought* the cavalry. The renegades had many tricks. After a raid, a band would scatter, making them far harder to track, and meet at a prearranged location several days later. Here they would set up a phony camp, complete with campfires and a broken-down horse or two staked out nearby. Then they would make their real camp several miles away. By the time the troops came roaring into the phony camp at dawn, the Apaches would be long gone.

They were constantly inventing new ways to shake the tracking scouts. They would double back and then zigzag over their trail, or they might reverse direction and retrace their trail while one or two Indians would peel off at a time until all had gone; they wrapped their horses' hooves and traveled across slickrock; they traveled down streams and along arroyos that would wash out at the next rain.

While most of the time Crook's Apache scouts could follow the trail, it usually took them more time to puzzle it out than it took the renegades to set up the confusion. Meanwhile, the gap between pursuer and pursued ever widened.

Crook soon realized that it was hopeless to chase the small Apache bands all over the Southwest and Mexico. To defeat them, he would have to locate and smash their main camps in the Sierra Madres. This became central to his policy of giving the Indians no rest.

Crook sent his best captains and scouts into Mexico. For months they followed old trails and scouted the Sierra Madres, sometimes penetrating territory that no Mexican, let alone American, had ever seen. Finally, in January 1886, one of Crook's captains discovered fresh Indian "sign" near the Yaqui River. They followed the trail through harrowing mountains and the roughest country yet encountered, country that shredded the soldiers' uniforms, ruined their shoes, and lamed their horses.

In the end they discovered Geronimo's main camp. What is more, so confident was Geronimo in the safety of his retreat that he had posted no guards. While most of the Apaches escaped during the ambush, the Americans were able to capture and burn the Chiricahua's food stores and possessions.

The defeat came as a great shock to Geronimo, as he had always been able to find a safe refuge in the Sierra Madres. One officer wrote later:

"When they found. . .that there was no place safe for them, no place even in the immense stretch of mountains beyond the regions penetrated by no others than themselves. . .they knew it was only a question of time as to their annihilation." Geronimo realized that, with Crook, he had met an officer who was his match.

The Apaches had two traditions when waging war that now came into play. The first was that, while they had only contempt for weakness, they had the "profoundest respect" for any man who got the better of them. Second, they recognized when the tide turned against them. Rather than fighting to the death, their traditions required that the war chief (in this case Geronimo) surrender on as favorable terms as possible.

A third factor came into play: the women. While they were not permitted to address any man during a war council, they were allowed to sit close enough to overhear what was being said. They would then make loud comments to one another on the proposals being discussed. The warriors, naturally pretending not to hear, nevertheless had to take into account the women's opinions. At this war council, apparently, the Apache women expressed their opposition to continued flight.

Later that day, after much thinking and discussion, Geronimo sent an emissary to the soldiers, saying he wanted to talk peace. Crook rushed down to Mexico and, in the Cañon de los Embudos, near the American border, they sat down to talk. Among the Apaches were many of their great leaders: Josanie, Nachez, Chihuahua, Nana, Noche, and Cayetano. "The whole ravine was romantically beautiful," one officer remembered. "Shading the rippling water were smooth, white-trunked, long, and slender sycamores, dark gnarly ash, round-barked cottonwoods. . . . Twenty four warriors listened to the conference or loitered within earshot; they were loaded down with metallic ammunition, some of it reloading and some not.* Every man and boy in the band wore two cartridge belts." A photograph taken at the occasion shows a row of young Apache boys—they can be no older than ten—carrying with aplomb rifles nearly half again as tall as they.

Crook opened the conference with a terse statement: "What have you to say? I have come all the way down from Bowie."

Geronimo responded by detailing the reasons he left the reservation, telling of the abuses of the Indian agents at San Carlos. He was particu-

---

*In other words, some of the Apaches had ammunition in magazines, which meant many shots could be fired before reloading was necessary.

larly outraged at a smear on his reputation: the gossip and newspaper reports that said he was a "bad man."

"I know I have to die sometime," Geronimo said, "but even if the heavens were to fall on me, I want to do what is right. I think I am a good man, but in the papers all over the world they say I am a bad man. . . . I never do wrong without a cause." As a primary condition of surrender, Geronimo stated: "I want good men to be my agents and interpreters; people who will talk right. . . . In the future I don't want these bad men to be allowed near where we live."

Unfortunately, this was the one thing Crook couldn't deliver, since he had no control over political appointees from Washington. Crook refused to make promises he couldn't keep. Instead, he told Geronimo: "You must make up your mind whether you will stay on the warpath or surrender unconditionally. If you stay out, I'll keep after you and kill the last one, if it takes fifty years." He hammered home the point that Geronimo would never, ever, be safe or at rest until he surrendered.

As Crook spoke, "perspiration in great beads rolled down [Geronimo's] temples and over his hands; and he clutched from time to time at a buckskin thong which he held tightly in one hand."

The chiefs retired to discuss the situation. The next day they came into Crook's camp to surrender. But it would not be unconditional; in the end Crook would have to make some concessions.

Geronimo was the last to surrender. "Two or three words are enough," he said. "Once I moved about like the wind. Now I surrender to you and that is all."

Crook had agreed to a number of things, including a promise that Geronimo and the chiefs would be reunited with their families (Geronimo's family had stayed behind at San Carlos). They would be removed from Arizona for a period not longer than two years, and then be allowed to return and live freely on the reservation. Crook further promised they would not be turned over to civilian authorities in Arizona for trial and (inevitable) execution.

The Tucson Ring was not pleased with the capture of Geronimo. The campaign against Geronimo had been a fantastic windfall for them. A man named Tribollet, a notorious swindler connected with the Tucson Ring, intercepted the Indians—traveling separately from the soldiers—at the border with a fifteen-gallon keg of whiskey. The Indians were still flush with cash from their raids, and Tribollet sold them the whiskey at a spectacular price. When they were drunk, he told them that he had overheard the soldiers talking and that he had learned they planned to murder all the Apaches as soon as they set foot in American territory.

Geronimo, his judgment impaired by the whiskey, took the report seriously. Geronimo and his nineteen warriors decided to make a break for it; the rest of the Indians voted to stay. Late that night they stole out of camp.

Geronimo's escape was a disaster for Crook, as the Apache had supposedly been under his control. The news was headlined around the country. Meanwhile, other problems had developed. President Grover Cleveland, the first Democrat elected to the White House since the Civil War, did not want to accept the surrender terms to which Crook had agreed. His party, in the process of disenfranchising blacks in the South, was also clamoring for Indian blood. He told Crook to renegotiate the surrender terms so that the only condition was the "sparing of their lives." Crook, an honorable man, pointed out the gross unfairness of renegotiating surrender terms after the fact.

Geronimo's escape gave President Cleveland the pretext he needed to relieve Crook. He replaced him with someone more to his liking: General Nelson A. Miles. The government also informed the Apaches who had not fled with Geronimo that the terms of their surrender were null and void. The men were separated from their families and were escorted in chains to the nearest train station, where they were packed in cars and sent off to Florida for imprisonment. They had no choice but to leave all their belongings, horses, and dogs at the train station. (Some of the dogs, howling with grief, chased the departing train for miles down the track.)

Miles was a vainglorious liar, a man without personal honor, a man whom Teddy Roosevelt would later call a "strutting peacock." If ever there was a contrast to Crook it was he. Miles wanted to be president of the United States and saw the capture of Geronimo as the way to achieve it. But Miles was also very intelligent, and he continued Crook's policy of hard pursuit.

Miles's crack officers and their scouts (Miles himself stayed at home) picked up Geronimo's trail in Mexico and chased him for four months. It was excruciating work. Among other hardships, the men's clothing became so filthy from lack of washing water that the only way to get rid of the vermin was to pile the infested clothing on a fire-ant nest. The ants would then swarm out and carry off the lice and fleas.

Geronimo, pressed closely by Miles's troops, called for a parley. Geronimo offered his conditional surrender to Captain Lawton,

Miles's field commander. Lawton wired Miles to hurry down and negotiate the terms. Miles, however, had other ideas. If negotiations bogged down and the skittish Apaches took off, Miles would face the same fate as Crook. Miles wired back an order to Lawton in which he suggested, in oblique language, that it would be much simpler if the Indians were lured into camp and then murdered. Lawton disobeyed the order and Miles, with great reluctance, concluded that he would have to make a trip to Skeleton Canyon. He arrived on September 3, 1886.

Miles instructed his interpreter to tell Geronimo that "General Miles is your friend."

Geronimo sized up Miles in a moment. He didn't like the man at all. He responded, sarcastically, to the interpreter: "I have been in need of friends. Why has he not been with me?" and roared with laughter at his joke, along with the Indians and then the soldiers (once the joke was translated), to the great discomfort of Miles.

Miles was ready to promise all kinds of things to Geronimo. Later the old Indian would recall: "General Miles said to me, 'The President of the United States has sent me to speak with you. . . . I will take you under government protection; I will build you a house; I will fence you much land; I will give you cattle, horses, mules, and farming equipment. . . . There is plenty of timber, water, and grass in the land to which I will send you. You will live with your tribe and with your family. If you agree to this treaty you shall see your family within five days.' "

Geronimo continued: "General Miles swept a spot of ground clear with his hand, and said: 'Your past deeds shall be wiped out like this and you will start a new life.' " He placed a stone in front of Geronimo and said his word and that of the president were as solid as the rock. (Geronimo's account of that meeting was corroborated by the other army officers present at the conference.)

Unfortunately, it was all lies. Miles wanted to get Geronimo back to the United States in chains and would have promised anything to accomplish it. It would be his word against a criminal renegade Indian who didn't even speak English.

On the strength of these promises, the Apaches gave up their arms and accompanied Miles back to Fort Bowie. There, violating all the surrender terms, they were separated from their families, clapped in chains, and shipped by rail to prison camps in Florida, where they were held as "prisoners of war." Only a few officers knew the surrender terms, and none spoke out at the time.

The war with the Apaches was over.*

Conditions in the Florida concentration camp were pestilential and many Apaches died. In 1894 the Apaches—still officially "prisoners of war"—were moved to Fort Sill, Oklahoma, where they were belatedly reunited with their families and instructed to become farmers.

Many of the old war chiefs drank themselves to death. Geronimo, on the other hand, became a Christian and joined the Dutch Reformed Church. He was sent to the St. Louis World's Fair as an "attraction" and sold his signed photograph for twenty-five cents (fifty cents if he signed in larger block letters). "He became a tireless promoter of himself," a biographer wrote, "hawking photographs, bows and arrows at various fairs and exhibitions." He spent a year with a Wild West show. During one of these shows he suddenly recognized General Miles in the audience and, abandoning his act, rushed into the grand-stand to kill him. He was restrained, unfortunately, before he could accomplish the deed.

He drank a great deal and became a foolish old man. One Apache described Geronimo's last years at Fort Sill: "Geronimo was very absent-minded. He would be looking for his hat and he would have it on his head. One time, when we were over to visit him, he was making a bow with a big knife. Pretty soon he began asking his wife where his knife was. All the time he had it in his hand, but we didn't let on. So there he was, scolding his wife and telling her to look for it for him. . . . But she wouldn't look. She said, 'You're old enough to look for your own knife.'

"Geronimo got pretty angry. 'Boys, you see how she is!' he said. 'I advise you not to get married.' Finally he saw the knife in his hand. 'Why, I'm nothing but a fool!' he said."

Geronimo never forgot Miles's broken promise that they could re-turn to Arizona. In 1905, to his biographer S. M. Barrett, Geronimo made one last plea: "We do not ask for all the land which the Almighty gave us in the beginning. . .the Almighty created [this land] for the Apaches. It is my land, my home, my father's land, to which I now ask to be allowed to return. I want to spend my last days there, and be buried among those mountains. If this could be I might die in peace, feeling that my people, placed in their native homes, would increase in numbers, rather than diminish at present, and that our name would not become extinct. . . .

"We are vanishing from the earth, yet I cannot think we are useless

---

*A few Apaches, however, remained in Mexico, where they live to this day.

or Usen would not have created us. . . . When Usen created the Apaches He also created their homes in the west. He gave to them such grain, fruits, and game as they needed to eat. . .He gave them a pleasant climate and all they needed for clothing and shelter was at hand.

"Thus it was in the beginning: The Apaches and their homes each created for the other by Usen himself. When they are taken from these homes they sicken and die.* How long will it be until it is said, there are no Apaches?"

On February 16th, 1909, Geronimo went into town and sold one of his tourist souvenir bows. He got drunk with the money. On the return trip he fell out of his wagon and lay all night in the freezing rain. He was found the next morning and taken to the hospital, where he died.

Geronimo's Christian funeral did not pass without one final clash between the ancient Apache way of life and the new Anglo-American way. The service was held at the Christian cemetery, and Geronimo's widow arrived with her husband's favorite sorrel horse. Suddenly, while the Reverend was intoning from his Bible, she drew out a knife and attempted to kill the horse—an Apache custom that allowed the departed warrior to ride to the afterworld. After a struggle the scandalized churchmen were able to disarm her and the funeral proceeded without further incident.

The Chiricahuas would never see the Sulphur Spring Valley or its surrounding mountains again. What is left of the Chiricahua tribe still live at Fort Sill or at the Mescalero Apache reservation in New Mexico, where some were allowed to transfer in 1913. When we rode through the ancient homelands of the Chiricahua in 1989, for all that we saw they might never have existed.

----

*Despite his professed Christianity, Geronimo apparently still followed the Apache religion as well.

11

·◁▷· ⊠ ·◁▷·

We left the Buckskin Ranch on April 28th and rode northward, through the foothills of the Galiuro Mountains, crossing a series of dry canyons that spilled out of the mountains. A coyote streaked away from us and two fat ravens burst out of a draw and flew over our heads, their wings rustling like satin through the air.

We rode for hours in silence. In the desert, during the heat of a windless day, we were submerged in a stillness as deep as the endless spaces surrounding us. As we moved, the only sounds were the thump and scrape of the horses' hooves, the rhythmic creak of leather, and the occasional whistling of hawks. When we stopped the silence would deepen until I couldn't tell whether the strange humming and ringing noises I heard were inside my ears or came from the landscape.

Around eleven o'clock, Walter, who was in the lead, suddenly reined in his horse. A low vibration, like subsonic thunder, had arisen from the earth at our feet. We looked about in wild surprise and saw a ridge in front of us liquify: its entire surface beginning to flow and undulate. For an instant I thought we were in the midst of an earthquake, or some great hallucination induced by heat. Then I realized that the ridge was carpeted with an immense herd of black-tailed deer, an uncountable sea of them, the same color as the landscape itself. We watched as wave after wave of them rippled up and over the ridgeline, until the last panicked stragglers bounded away. It was something you might expect to see on the plains of East Africa, but surely not in America in the late twentieth century.

We ate lunch at a stock tank near a stand of blooming century plants that looked artificial, like an abandoned science fiction movie set. A dead raven floated, face down, in the green water of the tank. We fired up the stove and I made some instant miso soup.

Eusebio eyed the brown liquid with deep suspicion, tasted it, and instantly spat it out.

"Ehhh! That Jap food tastes like piss!" he said.

Walter slurped his down with many loud grunts and sighs of satisfaction, a process calculated to irritate Eusebio. It had the desired effect.

"I don't know how you can *eat* that *shit*," Eusebio finally exploded. "That's the worst-tasting sum-bitch I ever ate."

Walter noisily slurped down a second bowl, exclaiming in exaggerated tones how delicious and nourishing Japanese food was, and how it took a true connoisseur to appreciate its delicate flavor. Eusebio went and sat underneath one of his horses, the only shade for miles around. Every time the horse moved, Eusebio would jerk her lead rope, screeching "Ho! *Cabrona!* Back!"

We rode past the mouth of Rattlesnake Canyon, where we could see the remains of an old horse trail winding up into the mountains. The trail, we had been told, led to a cabin where an infamous shoot-out had taken place. The gun battle would leave three lawmen dead and trigger the largest manhunt in Arizona since Geronimo had jumped the San Carlos reservation. It was a gun battle which would, in a larger sense, symbolize the confrontation of the Old West against the new, the final closing of the frontier.

In 1909, a drifter, miner, and part-time cowboy named Thomas Jefferson Power arrived in the Sulphur Spring Valley. Born in west Texas, T. J. Power had homesteaded 160 acres in New Mexico and settled down with his wife, mother, and family to ranch and farm. He probably would have finished his days there, except for a freakish accident. In 1894 his neighbor's house collapsed while his wife was visiting, killing her.

Something happened to Power as a result of his wife's death. He began one of those restless series of wanderings that were so typical of the Old West. He gathered up his family and moved to Texas, to Oklahoma, and then to Kansas. From there Power went to Colorado, New Mexico, Texas, and back again to New Mexico. He worked at whatever odd jobs he could find. His three sons got little schooling, instead hiring themselves out as farm laborers, blacksmiths, and cowboys. At one point Power scraped together some cash and bought a ranch, but just when it started to work a severe drought killed his cattle and then a great flood washed away his topsoil.

In 1909, T. J. Power and his family arrived in Klondyke, Arizona, the town a day's ride north of us. A cowpuncher, sitting on the porch of the Klondyke store, watched the Powers arrive. Fifty-three years later he told a reporter: "They were the scabbiest lookin' outfit I ever did see. Old wobbly wagons and skinny stock and old plow horses."

The rest of the townspeople did not much like what they saw either.

T. J. Power first worked a ranch at the mouth of Aravaipa Canyon and then moved his stock up into Rattlesnake Canyon in the Galiuro Mountains. He later staked four mining claims at some old diggings nearby, recording them simply as Abandoned No. 1, 2, 3, and 4. An ex-army scout by the name of Tom Sisson joined them and they all lived together in a log cabin deep in the mountains.

They were mightily disliked from the beginning. Most of the townspeople considered them trash. In the previous two decades, law, order, and propriety had settled down over the Arizona frontier, and misfits were no longer tolerated. The Powers got embroiled in various disputes involving cattle rustling, grazing rights, bootlegging, and mining claims. Local cowboys would stampede Power cattle and it was said that some of the town girls were once given five pounds of candy apiece to snub young Tom Power at a schoolhouse dance.

Then the daughter, Ola May Power, died under strange circumstances. The Powers asserted she had hurt her neck and had then been "poisoned," but rumors went around Klondyke (and persist to this day) that Ola May had ridden away to elope with a no-account cowboy, and that one of her brothers had chased her down the trail and roped her off her horse, accidentally breaking her neck.

When World War I started, the two Power boys, John and Tom, were called up, and a notice was sent to them. They never reported. (It is possible nobody in the Power camp could read.) To be a draft evader, a "slacker," was un-American, a disgrace. People began to talk. Something had to be done.

U.S. Deputy Marshal Frank Haynes swore out arrest warrants for

Tom and John Power. He enlisted three others to help him serve the warrants, sheriff Frank McBride and deputy sheriffs Kane Wootan and Martin Kempton. Both Wootan and McBride were long-time enemies of the Power brothers, which perhaps explains why county law enforcement officers would take it upon themselves to serve a federal warrant. One local man reported (forty years too late) that Kane Wootan told him in Klondyke that they were going to go up into the Galiuros to "shoot the hell out of" the Powers.

The four lawmen left Klondyke late on the night of February 9, 1918, and rode up Rattlesnake Canyon. They arrived at the Power homestead before first light and staked out the four corners of the cabin. Shortly thereafter their presence spooked two belled mares that grazed free around the cabin, and the horses ran past the front door. Old Tom Power, hearing the sound, came to the door carrying his rifle. A furious gunfight ensued; when it was over, three of the lawmen were dead and T. J. Power lay dying.

Tom Power later gave a fairly credible account of what had happened. Thinking a mountain lion might be after the horses, he said, his father went to the door with his gun. Someone yelled "Throw up your hands!" T. J. Power dropped his gun and was immediately cut down by three shots.

The two brothers, having no idea who was shooting at them, began firing from the windows, and in less than sixty seconds all was silent. It had happened so fast that Sisson was still in his bunk, looking stunned.

When the two brothers and Sisson went outside, they found the dead bodies of Wootan, Kempton, and McBride, and the mortally wounded T. J. Power.

Haynes, the only survivor, would tell his version of the shoot-out—or rather "versions," since his story changed as often as he told it. The only truth that can be gleaned from his accounts is this: Haynes, the man with the warrant, hadn't identified himself, hadn't asked them to give up, hadn't fired a single shot, and probably hadn't seen a damn thing while he was cowering in the dark. All he heard was some shouting followed by several furious bursts of gunfire and silence. He then snuck away to his horse and rode off.

The two Power brothers and Sisson decided to turn themselves in to a sheriff they knew in Tucson. On the way they ran into a cowboy friend who warned that they would be lynched the minute they showed their faces. The three dead men had left behind three widows and eighteen children, and the public was clamoring for vengeance. The newspapers were already referring to them as "murderers," "slackers," and "the Power Gang."

After hearing this they turned for Mexico, and a massive manhunt ensued. Over three thousand horsemen, including cavalry troops, were eventually brought into action, along with bloodhounds and trackers. For twenty-nine days the three men eluded the posse of thousands—mostly because the newspapers had painted such a terrifying portrait of the "bloodthirsty Power Gang" that the possemen spent most of their time in camp, drunk, doing their damnedest to avoid finding them. In early March the three fugitives crossed into Mexico. By this time a competent U.S. Cavalry officer had picked up their trail in the Big Hatchet Mountains in southwestern New Mexico. So great was the uproar that the officer authorized his troops to cut the fence at the border and pursue the fugitives into Mexico, an action that he knew would have international repercussions. They captured the three men in a thicket of mesquite and hauled them back for trial.

A trial of farcical solemnity followed. The judge barred evidence that supported the Powers' version. Gross contradictions in the testimony of witnesses—particularly Haynes—went unremarked. Several witnesses, whose earliest statements had been favorable to the Powers, strangely altered their stories after speaking with the prosecutors.

The three were swiftly convicted of first-degree murder. They undoubtedly would have been hanged had Arizona not abolished the death penalty two years earlier. (Such was the outrage against the defendants that it was immediately reinstated following the trial, and many editorialists regretted that it couldn't be made retroactive.) The Power brothers and Sisson were sentenced to life in prison.

Sisson, who had spent the entire gunfight in bed, died in prison in 1957 at the age of eighty-six. He was the oldest prisoner in state history.

The two Power boys also broke incarceration records. They spent forty-two years in prison, tying each other for serving the longest terms in Arizona's history. In 1962 they were finally released on parole; John was seventy and Tom sixty-eight. A dogged newspaper columnist named Don Dedera took up their cause and published a series of articles that showed the Powers had been unjustly convicted. As a result they were granted a full pardon by the governor of Arizona in 1969. They settled in the Sulphur Spring Valley—the only home they had known in all their wanderings—and lived out the rest of their lives as they had begun them, as poor, part-time laborers.

Once upon a time, the West had been a haven for drifters, misanthropes, outcasts, tuberculars, criminals, those with unpopular religious beliefs, and misfits of all sorts. These were the people who, for various reasons, could not or did not want to live in more settled parts of the country. It was an era that had begun in the 1820s with the mountain men and had continued with people like Ed Schieffelin, the silver prospector. Many of the homesteading ancestors of the cowboys and ranchers we would meet had been of the same type.

When the frontier "officially" closed in 1894, so did the West as a haven of tolerance. The Power shoot-out was a sign that the rural West would no longer countenance the kind of extreme (and sometimes unattractive) individualism that people like Thomas Jefferson Power represented. It wasn't coincidental that the early West had relatively high populations of blacks, Jews, Mormons, and (some evidence indicates) gay men and women. Many westerners have forgotten that individualism—which they extol in principle—cannot exist without tolerance. Today, the frontier as a refuge of tolerance and individualism has been replaced by large cities such as New York and San Francisco—hotbeds of Godless liberalism condemned by the so-called individualists of the rural West. Many of the qualities of the frontier— violence, crime, homelessness, drunkenness, craziness, abandoned and broken families—have become, for better or worse, qualities of our major cities. The wild West has moved to the metropolis.

On our trip we would still see, in out-of-the-way places, a few examples of the wanderer, the outcast, the crazy old coot in his cabin ready to blow your head off with a shotgun. But this would be the exception rather than the rule.

Since World War I the population of the Sulphur Spring Valley— like most of the rural West—has gone into a long, slow decline. The old Power homestead is now in the middle of the Galiuro Wilderness and Klondyke is about ten residents away from being a ghost town. It is probably safe to say that, with the exception of the town of Willcox, the human population of the Sulphur Spring Valley is lower now than it was when Coronado came through 450 years ago.

That evening we rode into the Eureka Springs Ranch, the outfit Dee Wear's father had once managed. Walter and I chatted with the ranch manager's wife, Kim Lackner, while Eusebio glowered in the blazing sun outside, refusing to put either himself or his horses in the shade.

"Let 'em burn up!" he said when Walter suggested he move them. "I don't give a shit! Good! I'll burn up with 'em!"

When I came back out Eusebio was picking his teeth. "This Arizona," he said, "this is the *sorriest* Goddamn country I ever seen."

I had heard this many times before from him. I said nothing.

"Lemme tell you something else," Eusebio continued. "We ain't getting nowhere fast. We been out two weeks and we gone, what, a hundred miles? Shit, man, we ain't *never* gonna get to Pecos."

I waited in the sun. Eusebio wiped the sweat out of his hat brim, flicked it off his fingers, and fitted the hat back on his head. He looked away.

"First chance," he said in a low voice, "I'm gonna take my horses and I'm gone, I'm *gone* back to East Pecos." He then rattled up a gobbet of phlegm from the depths of his throat and deposited it neatly at his feet, to underscore his point.

I did not argue with him. I was, on the contrary, greatly relieved. It was clearly time for him to go.

Walter was delighted when he heard the news. He clapped me on the back. "We're on our own now, partner."

Eusebio's leaving would create several problems. First, deprived of Eusebio's three horses and tack, I would need at least one new horse, so that Walter and I would each have a saddle horse and a pack horse. The second problem was that, after consulting the maps, we realized that we had a good five days of riding before we hit a paved road where Eusebio and his horses could be picked up. We were going to have Eusebio with us a while longer.

A solution to our problem suggested itself. We had realized that our horse Bobby was not going to make it. He was too fat and flabby when we had started, and he wasn't hardening up with the rest of the horses. He was clumsy among the rocks (we'd been riding in some severe country) and he had badly burned one of his fetlocks getting tangled up at night in the picket rope. On the other hand, he was a beautiful, gentle (if rather stupid) quarter horse who was worth good money. Walter called up his friend Wicks in Santa Fe and struck a deal. We would give him our horse Bobby, in return for the rental of two fresh horses and a saddle. Wicks also agreed to take Eusebio and his horses back to East Pecos.

The Eureka Springs Ranch, one of the oldest in Arizona, was located at the northern end of the Sulphur Spring Valley, at the headwaters of Aravaipa Creek. The ranch started off as a stage stop between Fort Bowie and Fort Grant. In the late nineteenth century it was owned by two brothers named Leitch, from Ohio, who got rich from swindling the army and the Indian agencies with beef, hay, and wood contracts. It was known for a strange, ever-changing mirage that appeared on the southern horizon every morning, giving the appearance of a lake, with trees, hills, and sometimes people. After the Apaches were defeated and the army reduced, it continued as a cattle ranch.

When Wear's father stopped managing the ranch it changed hands several times and went to hell again. By the time it went up for sale in the early 1980s, the cattle had gone wild and nobody knew how many there were. Since the quantity of cattle would greatly affect the value of the ranch, they were counted from a helicopter. Between six hundred and eight hundred were variously counted, and the final number was upped to cover those that had been overlooked. The ranch was sold for a price that included 1,200 cattle.

The present ranch manager, Don Lackner, was hired by the new owner to whip the ranch into shape. It took him and his cowboys three years to round up the maverick cattle. When he was done he had flushed over 4,400 head from the canyons, mountains, and brushy draws. The sale of the cattle alone, for several million dollars, nearly paid for the ranch in its entirety.

We slept in the barn on a pile of alfalfa bales. The next morning was bitterly cold, and while it was still dark I got our stove going outside the barn and boiled coffee. Just before sunrise the cowboys started arriving for work. The first to show up was a skinny, sixteen-year-old kid. He caught a black horse in one of the corrals and saddled it up next to the barn. More cowboys arrived. Soon the dusty flat in front of the barn was crowded with whinnying horses and cowboys murmuring and laughing and spitting tobacco juice, mingled with the sounds of slapping leather, the thump of the saddles on horses' backs, and the jingling of spurs. The dust rose in curtains in the still air, flooded by dawn light. The corral posts sent bars of shadow through the golden clouds of dust, silhouetting horses and men. It was a scene out of the nineteenth century, the living embodiment of a way of life I had thought extinct.

Marilyn McCoy arrived around eight o'clock and traded back Walter's horse Robin for Pepper. She eyed Eusebio's horses with disapproval.

"Good Lord," she hissed in my ear, "that's the worst shoeing job I've ever seen. Who shoed these horses?"

I told her Eusebio did.

"They should be reshod immediately. And look at this." She ran her hand down King's spine. I couldn't see anything wrong.

"See the bump here? Who's riding this horse?"

I said I was.

"Bring me your saddle."

I brought her the saddle that Eusebio had loaned me.

She snorted. "Look at that. That's a roping saddle. I bet it weighs forty pounds. That's no saddle for long-distance riding."

She slung the saddle on the horse's bare back.

"See that?" She pointed to the underside of the saddle right below the cantle. The bottom of the saddle was clearly pressing on the backbone where the bump had formed. "This saddle doesn't even *fit* this horse. He's going to have a serious problem, if he doesn't already."

Whiskey also had a bump coming up from a poorly fitting saddle.

Marilyn shook her head in disgust. "Let me give you boys some advice," she said. "You've got to inspect every square inch of your horses' backs, both in the morning before saddling them and in the evening right after unsaddling. You've got to know those backs better than you know your own ugly faces. You sore a horse's back on a trip like this and you won't be going *anywhere* for a long, long time."

She was visibly relieved when we told her Eusebio had quit. "I didn't want to say anything, but when I first met that fellow I knew you boys were headed for trouble. I mean *big* trouble." She grinned. "I guess, maybe, just *maybe*, you've got a shot at making it."

Seventeen miles down the road we pulled into another ranch, the Flying Diamond. It was named, like most ranches, after one of its brands, a diamond with two wings:

The Flying Diamond Ranch surrounded—and now owned—the little town of Klondyke. Klondyke had been founded by some disgusted ex-prospectors from the Yukon gold rush whose command of spelling was a little shaky. We were welcomed by the owner of the Flying Diamond, Gordon Whiting, a muscled young man with a bushy mustache and weight-lifting equipment in his barn. Whiting made his own shotgun ammunition, played country-western music for his horses, and relaxed in a galvanized stock tank turned into a hot tub. He was a savvy businessman who knew the ranching business backwards and forwards. His ranch ran like clockwork and was prosperous, unlike some of the old-time ranches in the valley.

There was some resentment over that. "They think that what was good enough for their granddaddies is good enough for them," Whiting said. "But you just can't make money these days operating that way. You gotta treat ranching like any other business."

He put us up in one of the cowboy trailers for the night.

The next morning, before dawn, I sat down on the crooked front porch of the Klondyke store to write in my journal, the very same porch the Power brothers had ridden by eighty years before. It didn't look like much had changed since then, except that the porch had departed a good five degrees from the horizontal, the roof had sagged, and the beadboards had curled and sprung loose from the ceiling.

A greenish glow rose over the mountains in the east, the kind of color that you see only in the desert at sunrise. There wasn't a breath of wind. A cow lumbered around the corner of the store and stopped in surprise, staring at me with dumb sloe eyes. An old rounded gas pump, of a kind I hadn't seen since I was a boy, stood in the middle of the dirt patch in front of the store. The red top had faded white and as the sun peeked over the distant mountains the pump threw a long, lonely shadow.

Klondyke was a typical dying Western town. The story of its demise was a common one. The mining and ranching booms of the late nineteenth century were long over, and the place had never recovered from the Great Depression. Across the dirt road from where I was sitting I could see the old tin-roofed Klondyke schoolhouse, boarded up tight. The playground swings were rusted and broken. The school had closed down sixteen years ago and the few remaining kids in Klondyke were now bussed forty-five miles to Pima.

Gradually the shadows shortened and the heat came up. The cow shuffled off down the road, sniffing at the weeds as she went, kicking up puffs of dust. I moved around the corner of the porch into the shade and propped myself against a post. Somewhere I heard a screen door slam, and then I nodded off.

After hearing our tales of lost horses, Gordon Whiting showed me how to hobble a horse with a lead rope, by twisting and tying it around the horse's front legs. Then he showed us how to tack on a horseshoe. He was full of useful information. All the time he had a radio going, wailing out songs about cheatin' women and lyin' men and long lonely nights.

"Horses like music," he said. "Calms 'em down."

While shoeing his horse he told a story about a stagecoach robbery that occurred near the ranch. A group of white men, dressed and painted like Indians, attacked the Fort Grant Stage. The men put enough lead in the air to convince the guards to hand over an army payroll box. Following the robbery, the impoverished town of Pima suddenly had a minor boom of prosperity, but the crime was never solved. Some fifty years later, the University of Arizona came into possession of a strongbox that was believed to be the one taken in the robbery. The owner of the 76 Ranch,* who had long been suspected as one of the robbers, was asked to come and take a look at the box, for historical sake, to see if it might be the one.

The old man eyed the box and screwed up his brow for a long moment.

"Well now," he said, "I ain't gonna tell you whether I was in on the robbery or not. But I will tell you this: that warn't the box."

After breakfast we paid a visit to the old Klondyke cemetery, where the Power family was buried. It stood on a bluff overlooking Aravaipa Valley. The cemetery was choked with cholla and prickly pear, and Indian potsherds and flint chips were scattered around the graves, the remains of a prehistoric midden heap. Perhaps, I thought, looking at the stony ground, it had been a little easier digging graves here. The cemetery had been abandoned; the last person to have been buried here was John Grant Power in 1976.

The Power headstones told the sad and somewhat strange story of the Power clan.

> T.J. Power, Sr. 1918
> Shot Down with His Hands Up
> in His Own Front Door

T. J. Power hadn't been buried here until 1972, when John dug up his father's skeleton and packed it out of the Galiuro Mountains to be interred with the rest of his family.

---

*This same ranch has a large ruin on it that some scholars believe might have been Chichilticale.

T.J. Power Jr.
1894–1970
Poisoned in LA, Calif.
Died at Sunset, Ariz.

The curious "Poisoned in LA" epitaph was, so they say, due to the fact that Tom Power became paranoid in his old age and had delusions that he had been poisoned.

O.M. Power 1917
Poisoned by Unknown Person

The family to the end had insisted that Ola May had been poisoned, not killed.

Martha Jane Power 1915
Killed by Run Away
Horse and Buggy Accident

And finally the last of the Power clan to die and the one who bought tombstones for all the rest:

John Grant Power
Sept. 11, 1892–April 5, 1976
"Rest in Peace"

12

We rode northwestward on a dirt road, paralleling the dry bed of Aravaipa Creek. The canyon walls slowly began to shut us in and the dirt road became more tentative, until it petered out for good in a deep grove of cottonwoods. Aravaipa Creek suddenly became a marsh filled with cattails, and from there a merry little stream debouched.

We passed a rattlesnake in the grass, which buzzed malevolently. Eusebio threw a rock at it. He had a terror of snakes and had brought with him a shriveled root, called *osha,* collected in the Pecos Mountains, which he claimed would drive away snakes. The root emitted a fearful stench.

"Sum-bitch rattler," Eusebio muttered.

"Is it big enough to eat?" Walter called out.

"Ain't nobody gonna eat that sum-bitch while I'm around," Eusebio said.

Walter needled Eusebio. "Why, they make excellent eating," he said. "You grab 'em by the tail and crack 'em like a bullwhip. The head snaps off and you gut 'em and coil 'em up in the fire."

"You ain't cooking that sum-bitch on my fire," Eusebio said.

The canyon was a panic of growth buried in the heart of a desert.

The water in the creek was crystal clear, and as the canyon narrowed the stream flowed faster, burbling and splashing over the rocks. The sun flamed off the honey-colored sandstone cliffs, and the musky, sweet smell of cottonwood catkins mingled with the cool scent of water and the tang of greenery crushed by our passage. A roar of sound issued from the depths of foliage: the motor-like whir of cicadas, the scratching of crickets, the droning of bees, the chirruping and humming and buzzing of thousands of insects. We could see the backs of fish darting about in the creek bed, their shadows projected like black torpedoes against the pebbled bottom.

The desert was never far away. A dozen feet beyond the banks of the stream, talus slopes of dry rock pitched upward to sheer canyon walls. Twenty- and thirty-foot saguaro cactus dotted the slopes, looking like Easter Island gods in the trembling heat.

The murmuring sound, combined with the swaying of the horse, the heat, and the humidity, put me in a kind of daze. Without my even being aware of it the scene imperceptibly dissolved around me and I found myself in the playground of my kindergarten. It was an astonishingly vivid scene, so real that I momentarily forgot where I was. I was hiding a cache of pennies in a hole in the roots of an old oak tree. It seemed so real I was startled to find myself suddenly back in a remote canyon in the Arizona desert.

It was as if my brain were relaxing in a most profound way, and as it slowly settled these memories popped up, a neurological artifact. In retrospect I believe that spending ten hours a day on a swaying horse's back, with little to occupy my mind, was a sustained meditation of sorts. Never before in my life had my higher intellect been so neglected; I had not even opened a newspaper in more than three weeks. My journal entries had become cursory at best, bald, short, declarative sentences, with the simplest words misspelled, reading like the labored scratchings of an illiterate.

The trail began to thin out. The pleasant gravel streambed turned into a deep arroyo jammed with rocks and boulders slick with algae. At each crossing the horses scrabbled and slipped among the boulders, trying to maintain a stable purchase. Soon they were lathered up and blowing hard, the whites of their eyes rolling in fear, and it became increasingly difficult to persuade them to cross. Eusebio became eerily silent, no longer cursing, hollering, or whipping his horses.

We stopped for lunch in a narrow meadow between Booger Canyon

and Hell Hole Canyon, two massive ravines that spilled into Aravaipa
Canyon.

We saw something we hadn't seen in 150 miles of wilderness travel:
hikers. A couple came jaunting by, dressed in colorful Gore-tex clothing and carrying collapsible aluminum hiking sticks. They looked so
bright and clean and new that we, in contrast, suddenly saw ourselves
as we must have appeared to them: three unspeakably foul (and no
doubt criminally dangerous) men. They eyed us with undisguised fear
and hurried past on the upwind side.

Past Hell Hole Canyon the going got much worse. We found ourselves in a very dangerous situation. The horses began to panic for real.
At one three-foot embankment, crowded with boulders, Robin, in a
spasm of fear, leapt into the air. She landed in the stream with a roar
of water and splashed about with the two-hundred-pound pack on her
back. My heart nearly stopped and I was certain she had broken a leg,
but she scrambled up with nothing worse than a few scrapes.

I insisted we stop on the far bank to look for an alternate route on
the maps. Unfortunately, there was really no way out, unless we rode
back seventy-five miles.

"Eusebio," I asked, "are we going to kill a horse in here?"

He shrugged.

I asked again without getting an answer.

Finally I became irritated. "Goddammit, I want an answer. *Are we
going to kill a horse in here?*"

Eusebio stared at the ground. "Maybe," he said slowly, "and maybe
not. I'm not saying *nothing.* You kill a horse in here, it ain't gonna be
my fault."

"What a load of bullshit," Walter said with disgust and got back on
his horse. We continued on.

The afternoon sun had wheeled around and was now glowing off the
eastern walls of the canyon. The canyon had become so narrow and
twisting that we lost track of how much farther we had to go. The trail
kept disappearing and reappearing. It wasn't a trail at all, just a place
where hikers had worn down the vegetation. In several places the brush
was so thick that the packed horses became wedged in it, unable to
move.

At one point the canyon narrowed to less than fifteen feet wide, with
sheer walls on either side. An uprooted cottonwood, with a trunk three
feet in diameter, was jammed in the gap, with just enough room for a
packed horse to squeeze through. Just beyond, Walter and I heard a

tremendous ripping noise followed by a torrent of curses. Eusebio's packhorse had caught a pannier on the jagged rock wall of the canyon and the canvas had torn nearly in half. Stuff was spilling out into the creek and the pack was listing to one side.

Walter, always resourceful, improvised a hitch that temporarily held the pannier together until it could be repaired. With the canyon walls flaming blood-red in the evening sun, we came upon a small meadow with a little flat spot for our bedrolls. We would have to camp.

We unpacked the animals, smeared gall salve on their bloody legs, and staked them out in the rich grass. Eusebio sat down to sew the pannier back together, muttering angrily to himself in Spanish.

Walter hauled a fishnet out of the bottom of a pannier.

"We're gonna have ourselves some trout!" he said.

We found a likely pool, and as we peered into it we could see the flickering of silver. Walter cackled and smacked his palms together. We each took an end of the net and waded into the pool, lunged and scooped, and hauled the net out.

It was empty.

"Dammit," Walter said, "you're letting 'em get out from under."

I was annoyed. "It's not my fault. I saw the fish going right between your legs."

We thrashed through the pool a second time, roiling the bottom. Again the dripping net was empty.

"Damn, Doug, I *saw* 'em get right out from under your end."

"If you spent more time holding your own end down we'd have some fish by now," I said.

We tried driving them upstream into shallow water.

"Hold your end down!" Walter shouted.

We argued a while longer and then I lost my footing and fell head-first into the pool.

When I surfaced Walter was stomping around, laughing. "I didn't want to mention it, but you needed that bath!"

"Shut up," I said.

We hauled in the net. Somehow, in the confusion, we'd managed to catch two fish, barely larger than minnows, which wiggled in the folds of the net. We untangled them. Two big, ugly, rubbery mouths were gasping for air.

"Son-of-a-bitch!" Walter roared out. "These ain't trout! These are suckers!"

We straggled back to camp, dripping wet and laughing.

"Where's dinner?" Eusebio asked.

"Right there," Walter said, kicking a pannier. "Rice and beans."
"*Que chinga'os,*" he said with infinite disgust, and went back to his
sewing.

That night, warm air pooled in the bottom of the canyon, and the
darkness thickened with sound. I lay in my sleeping bag and looked up.
The black canyon walls, visible only as absences of light, blotted out
most of the sky. Where they opened to the stars they looked like a great
crack in the earth filled with phosphorescence, a river of light.

We had camped not far from the site of the most brutal Indian
massacre in the history of the Southwest. Aravaipa Canyon was once
home to a band of Apaches who ranged from the foot of the canyon at
the San Pedro River all the way through to the Eureka Springs Ranch.
The Aravaipa Apaches were a small group and constant warfare eventually reduced them to abject poverty.

In 1871, five gaunt Aravaipa Apache women, dressed in tatters and
carrying a flag of truce, came into old Camp Grant, an army fort at the
junction of Aravaipa Creek and the San Pedro River. The officer in
charge, Royal Emerson Whitman, a Maine Yankee only recently transferred to the territory, treated them kindly and fed them. Eight days
later they returned with more Indians and some pathetic goods for sale.
They told Whitman that their tribe was *in extremis* and asked if their
chief could come in for a peace talk. Whitman agreed.

The chief, Eskiminzin, returned with a group of warriors. He explained to Whitman that his band—or what was left of it—wanted
peace. Whitman suggested that Eskiminzin take his people to the San
Carlos Agency, but Eskiminzin argued against that. "That is not our
country," Eskiminzin said, "neither are they our people." He explained that removal from his tribe's homelands would make them
physically ill. He asked only that they be allowed to settle along
Aravaipa Creek, where he promised they would plant and become
farmers. He requested that they be supplied with tools and food until
the crops came up.

That sounded like a reasonable proposition to Whitman, who was
unversed in frontier hatreds. Here were several hundred "hostiles"
who wanted to give up, become farmers, and generally act like white
men: this was precisely the goal of the current Indian policy. He told
Eskiminzin that the tribe could stay near Fort Grant while he for-
warded the chief's request to his commanding officer, and he issued the
starving Indians some food and clothing.

Whitman was as good as his word. Over the next few months several hundred of Eskiminzin's people came in. As the spring wore on and the lower reaches of Aravaipa Creek dried up, Whitman gave Eskiminzin permission to move his people deeper into the canyon. Meanwhile, Whitman's urgent message had been returned, unacted upon, because of a minor procedural error on Whitman's part. He corrected the missive and sent it back.

Whitman carried from Maine an honesty and respect for straightforward dealings. He closely monitored the quality and prices of goods sold the Indians. He even shifted buying his hay from the profiteers to the Indians themselves, paying them a penny a pound—a good price. Whitman arranged for the local ranchers to hire the Apaches as field hands for the barley harvest, and as a consequence there was little friction between the ranchers and the Indians. He also counted the Indian men several times a week to make sure that they were not slipping away on raids.

The citizens of Tucson were not at all happy with "Whitman's experiment." They did not like the idea of a band of Apaches encamped nearby, being fed at government expense. It may seem strange that they should be so angered at the surrender of a band of Apaches, until one remembers that this was in the middle of a tribal war. Tucsonans weren't interested in seeing the Apaches at peace and living like white men. They wanted to see them dead.

The Tucson Ring had its own reasons for engineering the failure of Whitman's experiment. They had already lost the hay business and Whitman had prevented them from cheating the Indians. If the Aravaipas settled down and became self-sufficient, successful farmers, they might become a model for other Apache bands. That disaster had to be averted.

When some Apaches raided a wagon train and killed two men, the Tucson Ring and its newspapers set up a howl. Phony evidence was advanced showing the depredation had been committed by "Whitman's Indians." Ten days later, a distant ranch was attacked by Indians. The Arizona *Citizen* charged the government with fattening up the "murderers" so they could continue their savage attacks. The propaganda campaign was a great success and the citizens of Tucson began crying loudly for Aravaipa blood.

The final campaign against the Aravaipa Apaches was organized by one William S. Oury, former Texas Ranger, Forty-niner, and ex-mayor of Tucson. Oury assembled a group of "civic-minded" citizens under the chilling name of the Committee on Safety. On April 28,

1871, Oury gathered together a force of forty-two Mexicans, six An-glos, and ninety-four Papago Indians—bitter foes of the Apaches—and set off for Aravaipa Canyon hauling a wagonload of food, guns, and ammunition.* Oury and his forces followed the San Pedro north to where Aravaipa Creek drains into it, sneaked past Camp Grant, and reached the Aravaipa camp just before dawn.

The Anglos and Mexicans stationed themselves on the rim of the canyon while the Papagos charged into the camp. "There was," Oury wrote, "no time for anything but a haphazard dash, and kill all we could." The Papagos clubbed and slashed and shot the sleeping Apaches in their wickiups. Indians trying to climb the canyon walls to escape were picked off by sharpshooters on the rim and then clubbed for good measure when they rolled back to the bottom.

Oury was elated by the success of the expedition, calling it a "memo-rable and glorious morning. . .the killing of about 144 of the most blood-thirsty devils that ever disgraced mother earth."

What Oury doesn't mention is that of the 144 killed, all but eight were women and children; the Aravaipa men had been out hunting in the hills when the attack occurred. The defenseless women and chil-dren were clubbed, shot, dismembered, and gutted; those who tried to crawl away were beaten on the heads with rocks until their brains burst. Almost all the dead were mutilated in the most ghastly ways and at least two of the women were raped. The only survivors were some women and twenty-seven children taken by the Papagos, and these were sold into slavery in Mexico. Not a single member of the attacking party had even been wounded, because there was nobody to defend the camp.

When Whitman heard of the massacre he immediately sent out a surgeon and wagon to bring in the survivors; the wagon returned empty. Deeply shocked, Whitman insisted on going to the camp him-self to bury the dead, despite the very obvious risks involved.

"The camp was burning," Whitman recalled, "and the ground was strewn with their dead and mutilated women and children. . . . I thought the act of caring for their dead would be an evidence to [the warriors] of our sympathy at least, and the conjecture proved correct,

---

*It is an unpleasant fact of Western history, not often noted, that at almost every Indian massacre, Indians of other tribes provided decisive help to the whites. In fact, Indians accompanied virtually every major American military campaign against other Indians.

for while at work many of them came to the spot and indulged in their expressions of grief, too wild and terrible to be described." The survivors, he added, were "so changed in 48 hours as to be hardly recognizable. . . . Many of the men, whose families had all been killed, when I spoke to them and expressed sympathy for them, were obliged to turn away, unable to speak, and too proud to show their grief. The women, whose children had been killed or stolen, were convulsed with grief."

Eskiminzin, who had lost two wives and five children, didn't blame Whitman or the soldiers. "They say," Whitman quoted, " 'We know there are a great many white men and Mexicans who do not wish us to live at peace.' "

What Eskiminzin told Whitman was not the full extent of his feeling. Not long afterward, the chief visited the ranch of a white man with whom he had become good friends. The rancher invited him to supper and they talked and enjoyed each other's company for several hours. Then Eskiminzin abruptly pulled out a pistol and blew his friend's brains out. "Anyone can kill an enemy," he said later. "But it takes a strong man to kill a friend." This was the lesson he had been taught by the Americans. The surviving Aravaipas became renegades, going off into the mountains.

When news of the massacre reached the East Coast, a deep revulsion took place. Easterners demanded that the perpetrators be brought to justice. President Ulysses S. Grant responded by declaring to Governor Safford of Arizona that he would put the territory under martial law if the murderers were not brought to trial. A show trial of the one-hundred-plus killers was quickly organized and conducted with great solemnity. The jury found the perpetrators not guilty in about the time it took for them to walk out and back in the courtroom. At that time, in Arizona Territory, it was impossible to convict a white man for murdering an Indian, even an Indian child. An expression current in Tucson summed it up: "Nits make lice." The trial showed only that the "evidence" connecting the Aravaipa Apaches with the raids and killings had probably been fabricated by the Tucson Ring and its supporters.

Whitman and other Camp Grant officers testified at the trial on behalf of the Indians, and as a result, Whitman became "the most vilified man in Arizona." The Arizona *Citizen* falsely accused him, among other things, of being a drunkard and of having a fascination with "dusky maidens."

Much later, Whitman was present at the final surrender of the

Aravaipas. The peace parley started off badly when General O. O. Howard, the commanding officer, got down on his knees and ostentatiously began to pray. Eskiminzin leapt up in horror and fled. "They scattered like partridges when they see a hawk," Whitman told a friend. "After a while I caught sight of the old chief peeking 'round the corner of a building and beckoning to me. . . . What did I mean [he said] by bringing that man there, to make bad medicine against them?"

Eskiminzin agreed to take the surviving Aravaipa Indians to the San Carlos Agency. Eskiminzin had been right when he said the Aravaipas would die if removed from Aravaipa Canyon. Once at San Carlos the Aravaipas lost their identity and today they no longer exist.

13

◁▷ ⊠ ◁▷

We broke camp early. It was May 2nd, and we had to reach the mining town of Winkelman on the 3rd to meet Wicks, the cowboy who was to give us fresh horses and take Eusebio home. The canyon walls gradually opened up and the creek flowed into a land of arid, stony hills, dotted with giant saguaro cacti.

At the very foot of the canyon, on a bench of land above the river, we spied a magnificent horse ranch. The most prominent landmark was a costly and beautiful horse barn, with room for dozens of stalls. Next to that were corrals, hot walkers, exercise rings, and a swimming pool for horses. On the near side were more barns, a large main house with a swimming pool (for humans), and several guest houses. The ranch was surrounded by fields with miles of white pipe fencing.

As we got closer, the place began to look strange. A barn door hung on one hinge, swaying drunkenly in the breeze. The dirt road we picked up was full of weeds. Blue sky shone through the shattered window frames of the main house. The pool was half full of tumbleweeds. An old chair, its stuffing ripped out, stood outside in a patch of dead grass. The head of a doll, cracked by the sun, looked out of a broken window.

It was one more ranch gone bankrupt.

We followed the road back toward the San Pedro River. We started passing ugly modern houses. There were clusters of signs along the road. House for Sale. Aravaipa Subdivision. Choice Lots. Century 21 Realty. And everywhere: NO TRESPASSING, KEEP OUT. I realized with a start that these were the first No Trespassing signs we had seen in some 175 miles of travel.

We had come down on the Tucson side of the mountains, leaving rural Arizona behind. These were the vacation homes of city folk. The road turned to asphalt and the heat became ferocious. Cars whizzed by, big American cars packed with plump women and men wearing brand-new cowboy hats. We had entered as ugly a landscape as I believe I have ever seen.

Twelve miles of riding brought us to a small group of prefabricated metal buildings and a sign announcing them as Central Arizona College. As we were watering our horses, the ground suddenly shuddered beneath our feet, and a moment later I heard an unearthly roar rolling across the desert. I looked up. A gigantic cloud of mouse-colored dust was rising up in slow motion from some hills to the west. It continued to expand like a grotesque balloon, until it blotted out the sun itself. Some infernal mining operation was in progress.

We crossed a highway and rejoined the San Pedro. We camped in a patch of sand at a bend in the river, not far from the supposed location of old Fort Grant. Nothing was left of the fort, and its precise site has been forgotten.

The soldiers at old Fort Grant also despised this landscape, and the fort had finally been moved because of its "unhealthy location."

"Beauty of situation or construction it had none," an officer posted at the old fort wrote. "Its site was the supposed junction of the sand bed of the Aravaipa with the sand bed of the San Pedro which complacently figured on maps of that time as a creek and river respectively. They were generally as dry as a lime-burner's hat. It was a hot-bed of fever and ague."

We pitched camp in the dusk. I got a fire going and started dinner. While I worked, I could hear Walter in the brush, talking to his three horses while they grazed. (After several weeks we had found ourselves conversing with our horses as if they were human.)

Then I heard Walter's voice raised: "Whoa, Ped."

And a little louder: "I said whoa."

Uh-oh, I thought.

Then: "Ped! *Whoa!* Bobby! Whoa, you son-of-a-bitch, *whoa!* Hey! Robin! Goddammit, *whoa!*"

I began to feel sick. Faintly, from the brush, I could hear one last despairing cry:

"*Motherfuckers!*"

Walter's hysterical voice disappeared into the darkness.

Eusebio stood up and spat. "Shit," he said, "he just lost his horses."

Walter returned an hour later. All three of his horses were gone. In a moment of trust, he had let two graze free; they had taken off, and in the excitement he had dropped the lead rope of the third horse, who also escaped.

It was now pitch-black, a moonless night. We would have to wait until morning.

We had a short, depressing dinner. Eusebio took a grim enjoyment in the disaster. "You watch," he said, "them horses, they shag ass. Them sum-bitches *gone,* man. Ain't nothing gonna stop them now. You ain't *never* gonna find them sum-bitches." He smacked his palms together and spread his arms dramatically, his beady, darting eyes flaming in the firelight. "They *gone!*"

He kept up a steady stream of dreadful predictions, involving horses run over and people killed on the highway, horses lost in brush for months, horses traveling forty, fifty miles in a single night. As he talked, Walter sank deeper into a depression.

I finally pointed out to Eusebio that, as Bobby was one of the lost horses, and as Bobby was our payment for getting Eusebio back to East Pecos, and as Wicks would probably not accept a promissory note on a horse lost somewhere in the Arizona desert, *ergo,* Eusebio would not be going anywhere until we found Bobby.

There was a momentary silence while Eusebio processed this information, his brows knitting together until his entire face was a mass of puzzled wrinkles. Then his eyes popped open and he slapped his hand on his thigh.

"*Aiee!* Sum-bitches! We'll get out there, catch 'em first thing tomorrow! There'll be a fence'll *stop* them sum-bitches, you'll see!"

I will not go into the painful details of our search for the lost horses. We could not track them; the brush was too thick and the ground, which hadn't been rained on in six weeks, was crisscrossed with horse tracks.

Our first step was to determine the area they were lost in. We located and rode the boundary fences and figured it at about seventeen thousand acres, or approximately twenty-seven square miles—virtually all of it dense salt cedar, willow, and cottonwood brush.

I would submit that you cannot understand despair until you have looked for lost horses in twenty-seven square miles of impassable brush, lousy with invisible rattlesnakes, under a white-hot sky in 107-degree heat with no wind and high humidity. (We learned later it was the hottest day southern Arizona had experienced at that time of year in forty-four years.)

We saw, during that long day, something of the way the West had changed since Coronado's day. This was mining country, and there is something about working in an underground hole that breaks the human spirit. I'll never forget coming across the mining town of Dudleyville, emerging from the brush like some Boschean vision of hell: houses of unpainted cinderblock; trailers shedding strips of aluminum; dogs behind chain-link fences, racing back and forth in a frenzy of blood-lust hatred, slobbering and digging to get out; No Trespassing signs with a full-frontal picture of a six-shooter.

Later I rode alongside the highway, through heaps of trash, broken bottles of Night Train, used diapers, beer cans, oil-soaked dirt, and cacti draped with torn plastic and toilet paper. The only breeze was the backwash from passing trucks. Nowhere could I escape the distant clank and grind and roar of men and machines in the surrounding hills, extracting minerals from the earth.

Wicks, the cowboy with our fresh horses, arrived at 2 P.M. I met him on the highway. When he opened the truck door a dozen Coors Light cans tumbled to the ground. He had been refreshing himself since five o'clock that morning.

We rendezvoused back at our camp. Wicks staggered about, mightily annoyed that we had allowed his payment to take hoof. He asked us a lot of questions, none of which we answered satisfactorily, and after some thought he emitted a stream of tobacco juice and the following assessment:

"What a bunch of greenhorn assholes."

He then proceeded to give us some of the best advice we had during the entire trip. Among his instructions were (a) the minute you reach camp, stake out or hobble the horses—never let a horse be loose, even for a moment; (b) train them to come back to camp in the morning by whistling and giving them some grain; (c) just when you think you can trust them, don't; (d) watch them particularly carefully when they are fed and rested, as that's when they'll start causing trouble; and (e) identify the lead horse and watch him closely, as he's the one who will initiate the trouble.

To horse people this advice might seem a little elementary, but to us it was a revelation.

Wicks was a short cowboy with a mustache and an Arizona drawl. He carried a coffee can in his left hand, into which he regularly deposited, with a ringing sound, a stream of tobacco juice. When riding, he wore Adidas, a Lacoste shirt, and a trucker's hat. He was a good enough cowboy that he didn't even have to look like one.

Wicks had once been a champion calf roper. His greatest moment, he told me, was getting thrown off a horse in Madison Square Garden in New York City, for which he received a standing ovation. "I roped fifty head a cows every night for ten years to git there," Wicks said, "and then this son-of-a-bitch horse threw me comin' right out of the gate."

He was a very good roper, almost a world champion. I didn't ask him why he'd quit; the pile of Coors cans explained everything. He now trained horses for the movies, teaching them how to fall down when "shot," how to rear on command, and other tricks.

We finally found the horses at nine o'clock that evening. They were grazing alongside the highway, not even inside the twenty-seven-square-mile wilderness which we had been combing for the past fourteen hours. Somehow, they'd found a hole in the fence or jumped a cattle guard.

The next morning I met my two new horses, Banjo and Popeye. They were both large, powerful quarter horses, with sorrel coloring. Popeye had a white blaze on his forehead and Banjo a snip of white on his nose.

Wicks was a little worried about my ability to handle Popeye. He gave me detailed instructions on what to do if Popeye ran away with me or started bucking. "If somethin' starts to happen, you either git off right away or stay on for the ride—you cain't change your mind halfway through a wreck. If he stampedes with you, reach around and pull the son-of-a-bitch's head sideways with one rein so he cain't see where he's goin'. But don't do it too fast or he'll fall. If that don't work, steer him straight into a bush; that'll stop him."

I was a little perturbed at the advice.

"Now look here," Wicks cautioned, "if he acts up, you gotta punish him."

And how does one punish a 1,200-pound horse?

"The way you do that is to ride him around in a tight circle while kicking the shit out of him. They hate that. Or get off him and kick him hard in the ribs. But kick him with the side of your foot, not the toe."

"I guess you have to be careful not to break his ribs," I offered.

"Hell no!" he said. "You don't want to break your *toe*." He roared with laughter and turned to Walter. "I had a friend did that once, broke his toe kicking a horse. What a dumbshit."

It came time to depart. We shook hands all around while Eusebio sat silently in the truck.

Wicks got in and leaned out the window with a big grin.

"Now that Banjo, he's a lively son-of-a-bitch. As soon as I drive away, he's gonna buck that pack into the river and take off and you're gonna have another lost horse."

We all laughed at the joke. While they lurched off Walter and I sat in a patch of dust under a cottonwood, eating peanuts.

"I'm glad we got rid of that Mexican," Walter said. "That bastard was *diseased*."

"At least he'll make a good character in my book," I said.

"Yeah, and when he reads what you write about him he'll come and burn down your house."

"What makes you so sure he can read?" I asked.

We laughed, feeling enormously elated. The real adventure was now beginning.

"I'll tell you something," Walter said. "*This* is more like it, God *damn*. We're on our own now." He whooped and danced by the side of the river, shedding dust.

Then we formally shook hands.

I mounted Popeye and lightly touched his flanks with my heels, to get him started. The horse acted like he'd just received a load of buckshot in the ass. He sprang forward and went blasting through the brush at a dead run. I held on for dear life and followed Wicks's advice for arresting a runaway horse. When I finally got him under control I saw what had spooked him. Banjo was in the middle of the river, leaping and twisting and kicking, trying to shuck his pack. Our gear was popping off every which way. Then, with the pack half undone, he galloped like hell up the river and disappeared.

We watched in stunned silence. I can hardly describe what my feelings were at that moment. We had lost another horse.

We tried tracking him without success, as he had galloped a considerable distance in the river bottom. So we wearily rode, yet again, to the southern end of the boundary fence and began sweeping north through the brush.

Three despairing hours later Walter found him grazing peacefully with a herd of mules.

We rode north and stopped at a farm in the middle of nowhere, where a restless man with a straw hat was watering a patch of corn. We asked if we could buy some grain. The farmer was angry and eager to talk. There were, he informed us, too many God Damn people in Arizona. Had we seen the God Damn traffic? And had we heard about that nucaleer waste they was dumpin' every which way? As for himself, he was moving to Mon-tan. He was going where a man could *breathe*, God *Damn*.

We told him about losing our horses.

"Why, I got jist the thang you need," he said, and returned carrying a rusty cowbell. "Put this on the lead horse. In the early morning you kin hear him ringin' a mile off. I'll take a dollar fer it."

Walter was furious. As soon as we were out of earshot he exploded. "Goddammit, if you think I'm tying a rusty old cowbell around my horse's neck, forget it. I ain't riding a cow. It's not *dignified*."

I packed the bell anyway. It would turn out to be the best dollar we spent the entire trip.

As we rode northward toward the Gila River, the paired mining towns of Winkelman and Hayden loomed in the distance. Our first inkling of what we were to encounter was the sight of two tall structures rising up on the horizon.

"Jesus, what the hell are those?" Walter asked. We peered at them through our binoculars and determined they were immense smokestacks, so large they almost defied comprehension. (One is, in fact, as tall as the Empire State Building.)

Soon we saw, looming over the brown landscape, a hideous, toxic, multicolored tailings pile several miles long and hundreds of feet high. We rode past a poisonous Gila monster, a three-foot lizard colored pink and black, which dragged itself away from us with insolent slowness.

On the outskirts of town we passed railroad sidings, several decaying industrial buildings, and a chain-link fence with the words "Hayden Country Club" on it. Beyond the fence we glimpsed a stretch of brown fairway, quickly reverting to desert. The bleached, decaying town of Winkelman clung to a hill on the far side of the Gila River.

It was a post-apocalyptic scene. Neither Walter nor I could bring ourselves to speak.

The Gila River itself was a brown, oily mass of water. We crossed on an abandoned footbridge and started looking for a place with grazing for the horses where we could camp. There was none. Grass did not appear to grow here. As we rode along the northern bank of the river we heard a gurgling sound and suddenly smelled the stink of methane: the town's sewage treatment plant.

Just past the plant, but not quite beyond its odor, we came to a ramshackle backyard with several horses in a corral. This we took as a good sign. As we tied up our horses a Mexican man in an old T-shirt emerged from the house. His name was Braulio Amauisca. His father, he explained later, had been a Mexican *charro* who had come to Arizona on a cattle drive. He decided to stay, and eventually became foreman of one of the Big Stacks, which were, at one time, the tallest smokestacks in the world.

Amauisca was very kind to us. He gave us as much hay and water as we needed, invited us to camp in his yard, and vehemently refused payment. It was humbling to see how human dignity and kindness could flourish in such a depressing place.

The sewage plant burbled and stank all night long.

The next morning, Walter and I walked into Winkelman looking for a breakfast. The town was named after an early stockman, Pete Winkelman, but it had long since become a one-company mining town. We walked aimlessly down the cracked streets in the long yellow light of dawn, past the tin facade of an abandoned garage, past a bar with a faded picture of crossed martini glasses, past a junked car packed with tumbleweeds, past the filmy window of a grocery, past a cemetery with plastic flowers bleached by the sun. The town trembled with desolation and loneliness.

As we reached the top of the town, a great smelting operation came into view in the mountains beyond. Every twenty minutes there would be a roaring sound, and we could see, as if in slow motion, a plume of slag come rolling down the side of the mountain. Even in the light of day we could see the slag glowing red-hot.

We sat down on a curb opposite a gas station where a man was hosing down the tarmac.

"Unbelievable," Walter finally said.

"I know," I said. "It's like a hell, isn't it?"

"It's *civilization*," Walter said. "As long as we're out there"—he pointed at the desert—"we're fine. It's civilization that screws us up. Coronado didn't have to deal with this shit."

Walter idly photographed a bridge over the Gila which had been blocked off with a pile of sand.

The gas station attendant called out:

"Body snagged up under that bridge during the flood of '83. They never figured out who it was."

He came over, eager to talk.

"That's a historic bridge there," he said, "one of the oldest in the state. Years ago some drunk busted up the railing, and they haven't had the money to fix it."

The man went on to explain he had sold automobiles in Phoenix for fourteen years. "I was good, so they got me down here to sell Chevys," he said, "but then the strike came and wiped 'em out. Nobody could buy a car. Hell, half the town was on food stamps."

What strike was that? I asked.

The man was aghast. "What *strike*? Why, the strike of '82. Or was it '81? Seems like yesterday. It was in all the papers, the *New York Times*, all of 'em." He spoke with pride, this man washing the tarmac at dawn, nearly a decade after the strike had ended his dream of selling Chevys. The strikers brought the company to its knees, he said, but the town had never recovered.

When I returned to our camp, I asked Braulio's wife, Joann, about the strike. We sat in her living room under a velvet painting of a conquistador. It was an immaculate and cheerful house, a sharp contrast to the drabness of the town.

"Oh, that strike was very bad," she said. "They struck against Kennecott and Phelps-Dodge. Most everyone lost their homes and cars. None of the companies cared. The mine controls everything in this town. The only nice thing they ever did was to build our beautiful school."

She took out a picture of her son, Simón. "He's learning how to rope, like his granddad. He's nineteen now, and a high school graduate."

She sighed. "I told him I didn't want him working in the mine, so he went to Phoenix. But he hates the city and wants to come home."

She folded up the photograph, and looked out the window at the cement yard and the shabby street.

"The mine owns everything. I hope my son stays away from the mine."

After passing through Winkelman and Hayden, we realized our struggle with civilization was not over. Our plan was to ride up the Gila River to a place called Dripping Springs, but as we set off we found that the canyon, the river, and the highway all converged at an impassable bottleneck. When we inspected our maps we realized there was no other way to go; the mountains surrounding Winkelman were riddled with mines and crisscrossed with chain-link fences.

We went as far as we could and tied our horses up to a lone mesquite tree and sat down in the dirt. We were not far below the slag pile and I could see the *nuée ardente* of slag roaring down the mountain, shaking the earth under our feet. The heat was so intense that it felt like the slag itself was baking us alive.

Walter was near despair. "Let's ride into town and buy a case of beer," he suggested as a solution to the problem.

"I suppose we could trailer the horses up the canyon," I said.

At the far end of a dirt area we could see a battered house trailer parked on cinder blocks. It looked deserted.

I idly cupped my hands and hollered. To our surprise, the door burst open and a big strong woman with a red face came tumbling out. Even before she had come within hearing distance her mouth was working and she was talking a mile a minute. She introduced herself as Norma.

When we told her what we were doing with packhorses, she really got going.

"Coronado came through here? Through my prop'ty? Well now, that is something. That *is* something. Why, these town officials ought to git off their butts and mark this historic trail or somethin' instead a sittin' around like a bunch a cows. Coronado you say? I'll be damned. Poor feller who sold me this place didn't know nothin' about that. Sold me a historic prop'ty, he did. . ."

We couldn't get a word in edgewise.

A horse came trotting over to check out the excitement. He stood about twelve hands.

"Now see this here horse, he's out a Chain Lightning (you boys a course know about Chain Lightning) and his sire was Noble Nix. We'll git him grained up and then you'll see some action, yessir! And this other one. . ."

We were waiting for a moment to explain our predicament. That moment appeared to be receding by the minute.

A pregnant goat came waddling over, her udders dragging in the dirt. Soon a dozen tiny horses appeared out of the brush and crowded around us, making a fuss and shoving their noses into our pockets.

"Lemme show you all something," Norma said, and charged back into her trailer. She brought out a photograph of a man on a rearing horse. The photograph had been lovingly shellacked onto a piece of plywood, the edges scalloped and burned.

"This is my daddy. He had polio when he was twenty-two, but he taught this horse all kinds a tricks. Had to strap his bum leg into the stirrup. Imagine that, polio at twenty-two, could barely walk, and here he is ridin' trick horses. He was quite a man, I'll tell you. . ."

There was no stopping her. She told us about her adventures packing into the Superstition Mountains and her plans to offer handicapped kids trail rides around her property. Despite her eccentricities, she had a sterling heart. She was struggling, like the others we met in the town, to maintain her dignity against something large and dehumanizing, the monster that was roaring every twenty minutes in the mountains beyond.

She had no telephone, so she drove us around town looking for someone with a horse trailer. Roundup was going on at the surrounding ranches, and as a consequence trailers were hard to come by, but we eventually located a cowboy with an open trailer.

We bought some beer and spent the day at Norma's property, drinking ourselves into a stupor. I saw a fat coontail rattlesnake in the shade under a cactus and squirted beer all over it; it coiled and reared and rattled quite satisfactorily.

Around four o'clock the cowboy showed up with his wife and a four-horse trailer. His name was Jack and his wife Darlene. Jack was a skinny fellow with a slight curve to his frame, like a flexed bow, and he walked with that peculiar cowboy lope that comes from spending more time on a horse than on foot. He was in his late thirties but he looked ten years older. The cowboy life had taken its toll.

It took us two hours to load Popeye, who had to be winched into the trailer with much sweat, commotion, and the utterance of terrible oaths. We bought another case of beer and drove up the canyon. Popeye was so frightened he twice sank to his knees in the trailer and we had to stop and get him back on his feet.

"I guess there are some things Wicks didn't tell us about this horse," Walter observed wearily.

I asked Jack how his family happened to come to Arizona.

"My step-grandfather," he said, "came out of Georgia. He had an accident, nobody knows what really happened. Had to leave the country. Came here in 1900, 1901."

"What kind of accident?" I asked.

"Chopped a hole in a nigger farm laborer."

He clammed up the minute I turned on my tape recorder. I slipped it in my shirt pocket and we cracked another round of beers.

"How big is your ranch?" I asked.

"Don't have a ranch," he said gruffly.

He drained his beer and pulled another.

We rode in silence.

"Hey," he said, pointing into the canyon, "see that open spot? Used to be a homestead right there. That's where I used to go to school, take the bus every morning. My stepdad, he went to school on a burro. His school bus had turn signals like this:" He put his hands up on either side of his head and wiggled them, imitating a burro's ears.

"Get your hands back on the wheel," Darlene said.

The beer was flowing freely now.

"The people first come out here," Jack said, "they came from back east. Farmers, most of 'em. They was used to farm ground. When they saw this country they thought, *Man*, this is a *terrible* son-of-a-bitch. They used the water up to irrigate and irrigate, and they don't realize you got to *section* your water. You can't use water like you do back east or your wells will dry up. And that's what they did. Most of 'em went bust."

We exited off the highway and bounced along a series of dirt roads that wound among desert hills. He finally pulled up at a set of corrals just past Dripping Springs. We unloaded the horses, put them in the corrals for the night, and stood around the truck, drinking.

"Yup," Jack said, "the old man, my stepdad, sold the ranch. Just before he died he sold it. It was down there, about fourteen and a half sections. It went from the top of the mountains, both sides there, about four miles long. It was a good piece of country."

He crushed his empty beer can in his hand, tossed it in the growing pile in the back of the truck, and pulled another. We settled down for a visit.

"In the past twenty years, lot of these ranches changed hands," he said. "I've worked for all these outfits, all of 'em. Some a these new people come in here, think it'd be kinda fun to own a ranch. Well shit. Kinda *fun*."

He chuckled evilly.

"These two guys bought a ranch down there, hired me on. Guy from Wisconsin, *dairy* farmer." He snorted. "Other guy was twenty-nine years in the air force. Didn't know Goddamn shit, what the cows were supposed to eat, if the Goddamn cactus had food on it or *nothin'*. And I'll tell you what, they gave me some buuuuullllllshit. I go down there at five o'clock in the morning and I saddle up my horse, and they come up there saying, 'How come you didn't saddle my horse?'" He imitated a whiny, high-pitched, effete eastern accent.

"So I say, 'If you Goddamn git up and go to work with me, you saddle your own Goddamn horse.'"

"They didn't know *how*," Darlene said incredulously. "The air force guy was kinda scrawny, couldn't even pick *up* the saddle."

"His name," Jack continued, "was Donald Dunnington Throckmorton *Esquire!*" He roared with laughter. "They called him Duck. Well, *Duck* wanted another horse so I went and bought this young horse, a buckskin. He was *fire*. He'd buck you off going right out, before you'd git anywhere. He'd go up and he'd twist one way and then another and come back down. But I hadn't paid for the horse all the way yet, paid half on him on a thirty-day trial. I was gonna send him back. Well, that stupid son-of-a-bitch Duck went in and paid him off and come back and say, 'Hey, it's mine now.' I said, 'You dirty shittin' no good son-of-a-bitch, you ride him then.' That Duck got on him and rode him from here to that mesquite and that dirty bastard got *phhsssssblaaat!*"

He sprayed a mouthful of beer into the darkness by way of illustration.

"That buckskin bust him off, I thought he was a dead man. I ain't shittin' you. I was about to give him Goddamn shittin' artificial respiration."

"Now, Jack," Darlene said, "you gotta admit, the guy had guts."

"No, Darlene," Jack said. "He didn't have guts. The son-of-a-bitch was *stupid*."

We talked a while longer. "You know how you can tell a real cowboy?" Darlene asked. "Have him pull his shirttails out. If one side is cut off you know he's a real cowboy."

"How's that?" Walter asked.

"When you gotta go out there in the brush, you ain't got nothing else."

"She got pissed at me, coming home with one shirttail off. She says, 'Why'n hell didn't you just tear the whole thing off?' and I says, 'Well, I might need the other half.' "

We all laughed. The massive form of El Capitan reared up in the east, blotting out the stars.

Jack pointed to a dark mountain on our left. "That's Sourdough Johnson Mountain there. Sourdough Johnson, he was a bootlegger and prospector around here. He had stills up in this old mountain, and there are a few still up there, too."

Walter turned to Darlene. "You must have fallen in love with this man, looking out at country like this."

"Aw," said Jack, "she chased me for a long time but I wouldn't slow down."

"I chased him for a year," Darlene said, "but he wouldn't stop. So I didn't speak to him for three months. The next time I saw him he asked me to marry him. I thought he was joking. Week later we were married, been married nineteen years."

"We have our ups and downs and our battles," Jack said. "We've got three daughters, all honor rolls except the youngest one. That youngest one, she likes to wear her spurs on, and keep her hat pulled down pretty good* with a faraway look in her eyes. She's an outlaw, kick your ass just as soon as look at you. Sixteen years old."

"She's just like her dad," Darlene said.

"Born and raised in this country, just like I was," said Jack.

"My girls," said Darlene. "You'll never find any like 'em. They can brand, they can vaccinate, they can fix fence, they can cut horns, they can help Jack worm—"

"They can saddle their *own* Goddamn horses," Jack said.

"They're self-sufficient," Darlene said. "Thank God, they don't *need* a man."

Jack told stories about stagecoach robberies and buried gold up on El Capitan, lost treasure from a Spanish mission in the mountains, how a friend of his found an old Spanish harquebus in a dried-up spring, and how the Apaches used to roam through here and then disappeared. We drank and drank and it started to get very late. Darlene dropped a number of hints about the hour and finally began to get mad. Jack asked us:

"Have you ever heard the 'Mormon Cowboy' song?"

---

*To keep your hat pulled down means you like to ride a fast horse.

We had not. Jack began to sing and Darlene got in the truck and slammed the door.

"I am a Mormon cowboy and Utah is my home,
To Tucson is the first place I did roam,
From there to El Capitan, a place you all know well,
That rough and brushy country, no mortal man can tell. . ."

There was a long pause. "Shit, I can't remember the rest of it."
"Are you coming, Jack, or what?" Darlene said.
Jack cracked a beer and started another song.

"Bill of an Arrow heard them say
In an Arizona town one day,
Them damn Apaches were up on the trail that day,
Heard them tell of murder done,
At Rocky Run. . ."

He stopped. "That don't sound right," he said. "My mother used to sing it to me all the time. God *damn*, I've forgotten 'em all."

There was a long silence. Darlene fumed in the truck.

"Well," Jack finally said, "a lot of things have changed around here." He crushed his last beer can, propped his boot on the bumper, and looked up over El Capitan.

"Yup, the old man sold it before he died," he said, almost as if he were talking to himself. "The only way that ranch would come back to me is if they don't make their payments. Then it come back. Fourteen and a half sections, down there all the way from the mountaintops to the mountaintops."

He tossed the can in the back and opened the door.

"All I got now is three acres."

We were too drunk to light a fire, let alone cook dinner. We unrolled our bags in the dirt and crawled inside.

We got up in the dark, which would have been too early even if we had not been indisposed. In front of us were the Pinal Mountains—scrubby, arid desert mountains sprinkled with witch mesquite, cactus, and greasewood.

While ascending the mountains we stopped at two points to argue about the route. I was right the first time and this threw Walter into an ugly mood. The second time I triangulated our position from nearby peaks, while Walter sat on his horse, scowling.

"We go this way," I finally announced, with no little satisfaction.

"Good," Walter said, and rode off in the other direction.

I caught up with him and we argued.

"I don't give a damn about your maps and compass and tricalations or whatever the fuck you think you're doing," Walter said. "Any damn fool can see this is the way to go."

Walter turned out to be right, which immediately reversed our moods. Walter began singing and reciting obscene poetry, while I rode in angry silence. We found a spring three-quarters of the way up the mountain range, marked by a burst of green cottonwoods wedged in a ravine. This was our first water of the day and the horses crowded and fought to get a drink. We passed a man shooting trees with a .357 Magnum and finally arrived at Pioneer Pass, at the top of the Pinal Mountains.

At the very summit we had a long view looking north.

Wave upon wave of mountains stretched as far as the eye could see, for at least seventy miles. This was the great *despoblado*, the howling wilderness that had nearly killed Coronado and his men. It was still mostly wilderness. We guessed that the farthest blue line must be the Mogollon Rim itself; later we would realize it was merely Board Tree Saddle, not even halfway through the Rim country.

Gazing across this restless sea of mountains, I felt a shiver creep up my spine. Up to now we had been passing through relatively settled ranching and mining country. Once in the *despoblado*, we would see few human beings until we arrived at Cíbola, the Seven Cities of Gold.

Walter and I were both unnerved by the view. For the first time, I questioned whether we really would make it.

We continued to follow old mining roads down the mountains. I soon noticed that Banjo, whom I was riding, was becoming exhausted. I put my horses in a string and led them on foot. We had traveled nearly twenty miles and had not seen even a blade of grass. We had to get out of the mountains before dark and find a camp with grass. A night of no feed after coming across this mountain range would seriously weaken our horses.

I remembered Coronado's report to the viceroy: "I entered the borders of the *despoblado* on St. John's Eve, and, for a change from our past labors, we found no grass during the first few days, but a worse way through the mountains and more dangerous passages than we had previously experienced."

The shadows lengthened. As we neared the town of Globe, the mining road entered Icehouse Canyon and turned to asphalt. There was still no grass. I got back on Banjo and we began to trot. It was now nearly dark; once cars started to pass us with their headlights on we'd be stopped dead in our tracks—to ride horses in the dark against glaring headlights was asking for trouble.

We couldn't enter the Rim country with starving horses, especially since we had no idea what kind of grass we would find in those mountains. If they were as barren as the Pinals, our horses would die. We had also heard that Arizona and New Mexico were in the grips of a severe drought—the worst in forty-four years—and the grass was dying. Cows were being shipped to Colorado and some of the great Indian mustang herds were being rounded up and many of the animals shot to save the lives of the rest. Beyond the Rim we would have to contend with the arid desert of the Colorado Plateau, far drier than anything we had yet experienced.

I wondered how we were going to find, every day, the 350 pounds of water we needed for ourselves and the animals, for the next six hundred or seven hundred miles of travel.

All these thoughts were going through my mind as we raced down Icehouse Canyon, in the growing dark, looking for grass that didn't exist.

14

In the fading light, we spied a horse trailer halfway up the side of the canyon, next to a house cut into the slope. The horse trailer was invitation enough for us. We trotted up the driveway and were met by an excited, skinny boy and his mother. Soon afterward the husband—Mark Shellenberger—came home from work.

Mark knew the mountains north of the Salt River and was deeply interested in our trip. After dinner we spread out our maps. He looked them over for a long time and, with a frown on his face, brought out some of his own.

"Is this the way Coronado is supposed to have gone?" he asked, in a doubtful tone, trailing his finger across the dark clusters of contour lines.

We said it was.

There was an unsettling silence.

"May I suggest another route?" he asked.

We asked what the advantage of his route would be.

"It's about thirty miles shorter," he said. And then he added, with a smile: "It does have one considerable advantage—it won't kill you."

The route we had mapped out was, in his view, impossible. Coronado was supposed to have ridden two days down the Salt River.

Well, he said, the Salt River is a deep, powerful river running through steep canyon walls. Nobody in his right mind would attempt to ride down the Salt, particularly with packhorses. A packed horse can swim about as well as a man with an anvil strapped to his back.

From there, Coronado was supposed to have turned northeast and ridden up Salome Creek or one of the other creeks flowing out of the Sierra Ancha. You could ride up them, Mark said, but you'd never get out of them. They boxed up (walled up) in the mountains. Finally, he said, nobody but a fool would try to ride across the canyons draining off the Mogollon Rim, as Coronado was supposed to have done. No, the entire route from the Salt River to the Rim was as savage and deadly a piece of country as you could find. It was not rideable; it was not even walkable.

Shellenberger then mapped out for us a much shorter route, one that crossed the Salt and continued north along Cherry Creek. It followed more logically the lay of the land. It would cross the Coronado "trail" at two points: once at the Salt River and once at Board Tree Saddle. At these points we could judge for ourselves whether the hypothetical Coronado route was feasible.

We were, more or less, stunned to receive this news. In fifteen minutes Shellenberger had demolished the heart of the argument for Coronado's far western route up through Arizona.

Shellenberger gave us one final piece of advice. After crossing the Salt, he said, we would see in front of us a hogback ridge. There would be no trail, and there was only one way over. We were to ride up the left-hand side of the ridge, climbing as high as possible up the steep sides of the mountain, even to the point of danger. Eventually, close to the top of the mountain, we would pick up a very faint animal trail that would take us over the top and down the other side to Cherry Creek.

The riding, he added, would look much easier on the lower slopes of the ridge, where there would appear to be a logical route, but on no account were we to go that way. Otherwise, we might never get out of the Salt River Canyon alive.

The town of Globe meandered along a narrow valley between steep mountains. Legend had it that Globe was named by a prospector who found a boulder of almost pure silver, tumbled into a globe-like shape, in a creek bed where the town now is.

We rode into downtown Globe on a street full of Sunday-morning traffic—people dressed up and going to church. It was so hot our horses' hooves imprinted the soft macadam.

In a moment of inattention, Walter hooked his lead rope under
Robin's tail and the horse went shooting out into the traffic, skidding
across the road on her metal shoes like a skater on ice, and then falling
down amidst braking cars. I could hear Walter's thick Texas brogue
erupt magnificently above the din, roundly cursing the horse with
earthy expletives. With great skill and horsemanship he managed to
stay on her back and get her up and out of the traffic.

We stopped to make some telephone calls, tying up the horses in a
parking lot. As I was walking along the street I passed a department
store with the doors hooked open. A river of air conditioning washed
over me, smelling richly of new clothes and leather goods. I experienced a sudden desperate longing to be back in civilization; I wanted
to go inside and bury my face in the racks of slacks and shirts and
doubleknit sportcoats and inhale the fragrance of fresh polyester and
Sea Island cotton. I had, in fact, turned to enter the store when a
pimply-faced security guard stepped across my path, making it clear
that the likes of me could have no legitimate business in a reputable
establishment such as this. My shower at the Shellenbergers had done
little to improve my appearance, since I had put back on the same
unwashed clothes, as stiff and greasy as old oilcloth.

We soon left Globe behind us and were back in the country on a dirt
road. We were now approaching the Salt River, the first great milestone
of our journey, the river that many sage and level-headed people had
predicted we would never reach.

As we passed a tumbledown shack with a yard full of junk, an old
man in a slouch hat charged out, followed by a growling mastiff.

"What you got in them packs?" he cried out eagerly, his beard
wagging. "Relics?"

We told him about our journey. He explained he was a prospector
and treasure hunter who made his living digging around old mining
camps and ghost towns.

"Jist last week I found me some sterling flatware," he said proudly,
and came back out with a fistful of half-melted spoons. "You boys
must've found some relics, Indian pots and sich?"

We had not.

He was crestfallen. "There's all kinds a treasure round here," he
said, "if you keep yer eyes open. Why up there in Nigger Warsh—
course yer not supposed to call hit that no more, the word 'nigger' ain't
perlite, though back in my day that's what they called themselves and
I'll tell you I knew some damn fine nigger cowboys—anyway, Nigger

Warsh up there was just about *paved* with gold nuggets and flakes, drift gold. But them Apaches was up in there and they told ever'one who wanted to come through that they better not bend down to pick up them nuggets. If they see one of 'em bend down he's a dead man, yessir. This one feller, he picked up a nugget the size of a cow's liver and they found his body so full a arrows he lookit jist like a porca-pine. But after that them fellers got to walkin' up that warsh in their bare feet, see, and they picked 'em all up with their toes. Them Apaches were none the wiser."

He wheezed with laughter, which quickly disintegrated into a racking cough. The mastiff, holding us responsible, advanced with a snarl.

The old man wiped his mouth and screeched at the dog, "Shut yer face, God *damn* you."

The dog whined and retreated behind an old car engine.

"I been up and down Nigger Warsh fer thirty year. Nothin' up there now but rattlers and sand."

He showed us some more of his finds: old bottles, half of a cut-glass candy bowl, some Indian potsherds. As we were leaving he called out: "I betcha you boys find some treasure. You cain't ride a thousand mile and come home empty-handed!"

Toward the end of the day we topped a hill and saw the H&E Ranch spread out below us like a cattleman's dream: miles of clean white fence enclosing emerald fields, a vast lawn rainbowed with hissing sprinklers, a cluster of new barns and dozens of horse stalls—all ringed about by blue mountains. We stopped at the main house, where we were greeted by a sunburned man in a T-shirt, gold chains, and Adidas. His name was Hollis Crim, the new owner of the H&E. Crim came from Florida and had bought the ranch eight years ago with his wife, an heir to the Anheuser-Busch fortune. Crim was delighted to meet us and ordered his Mexican cowhands to unsaddle and stable our horses. I doubt our horses had ever seen such luxurious accommodations, with spotless stalls, automatic watering equipment, and the leafiest alfalfa feed I'd ever seen. He invited us to sleep in his barn.

This was not a barn in the normal sense. It had a large tack room, a wet bar, a lounge, a kitchen, bathrooms, a bedroom, a utility room with washer and dryer, and a deep freezer packed with frozen bull testicles and livestock drugs. The place was as clean as an operating room.

We were more interested in the washing machines than anything else. We stripped to our underwear and wrestled and pounded our clothes into the machine. While they were washing I strolled back to the barn door, where I had left my precious journal, only to see a mangy cur worrying the plastic bag I carried it in. Another dog was trotting off with my only pencil. The journal itself had disappeared.

I panicked and rushed outside. A whole pack of dogs were lounging around. They scattered when I came bursting out of the barn, then turned and began baying hysterically at me. We pursued each other back and forth through the corrals and I eventually found my journal— slick with dog slobber but otherwise intact—next to a water tank. When I returned Walter was helpless with laughter.

"I wonder what they think of us now," he said, "after seeing you running around half naked after all those dogs."

A fellow named Roy Hicks came by the next morning. Hicks was the former owner of the H&E Ranch, he and his father having sold it in 1979.

Hicks spoke with a self-deprecating drawl and often looked at the ground while scraping a worn boot across the dust. He looked about the ranch with an amused, saddened look in his eyes, which were bleached the same pale blue as the back of his shirt, hanging loosely on his spare frame.

His family was one of the old pioneer families of central Arizona. His grandfather, Mark Hicks, had been known from Globe all the way up into the Tonto Basin and across the Mogollon Rim, and he was still talked of with a kind of awe.

Hicks's great-grandfather had originally come to Arizona from Waco, Texas, in 1887. Hicks said he had left Texas for health reasons. The health reasons, it turned out, were the members of a family near Waco, one of which old man Hicks had killed with a pruning hook in a dispute over water. The great-grandfather camped out near Miami (that's pronounced "Mee-YAM-ah"), Arizona, for six or eight months while scouting the country, and he finally found this little valley between the Salt River and the mountains. He purchased the valley from the squatter who occupied it, for a team of horses and a wagon, plus some cash. He then became a squatter himself.

It was Roy's grandfather, Mark Hicks, who filed for a homestead on the land and built up the ranch. He was a wheeler and dealer who bought up ranches and went broke and sold ranches and then bought them back again.

"At one time," Roy said with a smile, "he had a pretty good-sized chunk of ground, maybe a hundred and fifty sections [96,000 acres]. He had cowboys workin' for him all over the country. He was workin' towards selling a thousand head in one go, that was his dream." He shook his head.

The land was open and unfenced when the Hicks family settled outside of Globe. Mark Hicks built some of the earliest fences in the area, mostly drift fences—that is, unconnected stretches of fence going between two natural formations like a bluff or cliff—to keep his cattle from wandering off range. The larger corporate-run cattle outfits, the ones that severely grazed out an area and then moved to fresh pasture, had been expanding onto land used by homesteaders (which they derogatorily called "nesters"). They made some trouble over Hicks's fences but Hicks refused to be pushed around and soon the entire range was divided up and fenced.

Mark Hicks filed on the property in 1906 or 1907, and thereby acquired ownership to several hundred acres along Pinal Creek. The rest of the land he grazed still belonged to the government. Nobody thought of it then as "public land" in the modern sense of the word—it was just land made empty by the disappearance of the Indians.

"Why did you sell the ranch?" I asked him.

Roy pulled his hatbrim and scuffed the dirt. "Well," he said slowly, "it was a hard decision for us to make, my dad and me. We talked it over. And we talked again. We talked about how we'd come here with nothing, and we'd worked ourselves damn near to death, all of us, and we decided we weren't gonna let the bureaucrats take it away from us. We were gonna get out of here with something."

I asked what he meant by the bureaucrats.

"These doggone ranches around here are on public lands. It's not like it is in other places. It's public land and it can be taken away from you. There was nothing here when we came, and we never did make a lot of money out of this outfit because we put so much back. Heck, we put in the water, fifteen, eighteen windmills with wells, miles of fences and roads. At the time we sold, a lot of the older families were getting pressure put on 'em to conform to the Forest Service ways. The Forest Service wanted to get a rotational grazing system going, which was all right—it was their land. But they didn't want to invest any money in it. They wanted to use our money. We figured we'd already invested enough in the land."

I asked Roy if ranching was a tough business.

"Why, it's mostly like gambling," Roy said, with an amused crinkling around the eyes. "You're gambling on the market. You're gambling on the weather. It gets in your blood, just like gambling. You work for eighteen months from the time that cow conceives till you have something to sell, and if you don't have a market then you give 'em away. Oh, you'll hit a good market with good yearlings once in a long while, but most of the time for us it was just a get-by situation."

"How come?" I asked.

"There's just not the rainfall here. I remember growing up, these old-timers would tell me it used to rain in this country, but hell, I got to be damn near an old man before I ever saw it."

Hicks chuckled. "Back then, in real dry times, we'd burn the spines off this prickly pear and those old cows would eat 'em."

"Are many of the old-timers left?" I asked.

"Not any more. Right in this county used to be one of the strongholds of the old families. But in the last fifteen years, these ranches have started changing hands and there's very few of the old ones left. See, ranching today is kind of like owning racehorses." He grinned. "You don't see anybody that owns racehorses that don't have income from someplace else."

"Crim must've put a lot of money into this place," I said.

"Beautiful, isn't it?" Then he added quietly: "The cattle can't support this."

While we had been talking, Roy's son had arrived at the barn and was saddling a horse. He now worked as a hand for Crim. He led his horse over to us, a rifle slung over his shoulder. Walter also joined us.

"That's been through some mesquite," Walter said, pointing to the gun.

"Yeah," said Roy, "it's been drug around a spell. My dad got that rifle when he was a young man. That short barrel—it's sixteen inches—was illegal for years."

Roy's son hefted the gun and grinned. "When he gave this to me, he told me to wear this son-of-a-bitch out."

In the silence a horse whinnied in one of the stalls. The Mexican cowboys had arrived for work and were loading horses into a trailer.

"I'll tell you one thing," Roy said, "we were *good* operators. When we sold the ranch, we didn't owe anybody anything. Lot of 'em had to sell out because they were financially ruined. We done all right. We may not own cattle any more, but we still like to watch 'em."

He laughed. "We like to watch the gambling going on."

◦ ⚎ ◦

The H&E Ranch was not much different from many other ranches in the arid West: a tiny piece of private land embedded within vast tracts of public land. This land-tenure arrangement was an artifact of misguided homestead laws, and it is rapidly becoming one of the most explosive issues in the West today.

The homestead laws were originally conceived for farming ground and the richer pasture lands of the Midwest and Great Plains. In the beginning they restricted homesteading on more than 160 acres of land at one time, the idea being that 160 was sufficient to support a family through farming.

Not so in the arid West, where dry-land farming was impossible. In these areas, it took a minimum of four sections of land—at least 2,560 acres—to support even the poorest family through livestock ranching, and in most areas it would take at least five thousand to ten thousand acres. In 1875 the homestead laws were expanded to allow filing on a full section—640 acres—but this was still grossly inadequate. Nobody in the East could conceive of a place where it took more than a square mile of land to support a single family.

At the time few ranchers saw this as a serious problem. Ranchers such as Mark Hicks filed a homestead on acreage enclosing a water source, which gave them *de facto* control over large areas of empty, waterless grazing lands. That they did not actually own title to these lands seemed irrelevant.

The end result of this process was a crazy patchwork of private landholdings, in and of themselves worthless for ranching, embedded within huge tracts of land that wasn't owned by anybody, and thus became the property of the government—that is, public lands. It was only by combining the two—the private land with water and the public land with grass—that ranching could be made to work.

Belatedly, in the 1930s, the government exercised control over lands in the public domain. The Forest Service and the Bureau of Land Management—the two largest landholders in the United States—formalized these *de facto* grazing arrangements by issuing the ranchers grazing permits under the Taylor Grazing Act and similar laws. The rancher was required to pay a fee based on the number of cattle he grazed. Improvements, naturally, were to be the responsibility of the rancher. Overgrazing, which had occurred on a massive scale when the lands were open and unfenced, was prevented by limiting the number of "animal units" allowed per section of land.

For most of this century the system worked fairly well. The grazing permits were handed down from father to son or sold when the ranch was sold. No ranch could exist without the grazing permits; to strip a ranch of its grazing permits would be to leave the rancher with several hundred acres of land that was worthless for any kind of profitable ranching.

In the past twenty-five years, however, environmentalists have begun to protest the fact that vast tracts of public land in the West are leased to ranchers for grazing. This was, after all, *public* land. What gave the ranchers the right to run their cattle on it? A term was coined: "welfare ranchers." It alluded to the theory that a small number of ranchers were, supposedly, deriving a huge benefit from America's public lands.

Some former grazing lands have been turned into wilderness areas, national parks or monuments, and the grazing leases revoked. In other areas the Forest Service has pressured the ranchers to adopt the Savory grazing system—the rotational grazing system Hicks mentioned. This system was developed in Rhodesia by a man named Alan Savory. It is based on the fact that grass does better when it is intensively grazed for a short period of time and left to rest, rather than being lightly but continuously grazed. Savory range management is expensive to implement as it usually requires the building of many smaller pastures with miles of new fence. It also takes far more labor to move the cows from one pasture to another during the course of the year. There is no question that the Savory system is better than earlier range management practices; whether public lands are improved by the addition of thousands of miles of new fence is another question.

In recent years some environmentalists have been calling for nothing less than the removal of all livestock from public lands.

The ranchers suddenly woke up to the fact that the lands they had been ranching for three and four generations weren't under their control at all, and might soon be taken away from them. The ultimate resolution of this problem has not yet come. When it does there will be a big fight, and the nature of the West might be changed forever.

This is a problem with no easy solution. The land is public, and the public should have a say as to how it should be managed. On the other hand, the ranchers have a moral and ethical right—if not a legal right— to use of the land.*

---

*The fact is, in most instances the people with the highest moral right to the land are the Indians from whom it was taken in the first place. Which reminds me of a joke told

The ranchers are already losing the fight. They are a cantankerous, independent lot, who—unlike the farmers—are not good at organizing themselves and lobbying. There is no romantic image in the American mind of the rancher as there is of the "yeoman farmer," an image that powers so much of the farm lobby's oversized muscle and makes farm support a liberal cause célèbre. The old pioneer ranches of the West are going broke and being sold off, a way of life is passing, and nobody cares anything about it.

The final battle will focus on the presence of livestock on public lands. This anti-grazing movement has its roots in the great nostalgia that many Americans feel for the vanished American wilderness of the past, the Old West before it was stocked with cattle and cut up by fences. The more urbanized America becomes, the stronger this nostalgia grips our imagination. It is a powerful and largely unrecognized force in American politics today, the engine that drives the environmental movement, and it is strongest (not surprisingly) among urban and suburban dwellers on the coasts where the natural environment has virtually ceased to exist.

This romantic attempt to recapture America's Arcadian past may not be such a bad idea. Maybe getting the livestock off public land wouldn't be such a bad thing either. On the other hand, such a move would destroy, once and for all, the ranching industry between the Great Plains and the Sierra Nevada. Should livestock be evicted from public lands, most of the crazy quiltwork of private landholdings in rural areas would be sold off to developers.

Such a move would finish off, once and for all, the Old West.

The other question is, with the livestock removed from public land, would the lands be allowed to remain untouched, to return to true wilderness? It is not likely. Nothing will attract people to a place faster than designating it a national park or monument or wilderness area. Once people begin to arrive, then the Park Service or BLM or Forest Service is required to provide access. This means paved roads, RV campsites, graded hiking trails, Port-o-San toilets, gas stations, tourist cabins, and all the other improvements that make our national park system "accessible" to a public that prefers nature viewed through the tinted glass of a motorcoach window, and that class of weekenders who

---

in rural Maine: a farmer is asked, "Is this your land?" The farmer replies, "Yer damn right it is, and it was my daddy's before that, and his daddy's before that, and *his* daddy stole it fair and square from the Indians!"

find their excitement in breaking beer bottles and roaring around on ATVs. Edward Abbey's "Industrial Tourists" have multiplied exponentially since he published *Desert Solitaire*. Even wilderness areas have become overrun in recent years by hikers, backpackers, and outfitters. Trails get built, lakes become heavily infested with campers, permits have to be issued to control the flow of people, and all wilderness values are destroyed.

Having crossed hundreds of miles of ranches, I can say without reservation that most ranchers take better care of their land than "recreational" users take care of public lands. You never see litter, broken glass, beer cans, or ATV tracks on ranches. The most pristine, the most isolated, the most undisturbed wildernesses I have experienced have been BLM- or Forest Service-administered ranchlands. In some areas we rode for fifty or a hundred miles across ranches without seeing another human being (or, for that matter, a cow). On the other hand, some of the most trashed-out lands I've seen have been around campsites in the national parks and forests.

Very few environmentalists know anything about the history of Western land tenure, and not many understand the distinction between overgrazing, which is profoundly destructive, and controlled grazing, which has a minimal impact. Many environmentalists overlook the fact that it was not the ranchers who, over the past century, fouled up America; ranchers didn't build ill-conceived developments, erect factories, pollute the air, poison the rivers, dump toxic waste, and clear-cut the virgin forests—thereby making the need to preserve wilderness so imperative. The profits from environmental destruction flowed right back to the corporations and their shareholders in towns and cities. Many of the very people who are clamoring to return the rural West to its original condition, at the expense of the ranchers, have family money created from manufacturing, transportation, mineral development, oil, gas, and real estate—those same activities that wrecked the American wilderness in the first place. Many well-meaning people, while recycling and contributing to environmental organizations, continue to live in large houses, continue to build second homes in environmentally sensitive areas along coastlines and rivers, continue to drive several cars, and continue to hold stock in companies that are in one way or another degrading the environment. The Western rancher who rounds up his cows on horseback, who lives in a small house (often heated with a wood stove), and who pumps his water using windmills is not the villain. There is no small element of hypocrisy in the environmentalist who cries out that the "welfare ranchers" must bear the burden of restoring the American wilderness.

Environmentalists have made a great political mistake in attacking the ranchers. Ranchers are in the business because they love nature and the outdoors and hate cities, pollution, and development. Only a fool would operate a Western ranch thinking he was going to get rich. (There is no ranching equivalent, for example, to the multimillionaire farmers crowding the government slop-pile for subsidies and squealing loudly when any politician suggests a cutback.) At one time the ranchers would have been natural allies of the environmental movement. To be sure, they would be looking out for their own interests when it came to grazing and predator control, but in the really big environmental issues of the day—toxic and nuclear waste, uncontrolled development, habitat loss, destruction of the ozone layer, the greenhouse effect—they could have been a potent force. Now they drive around with bumper stickers telling the Sierra Club to go hike to hell.

⊯ ⚊ ⊰

When I brought Popeye around to be saddled I made a very unpleasant discovery: the packsaddle had left a serious burn on his back. (I hadn't seen it earlier because the Mexican cowboys had unsaddled our horses.) Roy inspected our equipment and said that the packsaddle was a little too narrow for Popeye's back, and a spot on the saddle blanket had become stiff and pilled from hardened sweat.

Roy said he thought we could get over the Rim with the horse but we would probably have to find a new horse shortly thereafter. He showed me a special way of folding the saddle blanket to keep pressure off the sore, but he didn't have much hope for it healing up until the horse was back in his corral, no longer being worked.

"Shouldn't I be walking?" I asked.

Hicks looked a little shocked. "Why walk when you've got a horse?"

I was furious at myself. There was really no excuse for what had happened.

We followed an old track into the desert, heading toward Horseshoe Bend of the Salt River. The idea that we were almost at the Salt filled us with elation. We set off (myself on foot despite Roy's advice) singing and talking loudly. I stopped at every windmill we passed and dipped my shirt in an effort to keep cool. The cactus and greasewood trembled in the heat and both land and sky were withered white. An odor of dust hung in the air.

We stopped to rest at one windmill, an old Chicago Aermotor spinning in the wind, threading a cool stream of water into a cement tank. As I sat on the tank's rim, wringing out my shirt, I noticed several names written into the cement.

FAT. CLoud T.
Mark Hicks July 14, 1938
L.H.

The names represented, respectively, an old Apache cowboy named Fat Cloud who worked for the Hickses, Roy's grandfather, and Roy's father. They must have been the builders of the tank. I imagined the day, fifty-one years ago, when the three had finished work and shook hands all around—a job well done. Maybe they also soaked their shirts in the tank and slapped them back on, wet, to feel the shivery sting of evaporation.

The inscription on the water tank filled me with a profound sadness. It reminded me of the Hohokam petroglyphs I had seen along the San Pedro River, a stray mark in time whose meaning was spinning off into chill autumn like leaves blown off a tree. I felt that we had made our journey too late to witness anything but the fluttery end of a long, quiet, efficient dying.

In the early afternoon, we reached the top of a sand-blown hill and had our first view of the Salt River.

The Salt was one of the great landmarks of our expedition. It represented the beginning of the Spaniards' *despoblado*, but it was also a psychological milestone of sorts. Before our trip many sober acquaintances had shaken their heads and wisely predicted that two green horsemen like us would never reach the Salt River. Well, I thought, we'd made it. (And allow me, at this time, to say to all you smug, self-satisfied doubters, go to hell.)

At the sight of the Salt River I felt a wave of emotion. The river looped in a shining arc through the canyon like the polished blade of a scythe, cutting into mountains the color of smoky amethyst. I could hear the faintest echo of its rapids, a distant hiss like wind in pines. The layered *despoblado* slanted upward from it, a sea of mountains to the farthest blue line.

It was May 8th, nearly a month into our trip.

Horseshoe Bend is located in the Salt River Canyon Wilderness.

Hollis Crim owned fifty acres of land alongside the river, part of an old homestead, which he had given us permission to use. The land had been cleared of mesquite and fenced, and it was full of lush green grass. I unpacked and unsaddled my horses, washed and doctored Popeye's back, and turned them loose. They took off, bucking and kicking and farting as they galloped around the pasture, the turf shuddering under their joy.

I collected my notebook and headed to the river for a dip. After exploring the banks I found a perfect swimming hole: a deep cold pool shaded by cottonwoods. I tore off my clothes and lay on my back in the water, looking through a screen of quaking cottonwood leaves into an infinite blue sky.

Suddenly a ragged face emerged into my field of view and I heard it speak:

"What t'hell you doin' at my pool?"

The man had hair nearly to his waist, an immense black beard, and was wearing a sleeveless shirt. His right shoulder was covered with scabbed-over scars and a big knife was tucked in his waistband. He was leaning on a long pole, staring down at me with eyes that peered with Rasputin-like intensity from his bushy face. He was just about the most frightening person I had ever laid eyes on.

I clambered out of the pool in fear and confusion, apologizing profusely while I hopped around trying to pull on my clothes. Momentarily I expected him to unsheathe his knife and cut my throat.

But he seemed satisfied by my explanations. "Well all right, then," he said, greatly mollified. "I just ain't used to seeing folks in my pool. Didn't mean to scare you."

He was quiet for a second and then asked, "You seen any rattlers?" I said no.

"Good," he said, and he poked his stick in some old roots and weeds along the bank. When he was satisfied that there were no snakes, he slid into the water.

He told me he lived in a camp a quarter of a mile upriver. He said he didn't "mix too good with civilization," and that he hunted rattlesnakes for a living, tanning their skins and making them into belts, hatbands, and buckles. He was utterly terrified of snakes. "Someday they're gonna git me," he said. "I've killed too many now."

He added he had caught a mess of catfish and invited Walter and me to join him for dinner.

· · ·

He showed up after dark with a sack full of catfish fillets. Walter rolled the fish in a mixture of pepper, spices, and salt, and fried them in hot oil.

"Blackened catfish," he explained with all the flourish and dignity of a gourmet chef. Walter was very proud of his cooking.

While the fish fried and a pot of beans simmered, we sat around the fire and talked. The splash and clink of water over rocks—that loveliest of sounds in a desert—filled the air around us.

It took quite a bit of persuading to get the man's first name once he heard I was writing a book. "It may be Rod," he finally said, "and then again maybe it ain't." It required even more cajoling for him to consent to being tape-recorded.

Rod had lived in his camp in the Salt River Canyon Wilderness for nearly four years straight, and seasonally for many more years. His camp consisted of a small tent, a high cot (for sleeping off the ground, where the rattlesnakes couldn't get him), a firepit, and a box for provisions. He went into town once a month to resupply. When he left in the morning, he raked the dirt in his camp so that he could tell if any rattlesnakes had come through during the day.

"Those fuckers are everywhere," he said, "and man, they're *lookin'* for me."

"How'd you come to live on this river?" I asked Rod.

He leaned back on his tree stump. "I first come out here with my mother's husband, Eulin," he said. "That was long after I got back from 'Nam. See, me and my sister was adopted. She went to court. Michigan had changed their laws, said kids had the right to know who their parents were. Course you're taking a risk: what you find you might not like."

He laughed through his beard.

"I never wanted to know. I used to figure, hey, the bitch left us, why look her up? It was my sister found my mother, and she gave me her address and a phone number, a Phoenix address. I thought about it for a month and then I said, hell, I'm going down, I'm gonna meet my mother. I was up in Michigan at the time so I hitchhiked to Sky Harbor Airport and called her from there. It took her about twenty minutes, I mean she thought somebody was playing a joke on her or shit like that. But she showed up, in a white Lincoln Continental with suicide doors."

"What did she say?" I asked.

"Hell, what *can* you say? It's your *son*. Anyway, Eulin—that's her husband—he come home on Friday and we pack up his truck and we come up here to go fishing.''

"What was it like?''

"I's so damn drunk I hardly even remember *seeing* the river. It was blood red and I ain't never seen it so red since. Where I come from in Michigan I was used to clear water, and I said, 'Shit, man, there ain't no fish in this damn thing.' Till Eulin pulled some of 'em out of here about half as long as that log there.

"After that, I started coming here and finally I moved out. The only way I can stay away from that shit, the drinking, is if I come out here. In town I'd be drunk all the time. If I didn't find this river, man, I'd be fuckin' dead, and that's a fact.''

The fish was sizzling and we heaped the wood up until the fire was blazing. Earlier, Walter had washed his shirt and hung it up to dry next to the fire. It now burst into flames, and there was much shouting and commotion while he stamped it out.

"I just got one more,'' Walter said forlornly, holding up the smoking rag.

The catfish was done.

"Were you here during the '83 flood?'' I asked. We had heard several people mention a terrible flood in 1983.

"You're damn right I was,'' said Rod, poking a piece of fish into his hairy face. "I lost my dog Digger in that flood.''

"What happened?''

"That year we had *beaucoup* snow up north along the Rim, then it rained almost the whole month of January, all of February, and damn near to the middle of March. That river come up, *man* I mean to tell you. It was March 27th, it was a Tuesday. I was comin' back from Cherry Creek. Beautiful day. I had a nice mess of catfish, and I was fishing this hole on my way back. I had a can of Bugler's out, rolling a smoke. And I turned around to see where my dog was at and Digger was out in the water. There was a hell of a damn big whirlpool right there and it sucked him under. He come back up, but I don't think he were even alive then. But I went for him, jumped in. I was in real good shape. I hadn't drank in six months.

"I got ahold of him but I couldn't hang on to him. When you hit that water, man, it was *ice* cold and all the air went right out of my lungs and I went down the river. I had to let go so I could get my own ass out. When I did get out I was four hundred meters down the river and on the opposite bank. As fast as that river was moving, and nothing but damn big rocks. . .shit.''

Rod had finished eating. He now rolled a cigarette and lit it with a stick from the fire.

"God he was a good dog too. Never did find him. He was mostly terrier. Hell, he was only about that big, but he was a gutsy little shit. Ain't nobody gonna come around your camp, animal or man." He inhaled his cigarette. "He'd stay with you, not like most people."

We could hear the horses whinnying and thundering around in the dark.

"So you hunt rattlers for a living?" I said.

"Yup, and I better git off my ass and git out here and start catching a few of 'em."

"How do you catch them?"

"See this stick? That's made out of a piece of sucker rod, and that cable I got in a garage sale. You slip that loop behind his poison glands and snap 'er shut. It breaks the vertebrae but his old jaws are still flapping. Generally I cut their head off, but that old mouth keeps on going. I always bury the head. Man, I don't care if I'm twenty miles back up in the Apache Mountains, I *bury* that head."

"Somebody might step on it?" Walter asked.

Rod laughed. "*Step* on it? There ain't *nobody* up in that country. No, I got this feeling if I don't bury it, well, it might show up lookin' for me."

"How many do you kill in a year?" Walter asked.

"I used to keep a logbook. That first year I got 375. And I kept a log of everything I made—belts, hatbands—and who I made it for and where they lived. And then I said, 'What am I keeping this shit for?'" Rod laughed and flicked his cigarette butt into the fire.

"What's the biggest snake you caught?" Walter asked.

"Right over there on them Indian Flats, five foot ten and a half inches. Jiminy *Christmas* I got him on the end of that snake pole and when I pulled him out of that hole he got to slashing around and he damn near whipped me right over."

"Those bastards are strong," Walter said. "They make good eating too."

"Not for me," Rod said.

"What's it like here in the winter?" I asked.

"It's nice out here. You listen to the sounds God intended you to. I've got all kinds of books. My camp is always open. Anyone can come and share my food. I hunt rabbits out here in the winter. I love rabbit stew and cornbread dumplings. You take the bones and break 'em in half, get all that bone marrow and make your stock out of 'em."

Rod had mentioned earlier that he had been shot up in Vietnam. I asked what had happened.

Rod scowled. "Too many things," he said. "I carried that fucker on my back for too many years and it's time to leave it alone."

We talked some more. Rod told about the river rafters that sometimes came through during the summer, about an escaped double-murderer who hid out in the canyon, about women who sometimes shared his cot. The crickets in the field had started a tremendous racket and the fire flickered down. A breeze stirred and the ashes slid off the banked coals. They glowed orange, illuminating Rod's wild face.

I asked Rod again about Vietnam.

"You're a persistent fucker, aren't you?" he said, laughing.

"Yes," I said.

"You know the motto of the Special Forces?" Rod asked.

I did not.

" 'Kill all the motherfuckers and let God sort 'em out.' " He repeated it for emphasis, and then said: "That's twisted. I mean, think about it: that's *sick*. At a certain point in your life, you gotta stop carrying that kind of shit around. That's what I'm talking about."

He waited, and then continued. "I was drafted. Then, after I got out of the hospital, I reenlisted in the army three years to go back there."

"How'd you get hurt?" I asked.

"The first time I got shot." There was a pause, and then he added: "By the North Vietnamese, not my own people."

"And the second time?"

Rod said nothing.

"Second time he got shot by his own people," Walter guessed.

"Yeah," said Rod shortly.

"I heard that was pretty commonplace," I said.

"You're damn right it was. You see, over there, everybody had an equalizer. You didn't go around chewing people's asses out, acting like a fuckin' lifer, man, because if you did you's gonna get your ass sent home in a garbage bag. You get a bunch of grunts come out of that jungle after they been out there two and a half months, in the same fuckin' clothes, and you get some fucker back there in the rear telling you you gotta get your hair cut and get your weapon G.I.'ed before you can have a beer, you set his ass straight real quick."

"How so?" Walter asked.

"You'd give him a warning first. You know, throw a concussion grenade in his hooch."

"That's a hell of a warning," I said.

"Fuck yeah, but the next one's gonna be a fuckin' frag if you don't straighten your ass up."

"How'd you get shot?" I asked.

"We got ambushed. Up in I-CORPS area, just south of Chu Lai about twenty-eight miles outside a little village called Dak Ho. We walked into an L-shaped ambush."

"Were you hit pretty bad?"

"Tore our ass up. Well, I'm still alive."

"Do you have any scars?"

"Fuck yeah. But I got more scars on me from falling down drunk than I ever got over there."

"After getting drafted and then getting hurt like that," I asked, "why'd you reenlist?"

Rod stared intently into the bed of coals, the points of his wild face highlighted in orange. He ignored the question.

"What about the second time you were shot?" I asked. "How did that happen?"

Rod continued to be silent. The expression on his face had changed, and it deterred me from following that line of questioning any further.

Finally he shrugged, raked a stick through the fire, and lit another cigarette. Then he said:

"Hey, everybody goes through their own war. I look at my sister. Left home when she was fourteen, quit high school, raised her kids on her own. She struggled all her life to make a *home* for her kids, working fuckin' tables at fuckin' Red Lobster, working in fuckin' cheap factories. She raised them kids, and she did a damn good job of it, and I'm proud of her."

He laughed a small laugh. "I got my ass to a phone and called her on her fortieth birthday. I wonder if she's gonna call me on mine?"

We crossed the Salt River on May 9th, with Rod standing on the bank shouting directions. Even in its low state the Salt was still a big, powerful river, full of treacherous channels and holes.

We had now officially entered the *despoblado*.

15

◐ ☲ ◐

Even today, the *despoblado* of Arizona remains one of the least inhabited places in the United States, most of it with a lower population density than Alaska. It consists of two distinct geological provinces: the mountainous, forested country below the Mogollon Rim, and the arid desert country beyond the Rim. Zuni Pueblo—the Seven Cities of Cíbola—marked the end of the *despoblado*.

When Fray Marcos came through in 1539, the Indians below the Rim warned him about the *despoblado*. "The natives," Fray Marcos reported, "begged me to rest here for three or four days, because the *despoblado* began four days' travel from here, and from its beginning until coming to the city of Cíbola is fifteen long days' travel. They wanted to prepare food and prepare me with what I needed for my journey. . .so I delayed three days without going farther. In this time I constantly tried to obtain information about Cíbola and all other places, doing nothing else but taking Indians aside to question each one of them separately. They all agreed in their accounts. They told me of the multitude of people, the arrangements of the streets, the bigness of the houses, and the type of doorways. . . .

"The three days being over, many people gathered to go with me. I selected about thirty prominent men, all very well dressed. . .and set out on my way. Thus marching, I entered the *despoblado* on May 9 [1539]."

In a curious coincidence, we entered the *despoblado* exactly 450 years to the day later.

"We traveled as follows:" Fray Marcos continued. "On the first day we marched over a wide and much-used road. We arrived at dinner at a spring which the Indians had indicated to me, and then at another one, where we slept. . . . There were also old shacks and many signs of dead fires of the people who had traveled this road on their way to Cíbola. In this manner I traveled twelve days."

From this description it is almost certain that the route Fray Marcos, and later Coronado, took was a major trade route between Cíbola and the thickly settled regions south of the *despoblado*.

We would be following no such well-traveled road.

On the north side of the river we passed through a grove of mesquite trees on a sandy flat. Here we found a half-dozen burnt corral posts poking up through the sand, the ruins of a homestead once belonging to a one-armed German named Rockinstraw or Roggenstroh. A rusted cable twisted through the ruins, once a ferry line that Rockinstraw used to haul people and horses across the river. The old Pony Express route between Globe and Young also used to pass through here, but the track had long since vanished.

Rod told us to look for an eroded diagonal cut in the mountain just beyond the Rockinstraw homestead; it was, he said, the remains of the Pony Express route and the only way to get up. The cut angled up a 45-degree slope, and it was choked with loose rock, teddy-bear cholla, saguaro cactus, and yucca. In a hundred years of disuse it had entirely washed out.

It was so frighteningly steep that both of us instinctively kicked our horses forward, knowing if we stopped to think we might never gather the courage to attempt it.

All the horses immediately began charging and plunging uphill, scrabbling and sliding among the loose rock. (A horse cannot walk or trot up an extremely steep pitch; he can only lunge.) Walter's horse, Robin, who was packed, began to panic. Her feet clattered among the rocks, her eyes rolled, and she lost her balance, her body slamming into the sides of several saguaro cacti. We continued upward; there could be no stopping.

As we gained altitude and found blue space yawning below us,

Robin was seized with a paroxysm of fear and sank trembling to her knees, teetering on the edge of the abyss. With much prodding and cajoling we managed to get her back on her feet. Several hundred yards up the hill she threw herself to the ground again. This time she hit hard and rolled to the uphill side.

We were barely able to get her back on her feet.

Walter, recalling Mark Shellenberger's directions, kept us climbing high up the hogback ridge. I myself began to panic and started hollering to Walter that we were going too high, that any fool could see the plateau below provided a natural route, and that he was leading us astray. Fortunately Walter ignored me.

The pitch leveled off slightly, and then began climbing steeply again toward the summit of the ridge. Close to the top, with Walter still ahead, we rounded a shoulder of the mountain. Walter stopped, and in an unnaturally calm voice he told me to turn around and go back. The route ended in a cliff and his two horses were standing on a narrow ledge; in chill disbelief I realized that Walter appeared to be trapped. I did not see how he could turn both his horses around. He couldn't even dismount, as that would simply have carried him over the side of the cliff.

There was a long silence. "Okay, Ped, go!" he said and turned the reins into empty space. I looked away, but when the expected whinny and crash of falling horses did not occur, I turned back. Walter was riding toward me with a weak grin.

"Just gotta trust 'em," he said, his face slick with perspiration.

We stopped for lunch near the top, with the horses (and ourselves) exhausted and shaking from stress. Walter pointed out, with some satisfaction, that my "much easier" route had ended in an awful chasm, just as Shellenberger had said. We spent fifteen minutes pulling cactus spines out of the horses' legs.

I then discovered that my watch—our only watch—was gone, having fallen off my wrist on the scramble up the ridge.

"Good," Walter said. "What the hell do you need a Goddamn watch for anyway? You got some appointments you gotta keep?"

"It *would* be nice to know the date and time," I said, annoyed.

"Needing to know the date and time: that's a *disease*, Doug. We're out here to cure ourselves of that disease."

"Which is why you're always asking me what time it is."

"I *never* ask you what time it is," he said.

"Bullshit."

"Bullshit yourself," he said. "I never met anyone so concerned about
the time and date. Maybe now you'll *learn* something." He crammed
a dried fig into his mouth and chewed noisily.

From where we were, we could see the Salt River crawling through
its gorge a thousand feet below us, shut in by cliffs on all sides. The sun
was shimmering off a broad riffle of water, and the sky arched over our
heads, a hot, flat pan of blue. The smell of horse sweat and sun-heated
leather lingered around our resting spot.

"Somehow," I said, "I don't think Coronado rode down that river."

Walter guffawed. "Those professors didn't know jack shit," he said.
"They just sat at their desks and drew lines on maps."

Horseshoe Bend of the Salt River was the point where the scholars
had Coronado turning west and riding downriver for two days. We
could now see for ourselves that Mark Shellenberger was right, and that
such a route was absolutely impossible.

In most places steep cliffs and thousand-foot talus slopes pitched to
the water's edge. There was certainly no place to ride in or alongside
the river, let alone drive livestock. (Coronado's army with its herds of
sheep and cattle, it should be remembered, eventually followed the
same route.) If, as some scholars have suggested, Coronado didn't ride
down the bed of the river itself but instead rode along the high country
to the north of the river, he would have had an even tougher time: we
could see a series of steep gorges cutting down to the river.

In fact, no travel anywhere near the river was possible. As far as I
could see there were no trails, no roads, nowhere even a man on foot
could go without technical climbing equipment. Certainly no Indian
trail would have gone this way, let alone the friar's "wide and much-
used road." We had just disqualified one of the proposed Coronado
routes.

"Fucking professors," Walter said. "We've ridden three hundred
miles for nothing."

Close to the top, Walter found the faint animal trail. I was starting
to respect Walter's uncanny ability to find a trail in a wilderness, as
well as his nerve in navigating across seemingly impossible country. I
had first noticed this ability along the San Pedro River, when he could
keep us going in a straight line through miles of thick, monotonous
brush without ever consulting a compass. This ability of his would save
our hides more than once.

The trail led us over the hogback ridge, and we could see Cherry

Creek in a deep canyon below us, a crevasse of green amidst stony mountains. A few miles up the creek lay a sprinkling of ranch buildings.

Coming up, Pedernal had torn off one of his horseshoes in the rocks, so Walter dismounted and let him pick his own way down. Robin was still in a high panic, and when we reached the flatland by the creek she sank, gratefully, to her belly. We stopped to rest and I propped my head against a log and instantly fell asleep. I woke up to see the lens of Walter's camera hovering in front of me.

"Get that thing out of my face," I said.

Walter laughed. "You looked just like a dead man," he said.

A mile up the creek we entered the ranch, a cluster of buildings and corrals nestled against the cliffs. A giant man was sitting in the shade of a barn porch. His wife and two daughters were saddling horses on the flat outside. They watched us ride up.

Walter called out a greeting. "We got a horse here, threw a shoe," he said.

The man stood up and grabbed Pedernal's leg and hoisted it up to look at the hoof.

"Oh yeah!" he roared out, dropping the leg, his giant voice reverberating down the canyon. Without another word he went in the barn and came back out with a fistful of iron: horseshoe, hammer, rasp, nippers, clincher, and nails. He started banging and rasping away at an anvil on the porch and in five minutes Pedernal was wearing a new shoe.

His name was Steve Smith, and everything about him was big: his voice, his frame, his hands, his walk.

While he was shoeing the horse, one of the daughters, who couldn't have been more than six years old, jumped up and grabbed the stirrup of her horse, swung herself up, and shinnied up the leather fender just like she was climbing a rope. She perched in the saddle, in perfect form, reins in hand, like a mouse on top of an elephant. I'd never seen anything like it.

"Hey," said Walter, pulling out his camera, "do that again."

The little girl grinned and slid down the stirrup, dropped to the ground, and then climbed back aboard.

"How long has she been riding a horse?" Walter asked.

"Ever since she could walk," Smith said.

Then he roared out: "Bunkhouse and showers over there. Cold beer in the fridge. Steak's in the pot, dinner in half an hour. You can turn your horses out in this corral here."

After that rough ride, I dreaded taking off Popeye's saddle. I feared the sore was going to look worse; and it did.

Steve Smith's ranch was called the Dagger Ranch. We went in for dinner. A substantially large percentage of a cow had been boiling in a huge pot on the stove, and we carved off dripping hunks for our dinner. It wasn't until we were settled down for our meal that Smith asked us what our business was.

"You boys ride in from Horseshoe Bend?" he asked.

We told him we had.

"Huh," he grunted. "That's tough country."

We realized we'd just been paid a tremendous compliment. If this man thought something was tough, by Jesus it was *tough*.

Smith was a rancher and one of Arizona's top hunting guides, taking people after mountain lion and bear on the Apache reservation.

"There are more lions in these mountains than anywhere else in the U.S.," he said.

I asked him why.

"Any blind idiot can track a lion in the snow," he said, "but there's only fifteen men in the world can track a lion in the desert."

"So how do you survive, ranching these days?" Walter asked.

"I fix my own fence," Smith said. "I'm my own vet. I round up my own cows. I fix my own windmills. I brand, worm, do everything around here. Nowadays, you hire a guy to do something for you, there goes your profit."

The Dagger Ranch covered 85 sections (54,400 acres) of rugged mountains bordering the Apache reservation, but had only 30 "patented" (that is, privately owned) acres. It had been homesteaded by Alf DeVore, who, it was said, originally stocked the ranch with livestock stolen from the Apaches. Alf DeVore had been a brave man.

Smith had bought the ranch ten years back. After dinner we sat in his living room, underneath the enormous skins of mountain lion and bear. Steve parked his frame in a chair and proceeded to speak his mind on a range of subjects. He was a man of few gestures; when he spoke, he sat motionless in his chair, his big hands gripping the armrests, his voice carrying all the power. When the telephone rang he picked it up and roared into the mouthpiece with such strength that I could almost hear the circuits sizzling with the overload. It was as if he wanted to make for damn sure the other party heard him whether the phone was working or not.

"Well, if you're going to turn on that tape recorder," he said, when

I brought it out, "then I've got a few things to say about the Forest Service. They won't like it, but you go ahead and print this."

He settled back in his chair.

"The curse of this country is the cedars," he began. "The cedar's not natural in most places; it's an indicator of overgrazing, overgrazing that occurred forty or fifty years ago. Cedar duff kills the grass."

"I heard there's a chemical in it that inhibits growth," I said.

"That's exactly right," he said. "So, to bring back the country, you've got to burn your cedars. But we're not going to do that. And *why* aren't we going to do that? Because the Forest Service makes too much money, and they sold the public Smokey the Bear."

He paused, looking around for comment.

"What do you mean, too much money?" I asked.

"We've got a whole plateau up there, you guys are gonna ride through it, a hundred miles wide and three hundred miles long. All cedars. Forest Service is managing it, and there's people making *big* money. There's 2.1 million dollars being spent every year on fighting forest fires up there. Hey, are those guys gonna cut their budget? That's big business, fighting for Smokey the Bear. Those cedars have destroyed, absolutely *destroyed* that plateau up there."

He paused again. The room was silent.

"You've *got* to let the country burn," he said. "That's nature's way. Fire is nature's *tool*. Before we came along everything was perfect. Like in Yellowstone, everyone said, 'That fire was a bad deal.' Well, it was a bad deal that we *stopped* all burning forty or fifty years ago because the fire that burned last summer was harsher than it would have been. Even so, that fire did a lot of good."

Steve Smith was angry and his voice rolled on like thunder.

"Hey, when I was a kid in this country, you could see twenty or thirty does in a bunch. You'd have a lightning strike and next year those deer would go to that little forty-acre deal that burned out. All that new growth that comes back, that's what the deer like to eat. The deer can't eat that tough old growth. And each doe, she'll have *two* fawns instead of one. That burn actually *stimulates* reproduction.

"But today, your deer herd's low, your elk herd's low, nothing does any good. That's Smokey the Bear. The public's been sold on that deal for the last thirty years.

"Now on the Dagger Ranch here, you guys can get on your horses and ride up the creek and go up every one of these ridges and you'll see perennial grasses. We've got this deal called bush muhly. There's only two places in Arizona that still has bush muhly, and this ranch is one of 'em. We've got your side oats, your curly mesquite, your grama grasses, all in good shape. When water falls, it doesn't rut the land, it percolates in. In ten years, *ten short years*, I was able to do this. This deal was abused terribly bad. Fifty years ago, they had fifteen thousand head, and right now there's fifteen hundred.

"There's this big movement today, an *environmental* movement. People are concerned, and there's nothing wrong with that. We *should* be concerned. But so much of this business that's been sold to the public is just not correct, like Smokey the Bear. A lot of people say, 'Hey, here's another rancher, wants to burn the country up.' Hell, when a cowpuncher tries to tell 'em something they say 'Aw, forget that son of a buck—he's a damn cowboy.' They did a *study*, said they should take my thirty acres here and turn this deal into a *recreational* campsite, so more people can get into that wilderness you come through. They'll put paved roads and trails and grade out campsites and this place'll be filled up with people. Now you tell me: is that ecological?"

He waited for comment. We nodded in agreement. The man certainly made sense. The thought of hikers and campers and day trippers overrunning the pristine landscape we had just come through made me sick.

"If they try to take away my thirty acres here I'll fight them every step of the way. I'll make them sorry they ever started this thing."

I said, "A lot of scientists have concluded exactly what you just said, about fire."

Steve nodded. "Any time, those Apaches over here could've told them *all* they needed to know about fire. They've been burning their country a hundred years and it's the best damn country around here."

I slept that night in a bed for the first time in a month.

The next morning I asked Steve to take a look at Popeye's back. I was becoming increasingly worried about the horse, and I did not want to lay out money to buy a new horse in Show Low. Smith showed me how to roll up a gunny sack and position it between the saddle blankets to relieve the pressure on the sore spot.

I asked him whether I should be riding the horse at all. "Maybe I should walk him for a while," I said.

Steve looked incredulous.

"Walk?" he roared out. "When you've got a horse? Heck no. *Ride the son-of-a-bitch!"*

There is a saying about the Mogollon Rim: "The country is so rough that a man on foot is no man at all."

We started up Cherry Creek, along a little ranch road. I still felt concerned about Popeye, so as soon as we were out of sight of the ranch I guiltily climbed off his back and began walking.

Around lunchtime we saw a pickup bumping along the road. It came to a stop and a man got out, limping and wincing as he came over. His name was Nate Ellison, and he owned the Ellison Ranch at the other end of the road. He was one of those tough, fit men with a belly hanging over the belt, who carry themselves so well one would never think of them as fat. He wore a dusty cowboy hat of indeterminate color, curled and stained from a thousand rainshowers and dust storms. He started talking as if he'd known us all our lives. He had a happy, innocent quality about him.

He said he was looking for a mountain lion that killed six of his calves. "I've been out there tracking that son-of-a-bitch," he said. "That tom's taken my profit this year." He winced as he shifted his weight. "Damned leg's been broke these last few weeks," he added. "With roundup on I ain't had time to take care of it."

I was astonished. Surely, I said, he could take a day or two off and get a cast. Why, he might cripple himself.

Ellison snorted, "Yeah, and see the ranch go bust. As it is now I'll just make enough to pay my grazing fees."

Walter asked how he'd broken it.

He said he'd just roped a cow when a maverick bull charged him. He couldn't get his leg out of the way, as it was pinned by the rope holding the cow, and the bull struck him full force, knocking down his horse. "That son-of-a-bitch saw me," Ellison said with a grin, "and he knew *exactly* what he wanted to do."

Walter, I had discovered, was never one to be stingy with advice, and what was worse, he was usually right. In the past two days he had been offering me a number of suggestions concerning Popeye and his sore back, advice which was increasingly unwelcome. Nate Ellison had suggested that I transfer my saddlebags from the back to the front of the saddle, to take more weight off the sore spot, and after lunch I proceeded to do just that.

As I fussed with the saddlebags, Walter said, from astride his horse: "Here, you're not doing that right. Lemme show you how to tie those saddlebags on."

This was, finally, one piece of advice too many. I became enraged. I told Walter, in exceedingly vulgar words of language, what I thought of his advice, his abilities as a horseman, his character, and his very worth as a human being.

Without saying a word, Walter started to get off his horse. From the look on his face I knew I was in trouble. Generally speaking it is unwise to get in a fight with a person under five feet seven inches tall, and this is particularly true of a short Texan. On the other hand, I was so mad I relished the chance, however unlikely, to knock down the greasy little Texas bastard.

At the last moment Walter changed his mind and swung his leg back over the saddle.

He said, merely:

"If you ever talk to me like that again, you'll be the sorriest white man in Arizona."

We continued up the track, furious at each other. I walked at a brisk pace, leading Popeye and Banjo, while Walter, finding my presence intolerable, dropped way back and was soon out of sight. As far as I was concerned, I'd have been satisfied never to clap eyes on the bastard again.

Even though I was afoot, my butt started to feel sore. The more I walked, the sorer it felt. Another eight miles of walking gave me an intolerable case of saddlesoreness. It felt like someone had taken a grinding wheel to my buttocks.

I stopped and rummaged in my saddlebags for some kind of relief. There I found a tube of Phillips Corona ointment. I read the label.

For Hoofs, Body & Legs, Head, Face,
Udder & Teats.
Antiseptic Emollient Treatment for Horses & Cattle,
Other Livestock, Small Animals

This was good enough for me. I dropped my pants and began smearing the stuff over my butt. When I was in my most compromising position, Walter appeared around the bend.

"What the hell are you doing now?" he roared out angrily. "Jerking off?"

When I stammered an explanation, Walter, despite himself, began to laugh. He laughed so hard he nearly fell off his horse.

I had just provided Walter with his favorite story of the trip. I have heard it many times since. "I rounded the turn," Walter would say, "still thinking how I'm gonna teach this Yankee son-of-a-bitch a lesson he'll never forget, and what do I see but this big old white ass, smack in the middle of the road. And here he is, with his drawers down, bent over, rubbing his ass. I didn't know *what* the hell he was doing. Turns out he's spreading horse liniment all over his butt! *Horse* liniment!"

We camped at an old set of corrals on a bench of land above Cherry Creek. We were still somewhere on the Ellison Ranch. The creek tumbled down a bed of burnished granite boulders and through pools filled with fish. Below the corrals, alongside the creek, we found a narrow fenced pasture, about a third of a mile long and two hundred feet wide, filled with dry filiree grass.*

We turned our horses loose in the pasture and pitched camp on the rise, with views up and down Cherry Creek Canyon. The horses had such good feed that we decided to give them a day off.

Nate came by the next morning, wanting to know if we'd heard one of his lost cows bawling. He had his rifle and he said that he and Steve Smith were looking for the lion. He went down to the creek and called us over, pointing to the sand.

"See this sign? That tom went through here yesterday." Even though the sand was soft and smooth, the track was exceedingly faint— you could scarcely tell something had even imprinted it. I finally understood Steve Smith's statement that only fifteen men could track mountain lion. A mouse would have left a better track.

Robin had lost a shoe, and Nate said he'd return that evening with his tools and tack it back on for us.

We spent the entire day in a most indolent condition, doing nothing but sleeping, eating, and bathing. We ate two breakfasts and three lunches, making serious inroads in our dwindling food supply.

While I was sleeping in the sun by the creek, I had a splendid dream of the men's-suit department at Brooks Brothers. I found myself in the elevator; the doors hissed open, revealing aisles of hand-rubbed cherry cabinets. Each cabinet held a row of dark suits, arranged as if in a

---

*Filiree grass, *afilaria*, is one of the staple grasses of the southern Southwest, and is very high in protein. It was brought to the New World accidentally, wedged in the hooves and tangled in the fleeces of sheep.

museum exhibit, softly illuminated by hidden lighting. Slender, obsequious foreign gentlemen stood around, and as soon as I stepped out one cast an inquiring eye in my direction. With the flick of a finger I summoned him over; he approached, softly as a cat, and his face broke into an ingratiating smile; a dazzling rack of white teeth were exposed; and he slightly inclined his head and inquired, "May I be of assistance, sir?"

Then I woke up, disgusted to find myself in the middle of the Arizona mountains with sand in my mouth.

I whittled a small arrow and tried to spear a fish. When that failed I turned over some stones and caught a few crawfish with the idea of eating them, but I soon felt sorry for them and let them go. I then watched a turtle paddle over and wolf down some grains of rice that had been rinsed into the pool from dinner the night before. The expression of delight on the turtle's face as he made the discovery decided me against the idea of turtle soup. The poor fellow was as hungry as we were.

At sundown Nate reappeared driving two steers, a cow, and a heifer he thought had been eaten by the lion. He was in an expansive mood. "Like finding a thousand dollars by the side of the road," he said.

Walter went off to get Robin to be shod while I switched on my tape recorder and chatted with Nate. He said he'd killed 257 mountain lions, mostly on trips into the Apache reservation where hunting mountain lion is legal. Like his neighbor he was one of the top lion and bear guides in America. I asked if he'd gotten the lion that had killed his calves.

"Not yet," he said.

"Is this his territory?" I asked.

"It isn't his totally," he said, "there're just too many lions around here. He'll make a circuit, maybe eighteen to twenty-two days, go clear from here round to Roosevelt Lake and back."

"So there are other lions in here?"

"You're damn right there are. Sometimes these lions cross paths. Now that's something to see. Once I caught one lion off another. They'd fought, and he'd killed him and was eating on him. The survivor was the most bruised-up, skinned-up lion you ever seen. He was bitten clear through the ribs, his tongue was split, his ears was split, his nose was split, and his chest was just black from being bitten. The ground and the little bushes was just tore and there was hair everywhere. I'll tell you, that must've been a *noisy* thing."

"How will you find this lion?" I asked.

"When I used to hunt all the time, I'd learn one like this and then I'd hunt steady for ten days just for him. It's persistence. You *learn* him."

"Do they kill your cattle often?" I asked.

"You betcha. If I got to keep all the livestock I've lost to predators, I could be semi-retired by now. You know these people say a lion don't kill for nothing but to eat. Well, last year I bought eight heifers, they was two-year-olds, and they was bred to a University of Arizona bull and I paid more money than I could afford for 'em. I figured I'd get me three *good* calves out of those. But this big old tom, he come down off that mountain there, and he wrastled one of these heifers on the ground, and he just eat up into her bag, and here was this little bull calf stickin' out of her womb. Then this tom come down on this little flat right here, and he catch another calf, killed him but never touched him. Then he killed another calf right over there, and he ate just about a baseball size out of him."

"What is ranching like these days?" I asked.

"It's tough. I've got eighteen sections but they'll only let me run fifty-five head. I grow apples and peaches, guide now and then. I make just about enough money from one thing to get me to the next thing."

We talked some more and a golden eagle flew up out of the canyon and circled over our heads.

"See that son-of-a-bitch up there?" Nate said. "I saw one of 'em kill a fawn. I was on one of my bear hunts, guiding this fellow from California. We was settin' on a point waiting for bear to come out. We heard *whooooooshhhh* and this golden eagle come right over our heads and he landed on a fawn right in front of us. He just dropped down real quick and clinched it right on top of the shoulders. He was so big that he was able to fly about twenty or thirty feet, just kind of dragging it. And he just set there pecking on its head, pecking out its eyes. And then all at once that was it, the fawn was dead, and he start eating on him. They say that's an endangered species but I say he's a cruel son-of-a-bitch."

The story was told with particular force, but it wasn't until later that I realized the meaning behind it. Out here, where one lion could put a ranch out of business, people have a different attitude toward nature. Man and nature were still clasped in a struggle for existence. A lion killing three calves for pleasure, a golden eagle killing a fawn: these were looked on as moral outrages. There was a presumed equality between man and beast: if a lion killed a man's calf, then the man had a right to kill the lion. Only do city and town folk have the privilege to look on nature as benign, since where we come from nature has already been subdued. I wondered how people in New York would feel if a mountain lion moved into Central Park and began killing all their dogs and cats.

Ellison's great-grandfather, Colonel Jesse W. Ellison, was one of the most famous and colorful stockmen of the Rim country. Born in Brazos County, Texas, in 1841, he grew into a "reed-thin, habit-bound, hawk-faced" man whose conviction in his own rightness was unshakable. He relished being on the "right" side of a good fight. He started off as a Texas Ranger fighting Comanches and Kiowas, and then he enlisted for the South in the Civil War. He remained an unreconstructed southerner thereafter, went into the ranching business, and drove cattle up the Chisholm Trail to the Kansas railheads. Texas became a little too crowded for Ellison, so he moved his family and livestock farther west. In July of 1885, he arrived at Bowie Station, Arizona, with a line of railcars containing two thousand head of cattle and horses.

His arrival would be remembered for over a hundred years. Through an oversight the stock had not been given enough water for the summertime journey, and as soon as the doors opened the cattle, crazed with thirst, burst out and stampeded down the main street of Bowie "knocking houses off foundations, shattering windows, carrying off clotheslines, and sending women and children screaming ahead of them," one witness recalled. Ellison lost eight hundred fine animals in the melee.

He found a good-looking ranch just west of Cherry Creek, which he purchased from the owner. Ellison's cows had come from Texas with his Texas brand, a "Q," and his ranch became known as the Q Ranch. The fact that the previous owner and many of his neighbors had been ruined by cattle rustlers meant nothing to Ellison: it was just one more fight he was willing to undertake—which, we shall see later, he did with devastating effectiveness.

Ellison had mostly daughters, of which he was very proud. "They were all good ropers and good shots," he told a newspaper reporter in 1887. "They drove cattle instead of playing bridge and they lived on beans when we could get 'em." One of his daughters, Duette, married Arizona Territory's first governor, George W. P. Hunt, becoming the first of Arizona's first ladies. She liked to be photographed with her gun.

Like his great-grandson, Jesse Ellison was a bear hunter. According to one historian the "skins of Arizona's greatest trophy bears were tacked upon Ellison's outbuildings, only to rot away and leave their awesome dimensions outlined in rusted nails."

Walter finally brought Robin up from the pasture, and Nate handed him the tools. "You're gonna do it yourself," he said. "You've got to learn sometime."

While Nate gave instructions, Walter tacked the shoe back on. Then Nate inspected the other shoes and said Walter's horses would have to be reshod as soon as possible. The only place we might find a farrier, he said, would be in the little town of Young, about thirty-five miles to the north in the middle of the Rim country.

Then Nate said: "I guess you know your horse's got a big old water bag."

"What?" Walter asked.

"Right here," Ellison said, feeling Robin's hindquarters.

We inspected it. It was an enormous swelling, a large accumulation of fluid in the tissues right where the horse had fallen coming up the hogback ridge. It was the size of a honeydew melon and as tight as a steel-belted radial.

"You're gonna have to slit and drain that bastard," Nate said. "If it comes out water, even if it's bloody, it'll probably be okay. But if it comes out pus, she's got an infection and you'll have to do something about that."

The evening light burned off the canyon walls and flamed out. A chill crept into the air and we could suddenly see our breath.

"You must know this country pretty well," I said.

"Fifty-six years old," Ellison said, "and I was born right here. My dad and I built these corrals. I used to swim and fish in those holes down there in the creek. I know every rock, every tree, every thing you're looking at here." His voice had dropped nearly to a whisper, but I could feel, across the intervening darkness, the surge of emotion behind it.

He then wished us luck and we shook hands all around. I watched him limp off into the twilight, with a small sharp intake of breath at every other step, the small price of keeping his ranch going just one more year.

The next day, before sunrise, in the great stillness of an Arizona morning, the sound of a single shot echoed down the canyon. Ellison had found the lion.

16

⬧ ⧖ ⬧

We climbed the little jeep track for about fifteen or twenty miles, following the contour of the canyon. We had climbed over three thousand vertical feet from the Salt and had nearly three thousand more to go before we topped the Rim. The Salt River Canyon, while not as dramatic as the Grand Canyon, is almost a thousand feet deeper. We had left the desert behind and were now in high, cool forested country.

Just below Board Tree Saddle we found an old cowboy camp next to a spring, surrounded by ponderosa pines, oak, and manzanita. The camp, used once a year during roundup, consisted of several stumps arranged around a firepit and a box nailed sideways to a tree, creating a shelf. On the shelf were two dirty spoons and a mayonnaise jar half full of rotten sugar.

We pitched camp. A very dead, desiccated calf lay about twenty yards from the spring. The spring itself had been boxed and a length of pipe stuck in it. With the drought, however, only one drop of water fell from the pipe every thirty seconds. I rigged up a sling to hold our canteens and over the course of the night we were able to accumulate two gallons of cool, delicious water.

We staked three horses in a grassy patch of ground behind the camp.

I decided to hobble Popeye. This was the first time I had hobbled a horse, as we had either gotten feed at ranches or been lucky enough to find a fenced pasture with grass. I followed Gordon Whiting's instructions, twisting and tying the lead rope around both front legs. I then tied the cowbell on his halter.

Walter took a dim view of the proceedings.

"That old cowbell is gonna be ringing all night long," he said.

I made raspberry biscuits for dinner, burying them in a baking hole excavated in the ashes of our fire. We ate the biscuits with a stew made from a mixture of instant scalloped potatoes, sardines, and quinoa. We had started to run low on some foods and our dinners were, by necessity, becoming more creative in execution.

I went to sleep listening to the comforting clanging of the bell as the horse grazed.

Then, an indeterminate time later, I woke up in a cold sweat, suddenly aware that a profound silence had descended on the camp. I shook Walter awake. "The bell," I cried. "I can't hear the bell."

"I thought you knew," he said grumpily. "That horse went off down the canyon. I heard that Goddamn bell get fainter and fainter until it was gone. I guess he must've broken his hobbles and taken off."

"Broken his hobbles?" I shouted. "Jesus Christ, why didn't you wake me up?"

"I thought you were awake. It's pitch-black out there. Nothing we can do now." He rolled over and started snoring.

I was beside myself. The horse was gone. We would never find a loose horse in this country, and the last fence we had passed through was a good twenty miles back. I fell into a fitful sleep, dreamed of two women in a health food store kissing and fondling each other, and sprang awake, certain I had heard a ringing bell. There was nothing but silence.

As soon as the first glimmer appeared in the eastern sky I got up and began following the horse's tracks.

The trail was difficult to follow, particularly for someone as ignorant of the science of tracking as I was. Popeye had indeed gone down the canyon. In some places I had to get down on my hands and knees with the flashlight to see his tracks.

About a quarter mile down the trail, Popeye's track turned off and went down a dry, rocky wash. Once again I had to crawl on my hands and knees, inspecting the rocks with my flashlight. There was no dirt to imprint the horse's hooves, and the only sign I could locate was an occasional whitish mark where a metal shoe had chipped or abraded a rock. I painstakingly followed these marks for another quarter mile or so. The wash descended into dense woods and brush.

I soon lost his track. I backtracked and finally saw where the ugly brute had veered out of the wash into dense brush. By minutely examining the ground, looking for a crushed stem of grass, a whitish mark on a pebble, and other vanishingly small signs, I was able to follow his trail for another hundred yards.

Then I lost the trail entirely. No matter how carefully I combed the brush and the ground underneath for sign, I could find none. In my ignorance I made one of the cardinal mistakes of tracking and roamed back and forth over the area. Soon I picked up an unmistakable trail, which I followed around back to where I had started and realized, with infinite disgust, that I was tracking myself. By that time my efforts had so disturbed the ground that what faint sign might have been there was now obliterated.

I stood up and looked around. Ahead of me stretched Cherry Creek Canyon and dozens of tributary canyons, choked with boulders and trees and brush. It was the roughest imaginable country. It would take a tracker like Nate Ellison to find a horse lost in here.

I can hardly begin to describe my state of mind. First off, I decided, I was going to thrash Walter for failing to wake me up when the horse started off down the canyon. And if I ever did find that swinish, cretinous, glue plug bucket of guts I was going to whip him within an inch of his life. I stood in the brush, trembling with rage and despair. This was truly the end.

And then, in the deepening silence, I heard the faintest sound. I listened. It was a ringing bell.

I went crashing and stumbling through the brush, yelling Popeye's name and whistling as loudly as I could. I finally collected my wits and stopped to listen. There was no sound. I waited five minutes, ten minutes. He would have to move at some point. I then heard another distant clang. This time I quietly followed the sound, pausing every few minutes to listen and get my bearings. The horse had gone into dense brush which I had to push through with considerable force. Gradually the sound got louder and louder, and suddenly there he was, ten feet in front of me, still hobbled, eating oak leaves and peering at me out of the corner of his eye with a marked lack of enthusiasm.

The hobbles and bell had worked exactly as they were supposed to have done. It seemed to me that finally, after three hundred miles of misadventures, we were starting to figure things out.

I found Walter poking at a roaring fire. The sunlight was just starting to pour over the canyon rim. A few puffy clouds, shot through with vermilion light, drifted across an infrared sky. It was a glorious morning.

"Maybe that bell wasn't such a bad idea after all," he grunted, stabbing the stick into the fire.

We rode up to Board Tree Saddle. This was the second point where our trail would cross Coronado's hypothetical route, and once again we had an illustration of the illogicality of it. At Board Tree Saddle, the professors had Coronado heading northeast for fifty miles, crossing at right angles a series of deep canyons draining off the Rim. This made no sense. A natural route from Board Tree Saddle ran north along Squaw Mesa to a broad valley aptly named Pleasant Valley. From there the top of the Rim was an easy two-day ride. Why would the Spaniards (and the Indians before them) not follow the route of least resistance; which is to say, follow the lay of the land? That Coronado would have turned northeast here into dreadfully rough country, where he would have been lucky to make five miles a day, was patently ridiculous.

Perhaps you have to be there, on a horse, with a sore ass, contemplating riding over that country, to understand what I mean.

We traveled along the top of Squaw Mesa, through an open ponderosa forest, moving in and out of patches of sun. The smell of baking pine needles rose from the ground litter and I alternately felt the warmth of sun and the cool of shade on my back. That and the rhythmic shuffle of the horses had a kind of soporific effect, and I found my mind wandering over all manner of strange and fragmentary recollections. I remembered the first time I'd kissed a girl. It was during a terrifying game of spin-the-bottle; the bottle had ended up pointing at me and before I could protest I found myself clasped in a bony embrace by a girl named Cindy Brewster. And now, in the middle of Rim country, I suddenly remembered—in fact I actually *smelled*—for the first time since that dreadful moment the fragrance of the peppermint gum she had been chewing. How very odd, I thought, that the mind would bother to store such a minor fillip for such a great length of time. With death, I thought, all these trivial moments and stray memories suddenly become extinct, vanishing not only from the dying brain, but (perhaps) from the universe itself. It was inconceivable and frightening to think that, on my death, that memory of Cindy's peppermint gum would evaporate completely, and forever.

That's when I decided to put it in this book.

I woke up to a shout and the sound of thundering hooves. Robin was off and running down the road with Walter cursing hopelessly at her retreating form. She was becoming increasingly skittish and unpredictable, always trying to kick or bite the other horses, shying away from stock tanks and streams, having to be watered out of Walter's hat. As I found in myself a growing understanding and rapport with horses, I found myself disliking her more and more. Popeye was a bad horse; Banjo was a good horse; Pedernal was a great horse; but Robin was a piece of shit.

Eventually the trees thinned out and we came into a broad, green valley, carpeted with lush grass. In the middle of the valley lay a scattering of battenboard houses with long emerald fields radiating from each homestead. Two dirt roads led into the valley, one from the north and one from the east. The sun was beginning to set and the valley was flooded with a golden light. Small herds of cows and horses dotted each pasture. Mountains, hills, and forests swept down to the margin of the valley and stretched outward in all directions as far as the eye could see.

This was the town of Young, and the valley called Pleasant Valley. As we rode into town, we began to feel as if we had entered a time warp. Aside from a few dozen pickup trucks and some telephone lines, we could just as easily have been transported to the nineteenth century.

⊲ ⊠ ⊳

Gazing at this bucolic scene, it was hard to believe that Pleasant Valley was the site of one of the bloodiest feuds in American history. Some say nearly 50 percent of the adult male population of the Rim country died by the bullet or the rope, in what came to be known as the Pleasant Valley or Tonto War.*

The war started as a simple feud between two families. But in Arizona, in the Rim country in the 1880s, there could be no simple

---

*The Tonto Rim is an old name for this section of the Mogollon Rim, and the area below the Rim between Cherry Creek and Tonto Creek was often referred to as the Tonto Basin.

resolution of a simple feud. All the paradoxes and conflicts engendered by the settling of the West came together in this little valley in the 1880s. It took little more than spilled blood to start a war that would eventually engulf the region.

These paradoxes and conflicts were numerous. First, many of the older residents of Pleasant Valley, like many of the early settlers of the West, were veterans of the Civil War. Much of the legendary violence of the Old West was a direct result of the Civil War; discharged veterans carried guns and knew how to shoot, and after living through the carnage of the war little frightened them. Since the law had not yet come to much of the West, these people preferred to settle disputes immediately, among themselves.

The second conflict was caused, not surprisingly, by misguided homestead laws. You couldn't homestead land that hadn't been surveyed by section and range, and in the 1880s the Rim country hadn't been surveyed. As a result no one could legally homestead, buy, or sell land. The owner of land often ended up being the man with the fastest gun.

There were other problems. The range was unfenced so everyone by necessity ran their livestock together. The theft of cattle was so rampant that honest settlers were forced to rustle just to even things out with their neighbors. In addition to the conflicts between cowmen, sheepmen also moved into the valley, as did a soulless, ruthless cattle corporation based in New York City. The breathtaking remoteness of the valley attracted more than the unusual number of crooks, murderers, and thieves from the played-out Nevada silver mines and the overcrowded Texas range. Even today, Young is one of the most isolated rural towns in America; the nearest supermarket is a round-trip drive of 120 miles, 60 of those over boneshaking washboard dirt roads. Back then it was almost a country unto itself.

With this kind of mixture, something was bound to happen.

The people who first settled the Rim country in 1881 and '82 were extraordinarily tough. In the early days, the Apaches would regularly sweep through the valley, killing and burning out the settlers. They acted as a kind of sieve, filtering out all but the stoutest of heart.

"It was early in the morning," one Mrs. Meadows would coolly recall of her first year in Pleasant Valley in 1882, "and we heard the dogs barking. My husband said, 'My dogs are baying a bear. I'll take my gun and go over there and kill it.' I saw him pass that bare spot and just as he entered those vines on the other side, the Indians opened fire. I saw him fall. They kept up one continuous war whoop and a continual rain of bullets were falling on the house and yard. . . . [Henry, the oldest son,] had us pile up sacks of flour or any other sacks in such a way as to furnish protection from any stray bullet. . . .

"I noticed that the boys looked pale. John came to me and said, 'Ma, can you get me some splints?'

" 'Yes, what's the matter?'

" 'My arm is all shot to pieces.'

"A little later Henry came to me and said, 'Ma, have you a pair of scissors?'

" 'Yes, here they are.'

"He made a quick movement and I saw something fall to the floor. It was part of his entrails. He said afterwards that he knew he could not live long, and that he wanted to save his mother and the children before he passed on."

This was early life in Pleasant Valley.

When the Apache troubles died down after the surrender of Geronimo, settlers began coming into the valley in increasing numbers. They were very pleased with what they found. One settler, Mart Blevins, wrote his sixteen-year-old daughter back in Llano, Texas:

feb the 20 1887
well this leaves us all well—hopping you all the same—well i am here in canion creek in arizona—wee have got a veary fine outfit here. . .we have got as fine timber and water and land and grass as eveary was seen in any country—we air rite under the foot of muggaown mountain. hit snows some here. . .hit tis the finest country to raise vegatabuls that i eveary seen—our places has got 2 veary fine running creeks on thim. wee can irigate all of the land that we wants—horses will winter here fine—you can turn a pore horse looce here in the winter and he will get fat. . .there is a good chance for a pore man here. . .

The author of this letter would not live to see the fruits of his labors. In just four months he would disappear, almost certainly murdered and buried in some lonely canyon—one of the first casualties in the Pleasant Valley War. By the time the war ended, four of his sons would die by the bullet and a fifth be grievously wounded. The "good chance for a pore man" would go terribly bad.

One of the early homesteaders in Pleasant Valley was a fellow named

James Dunning Tewksbury. He came from Boston, where the variant spelling "Tewkesbury" is even today a distinguished Brahmin name. But something got Tewksbury moving, and he sailed around the Horn to California, perhaps to try his luck in the goldfields. He had soon settled in Oregon with his bride, a Shoshone Indian of legendary beauty. His ranch was prosperous and he began breeding a stable of fine racehorses.

But Tewksbury had that irresistible wandering impulse that was so common in the early West. Despite a well-respected, solid life in Oregon, Tewksbury moved his family on to San Francisco and then the silverfields of Nevada. His wife died and he moved again—now with five children—to Prescott, Arizona. In 1879, while pursuing a herd of stolen stock, Tewksbury found himself at the edge of the Tonto Rim looking down on an impossibly green valley, a cattleman's Shangri-La. It was such an impressive sight he gave up the chase and rode down to investigate.

He had found what he'd been looking for.

He married a woman from Globe, twice widowed, who owned cattle. His four boys drove their horse herd to Pleasant Valley and built a homestead along Cherry Creek, with a cabin, barn, smithy, corrals, and a stable. With his wife's cattle forming the nucleus of the herd, the ranch prospered. His sons grew into extremely handsome men, with that strange grace that comes from mixed blood.

In 1882, Tewksbury's son Ed met a man in Globe named Graham. Graham and his brother were looking for a place to run a small herd, and Ed enthusiastically recommended Pleasant Valley. The place was still wide open and blanketed with seemingly inexhaustible grass, and the Tewksburys wanted company. Graham traveled to the valley, looked the place over, and came back with his brother to set up their outfit about two miles up Cherry Creek from the Tewksburys. Like the Tewksburys, the Graham brothers were also wanderers: from Alaska to Mexico and parts in between. Like the Tewksburys, they had found in Pleasant Valley exactly what they had been looking for.

The range was open and unfenced, and everybody ran their cattle together. The brand was the only mark of ownership. This left a great deal of room for creative brand manipulation and the rustling of un-branded calves. Trouble soon developed.

One of the largest ranchers in the area was a fellow named Stinson. Stinson, rather shortsightedly as we will see, chose as his brand a simple

T: two impresses with a hot iron bar. Almost immediately, a proliferation of brands incorporating "T" sprang up:

$$\underline{\mathrm{I}} \quad \mathrm{J} \quad \mathsf{HT} \quad \underline{\mathsf{R}} \quad \overline{\underline{\mathsf{T}}} \quad \mathcal{B} \quad \mathsf{TEQ} \quad \mathsf{TC}$$

A man handy with a running iron, a ring of metal that could be heated in a fire and used to "draw" on a cow hide, could transform a Stinson cow into his own cow in a matter of seconds. Often the only way to tell that the brand had been altered was to kill the cow, skin it, and examine the brand from the inside of the hide. This form of rustling was common, and there was a certain period in the West when mere possession of a running iron was enough to get you hanged. Sometimes the brass ring in a piece of (phony) saddle rigging was used instead.

Stinson's cattle leaked away like water through a sieve. Meanwhile, other herds increased mightily, including those bearing the TE Connected brand, not yet registered, shared by the Grahams and the Tewksburys for (supposedly) maverick cattle they caught in the mountains. ("Mavericking," the capturing of wild, unbranded cattle, was a favorite cover for rustling. Your cow herd could appear out of nowhere and nobody could prove a thing.) Stinson's T could be changed into a TE Connected in about 5 seconds:

$$\overline{\mathsf{E}}$$

On January 12, 1883, the foreman of the Stinson Ranch, a man named Elisha Gilleland, along with two assistants, paid a visit to the Tewksbury homestead. John and Tom Graham were there. Words were exchanged, somebody was called a black-hearted damned thieving son-of-a-bitch, and a blaze of gunfire followed. Two of the Gilleland party were shot.

Although arrest warrants were originally issued for Ed Tewksbury, the grand jury that convened to examine the witnesses indicted Gilleland and an assistant instead, concluding that they had instigated the shoot-out.

Somewhere, somehow, during the trial or immediately following, Stinson had a chance to talk to the Grahams. Stinson operated on the "to catch a thief theory," and a secret agreement was drawn up: Stinson hired the Grahams to be undercover range detectives for him. For a price, the Grahams would now turn informant against their former partners.

A second event followed hard on this one. John Graham rode to the seat of Yavapai County and registered the TE Connected brand—but he registered it in the Graham name only. In one fell swoop the Tewksburys had been dealt out of their half of the herd.

In the months following this event, the Tewksburys quickly registered a slew of brands of their own. Lydia Tewksbury recorded her brand, LT:

LT

Ed recorded the JK Connected:

JK

James, another brother, recorded the JDT Connected.

JP

In turn, the Grahams registered a brand nicknamed the "pigpen," into which Lydia's LT brand could be transformed with a few quick strokes of a running iron:

LT→#

If the brands are any indication, the two families were doing their damnedest to rustle each other blind.

On March 29, 1884, John Graham thought he had enough information to swear out a complaint against the Tewksburys and some of their associates for altering brands on sixty-two head of Stinson cattle. The complaint was thrown out of court and the Tewksburys immediately brought a charge of perjury against the Grahams and Stinson. Both sides were spoiling for a fight.

Several months later, a furious shoot-out between the Tewksburys and several employees of Stinson took place at the Stinson Ranch. Nobody was killed, but Ed's brother John Tewksbury was wounded along with a Stinson employee. As the Pleasant Valley War historian Don Dedera noted: "Now, the tortuous, boulder-strewn bed of Cherry Creek became the natural demarcation of feudal territory: Grahams to the west, Tewksburys to the east."

The Tewksburys took their own revenge: they contracted with a man named P. P. Daggs to run sheep on the range. This was done not for mere profit: the Tewksburys knew the action would infuriate the cattle-running Grahams and Stinson. (Cattlemen hated sheep, believing they killed grass by cropping it too closely to the ground.) By this time, it had become obvious that the grass of Pleasant Valley was not inexhaustible; in fact, it was becoming severely overgrazed.

During this time, a third force came into play. The U.S. Congress, in an effort to promote westward expansion, had offered the railroads an incentive: any railroad would be given free land for building tracks. The land would consist of alternating sections for twenty miles on either side of the tracks; thus every mile of track laid would yield 12,800 acres of free land to the railroad.

The end result of this absurd law was a vast checkerboard of alternating private and public landholdings.

When the Atlantic & Pacific Railroad extended its rail lines across the Colorado Plateau, its checkerboard landholdings extended over the Rim itself, into large tracts of unsurveyed land. The railroad barons of New York wanted to do something with this newly acquired land, and so, with the help of New York investment banks, they incorporated the Aztec Land & Cattle Company, purchased a million acres of railroad land south of the tracks (where the grass and water were more abundant), and turned immense herds of cattle loose. The initial stocking of the range filled up four hundred rail cars.

The Aztec Land & Cattle Company took as their brand a familiar chuck-wagon utensil, the hash knife:

$$\underline{\text{T}}$$

The "Hashknife Outfit" expected that the other million acres of land in the checkerboard grid would also be at their disposal, for without that land they couldn't even move their cattle from one section to the next, let alone run a livestock operation. Naturally, anyone found on either railroad land or the checkerboard lands in between was going to have to move on. These people included sheep herders, peaceful Mormon farmers, small-time ranchers, and old families of Spanish ancestry—most of whom had been living and working the land for years. The Hashknife recruited enforcers from the idle murderers, thieves, and gunslingers who had made the Rim country their home, and these men quickly went to work.

What was particularly outrageous about these actions was that land claimed by the Hashknife Outfit hadn't been surveyed; the company actually had no legal title to it.

The sheepmen in particular were affected. Traditionally they fattened their sheep in the winter along the lower grasslands of the Salt River, and then drove them to the top of the Rim for summer pasture. This brought them into Hashknife-controlled land, and the Hashknife enforcers went to work. They cruised the Rim country, beating defenseless shepherds, shooting into their cooking fires, quirting and shooting at unarmed Mormons and driving them from their lands, killing sheepdogs, and clubbing herds of sheep to death or driving them over cliffs.

And since the Tewksburys were now sheepmen, the Grahams and Stinson allied themselves with the Hashknife Outfit. Many of the Daggs-Tewksbury sheep were killed and their shepherds threatened. Then, in the winter of 1887, one of their shepherds, a Ute Indian, was murdered and decapitated. No one knew exactly who had done it—or even if the story was really true—but the flash point had been reached.

Almost immediately afterward a savage gunfight took place between the Tewksburys and the Graham-Stinson-Hashknife crowd. Two of the Graham faction were killed and several others grotesquely wounded; the scene of the shoot-out was so gruesome that a band of Apaches, painted for war, accidentally encountered the scene moments after the shooting had stopped, took one look at the carnage, and fled, crying out *chindi!* Ghosts!

A short time later a herd of saddle horses vanished from the Graham corral, and the youngest Graham boy, Billy, went to track them. Either he was ambushed or (as the Tewksburys claim) he started shooting at a member of the Tewksbury faction. Billy was struck by a large-caliber bullet, and he rode back to the Graham homestead with his intestines hanging nearly to the ground. He lived just long enough to name his killers, and then died in "indescribable" agony.

Such a killing could not go unavenged. The Grahams and several accomplices surrounded the Tewksbury homestead on Cherry Creek. Firing from hidden positions, they hit John Tewksbury in the back of the neck as he emerged to get a horse. They also struck one of his partners, a man named Jacobs, in the back. Tewksbury, the historian Don Dedera wrote, "collapsed in a rage of pain so unbearable he grabbed and tore out fistfuls of hair from his head. One of the attackers walked to where Tewksbury writhed, and shot him three more times.

Then the assailant lifted a great stone, and dashed it downward onto Tewksbury's head. The skull was crushed."

Worse was yet to come. Mary Ann Tewksbury, John's pregnant widow, went out to bury her husband's body but was driven back into the house by fire. For over a week Graham snipers hidden in the rocks along Cherry Creek peppered the ground with fire every time Mary Ann tried to bury her husband. She and her children were forced to watch as half-wild hogs, foraging along Cherry Creek, gutted and devoured the bodies. When Mary Ann begged the gunmen to let her bury her husband and Jacobs, they replied: "No, the hogs have got to eat them."

The siege was lifted only when the justice of the peace from Prescott arrived eleven days later to investigate the shootings, but by that time little was left. The Cherry Creek tributary where the remains were rolled into a hole became known as Graveyard Canyon, and the grave itself is still a kind of landmark (marked on the official U.S.G.S. maps of the area).

"No damned man," James Tewksbury declared afterward, "can kill a brother of mine and stand guard over him for the hogs to eat him, and live within a mile and a half of me."

By this time the Pleasant Valley War had become news across the country, one more example of lurid bloodletting in Arizona Territory. The killings escalated. Strangers passing through were routinely shot by one side or the other; to be a stranger was in itself to be suspicious.

Eventually a sheriff's posse from Prescott came to Pleasant Valley to arrest all the disputants. The Tewksburys wisely gave themselves up, but the posse ambushed John Graham and killed him before he even knew what was happening. Tom Graham then surrendered. The grand jury proceedings in Prescott were a complete failure; witnesses lost their memories or didn't show up, and all the men were dismissed for lack of evidence.

Meanwhile, a group of Rim country citizens had gotten together and formed what became known as the Committee of Fifty. While the exact membership in this committee has been lost to history, the evidence is strong that none other than Colonel Jesse W. Ellison founded it. The committee's goal was to rid the valley of not only the disputants, but all undesirables. This extended to all those passing through Pleasant Valley who "were unable to explain their presence satisfactorily."

Their efforts were mostly directed against the shadier members of the Graham faction. Opinion by this time had more or less swung around in favor of the Tewksburys, with the war being blamed on the Grahams and the Hashknife Outfit.

The Committee of Fifty was an efficient operation. They got to work, hanging everybody suspected of rustling or shady dealings. One Pleasant Valley old-timer recalled: "My dad told me, one time, he said he seen many men. . .hanging all up and down along Cherry Creek and all different places around that country. You would find them hanging down there for several days and the maggots were dropping out of them!"

The Committee of Fifty brought an end to the war. If innocent men were hanged (and the record shows some probably were), so be it. "Mostly in any country," Jesse Ellison was reported to have said, "there always has got to be a cleaning up process. . ."

By the end of the war, only two male members of the original feuding families had survived: Ed Tewksbury and Tom Graham. Tewksbury settled down and quietly worked his ranch on Cherry Creek. Tom Graham felt that he'd better leave Pleasant Valley, and he and his wife, Annie, moved to Tempe, just east of Phoenix, where he became a prosperous farmer.

Almost six years went by. Tom Graham became a popular and solid citizen of Tempe. Despite the urgings of many friends, he refused to wear a gun. "The war is over," he would say.

While on the surface Ed Tewksbury appeared to have let the feud die, a bitter hatred was apparently at work. Over many months, possibly even years, he devised a plan of murder.

During the evening of August 1, 1892, Ed Tewksbury made a great show of himself in Pleasant Valley, riding around on his prize horse Sockwad, buying fruit, chatting with everyone, standing a round of drinks at the saloon.

Then at midnight, he took off on Sockwad heading west, along back trails of the Rim country, galloping, loping, and trotting, pushing the horse as hard as he dared. At various secret locations he corraled or tied up his horse, threw his saddle on a fresh mount, and continued.

Somewhere along the way he met up with his great friend John Rhodes, who had married Mary Ann Tewksbury, his brother John's widow. They arrived in Tempe early. Tewksbury and Rhodes went into the Tempe Hotel at around five o'clock in the morning, where

Tewksbury swiped a drunk's morning cocktail off the bar and tossed it down.

Two hours later, in the golden light of sunrise, Rhodes and Tewksbury found Tom Graham driving a wagon. A child of ten, fishing at a bridge over a stream, would later recall:

"[Tom Graham] stopped for a minute, waved, asked if I wanted a ride to town. No thanks, I told him. He was on a high-seated wagon, grain bags as high as the back of the seat. He drove on. I heard a shot. Turned. Tom was just falling slowly back on the grain bags. . . ."

Ed Tewksbury rode up to the wagon, looked down at the supine figure, and was satisfied. He then turned his horse of the moment, a big bay gelding named Jack, and rode, hard, back the way he had come. John Rhodes went elsewhere by another route.

Tewksbury then worked his relay in reverse. He threw his saddle on another horse north of Mesa, riding it for thirty miles; switched to another at Reno Pass; yet another and another. Finally, at Bouquet's Ranch, he once again mounted Sockwad.

These were not ordinary horses, but superb mountain horses—crosses between English thoroughbreds and tough Spanish horses—from Tewksbury's ranch. He pushed each one to the limits of its endurance, and some beyond. "For decades," wrote Dedera, "engraved in the lore of the Tonto, old men and children told and retold of the pitiful sight of a splendid horse, standing spraddle-legged in Bouquet's pasture, trembling, heaving strings of saliva and blood." Nobody knows how many other horses Ed Tewksbury rode to death on his errand.

At each change of horses he also altered the appearance of his hat, bandanna, arms, or saddle rigging: things people would notice. Along the way he passed a dozen or more witnesses, making little effort to conceal his identity.

Tewksbury arrived back in Pleasant Valley by noon of August 2nd, having ridden 170 miles in 12 hours. To the ranchers of the Tonto Rim country this would not seem an impossible piece of work. But, as Dedera wrote: "If Ed ever had to stand trial, it would be before a jury of sodbusters and merchants [that is, residents of Tempe or Phoenix] who had forgotten (if they ever knew) the feeling of a real mountain cowhorse at the peak of its age and condition between your legs." No jury outside the isolated Tonto country would ever believe a man could ride from Pleasant Valley to Tempe and back, straight through Rim country, in twelve hours—relay or no relay.

. . .

Incredibly enough, Tom Graham, paralyzed by a ball through his spinal cord, lived for more than a day. He told dozens of witnesses that Ed Tewksbury and John Rhodes were the murderers. Knowing he was dying, Graham himself filed the murder charges.

Tom's death would be described very effectively by his widow at the trial. "They had a talk in regard to his leaving his family. He bade his wife farewell. They held his baby up for him to kiss. He asked his wife to hold the baby up once more. He kissed his wife and said: 'I am gone.' "

Rhodes was quickly arrested in Tempe and put on trial. The second day of the trial, Tom Graham's widow, dressed in voluminous black mourning clothes, rushed the prisoner and shoved a Colt .45 against his back and pulled the trigger. The hammer caught in her clothing and jammed against the cartridge, preventing the gun from being fired or recocked. She was quickly seized and was led from the courtroom shrieking: "Oh, my God! Let me shoot! Oh, do let me shoot! Oh, God, let me shoot! Oh, God, he killed my husband! Oh, God, let me shoot! Oh, Jesus, let me shoot! Oh, God, he killed my husband! I have no one! They ain't doing anything! Oh, somebody help me!" Her cries so aroused the citizenry that Rhodes was nearly lynched.

Annie had good reason to be worried that Rhodes would escape the noose. He had an extraordinary alibi. There were still many Tewksbury friends and Graham enemies around. One of Tempe's most upstanding, respected citizens took the stand and said that Rhodes was working on his ranch all that morning, testimony that was corroborated by his ranch hands and employees. The alibi simply could not be taken apart and Rhodes was acquitted.

As Rhodes was leaving town (under armed escort, for his safety) Tewksbury was being led in, having been arrested in Pleasant Valley.

As with Rhodes, the evidence against Tewksbury was overwhelming. Witnesses actually saw him commit the murder. Witness after witness identified him as the mysterious rider galloping back to Pleasant Valley after the morning shooting. There were problems, however, with the testimony: they swore that he was riding a big bay gelding; that he was riding a sorrel horse; that he was wearing a straw hat; that he was wearing a cowboy hat; that he was carrying two revolvers and a rifle; that he was unarmed; that he was riding a roan horse with no brands visible.

The defense made the most of these contradictions and then mustered a number of unimpeachable witnesses who testified that Tewksbury had been seen in Pleasant Valley at midnight on the 1st and at noon on the 2nd. They worked the trump card: it was, after all, a 170-mile round-trip from Pleasant Valley to Tempe! Surely even the most expert rider, on the finest horse, could not accomplish such a piece of riding.

The jury found Tewksbury guilty, but the verdict was thrown out on a technicality. At the next trial, Tewksbury's elaborate deception worked better and the jury deadlocked. Eventually the case was dismissed and Tewksbury was set free.

When we came through the war had been over for a hundred years, but the participants, either direct or indirect, left their names on the landmarks we passed: Colcord Mountain (William Colcord, member of the Committee of Fifty); Ellison Creek; Graveyard Canyon; McFadden Creek, McFadden Peak, and McFadden Horse Mountain (William McFadden, a "good-natured Irishman" and member of the Committee of Fifty who hanged an innocent man named Stott, and who, "when in his cups, whined that he never thereafter lay down his head for a night's sleep but that Jamie Stott at the end of a lariat clawed and gasped and kicked"); Aztec Peak (Aztec Land & Cattle Company); and Tewksbury Spring.

The blood went into the ground and the names went on the mountains, creeks, washes, and springs.

17

⬭ ⊠ ⬭

Steve Smith had told us to look up Tobe Haught, one of the old-timers in Young. We found Haught at his ranch, behind the barn, feeding tree trunks into a huge circular saw: timber, he explained, for his mine.

He powered down the saw and came over. He was an old man with a face crisped by the sun, iron-gray hair, and knobby hands. There was a fierce look in his face of determination, even truculence. He spoke softly and gently, but as he talked he stood a little closer to you than was comfortable, and you could feel the radiation of his intensity. He did not look like a man you would want to have as an enemy.

Tobe immediately offered us the use of a corral and invited us to bed down on the hay-covered floor of his barn.

As soon as the horses were turned loose Walter and I walked down the road to the local saloon, the Antlers, where we heard we could get a good steak. On the way we passed a mysterious house, its door wide open. It looked as though the people had merely walked out and never returned. Nothing inside had been disturbed and nothing had been stolen. A perfectly good cowboy hat, now moth-eaten and cloaked with cobwebs, was sitting on the kitchen table. Tools frozen with rust sat on a windowsill. A rotting towel was draped over a rack in the bathroom. A frying pan and pot sat on the stovetop.

The Antlers was dark and smoky, with a long bar in the front and a dining room on the left. A group of old men in cowboy hats and silver bolo ties sat at a table, playing poker around a pile of soiled greenbacks. Some of the men wore green eyeshades. One man at least was wearing a six-gun strapped around his hips. Each man had a small glass of whiskey, neat, in front of his hand. They played in silence, the only sounds the riffle and snap of cards and the creak of a chair.

The walls of the Antlers had collected odd things: an old door nailed to the wall, displaying a collection of rusted snaffle bits; a photograph of a horse at the bar with mouth open and a cowboy pouring beer down its throat; a picture of John Wayne; a 1932 California license plate; an ad for Old Gold cigarettes ("Not a Cough in a Carload"); a postcard of a Vermont covered bridge in winter; a newspaper clipping about Commodore Perry Owens, gunslinger and sheriff.

A cowboy clumped in on bow legs and sat at a table next to us and ordered a whiskey. Walter turned to him.

"Was this place ever wild?" he asked.

The cowboy shoved his hat back on his head. "You're Goddamn right it was," he said. "This ceiling's new, but before they covered it up that son-of-a-bitch was so full of bullet holes you wouldn't believe it."

"What, gunfights?" I asked.

"Naw, they'd be shooting just for the hell of it."

"When was this place built?" I asked.

The man screwed up his face. "Hell," he finally said, "been here since God created the world, I guess."

We had a huge steak dinner and I bought a bottle of Jim Beam to take with us.

The next day Tobe offered to take care of Robin's water bag himself, the nearest vet being sixty miles away. "We do our own doctoring here," he said. His son Carrel would reshoe the horses.

Walter asked what he meant by "take care of" Robin.

"Operate," he said.

He tied Robin to a snubbing post, pulled up one of her front legs, and wrapped a rope tightly around the folded leg, which prevented the horse from putting the leg down.

"With only one front leg on the ground," he explained, "she won't be able to kick."

He slid an old penknife out of his pocket, spat, and began sharpening it on a whetstone. He hummed to himself, to the rhythm of the rasping blade.

Walter looked nervously on the proceedings. "What are you planning to do, exactly?" he said.

"I'm gonna cut that old bag open. And you're gonna have to keep the cut open for as long as that thing drains. Every morning and evening, you're gonna have to work your finger into the cut, reopen it, drain the bag, squeezing from the top down. Don't let it heal up until the bag stops draining, otherwise you'll have to cut it all over again."

Walter nodded.

When the knife was good and sharp, Haught dipped it in alcohol and stood behind Robin, bracing his legs. Then with one swift, hard motion he rammed the knife deep into her hindquarters, slashed sideways, and jumped back.

A shock wave detonated through the horse. She coughed, wheezed, tried to rear up, and fell sideways, her eyes rolling in terror. At least a quart of bloody water spurted out, streaming down her leg. The "operation" had taken less than a second.

Haught nodded with satisfaction.

"If it were heavy pus," he said, "you'd have been in trouble. She's gonna be fine." His son, Carrel, then gave the horse an injection of penicillin.

Carrel started shoeing Robin and Pedernal while I got out my tape recorder and struck up a conversation with Tobe. His grandfather, Samuel A. Haught, had come to Arizona from Texas. He must have been a remarkable cowman: in 1885 he trailed 115 head of cattle from Dallas to the Tonto Basin without losing a single animal.

Tobe was exercised about the environmentalists and the Forest Service. The Forest Service had been buying private land at the edges of Young and incorporating it into the national forest, slowly shrinking the town. In addition, most of the land around Young had been turned into designated wilderness. Grazing permits had been cut back on what land was left. Most recently, environmentalists had proposed restocking the wilderness around Young with wolves and grizzly bears.

Tobe had propped his elbow on the corral fence, and pushed his hat back on his head.

"So you're writing a book?" he said. "Well I wish you'd say something about these Goddamn environmentalists."

"How so?" I asked.

"They talk about us ruining all the damn country, the natural habitat. Well hell, we ain't stopping no natural habitat. But they're wanting to make every place a wilderness area. Well that's not for the public.

That's big baloney for a bunch of them sons-of-bitches back east. I can show 'em wilderness area that'll be a *real* wilderness area from now on. Why, this whole *country's* a wilderness area. There it is." He tossed his hand toward the mountains ringing the town. All this was spoken with a quiet voice, barely audible in the wind, drowned out now and then by loud cursing from Walter and Carrel as they struggled to shoe Pedernal.

"Now they're talking about replenishing this country with grizzly bear. Then they's gonna put some damn wolves back in here. They're just like these lion that're all over the place here. Lion kill your horses, they kill your cattle, they kill your deer and your elk and threaten your kids and everything. A goddamned lion caught a kid down here on Apache Lake, tore him up, put a hundred and forty stitches in his head."

Tobe snorted and cleared his throat. "You know what I'd like? I wish one of them bastards'd get one of these environmentalist sons-of-bitches. But *hell* no. Lion won't get 'em because they're setting in some city *office* somewhere, telling you what goes on out here."

The Haught family had been one of the few who had avoided becoming embroiled in the Pleasant Valley War. At times people had tried to enlist Samuel Haught on one side or another, but he would have none of it. The Haughts owned the old Perkins store (now a house), from which lawmen had ambushed and killed John Graham and a friend, shooting them through slanted gun ports built in the walls. It was an old house of thick stone, built from rock taken from an Indian ruin several hundred yards away. The gun ports were now stuffed with rags.

I asked Haught about his mine.

"I've got fourteen claims up there."

"Any really good claims?"

"Oh they're *all* good. Hell, in '46 or '48 we shipped thirty tons of copper, and they paid us for nineteen ounces of silver. There's a hell of a lot of that ore you can just whittle."

"What do you mean, whittle?"

"It's pure metal. I got probably another six or seven sets of timber to put in and we'll go and shoot around. I believe it's about thirty-five feet or forty feet to the top of the vein."

"Is there any possibility that you might strike it rich?"

"Oh," he laughed, his brown face breaking into a mass of lines, "it's *always* a possibility. Hell, it's not so remote. I think somewhere be-

tween Canyon Creek and Salt River will be one of the biggest mines
there ever was. Right here on Diamond Butte they find nuggets, and
where they come from nobody knows. Not only that, but this fellow
found a gold boulder here by Payson. Thirty thousand dollars' worth
of gold, wire gold, kind of spun around in there through the rock. Of
course they spent the thirty thousand back in there looking for more."

"How did you get these claims?" I asked.

"It was before I was born. My dad was runnin' a wild bull, maverick.
And he jumped him up there on this creek, run him right on top of the
hill and tied him to a bush. And he saw this ledge and seen these specks
of gold. When he got home, my brother was sick, and he died when he
was young. So it wasn't until later years my dad went back and located
it.

"We used to go over there and drill, with hand steel. You'd hit it
with a sledgehammer and shoot it. And I'd generally be mucking it out
while my dad was drilling another round. Oh I'll tell you that's *hard*
work. In 1937, or '38, we built a road in to the top there, with a pick
and shovel."

"How long was the road?"

"About twelve miles. Took us a little over a year to build. I was just
a kid but I worked a hell of a lot on it. My dad hired a guy named
Penrod. They called him Pickitis because he was a lazy bastard."

"Pickitis?"

"See, he had to pick the damn dirt. He was allergic to that pick."

We all laughed.

Tobe looked up toward the mountains below the Rim. "This is a
pretty piece of country, but it's changing. Land prices gone way up,
and they're starting to build vacation homes down there." He nodded
his head. "You can't buy ranchland now and make it pay.

"Then this son-of-a-bitch, this cedar, has moved in, killing all the
grass, and when you get a hard storm it just ruts your ground. All that
through there, all on top of those ridges, used to be grass, beautiful tall
grass. Now look at it, infested with cedar. Forest Service won't let you
clear it out. For years they fought fires in this country till it was so
infested with brush and snags that the damn bees could hardly get a
drink of water.

"Now this place up here had ten thousand acres, and some God
damned idiot in the Forest Service says all you can run is fourteen or
nineteen head. Environmental *study*, he says. There was originally
eighty head and eighty head of yearlings on that land. So how're you
supposed to make a living? The miners and cowpunchers opened up

this country, built all the roads through here, killed out the grizzly bear and wolf. So then they turn it into a wilderness area, want to put those sons-of-bitches back in. Now you can't take no vehicles in there, can't cut no timber or graze or nothing. *Hell* no. To mine, you'd have to pack it out on a *jackass*. So it's a wilderness for some son-of-a-bitch from back east to go around and say, 'Oh, isn't this *beautiful*, it's a *wilderness*.' Well, what about us? What about the people who opened up this country?"

He whipped off his hat, swiped a shockingly white brow with a bandanna, and looked around to his barn, his corrals, his horses and cattle, his green irrigated fields of alfalfa and timothy grass, his stone house with the rags sticking out of the gun ports.

"If they think they're gonna take this away from me," he said softly, with fearful intensity, "then those sons-of-bitches got another think coming."

By the time we had reached Young, we had ridden off our maps, being considerably west of our plotted route. As a result, we would be riding blind for the next fifty miles. Haught suggested we follow a sheep trail from Young to the top of the Rim. It was a very old trail, opened by the Tewksburys and other sheepmen in the 1880s, and it was still used twice a year by Basque shepherds in driving their flocks to and from summer pastures on top of the Rim. Some weeks ago, Haught said, the Basque had passed through with three bands of sheep, saddle horses, and pack mules. "Only a blind fool could miss the trail," he said.

We set off early the morning of May 15th. I had accidentally left Popeye's bridle back at the old cowboy camp, so I bought a cheap curb bit and headstall from a man who ran a small tack shop out of his garage. At the edge of town the horse chomped down on the steel bit and literally snapped it in half—another demonstration of power from this supernaturally strong horse. There were no more tack stores—let alone towns—between here and Zuni.

I did not feel it wise to ride a slightly crazed horse for 250 miles without a bridle, so, at the edge of town, we flagged down a passing police car. A deputy sheriff named Bill Lee listened to our problem and returned with an old curb bit on a shaped-ear headstall. The bit had a lovely, curvilinear shape and was as brown as an old bone. It had a trace of fine silver engraving on the shanks.

"It belonged to my granddaddy," Lee said. "Take good care of it."

.   .   .

The old sheep trail was not a trail in any normal sense of the word. The sheep were simply driven pell-mell through the thick Rim forest. We had the devil of a time following the tracks made by hundreds of sheep and a half-dozen horses and mules only a month before—a trail, moreover, in use for over a century. Every time we lost the trail I could hear Haught's parting words ringing in my ears.

The actual tracks themselves had been obliterated, and our only clues were a scattering of droppings, like black peas, and clumps of grass cropped by the passing sheep. Adding to our difficulties was the fact that sheep do not trail in a line, but spread out and trail in dozens of little parallel groups. Whatever faint marks we followed would often peter out, leaving us wandering and frustrated in the endless forest. We spent some time "cutting for sign"—that is, circling at right angles to the presumed trail trying to intersect it.

The old sheep trail eventually crossed a dirt road and a broad meadow, and began climbing a hill. We lost the trail two or three times and spent over an hour hunting for it. Near the summit Robin's pack, which had been poorly balanced, turned upside down and had to be cut off. While Walter spliced the rope and repacked I scouted ahead on foot.

At the top of the hill I had a view looking north, across a grassland dotted with cedars. About two miles ahead rose a thousand-foot hump of rock, called Naeglin Rim, covered with a prickly mantle of spruce. Although I knew the sheep trail must go over it, I was damned if I could see how.

I considered our situation. We had no map, and if we missed the trail we would be lost in one of the largest uninhabited areas of the lower forty-eight states. Even if we kept to the trail we hadn't the foggiest notion of where water might be found. Our horses, despite good feed and a day's rest, were still showing their backbones and ribs. It was now late afternoon and the Mogollon Rim was two days ahead. I remembered the words of Walter's friend who knew the Rim country, and who had predicted we just might kill ourselves in it. Continuing along that almost nonexistent sheep trail seemed foolhardy in the extreme.

I retraced my steps and found Walter finishing up his packing job. I told him that, in my opinion, we should forget the sheep trail and follow the dirt road over the Rim.

Walter was disgusted at what he considered rank cowardice, but I was insistent. We backtracked to the dirt road and began following it.

As the sun set the temperature plunged. The grass disappeared and we could find no trace of water. The road eventually circled west of

Naeglin Rim and dropped down into a small ravine. Although the ravine was dry, enough fresh grass was growing in the bottom to encourage us that there might be a water source somewhere farther up. Sure enough, a quarter mile up the wash we discovered a few puddles of fetid water, which the horses promptly sucked dry. Walter tied up his horses in a patch of clover while I hobbled Banjo and Popeye and pitched the tent on the only level spot in the entire ravine, a nice sandy flat in the creek bed.

It had grown very cold. We chunked a pot of lentils and rice on a roaring fire and broke out the bottle of Jim Beam.

I took a long pull on the bottle and handed it to Walter. It had been a month since we had had a drink. (In Arizona, beer is not counted as drink.) We passed it back and forth in silence. The amber liquid, sloshing about in the bottle, refracted the light of the fire in a most pleasing way. The whiskey was cold and raw in the mouth, but it burned nicely as it went down. The juniper wood crackled and smoked and smelled like a cigar box.

"So," I said after a while. "Are you glad you came on this trip?"

The wind breathed softly through the spruce canopy above our heads.

"Shit, Doug, I really don't know," Walter finally said. The firelight played on his dirty face. He was silent and then gave a short laugh.

"I been thinking a lot about that," he continued. "At my age, sometimes I wonder just what the hell I'm doing with my life. I mean, I'm forty-seven years old, I'm flat broke, my girlfriend's about to dump me, and instead of earning a living I'm sitting in a Goddamn canyon in the middle of fucking nowhere drinking whiskey. It just ain't responsible behavior."

"You're talking like an old man," I said.

"Goddamn, Doug, you forget that I *am* a lot older than you are." His mouth was temporarily stoppered by the bottle, his voice muffled. He wiped his beard and exhaled noisily.

"It's real strange when you start getting old. You start thinking about your life and who you are. You don't ever want to grow old. You *always* want to be young. To have that feeling of power and drive, I mean of *sexual* power. You'll know what I'm talking about soon enough."

"At least you're not moving pieces of paper from one side of a desk to another," I said.

Walter laughed and slapped the bottle down in the sand. As his beard filled out and his sideburns grew, his face had become almost Talmudic.

"You know what?" he said. "You and me are *different* from other people. That's our problem. But our view of life is very close, and this is why we've been able to relate to each other. Look around, look at all the people sitting behind desks, houses in the suburbs, all that shit. We chose something different. And here we are."

"Why didn't you turn out like them?" I asked.

"I *was* like them, once. I got married when I was twenty-one. Back then that's what you did. We were starting a traditional way of life."

"So what happened?" I asked. "How long were you married?"

There was a sudden, profound silence. "Eleven months," he finally said.

"That was pretty short," I said with a laugh.

"Drunk ran into her and killed her when she was seven months pregnant," Walter said.

I could not find words to respond to that. A piece of juniper popped in the fire.

"My adopted cousin," Walter said, "was in the car with her. Truck pulled in off the highway going into a beer joint, hit her broadside. My cousin was thrown forward, got brain damage. She was seven months pregnant. She wanted to go down to Possum Kingdom Lake, wanted me to go with her. I was working, going to school, building houses at the same time. I told her I couldn't go. We had a 1957 yellow Mustang. So she took Johnny. I remember telling her goodbye and I remember feeling I wasn't ever going to see her again."

He stopped and moved closer to the fire, rubbing some warmth into his shoulders.

"Several hours later Dad came out and told me that Jan was in an accident. We had to drive to Graham and we drove up to the back of the hospital. I jumped out, just ran in. Started running down the hall. There was this emergency room door and I jumped in and there was my cousin on one table, with blood all over the place, all over the floor. And I wanted to know where she was and the doctors wouldn't tell me. I told them, 'Well, if you don't tell me I'm going in every room in the hospital.' I started going through all the emergency rooms. And I banged into this one room where this man was on a table, broken leg, broken bone sticking out. This was the driver that ran into her.

"And then I kept going down the halls and finally someone stopped me and told me that she was dead. And I said 'Take me to her.' He said

'I can't do that.' And I said 'If you don't, this hospital's gonna be torn to pieces.' And he did, he took me in there."

He paused, then continued.

"There was a body on the bed. Had a white sheet over it. I pulled the sheet back and there she was. I went running out of the hospital. Crawled through a barbed-wire fence, started running out into the mesquite pastures. And I stopped by an anthill. An ant bed. And sat there, squatted down, and watched these ants, talked with these ants for a long time. Finally went back. Sat down beside her. Strange sensation. And the body has reflex actions after death and it was like, you know, like she was *moving*. The body was *moving*."

He stopped again.

"But I stayed in there with her. By that time all the rest of the family came down, her family came down, but I stayed in there with her, was the only one to see her.

"They put her into a mummy bag, put her in a hearse. Took her back to Wichita Falls. I rode back with them. Rode in the front seat, I had these sensations at that time of just jumping out of the car. I had no desire at all to live."

He took a deep breath and issued a short laugh, the sound dying suddenly in the trees.

"From that point, it was a strange life and existence. I was really in a trance, didn't eat anything for a long period of time. I never accepted her death. At the funeral service I knelt on one knee. Never moved. *Feeling* this pain. I went up and kissed her when she was dead, and I went to the burial and I buried her. *I* buried her. I shoveled all the dirt. That's the time I seriously started drinking."

I still could not think of anything to say, except, "Did you stay in Texas?"

"For about three months. Then I took a Brittany spaniel and a German shepherd and a Westphalia Volkswagen camper, and I went to California. I ended up moving everything I had from Wichita Falls to Del Mar. I lived in Del Mar, overlooking the ocean. Bought a motorcycle. Did a lot of cruising on the motorcycle, just traveled around the country. Pretty disorientated. Came back, went to Houston, met Vincent's mother, got married. That was too quick at that time, but that's the way reality in life happens. And I got a wonderful son, Vincent, from it. But it was just too quick in happening and our relationship never worked out to understanding."

He stopped talking for a moment, staring into the ashen fire. He shook a piece of cedar out of the pile and pushed it into the coals. It flickered up, widening the circle of light.

"I realized something, when I was going through this stage. One day I looked in the paper. This was during Vietnam, and there was a photograph of a mother and her dead child. I *realized* at that point I wasn't the only hurt person in the world."

He stopped and looked at me. "I'll tell you, Doug, this is a *hard* thing for us to realize, being creative people. You and me. Because we live in a very small microcosm. We create our own microcosm. We *create* the thing which is traveling around in our head and our body. To ourselves, we are the greatest, most unbelievable person. To *us*. But actually we're just one thing in billions of trillions of other little things out there. That's what we really are. You *have* to realize that, and when you realize that, your creative work will start having a lot more validity. That's a step beyond in your awareness. It's like taking your first drug to try to *feel* your creativity. When you start realizing that you're just one person among billions, the work that you do start producing, it can end up being *unbelievable*. It can actually deal with the unknown."

I could still say nothing. What was there to say? In rereading this tape transcription as I write now, I believe what Walter said was one of the most profound things I have ever heard about art, life, and the connection between the two.

The bottle was empty. I crawled into my tent while Walter pitched his bedroll outside, and for a long time I listened to the horses chuffing and cropping clover, while the flickering firelight danced on the tent roof.

Some time later I awoke, hearing a few raindrops splattering on the tent. I got up and put the rainfly over the tent. While I was tromping around, Walter, who was half asleep, thought I was a horse and started hollering: "Whoa Robin! Easy girl. *Easy* there, Robin!"

I woke him up and suggested he come inside the tent.

"It's just a few drops," he said. "I'll stay out here."

I crawled back inside, and the few drops turned into many. I heard Walter at the door. "I think I'll take you up on your offer," he said, crawling inside.

I awoke a little later. The rain was now pounding the roof of the tent like a thousand maniacal elves beating tom-toms. Then I heard an extremely ominous sound: the gurgle of water. I shook Walter awake. "You hear that?" I asked.

"It's nothing," he said thickly and rolled over.

I lay awake. The gurgle became a splashing and then a thrumming.

I shined my flashlight outside. Within the faint circle of light I could see nothing but rushing water.

"Walter!" I cried.

He bolted upright and shouted, "*Whoa you son-of-a-bitch!*"

"Wake up you fool," I said, "we're flooded."

The water was actually flowing under the tent, buoying up the nylon floor. Walter pressed his hand into it.

"Oh my God," he said, "we're floating away. Damn, Doug, why'd you pitch the tent here?"

I went outside with my flashlight to search for a fresh campsite. The rain was lashing down violently and the dry ravine was quickly turning into a roaring stream. It was bitterly cold, and I could feel chill water running in rivulets down my back and chest.

There was no place to pitch a tent, save the ex–clover patch where we'd tied up the two horses. The horses had eaten the clover down to nothing, dropped quite a bit of manure, and churned the whole thing into deep, foul mud.

"We've got to move the horses," I said.

Walter crawled out of his bag and joined me in the rain. We thrashed about, half drunk, half hung over. I caught Popeye, whose hobbles had become soaked, and the immense force of the horse's pulling had tightened the knots until they were as hard as croquet balls. In a fury I sliced the hobbles off with my knife, ruining a good lead rope in the process. Banjo was missing.

We tied the three horses a little farther down the ravine. Then we unstaked our tent and dragged it over to the new spot. When we crawled back inside, I could feel the mud and manure squishing under my hands and knees.

When we awoke late next morning the rain had stopped. The sky was piled with swift-moving clouds that boiled and whirled over our heads. It couldn't have been a few degrees above freezing. Banjo was still gone.

Complaining loudly, with a throbbing headache from the Jim Beam, I dragged on my icy, saturated clothing and went looking for him. I cut for sign and intersected his trail going up a steep slope out of the ravine. Banjo had not been belled; finding him in this forest would require close tracking.

The rain had turned the forest floor to mud and made the trail relatively easy to follow. I kept climbing for fifteen or twenty minutes, and the clouds began to break. At the top of the hill I came out into a clearing. The clouds tumbled along only a few hundred feet above my head. They parted and a shaft of sunlight glittered through.

There, ten miles away, rose a thousand-foot wall of rock, the Mogollon Rim itself: a sinuous escarpment dusted with fresh snow. Shreds of mist clung to the Rim's face, rotating slowly in the sunlight. God, I thought, there it is at last: that great landmark of our journey, the halfway point, the thing that was supposedly going to kill us and our horses. It was beautiful.

And there was Banjo, on the other side of the clearing, steaming and miserable.

We continued along the dirt road, climbing steeply, winding back and forth, up one mountainside after another. As we climbed our feelings began to soar.

We paused at a point of granite thrusting out of the trees, and found ourselves looking south over mountains that appeared to have no end, layer after layer, dissolving into a gray-blue indistinctness, merging with the sky. It was a well-muscled landscape, an orogenic flex in the earth's crust. The Mogollon Rim country is the backbone of Arizona, controlling most of Arizona's weather, accepting most of its rainfall, and determining much of its settlement patterns from prehistoric times to the present. It is an immense geological formation with a half-billion-year history; compared to the Rim, the Grand Canyon is a mere notch in the ground.

We ate lunch at the overlook, watching dark clouds roll in across the great sea of mountains. It began to rain. The rain turned the mountains blue, and then gray, and then they faded away in the mists.

"It's hard to believe we rode through that country," Walter said, unhooking his canteen from the saddlehorn. "Remember those people back in Santa Fe who said we were gonna die up here in Rim country?"

"Yeah. There are always people telling you that something can't be done."

Walter took a swig from his canteen and raised it to the clouds. *"Fuck you!"* he cried out. His voice tumbled off into gray space, with no answering echo. The rain misted down, covering everything like a cold blanket.

Our horses' hooves became balled with mud. The rain penetrated our riding gloves, ran into our boots, collected in our saddles, and crept between our legs. It became intolerable; we stopped to camp at two o'clock.

We camped underneath the oldest, deadest alligator juniper in Arizona. There was no fresh water or grass anywhere and the slope was pitched a good 20 degrees from the horizontal, but we had reached a state where we no longer cared. The horses drank from a mudhole and I crawled into my bedroll at three and was asleep by six.

My night was filled with restless dreams. Twice I woke up thinking I heard the sound of thundering hooves; each time I shook Walter awake, hollering that the horses were loose and running away. But each time the horses were standing, hunkered down and miserable, in the rain.

Then I dreamed I was back in Wellesley, the town where I grew up. I found myself wandering about the backyard of the house of my best friend, Chip. Everything was different. Most of Chip's modest, brick house had been torn down and a vulgar mansion erected in its place. I knocked on the door and a woman answered, demanding to know, in a crisp Brahmin accent, exactly what it was I wanted. She didn't know Chip or his family. I tried to explain that he had once lived there, but she shook her head. She had never heard of my street or my family. She disappeared and came back with an ancient, tattered directory of the town, but neither Chip's family nor mine was listed. It was as if we'd never existed. She thought I was lying and slammed the door in my face.

I wandered around the town, lost. Everything I knew was gone. All the old maple trees had been cut down. Futuristic mansions, encrusted with copper gables and chrome windows, had replaced the wood or brick houses. Shiny cars with fins roared at high speeds down the roads, now widened and straightened. There was the smell of steel and internal combustion in the air. I caught sight of one of the drivers, a man in a houndstooth jacket grinning diabolically as he peered over the wheel.

I was overwhelmed with loneliness and stood at a street corner, weeping into my hands. What had happened to my town, my country?

By morning the rain had ceased and we continued along the muddy road. The woods were piney and sweet, filled with blooming wildflowers and the thick smell of wet moss. The sound of dripping water was loud in the green life of the forest. It was impossible to imagine we were still in Arizona. The clouds began to lift and we came to a rich meadow, where we stopped to let the horses graze. They attacked the grass with loud cropping sounds and grunts of satisfaction, and in several hours had mowed down a good quarter acre.

The muddy road wound upward along the steep slopes of the Rim, following ravines and draws through the granite face. Just underneath the Rim the trees parted and we were shocked to find ourselves in a brand-new development. A short man with a bald head came tearing out of the first house and stood in the road, blocking our way.

"This is private property," he said belligerently.

I explained that we were retracing Coronado's route and would just be passing through.

"Well, Coronado didn't come through here," the man said. "We built this road ourselves with a dozer when we opened this old ranch for development. Now you just turn your horses around and get out."

I tried to explain who Coronado was and what we were doing.

The man was adamant. Coronado couldn't have come this way. This wasn't no Forest Service road. This was an exclusive development. And even when this was the old 33 Ranch, he added triumphantly, Coronado wouldn't have been allowed through: they didn't stand trespassers either. So whoever told me Coronado came this way was either mistaken or a liar. He concluded this unassailable argument with a vigorous nod.

Temporarily rendered speechless by this remarkable man and his logic, I went to confer with Walter, who was tending the horses.

"You ain't talking to him right," Walter said. "Look, you got him all worked up."

Walter went over. "Howdy!" he cried out, seizing the man's limp hand and vigorously shaking it. "Name's Walter Nelson."

The man grunted.

"Now we've got a little problem," Walter said, "and maybe you can help us. We're trying to get over the Rim."

The man looked disgusted. "This road don't even *go* over the Rim," he said. "You're lost, Nelson."

We backtracked and found the right road. We passed a turkey hunter, all gussied up in a pressed camouflage jumpsuit, who said he was "checking out the scene" before hunting season began. Then we passed some loggers skidding trees down to the road. The great slope of the Rim plunged down through massive stands of timber, and then, suddenly, we found ourselves on top. The Colcord Mountain Lookout firetower rose up in front of us. We had made it.

We climbed the tower. The observation deck surrounded a glassed-in booth, in which a very fat woman in a Forest Service uniform was doing needlepoint. Walter, always the friendly one, tapped on the window and hollered out a greeting. The woman did not even look up.

"Must be hard of hearing," he said and hammered again.

The woman glanced up momentarily, giving us a look that, in one instant, communicated that she had indeed heard us, that she found us a gross imposition, and that she would have nothing whatsoever to do with us.

Walter was furious.

"Now there's a sick woman, a very sick woman," he muttered. "No wonder she's holed up all by herself in this firetower."

He looked out over the mountains we had come through.

"So this is supposed to be the place where we would kill ourselves. Ridiculous. We were riding roads practically the whole Goddamn way. Some challenge." He stomped down the stairs.

Once on top of the Rim the land became almost perfectly flat, carpeted with long grass and towering ponderosa pines. Here and there were natural water pans, now dried up and blanketed with timothy and clover.

I immediately recalled Coronado's description of coming off the Rim:

"The way is very bad for at least thirty leagues [ninety-three miles] and more, through impassable mountains. But when we had traversed these thirty leagues, we found cool rivers, and grass like that of Castile . . .[and] many nut and mulberry trees."

These "rivers" were the gentle streams that flow northward off the Rim into the Little Colorado River.

By the time Coronado topped the Rim, he and his men were *in extremis*. Just beyond the Rim disaster struck. "The horses were so exhausted" in coming through the Rim country, Coronado wrote, "that they could not stand it, so that in this last *despoblado* we lost more horses than before; and several Indian allies and a Spaniard named Espinosa, who died from eating some herbs because they were out of food."

The men were buried with a quick ceremony in shallow graves and the expedition hurried on.

We heard the roar of traffic and came out on a highway, the main road from Payson to Heber. For about five miles we rode parallel to the road.

Suddenly we came across a beautiful woman with long blond hair sitting on a log.

"Hi," she said, as if she'd been expecting us, and smiled a radiant smile.

Walter and I were speechless. If we had encountered Margaret Thatcher barbecuing a pig we wouldn't have been more surprised.

"Where are you coming from?" she asked.

"Why," Walter said, recovering his composure, "we've ridden from Mexico. And I have to say, that the sight of you is the most welcome vision of beauty we've seen in four hundred miles of riding." He took off his hat reverently.

"Thanks," she said, and stood up, brushing herself off and extending her hand.

I practically tumbled off my horse to shake it.

"And," Walter continued, "if I may ask, what are you doing here, in the forest, by yourself?" His voice dripped with charm. I had never heard him talk like this before.

"I own the place," she said, nodding toward some cabins just visible through the trees. "Forest Lakes Touring Center and Cabins."

"Cabins?" Walter said.

"Yes, cabins. You need a place to stay?"

Her name was Brenda Grier. With his usual charm Walter managed to strike a deal for one of the cabins, and we unpacked our gear and took showers.

Later Brenda came by and demanded our dirty clothes.

"Oh no," I said. "You're not going to wash these clothes. I'll wash them myself."

"Don't be ridiculous," she said. "I used to work on a fire crew. After ten days fighting a fire, I know what dirty clothes look like. Your clothes are not dirty. Now let me have them."

I turned them over.

She pointed at me. "Now all I ask is that you put this in your book, that I washed your clothes," and she laughed a lovely laugh and went tripping into her house, blond hair floating behind her. My heart ached.

After making inquiries, we figured out we were about twenty-five miles west of our plotted route. To get back we would have to ride down a main highway. It would be a long, boring, and unnecessary ride. We decided to trailer it.

We spent part of the next day splitting wood to pay for our cabin and looking for a trailer to hire. We also heard more ominous news about the ongoing drought. North and east some of the great Indian horse herds were dying of starvation, as the grass had disappeared from lack of rain; as an emergency measure some horses were actually being shot.

Many ranches were rounding up their livestock and trucking them to Colorado. The drought was particularly bad east of Zuni, and we would be riding right into the heart of it. This was a severe drought in what was, in a normal season, already one of the harshest deserts in the Southwest.

While chopping wood, Walter and I talked about this and other problems; which is to say, we did a lot of arguing, shouting, cursing, and shoving each other. I had long ago concluded that Walter was right about the length of time the trip was going to take. After four and a half weeks of riding we had barely reached the halfway point, so we could expect spending another four or five weeks riding to Pecos. Even getting to Zuni Pueblo would require crossing nearly one hundred miles of harsh desert in the throes of drought.

Walter, for all his bravery, was frightened by the possibility that we might not find water. While this was a sensible fear, he wanted me to rent a plane to scout out the route; I thought that too expensive; Walter figured his life was worth more than the few hundred bucks a plane would cost; I doubted it was; Walter offered to break my nose; and the discussion proceeded apace. When we cooled off we concluded there was nothing we could do about it: either we would find water or we wouldn't. If we didn't, so be it. We would deal with that situation when it happened.

We did arrive at one firm conclusion: we would temporarily break the journey at Zuni Pueblo—the Spaniards' Cíbola, the Seven Cities of Gold. There were two excellent reasons for this. First, the Spaniards themselves had broken their trip at Zuni, not resuming their expedition until late August. By delaying until August, we would continue to travel at approximately the same time of the year as Coronado.

Second, the summer rains would begin in early July, and by August the grass and water would be somewhat replenished. Walter agreed that maybe, by going in August, provided there had been good rains, we wouldn't need to scout the route by plane.

We would, therefore, end the first part of our journey when we reached Zuni Pueblo, and resume it on August 1st.

18

The next day our hired trailer drove us to a place called White Mountain Lake. Our map, dated 1970, showed the area as vacant land, but when we arrived we found a sad little resort development around a cloudy lake.

For the first time since Winkelman, nearly three weeks ago, we found ourselves out of the mountains and on relatively flat land. As we rode northward, we rode out of the ponderosa pines and into a dry country of piñons and junipers. The rain that had fallen on us back at the Rim had not extended out here. The horses' hooves sank into the powdery dust. Volcanic rocks lay on the ground like black bones, the wind scooping the dust out from under them.

We knew the country would only get drier as we approached Zuni. In a few days we would be out of the trees entirely and into the white, featureless topography shown on our maps. What it would look like in reality we did not know.

Now that the mountains were behind us, there was no longer a need to follow trails. We merely took a compass bearing and rode off into nowhere.

It was a strange, rolling, monotonous country. At one point we rode across a tight grid of dirt roads, posted with "Real Estate for Sale" signs and lot numbers. The signs were riddled with bullet holes and the roads had grown up with snakeweed. Whatever development this was, it had clearly gone bust. We dropped into a broad piñon-covered valley and passed another pathetic development, mostly trailers and prefabricated houses surrounded by barbed wire as tight as catgut. We ascended a great volcanic mesa and camped at a pool of scrofulous-looking water in a large grassy basin on the far end. A herd of cows watched us approach and shuffled off.

We were too lazy to haul firewood from the distant trees, so we burned cow chips instead. They were as light and stiff as balsa wood, and they burned merrily and gave off sweet smoke, like burning grass or Irish turf.

When I unsaddled Popeye I noted, with great relief, that his sore was beginning to heal. I had cut a hole in the saddle pad, and that combined with the special folding of the saddle blanket was working. We wouldn't have to change horses after all.

As I was cooking dinner, I heard a furious ringing of the cowbell. I looked up to see Popeye, at a hobbled gallop, charge right over Walter.

I was sure that Walter had been killed. But he quickly stood up, slapping off dust and cursing loudly.

"What happened?" I asked.

"That old cow poked his head up over the dike," he said, "and the horse spooked." He mopped his brow with a bandanna. He said later he could feel the whiffle of wind from the horse's flying hooves pass his ear.

The cow was still peering over the dirt catchment dike, chewing its cud, with an expression of profound philosophical detachment on its face.

Walter poured a cup of coffee from the pot, took a gulp, and spat out some grounds. "*Damn*, I'm glad I'm not riding that horse," he said. "Someday he's gonna kill somebody."

On that reassuring note we began our dinner.

Finding water was constantly on our minds and in our conversation, and as our water dwindled our fear increased. If we ran out of water, we didn't even know in which direction to flee: many of our maps showed no human habitation whatsoever.

As we traveled, we periodically searched the horizon with our binoculars, looking for windmills or clumps of brush. The following day we spent mostly in a panic, looking for water; in late afternoon we finally did see a distant patch of brush. Brush in this treeless desert meant water, and there we did find our water: a small stock pond. A black man, his wife, and two kids were sitting in aluminum chairs in the shade of a lone salt cedar, fishing. Their pickup truck was parked nearby. The road they had come in on was little more than two tire marks winding off toward the horizon.

As we approached, the man handed his rod to his son and stood up, pushing back the brim of a battered fedora.

"What are you doing out here, in the middle of nowhere?" Walter called out.

"Oh, just wasting a little time," the man said.

We dismounted and shook hands all around. The two kids crowded around our horses, patting and stroking their necks.

"Does he bite?" the boy asked.

"He took a man's arm off once," Walter said.

They hastily backed up.

"Naw," said Walter. "They're friendly as puppy dogs."

"Get away from them horses," the mother bellowed from her spot in the shade.

We watered the horses and talked. The man's name was Bill Davis.

"What kind of fish you get in here?" Walter asked.

"Catfish," he said.

The boy ran over with a Tupperware tub containing two fish, each about the size of a Parker pen, and proudly displayed them.

Bill Davis had come to Arizona when he was seven years old, he told us. It was during the war, 1942. His daddy came here to pick cotton and they decided to stay. He lived in Snowflake, Arizona. Snowflake was originally settled by two Mormons, one named Snow and the other Flake.

"Have you seen any changes in this country?" I asked.

He shook his head slowly, back and forth.

"Nothing's the same," he said. "These days all people think about is money. Now take this old ranch. See that dozer over there?"

He pointed off toward the horizon. To our surprise we saw a distant puff of diesel smoke drift upward and could hear a throbbing at the edge of audibility. A yellow spot crawled up a rise, like a carrion beetle.

"Fellow who owns this ranch is dividing it up. Forty-acre parcels, going to sell 'em off."

"Who would buy forty acres of this?" Walter asked, with a short laugh.

Davis shook his head again. "There's people'll buy anything these days. Or at least, there's people who *think* people'll buy anything these days." A rumble developed in his interior which shortly erupted as a chuckle.

"Probably going to call it a retirement resort," I said.

"People so anxious," Bill said, "they gotta build a hell for themselves right here, even before they die. They's making money 'cross this whole area. Now back in Snowflake. My brother and me put in a well, cost two thousand dollars. Then the town decide they going to expand, spend a lot of money laying out water pipe. They condemn our well, make us buy water from the water company. Ec-o-no-mic development, they call it."

"That's crazy," I said.

He leaned toward me, lowered his voice, and touched my shoulder with his finger. "They ain't crazy. They's making *money.*" He rumbled again.

Walter asked if he knew where we might find some better drinking water than what was offered by the tank.

"Well *now,*" Davis said, "I got a twelve-gallon tank of water in my truck."

The water was inside the camper shell on his pickup, a big orange jug with a spigot. We filled up.

The wife called out: "He been telling me ten years he gonna save somebody's life with that old water jug. Cost twenty dollars."

"Only a damn fool goes into the desert out here without water," he said to his wife.

She flapped her straw hat at him.

We tied the canteens on our packs, thanked him profusely, and remounted.

"Hope you catch that ten-pound catfish lying down there at the bottom," Walter said.

Davis laughed.

We rode toward the sound of the bulldozer, crossed a deep arroyo, and climbed a rise. By the time we arrived the machine had been turned off, the men gone for the day. It still smelled of hot crankcase oil. A grid of roads had been freshly bulldozed into the desert floor, laying open the red earth underneath, like the skinning of an animal.

At the top of the rise we had a long view looking northeast. In the near distance were a series of low hills, covered with a peppering of junipers. Beyond that was an immense, treeless plain. At the western end of this plain, according to our maps, was the junction of the Little

Colorado and Zuni rivers, another great landmark on our trip. This is the place where the Zuni Indians believe the spirit of their dead live. On the eastern side of the plain we could just barely see the Stinking Springs Mountains, two low mountains also sacred to the Zuni.

We were finally closing in on the Seven Cities of Gold.

I spread out my maps and found a symbol on the map marked "tank" about seven miles distant. If this meant water, we figured it might be a nice place to camp. Finding Bill Davis and his jug had been freakish luck. Our paranoia about water had not lessened.

I took another bearing with my compass and we rode up and down some rolling hills, through little outcroppings of rocks, and laid down a rotten old fence. We finally found the "tank"; all that was left of it were a few planks of wood lying on the ground. I kicked one and it burst in a cloud of dust.

"What's the damn date on your map?" Walter asked. "Eighteen-ninety?"

It was six or seven o'clock and we did not have much daylight left to find water. The day, May 20th, was my thirty-third birthday, and we wanted to camp soon to celebrate.

We rode to the edge of the hills and looked down on a broad draw with several dry water pans covered with cracked silt. The wind whirled across them, raising curtains of white dust. Through the binoculars I could see a herd of cows bedding down alongside a thicket of salt cedars about half a mile away.

"Where there're cows, there's water," I said, handing Walter the binoculars.

"You go down to where the cows are," Walter said, peering out. "I'm going to check out that corral." He pointed to a black dot several miles off.

I loped across the pan and pushed into the brush. In the middle was a creek bed that didn't look as if it had flowed in ten years.

I caught up with Walter at the corrals. They were in ruins and there was no water there either.

Walter panned the binoculars across the horizon.

"I see something," he said. "An electric pole."

"No way," I said. "Not out here."

We rode toward it. It was indeed an electric pole with wires, the last in a row leading from the northeast. A small cabin stood at its base. I heard a humming noise and then Walter, who was ahead, shouted "Water! Tons of it!"

I came around the cabin. An enormous electric motor was pumping at least a thousand gallons a minute of water into an immense irrigation ditch, a surreal eruption in the midst of desert. It was flowing off toward a vast, newly plowed field. I dipped my hand into the gusher. Aside from a faint taste of oil the water was excellent. The wind howled.

I explored the ruined cabin. It was a lonely, forlorn place. It had slumped on its foundation and was heading for imminent collapse. A dead tree, the only one within miles, stood next to the ruin, stripped of its bark by scouring winds. A kid's ladder ran up into its branches. Inside the cabin was a mattress with a packrat nest built inside, a rounded 1960s-vintage Frigidaire, a shard of mirror carefully tacked to the wall, a warped schoolbook, and *The Yearbook of Agriculture 1966*. The interior smelled of rat urine and dry rot.

Scrawled in chalk on the doors and walls were a series of messages. The words were barely legible, having been abraded by wind and time.

> Got lay off 6/28/66 Tue a.m.
> Time 12:35

And then, in a childish hand,

> Willis the Great
> Keep Yard Clean

On the back door was another message, barely legible:

> Sandy
> Skinney
> Willis
> Van

> Sorry We had to Leave You

I wondered where this little family had gone. Once gone, the tree where the two kids played (Willis and Van?) had died; there was nobody left who cared. What had they done, just loaded up the pickup and left?

A rather sudden, disturbing image came into my mind, of the man and woman making love on the mattress in the blackness of the night, conceiving their first child, with the desert wind buffeting the batten-board. And then: buying the ladder for the tree, the kids laughing in the branches, the father mad about the yard, the broken mirror tacked back to the wall, the nights of shaking wind with whispers and arms encircling a heaving back, Sorry We had to Leave You.

We celebrated my birthday with a special dinner we had been hoarding for some time: instant corned-beef hash and scalloped potatoes. Walter gave me a small pin that said "Arizona" with a picture of a saguaro cactus, a sunset, and a red butte.

A full moon rose as the sun set, turning the cabin a ghostly blue.

We rose when it was still dark. The full moon was setting in the west, a dollop of buttery light, while a dusky violet color crept around the horizon. The wind had stopped and the stillness had a cathedral intensity. The bowl of the sky was as deep as a thousand feet of water.

We cooked a pot of oatmeal and broke camp. As we brought around the horses to be packed, the sun erupted over the horizon, its hydrogen plasma boiling, throwing radiant heat into our faces. The heat started the engine of the wind, and the first puffs stirred the horses' manes. It was going to be another ferocious day.

Several miles down the draw, a herd of range horses came galloping up and tore past us, circling at a full run. Pedernal, who was packed, got so excited that he yanked the lead rope out of Walter's hand and ran off with the horses. They galloped away and disappeared over a hill.

"There goes my eight-thousand-dollar Deardorff," Walter said to the departing cloud of dust.

Just then the herd came back around, with Ped flying along with them. Walter galloped off and managed to run him down and peel him away from the rest of the herd.

We rode past the old mail stage stop between St. Johns and Holbrook, now four eroding stone and mud walls. Beyond the ruin we happened on a herd of cows, and as we rode up a rancher came bouncing along in a pickup truck with his ten-year-old son. He chucked some bales of alfalfa to the herd, which lumbered over and began stomping, butting, and chomping in a cow feeding frenzy. The rancher waded among the herd with his lariat and tried to rope several calves, but they wouldn't let him get close enough to throw the loop.

He hailed us and we rode over.

"Say," Walter asked, "can we buy a bale of that alfalfa off you?"

"I got a better idea," he said. "I need to push this herd to a set of corrals across this pasture, so I can brand these calves. If you fellows drive this herd for me I'll give you a bale for free. You know how to drive cows, don'tcha?"

"No problem," Walter sang out. I was about to protest but Walter caught my eye, giving me his shut-up look.

"I'll meet you over there," he said, and gave us directions on how to go.

I turned to Walter. "For chrissakes," I said, "we don't know how to drive cattle."

"There's nothing to it," Walter said.

"Yes, but have you actually done it before?" I asked.

"I know how it's done."

"I don't think it would be too cool if we stampeded this guy's cows."

"Relax," Walter said. "Don't make any loud noises or quick movements with your horse. Walk, don't trot. Keep them calm."

We waited until the cows and our horses had finished their lunch, and then we split up and moved toward them, with Walter saying, in a low voice, "Hoooo cow. Hoooo cow."

The herd turned and started lumbering away in the wrong direction.

"Shit!" I called out. "Now what?"

"Don't tail them," Walter said. "Circle round to the side and push them back this way."

I did as I was told and the herd shuffled back in the right direction.

"Don't follow directly behind," Walter called out. "Ride on the right side, I'll take the left. Slow and easy, stretch 'em out into a line. Get them following each other."

To my astonishment it worked. Once in a while a cow and calf would try to peel off, but one of us would circle outward and bring them back in.

"Think if all your fancy New York City friends could see you now," Walter said. "Why, they wouldn't even recognize the dirty-ass cowboy you become."

Several hours later we reached the corrals. Walter knew exactly how to manueuver the cows through the gate.

"You fellows look like pros," the rancher said. His name was Larry Heap, owner of the HT Ranch.

The herd was milling about in the large corral, lowing anxiously. Heap cut out the first calf he wanted to brand and drove it (along with its mother) into a smaller corral. Then his little boy roped the calf, wrestled it to the ground, and tied up three legs while the calf bawled bloody murder. The mother nudged her calf with her muzzle, looking as upset as a cow can look.

Heap had laid the branding irons into a small depression dug into the ground. A propane torch roared into the pit, heating the irons red. Larry gave the calf a shot, tied off its testicles, and then branded it with the HT brand: five impresses with a hot bar.

$$\mathsf{H}_{\mathsf{T}}$$

The blue, acrid smoke was whisked away by the wind. He repeated the process on three calves, taking only about ten minutes to finish the job. As soon as the calves were released they stopped bawling and went off with their mothers to rejoin the herd.

"So you don't cut the balls off," Walter said.

"I put a tight rubber band around 'em," said Larry, "and they just drop off on their own." He grinned and leaned toward us. "You know what we call that? Changing their minds from ass to grass."

We asked him to examine Robin's water bag, which Walter had been diligently draining every morning and evening. The walking during the day kept it open, and a crusty fluid had dried all the way down her leg. She was also thin and undernourished, and the combination gave her a pretty sad look.

He thought the wound looked all right, but gave her a shot of penicillin to be sure.

"Her main problem," he said, "is that her weight's way down. This old grass here is all burnt up and there's nothing left even for the cows. This drought is killing us."

We finally came to the edge of the immense plain we had seen the previous day. It was marked Hunt Valley on the map and was about twenty or thirty square miles in extent.

We had reached the final end of the trees and scrub. To the north and east, as far as the eye could see, stretched nothing but barren, empty desert.

"So where the hell are these rivers?" Walter asked, scanning the horizon. Although the Little Colorado and Zuni rivers were out there somewhere, we could see nothing but a low, scabby line of brush. A chill wind howled like a madwoman out of the valley, slapping the tarps on our packs, pulling at our clothes, lashing our horses' manes and tails, and prodding our faces. While we gazed out over the wasteland, the horses pranced and twitched, their nostrils flaring. Popeye issued a loud irritating whinny, which scratched across the wind.

I examined the maps. "They're out in that plain there somewhere," I said.

We started forward. An unsettling, eerie feeling enveloped us as we moved into the soft dust of the valley floor. Each step sent up a rocketplume of dust and the wind vibrated through our saddle rigging.

We struck the line of brush. An arroyo, not more than a ditch, wound through the brush. There was a single puddle of slimy red water in it. The rest of the ditch bottom was covered with a leprous crust. A few clumps of four-wing saltbush gripped the banks.

"Jesus," Walter said. "This *can't* be the Little Colorado River. You fucked up, got us lost."

I examined my map. It was most definitely the Little Colorado River.

We stood on the bank, appalled, contemplating the two-inch-deep mud puddle that was the Little Colorado River.

19

⊲ ⊠ ⊳

The mighty conjunction of the Little Colorado and Zuni rivers turned out to be the dry siltbeds of two arroyos. There was no water anywhere.

This place, about sixty miles from Zuni Pueblo itself, marks the outer edge of the Zuni world, a place of dust, plains, wind, sky, and ghosts. It is called *Koluwala:wa* by the Zuni: Zuni Heaven, the city of the dead. Our trip from here to Zuni would be not only retracing Coronado, but also the mythical journey of the Zuni people during their search for the Middle Place of the World.

According to the Zuni epic story of the Search for the Middle, the Zuni emerged into this world through a water-filled opening in the earth in a canyon near the Colorado River. The nascent tribe then embarked on the search for the Middle Place, a powerful concept in Zuni cosmography. The Middle Place, the *Halona:Itiwana*, was the center of the world, the lap of the earth-mother, the midpoint between all the oceans and lands, the correct and balanced place where the Zuni were destined to live.

The search was a difficult one. When the Zuni emerged, they had no knowledge of where the Middle might be. According to the epic (of which there are many variations), they held a council. A priest who had a daughter and four sons volunteered to send his eldest son northward to search for the Middle. The young man left and did not return. The priest then sent his two younger sons south. They also did not return. Finally the priest sent his youngest son, Síwelhsiwa, and his daughter, Síwiluhsitsa, to search eastward. The boy had long, black hair and was very handsome, while his sister was the most beautiful girl in the tribe.

They walked until they saw, in the distance, a high mountain. They decided to camp at its base. Síwelhsiwa built a juniper-brush shelter for the night, and his sister lay down for a rest while he went hunting for food. When he returned with game his sister was asleep. He sat down beside her, and a gust of wind brushed her cotton mantle aside, exposing her long naked body. Síwelhsiwa was overcome with desire and he lay down with her and possessed her.

Síwiluhsitsa awoke in horror. She berated her brother, while he covered his face and wept. They both began to change. Her face became mottled with anger and her hair turned white; while he, slick with sweat from his sexual passion and wet with tears, threw himself into the red dust and thrashed about, until the dust that clung to him hardened forever.

She cried out that they could never rejoin their tribe, and said: "By my power I will divide this mountain and you will live in the north and I will abide on the south." She drew her foot through the ground, dividing the mountain in two. Water welled up in the furrow formed by her foot, in one spot flooding into a lake. The furrow became the Zuni River, flowing between the twin Stinking Springs Mountains.

Meanwhile, the old priest in the west heard nothing from his daughter and son. Nevertheless, the Zuni decided to journey eastward. When they reached the lake they were dismayed at its size, but they waded into it anyway. "Fear filled the hearts of many mothers," the story went, "for their children grew cold and strange, like other than human creatures, and they dropped them into the waters, changed indeed; they floated away, crying and moaning, as even now they cry and moan as the night comes on."

The dead children and others who had drowned in the lake prepared a city of the dead under the lake's waters. It was a place "where it is delightful, and filled with songs and dances; where all men are brothers."

The Zuni called the pool the Lake of the Whispering Waters and they said that at night, along the shores of the lake, one can hear strange voices and music and sometimes see a light shining in its depths.

The brother and sister continued to inhabit the two mountains. In the end they could not master their unnatural passion and live totally apart, and their offspring were sexless men caked with mud like their father, called *Koyemshi* or Mudheads. One moment the Mudheads would speak idiocies and gross obscenities and the next utter profound truths and prophecies. The Mudheads still live in North Stinking Springs Mountain with their father and are among the most sacred deities in Zuni cosmography.*

The tribe continued to follow the approximate course of the Zuni River toward the Middle Place. When they had come into the area near where they now live, a great water spider helped them find the exact point. It spread its six legs until each foot had touched the four oceans and the zenith and nadir of the earth; the Zuni then recognized the Middle as the spot directly under the spider's heart. That is where they settled, calling the place *Halona,* the Middle—the name the old part of Zuni Pueblo bears today.

We set off eastward, toward the Stinking Springs Mountains, seven miles across the valley. We could see the two mountains, North Mountain and South Mountain, and the notch where the Zuni River flowed between them. The Lake of the Whispering Waters no longer existed, having dried up in the late nineteenth century due to Anglo abuse of its water for irrigation.

We urged our horses forward, into the dead lake bottom.

We rode into a vast nothingness, a landscape of Zen-like spareness. The wind hummed and whispered and chuckled along the bare ground, unrolling skeins of dust before it. We passed a dead saltbush, clacking and gyrating as if possessed. A tumbleweed bounced past us, spiraled upward in a dust devil, and vanished.

As we rode deeper into the dead lake bottom, for some reason—whether wind, emptiness, or dust—the horses became increasingly agitated. I could feel a clonus of fear, a trembling of suppressed energy, take hold along Popeye's flank.

---

*Every year, some Zuni at the pueblo are assigned the task of being Mudheads. They spend the year in a particular costume, wearing warty masks and visiting people's homes. When a family's home is visited, they are obliged to give the Mudheads as much food as they can carry off, which the Mudheads then redistribute to needy families. During sacred dances, the Mudheads go about making obscene gestures and mocking the religious ceremonies; they also seize and eject from the pueblo any tourists caught taking pictures.

All at once Popeye exploded with a powerful series of bucks that sent me flying.

When I got up and dusted myself off, I saw that I wasn't the only one having trouble. Pedernal had also spooked and was galloping in circles around Walter; Walter finally dropped the lead rope and turned him loose. He ran about in a panic and skidded to a halt, amidst clouds of dust roiling off toward the horizon.

"What happened to you?" Walter asked when he had finally caught Ped and calmed him down. "Were you thrown?"

"Yeah," I said.

"Goddamn, Doug, ain't that the first time you've been thrown from a horse?"

"There's nothing to it," I said.

I got back on Popeye. He felt like a bundle of crazed nerves between my legs. Not three minutes later he began pitching again with tremendous force. It felt like a land mine had gone off underneath me and I went over the saddle backwards, my leg catching in the stirrup and coming down hard on the cantle. I lay in the dust with my wind knocked out and a pain shooting through my leg.

Walter dismounted and helped me to my feet.

I was furious. "Let me at him," I said, and grabbed Popeye's reins and gave him a kick in the ribs. Walter was greatly amused at the spectacle of me hopping around on one leg, shouting and cursing at the horse.

I walked out the pain and got back on him. Having successfully shed his odious burden twice, Popeye decided this bucking was a pretty good idea, so in less than five minutes he tried it again. This time I felt the gathering explosion and was ready for him, jerking his head to the side and up, causing him to skid out sideways. I managed to fight him to a standstill.

"Must be the wind," Walter shouted. "Coming from behind like that, it's blowing straight up their assholes."

Half a dozen times Popeye tried to throw me, but each time his heart was a little less in it and I was able to anticipate his moves.

My map showed a potential water source at the base of the Stinking Springs Mountains, a little symbol marked "West Zuni Windmill." We scanned ahead with our binoculars but could see nothing.

"What if there's no water?" Walter asked.

"There's East Zuni Windmill on the other side of the mountains," I said.

"And if that's dead too?"

I unfolded the map. There was no more water to the edge of the map, at least.

"One or the other'll be working," I said.

"You better be right," Walter said. "It doesn't look like it's rained in this country in three years."

The Stinking Springs Mountains loomed before us: dry, barren, covered with cleaved ocher boulders that looked as if they'd dropped from the sky. At the base of North Stinking Springs Mountain stretched badlands utterly devoid of life. As the shadows lengthened a stark yellow light fell upon the mountains.

We continued scanning ahead looking for the windmill, with a creeping, obsessive feeling of fear. What if there were no water?

Just when we had decided that West Zuni Windmill no longer existed, I saw sunlight flash off a turning vane. We whooped and cheered with intense relief, and urged the horses into a trot.

The windmill was spinning like a propeller, the pump rod wheezing up and down, pushing water into a metal tank. The tank itself was overflowing, with water dribbling over the lip into a sea of mud. A small herd of emaciated cows was bedding down about a quarter of a mile away. A single dying cow stood near the tank, swaying on match-stick legs, bawling loudly. As we unpacked the cow sank to its front knees, struggled back to its feet, and weaved away into some brush.

The horses had calmed down considerably since we had left the dry lakebed, but when led to the tank they refused to drink. They snorted and blew on the water a great deal and then backed away. I knew they had to be thirsty, as the last water they had drunk was at the HT corral that morning.

"Maybe they don't like that mud around the tank," Walter said.

I dipped a canvas bucket into the water and held it to Popeye's nose, but still he turned away.

Walter went off to photograph before the light died, while I hobbled the horses and turned them out some distance from camp. The grass was very sparse and cropped almost to the dirt by cattle.

I found the vanes of an old windmill scattered about and hammered them into the ground to make a windbreak for the fire. The ground was so hard I had to chop into it with our axe to make a firepit. I lit a cow chip and salt-cedar brush fire.

Walter returned without having taken any photographs, but he was elated with the landscape. He had left his 8 × 10 camera up on North Mountain, ready to photograph at dawn.

"There's a *power* here," he said. "I can feel it."

We decided to stay an extra day—partly because of the landscape and partly, I think, because we were both afraid to leave the water.

Since topping the Rim we had begun making extraordinary progress, riding up to twenty miles a day. What was more, these were straight-line miles. (Below the Rim we might cover perhaps twenty ground miles but make only five or six airline miles by the map.) Instead of taking a day to cross one of our U.S.G.S. maps, we were crossing two and sometimes three maps each day.

The wind howled incessantly. We could not escape it. Within two feet of the ground, a permanent layer of dust, sand, gravel, and pulverized cow dung blasted along. Anything you set down was instantly caked with dirt. You couldn't put food on a plate without it being browned with dust; lift a lid off a pot and a thick black scum instantly coated the food. Our tent filled with fine dust, which collected in drifts in the corners and blew deep into our bedrolls. Any object lighter than a few pounds had to be weighted down; empty metal pots rolled off; saddle pads and blankets flipped over and over and were gone; hats went flying. What began as an annoyance eventually became extremely debilitating: the wind became a constant, grinding presence, far worse than rain, snow, freezing cold, or roasting heat. It made us tired of life.

The next morning we climbed North Mountain. The wind was still blowing hard and very cold.

The peak was a shelf of naked limestone heaped around with loose rock. I wedged myself behind two rocks and began writing in my notebook.

At the limit of visibility I could see Mesa Redonda and a dark line marking the edge of the great Rim forest. To the south lay some blue humps, the White Mountains of Arizona.

A ghostly veil of cirrostratus clouds had spread across the sky, filtering the pre-dawn light. A strange play of light began on the dead surface of the lake, a shimmering of air, shadow, and color, unearthly hues of magentas and lime greens, oranges, yellows, grays, and purples. As the sun rose the colors pooled and marbled until the dry lakebed was a pointillist surface of light. As quickly as it had occurred the phenomenon vanished and the landscape returned to solid reality.

I returned to camp and made a breakfast of biscuits and oatmeal. When Walter got back we collected the horses to be grained and watered. They made another great show of not drinking, snorting and blowing on the water and flicking it with their muzzles.

Walter and I sat on the fence, giving them plenty of time to drink. We got to talking and the next thing we realized, all four horses were walking away. We began following them slowly, as not to spook them, but Pedernal (the lead horse and a real troublemaker) took one look behind, curled his lip in scorn, and whipped off in a gallop, followed by the others. A half mile off, still running, they disappeared around the southern flank of South Mountain.

"Damn!" Walter said, laughing. "Just when you think you can trust 'em."

I wasn't quite so amused. "We're just a pair of Goddamned idiots," I said. "How many times do we have to lose our horses before we learn?"

"It *was* stupid," Walter said unconcernedly.

"So what the hell are we going to do about it?" I said, getting more and more excited.

"Go get 'em," Walter said calmly.

"They could be ten miles off by now!" I shouted.

"You follow the tracks," Walter said. "I'll take a shortcut over those hills."

Tracking them was easy. Around the side of the hill, once we were out of sight, they had slowed to a trot and eventually dropped to a walk. I began noticing that each horse had a peculiar track, that the rear hoofmarks imprinted themselves on top of the front hoofmarks in a pattern that was unique to each horse when it walked.

It was actually a pleasant hike. I soon found myself on the backside of South Mountain, in an area of arroyos and sandhills. I passed an old ruin with a dead cottonwood in the front yard and just beyond it I saw the horses standing around, grazing.

I walked slowly up to Pedernal and took his lead rope, and gathered the other horses around.

"Bad horses!" I said. "Bad, bad horses!"

They looked at me with vacuous expressions.

I turned Banjo's halter and lead rope into a primitive bridle and reins, and climbed on him bareback.

"You're gonna carry me back as punishment," I said, and nudged him in the flank. Soon Walter came hiking out of the hills; he climbed on Pedernal and we rode back to camp with Walter singing a strange tuneless song of his own composition, the other two horses following sheepishly behind.

. . .

Walter came over with his tin cup full of water as I was making lunch. "Now I know why the horses won't drink this water," he said, pushing the cup in my face.

The color of the water was about the same as Lapsang souchong tea. I took a sip and immediately gagged. It was salty, fizzy, bitter, rusty, sulfurous, and it smelled like a fart. It was absolutely the foulest water I had ever tasted, or could even have imagined. The minute it touched my lips my throat would involuntarily close off.

"How much good water do we have left?" I asked.

Walter rattled about a pint of water around in a canteen. "Hey," he said, "the cows drink this stuff. It can't be poisonous. It's coming out of a well."

"Maybe we should purify it," I said.

"Hell no," Walter said. "If you add those pills you'll never be able to drink that shit."

We now knew where the Stinking Springs Mountains had gotten their name.

We tried mixing it with Tang. We tried mixing it with powdered milk. We tried making it into coffee. Nothing would improve the flavor. It was so salty that I wondered if it was hydrating us at all.

Walter hiked off behind North Mountain while I wrote in my journal. The wind continued to blow and I finally took off my clothes and lowered myself in the tank in order to escape it. I floated on my back in the stinky brew, gazing at the spinning windmill against the blue sky. The chill of the water took the edge off my thirst, but as soon as I had dried off it came back.

I began craving water. I picked up the canteen that Walter had filled from the tank and took a sip. The instant my mouth filled with water my thirst vanished. I spat it out.

I wrote some more. Again I floated in the tank. I collected up some pieces of agate and petrified wood around the camp. Then I counted the wounds on my hands, which I duly recorded in my notebook: fourteen scabs and cuts on my left hand, eight on my right. Finally I went back to the canteen. This time I pinched my nose, closed my eyes, and drank as fast as I could before the first wave of nausea hit. It worked, to a certain extent, reducing my thirst to a tolerable level.

The grass had been so sparse that the horses spent the entire night searching for it instead of sleeping, and twice Robin nearly keeled over in a stupor while we were packing her.

We followed the Zuni River between the Stinking Springs Mountains. East Zuni Windmill was not operating, but there was a scum of poisonous green water in the tank which the horses snorted at and again would not drink. We scanned the horizon, looking for signs of water. At this point the horses had not had a good drink in two days.

"When they get as thirsty as we are," Walter said, "they'll drink."

"Maybe they know something about the water that we don't," I said.

"I hope not," he said with feeling: the sulfur in the water had begun boiling out of our systems, making us stink.

We rode through the high country south of the river, where we felt we'd have a better chance of spotting water. It was a desert as spare and wide as the ocean, with only a few mesas notched against the distant horizon. A lonely tumbleweed appeared out of nowhere, rustled past us, and rolled into the distance until it was gone, as if on some forlorn errand known only to itself.

We rode and rode and hardly felt we were moving at all, while Walter sang his strange songs filled with nonsense, perversion, and obscenity.

Then Walter hollered: "Goddammit, Doug, you're the writer! Tell me a story."

I had been thinking about food, so I detailed, minute by minute, a description of a dinner I had once enjoyed at La Tulipe in New York City. We started with *blini au caviar,* with the little gray eggs popping in the mouth, followed by an ice-cold shot of Stolichnaya; then a *le gaspacho de Thon de saumon frais* and a bottle of flinty Puligny-Montrachet; followed by *l'entrecote de charolais a la fondue d'anchois et aux herbes* with a Chateau Margaux; and so forth down to the *tarte fine aux reinettes a la compote d'abricots* with Chateau d'Yquem. Each course was consumed, mouthful by mouthful, sip by sip, in real time, while Walter listened with rapt attention.

Finally he cried out, "You haven't said anything about the girl you're eating with! Tell me about the *girl!*"

I then described the woman I was dining with, how her stockings rustled when she crossed her legs, the expression on her face when her mouth was full of caviar and vodka, how she shook out her long blond hair, how she giggled as the juices of the steak escaped from between her lips and ran down her chin. Then I described walking outside with her leaning, just a little tipsy, against my shoulder, her hair smelling faintly of shampoo; I told how I flicked my finger for a cab, which screeched to a stop at our feet, and how I ordered the cabbie to take us to Rockefeller Center. I described the Christmas tree and the Rainbow

Room coruscating with light and people whirling on the dance floor and the band playing "Stomping at the Savoy"; I described holding the warm, strong body of the girl in my arms, and so on and so forth. The story went on for hours.

Then I was finished. The band was packing up; the evening was over.

"*Well?*" Walter demanded.

"Well what?" I said.

"What happened then?"

"Why, nothing," I said. "The evening was over."

Walter was beside himself. He stood up in the saddle and turned around, the cords in his neck standing out.

"Over?" he shouted. "Get outta here. *Over?*"

I had no idea what he was talking about.

"Jesus Christ," he cried out, "*what* did you *do* with the *girl?*"

"Now hold on," I said, laughing. "I'm not going into that."

"The hell you're not," he cried out. "Goddamn, I didn't listen to a three-hour story just to hear that you went home. *Did you fuck the girl or what?*"

I still refused to continue the story. Walter declared the story was as poor a one as he had ever heard, and went back to singing his tuneless songs.

20

⊙ ⊠ ⊙

$\mathcal{S}$omewhere in this barren country the Spanish first encountered the Zuni Indians, the builders of the Seven Cities of Cíbola.

Coronado was probably a two-day ride—about forty miles—from Cíbola when his scouts first spotted Indians. Coronado's two accounts of this meeting differ slightly. In his later testimony before a judge on his management of the expedition, he would say that the group was seen "near a lake" and that he sent two of his captains to the Indians "in order to get information from them and an interpreter." In another report he said the Indians approached them first: "Four Indians came out with signs of peace," Coronado wrote the viceroy, "saying that they had been sent to that desert place to say that we were welcome. . . . The maestre de campo gave them a cross, telling them to say to the people in their city that they need not fear."

This is an intriguing description. Scholars have wondered what the party of Zuni were doing forty or more miles from their villages. Some scholars have suggested that Coronado, who came through in early July, might have surprised a group of Zuni on a religious pilgrimage. Even today, once every four years certain Zuni religious leaders make a pilgrimage to the Stinking Springs Mountains and the Zuni city of the dead. The pilgrimage takes place in early summer. (In fact, 1989 was a pilgrimage year and the Zuni had asked us not to ride through the area in June, when the pilgrims would be conducting religious ceremonies.) If Coronado surprised a group of pilgrims, then the lake mentioned by Coronado could have been none other than the Lake of the Whispering Waters, the Zuni city of the dead.

The arrival of the Spaniards must have been a great shock to this group of Indians, whether they were pilgrims or not. What Coronado had to say to them was not reassuring. The Spanish general told them that "he had come in the name of his Majesty to place them under his dominion and to bring them to the knowledge of God; that they should become Christians, and that no harm would be done them in their persons or properties, provided they submitted peacefully to the obedience of his Majesty."

It is unclear just how much of this the Zuni understood, but they must have caught enough to realize that this strange group of men were by no means friendly. But now was not the time to resist. Smiling and gesturing, the three or four Zuni assured the Spanish (Coronado wrote) "that we were welcome, and that on the next day all the people would meet us with food." By this time Coronado and his men were emaciated and obviously in need of nourishment.

After the Indians left, Coronado, taking no chances, ordered the maestre de campo to ride ahead with an armed party to "go and see if there was any bad passage which the Indians might be able to defend, and to take it and protect it until the next day, when I would come up." The maestre de campo left while Coronado set up camp farther down the river. Sure enough, the Spanish discovered a narrow canyon along the Zuni River that would have made an ideal place of ambush. They quietly set up guards.

That night, the Indians secretly came to the canyon to fortify it. Finding the Spanish already there must have been a nasty surprise, but they attacked anyway. "According to what I have been told," Coronado wrote, "they attacked like valiant men, although in the end they had to retreat in flight, because the maestre de campo was on the watch and kept his men in good order. The Indians sounded a little trumpet as a sign of retreat, and did no harm to the Spanish. The maestre de campo sent me notice of this on the same night."

Now all pretense was dropped. There would be no peaceful encounter: the Zuni and Spanish began preparing for battle.

We met no Zuni pilgrims, nor did we see any sign of human life at all as we followed the dry bed of the Zuni River.

Later that day we crossed an old silt pan covered with an alkaline crust and found a skimming of water in the center. All the horses except Robin finally drank, although the water looked and smelled a lot worse to us than our Stinking Springs water, being (it seemed) mostly cow piss concentrated by long evaporation.

We stopped for lunch at a dry windmill, which Walter banged and rattled and levered on. We watched the machine shriek and groan in the wind while we ate our lunch, a dry biscuit and a spoonful of raspberry jam each. In the end nothing came out of the windmill except some powdery iron oxide; the well was bone dry.

"This is devastating," Walter said. "I don't know how much longer I can stand this Stinking Springs water."

"If we don't get to Zuni soon," I said, "we're also going to run out of food."

We camped at a splendid set of corrals in the middle of nowhere, and to our great surprise and pleasure we found a shed stacked with bales of alfalfa. We turned the horses loose in one of the corrals and broke open a bale. I wrote a little note thanking the unknown rancher, wrapped it around a five-dollar bill, and tucked it into the stack of hay. From horizon to horizon there was no ranch house or road visible; this was one hell of a large ranch.

We were both cranky from hunger. A truly heartbreaking sunset ensued, with all the requisite deepening of colors and tinting of clouds, but when I called Walter's attention to it he merely hawked up a gobbet of spit and called it "more bullshit scenery signifying nothing."

As we boiled a pot of rice for dinner, I sat cross-legged on the ground, munching a cracker and dropping crumbs. A stink bug on mysterious stink-bug business came by, walking as stiffly as a little machine. He discovered the crumbs, practically hopped in the air with excitement, and began eating frantically. I was struck with amazement at the philosophical implications of a stink bug with a taste for Stoned Wheat Thins. It was a stunning confirmation of the interrelatedness of all life.

I watched the bug in the twilight with much affection. He seemed luckier than us, this bug with a nice corral for a home, with lots of oats and cracked corn and hayseed to munch on. And here we were, so far from home, with nothing to eat but boiled rice. Then it occurred to me that a corral was not exactly a great place for a stink bug to live. At any moment a horse, oblivious, running eagerly to its feed, could step on him just like that. I wondered what the human-scale equivalent of the oblivious-horse-stepping-on-happy-unsuspecting-bug would be. I thought of the bug's family clustering around his corpse, saying, Who could have done this terrible thing? How could a loving God have allowed this to happen?

These were frightening thoughts indeed.

The next morning, as we were ready to leave, a cloud of dust appeared on the horizon, and soon a pickup truck had pulled up at the corral. An old man came gimping out on a bad leg. He took one look at us and roared out:

"Just what in blazes are you boys doing in my corral, helping yourselves to my feed and water?"

I began to explain, telling him about our trip, and how this barn full of alfalfa was a real godsend to our starving horses, and how we'd looked for the ranch house but could not see it, and how we'd left five dollars in the barn.

There was a silence. He hooked his bootheel on the corral fence and tilted up his hat.

"Coronado, you say?" he said. "Now that's interesting. I'd like to hear more."

We described our trip.

"Well now," he said. "I'm glad to know you," and he shook our hands.

He explained that this vast ranch we'd been riding on was called the St. Johns Stake Welfare Ranch. It was run for the benefit of the Mormons of the local "stake," the equivalent of a diocese or parish. The income from the ranch was dispersed among those Mormons who might need emergency financial assistance, were unemployed, or were just having hard times.

Just before we left, the old man came out of the barn holding the five-dollar bill.

"You boys forgot something," he said.

The wind was blowing harder than ever. No matter how vigorously I crammed my hat on my head it simply wouldn't stay, so I stuffed it in a saddlebag. The wind also made the horses bad-tempered, and at one stop to unwire a fence Pedernal and Robin got in a terrific fight, screaming, rearing, kicking, and biting. They both ran off and Walter had to chase them for two miles.

We heard the highway before we saw it, the sound of a distant jake-brake Doppler shifting as it went by. We searched ahead with the binoculars and could see the sporadic glint of speeding metal at the horizon. This was Route 666, the so-called Coronado Highway, named by highway department boosters trying to attract tourist traffic.

We rode along the right-of-way fence looking for a gate, while machines with people sealed inside them whooshed back and forth, with disembodied hands waving from windows. The highway seemed a peculiar thing, a frenetic, jumping nerve of late-twentieth-century civilization in the middle of nowhere. It gave me a strange feeling to be seeing so many people so suddenly, when we had encountered barely half a dozen in the past hundred miles of travel.

Ahead of us rose a country of deep canyons and towering mesas capped with black rimrock. Somewhere in this country was the "bad passage" described by Coronado, a sharp narrowing of the canyon through which the Zuni River flowed, the place where the first skirmish between Europeans and Indians occurred in the Southwest.

Several miles up a deep canyon we found an extraordinarily beautiful campsite. The dry riverbed became a bed of sand as white and soft as a Cape Cod beach. It lay in a hollow, entirely protected from the wind. Next to it was a cool grove of cottonwoods, the first live trees we had seen in days. Above the riverbed stood a windmill, cranking like the devil, and a tank of fresh water. Water spilling over the lip of the tank had created a little marsh and a rich meadow for the horses. On the far side of the canyon stood a picturesque ruin, a mud-and-stone cabin whose two empty windows looked out at us unperturbed, like two solemn eyes. The walls of the canyon soared up on either side of us, layers of yellow and white sandstone ending in black volcanic caprock.

After we'd unpacked, I spread out the maps and realized I had made a serious navigational mistake. We had ridden up the wrong canyon entirely, following an arroyo called Jalarosa Draw instead of the Zuni River. To ride back around would have taken half a day, at least. I was furious with myself, and stamped around camp cursing and kicking sand.

Walter took the mistake good-naturedly. "We'll ride over that ridge and hit the river on the other side," he said, pointing to a savage-looking volcanic cliff.

"That looks pretty dangerous," I said.

"Naw," said Walter.

We built a fire and cooked what we hoped would be our last meal before entering the Seven Cities of Gold.

That night, sleeping in the open, I woke suddenly and found myself staring into a boundless pasture of stars; for a moment I panicked, thinking I was falling upward into space.

⮞ ⚎ ⮜

Coronado's advance guard drove the Zuni from the "bad passage" the night of July 5, 1540.* The following day, Coronado tells us, "I started with as good order as I could, for we were in such great need of food that I thought we should all die of hunger if we were to wait another day. . .so I was obliged to hasten forward without delay." He added: "The Indians lighted their fires at various places and were answered from a distance, a method of communication as good as we could have devised ourselves. Thus they warned of our coming and where we had arrived."

Coronado probably camped that final night just beyond the bad passage, about six miles from the pueblo itself.

That evening, July 6th, the starving men—not knowing what to expect—were desperate and fearful. It is not hard to imagine their state of mind. For most of them, all their worldly possessions and aspirations were tied up in the expedition—as well as months of demeaning labor and suffering. The events of the next day would determine, to a large extent, the rest of their lives. Everything would depend on what lay stored in the as-yet-unseen City of Cíbola. They might end up like Cortés and his followers, rich beyond any rational measure of wealth. Or they might end up penniless, without honor or rank, perhaps even beggars on the streets of Mexico City.

This was as true of Coronado as it was of his poorest foot soldier. Coronado, the second son of a Salamancan nobleman, had frittered away his small inheritance back in Spain; he had married money but had mortgaged most of his wife's property to raise the 50,000 ducats he himself invested in the expedition. At thirty, Coronado was probably wise enough in the ways of the court to know that to return empty-handed (even through no fault of his own) would be the end of his promising career.

Tensions in camp that night must have been nearly unbearable. The soldiers already knew that Fray Marcos had exaggerated many things. His descriptions of the fine southwestern landscape had been proven

---

*The narratives are a little unclear about the date on which this and other events occurred, but a close reading has convinced me that, indeed, the first fight between native Americans and Europeans took place on this date.

false, and this alone must have made the soldiers sick with apprehension: might Cíbola prove similar?

The Spaniards did know one thing: the Indians of Cíbola were not going to welcome them. They would have to fight, if not for gold, at least for food.

As they pitched camp that evening, an incident occurred that might have been amusing under other circumstances. A group of Zuni gathered at a "safe place" and began hollering and shouting at the Spanish. If their intention was to frighten they certainly succeeded. Pandemonium and confusion broke out in the Spanish camp—so much so, Castañeda tells us, "that more than one [horseman] put his saddle on backwards."* The more experienced horsemen quickly mounted and rode out over the field, but "the Indians, well acquainted with the land, fled, for none could be found."

The next morning the soldiers rose and prepared for battle. Those who had plate armor or coats of mail now put them on; others donned thick buckskins or rawhide for protection. Some strapped, donned, or buckled on daggers, swords, cuirasses; gorgets, beavers, and sallets. A few had crossbows and harquebuses.

That morning—the date was July 7, 1540—they rode "in good formation" northeast through a thin juniper-piñon forest. The eastern edge of this forest marks the present-day boundary of Arizona and New Mexico and the beginning of the Zuni Indian reservation.

At the border itself the forest sloped down to the Zuni River. Beyond the river lay the Plain of Hawikuh, on the far side of which rose up the first of the Seven Cities of Gold. It was in this scrubby forest, in 1539, that Fray Marcos had come "within view of Cíbola, which is situated in a plain, at the base of a round hill." At that spot, about three miles from the pueblo, the friar had gathered a pile of stones and erected his slender cross. Here he recited the act of possession and named the new land the "Kingdom of St. Francis."

Coronado and his soldiers attained the top of the rise, probably very close to this spot. If the cross was still there no one remarked upon it, for the city of Cíbola, the first of the Seven Cities of Gold, had finally come into view.

The soldiers stood for a moment gazing across the sandy bed of the river to the fabulous city, three miles distant.

---

*The sixteenth-century Spanish saddle did not have a saddlehorn and no obvious front and back.

Castañeda tells us the soldiers' reaction:

"The curses that some hurled at Fray Marcos were such that God forbid they may befall him."

Instead of a magnificent shining city of ten-story buildings, larger than the City of Mexico, "it was a small rocky pueblo, all crumpled up, there being many farm settlements in New Spain that look better from afar."*

From their vantage point they could also see that the entire province was up in arms. "The people of the district," Castañeda wrote, "had gathered there, for this is a province comprising seven pueblos, some of which are by far larger and stronger pueblos than Cíbola.† These people waited in the open within sight of the pueblo, drawn up in squadrons." The smoke signals sent out the previous day had apparently called in warriors from the other Zuni pueblos.

The first major battle between Europeans and Native Americans in what would become the United States was about to begin.

Coronado sent the maestre de campo, two friars, his personal secretary, and some horsemen a little way ahead to confer with the Indians. They told the Zuni that "we were not coming to do them any harm, but to defend them in the name of our lord, the emperor." An interpreter then "made intelligible" to the Indians the order requiring them to submit to his Majesty and to God.

The Zuni sent back their logical reply: a shower of arrows. Some of the horses were wounded and one of the friars had his gown pierced.

"Meanwhile," Coronado wrote the viceroy, "I arrived with all the rest of the cavalry and footmen and found a large body of Indians on the plain who began to shoot arrows. In obedience to the suggestions of your lordship and of [his Majesty], I did not wish that they should be attacked, and enjoined my men, who were begging me for permission, from doing so, telling them that they ought not to molest them, and that the enemy was doing us no harm, and that it was not proper to fight such a small number of people. On the other hand, when the Indians saw that we did not move, they took greater courage and grew

---

*Some popular writers have claimed that the Spanish saw the setting sun glowing on the pueblo's adobe walls and mistakenly thought the entire city was made of gold. This is complete nonsense; at no time did the Spanish ever believe the city itself was built of gold.

†The word Cíbola was probably a corruption of a form of "Ashiwi," the Zuni word for themselves. The Spanish used "Cíbola" to refer to both the province (that is, all the Zuni pueblos) and this particular pueblo, which the Zuni called Hawikuh.

so bold that they came up almost to the heels of our horses to shoot their arrows. On this account I saw that it was no longer time to hesitate." He got the quick blessings of the friars for the assault, gave the traditional cry *Santiago! Cierra España!** and charged.

The Indian line in front of Hawikuh broke almost immediately, and the Zuni fled across the plain toward the pueblo. Coronado claims in his report that only "some" Indians were killed, as he did not allow the soldiers to pursue them. This information is suspect: Coronado was under strict orders not to harm any natives unless absolutely essential; reporting a massacre would have gotten him into trouble. An anonymous report written only ten days after the battle at Hawikuh presents a more likely scenario. It has a petulant, querulous, self-justifying tone that would be consistent with the disappointment the soldiers must have been feeling.

Coronado and his men, it reads, "were not received as they should have been, being then all exhausted from the hardships of the trip, of packing and unpacking like muleteers, of not eating as much as they would have liked to. . . . The general [Coronado] approached [the Cíbolans] in person. . .to request them to surrender, as is customary in new lands. Their answer was the large number of arrows which they shot. . . . The Indians turned back and thought that they would retire to the city, which was close at hand, but before they reached it they were overtaken and many of them were killed. They [the Indians] killed three horses and wounded seven or eight others."

If this document is to be believed (and I think it should be) more than just a few Indians were killed. But whether few or many, for the first time Europeans had spilled a significant amount of Indian blood on what would become American soil. It was the beginning of a terrible conquest that would not end until the Battle of Wounded Knee exactly three and a half centuries later.

The first skirmish was over, but the Zuni had now fortified themselves in the pueblo itself. Just before the arrival of Coronado the Indians had evacuated from the pueblo all the women, young boys, and men over sixty, except two or three old men who remained to command the warriors.

"The hunger which we suffered," Coronado wrote, "would not permit of any delay." He divided his forces and dismounted to lead the final assault himself.

---

*The ancient Spanish battle cry, meaning "St. James! Spain! Close on them!"

The crossbowmen and harquebusiers fired upon the warriors on top of the pueblo's walls to drive them back so the walls could be scaled. "But the crossbowmen," Coronado wrote, "soon broke the strings of their crossbows and the musketeers could do nothing, because they had arrived so weak and feeble that they could scarcely stand on their feet."

As Coronado and his soldiers stormed the pueblo walls, the warriors rained "countless great stones" from above. "The Indians," Coronado wrote, "all directed their attack against me because my armor was gilded and glittering, and on this account I was hurt more than the rest, and not because I had done more or was farther in advance than the others; for all these gentlemen and soldiers bore themselves well. . . . They knocked me down to the ground twice. . .and if I had not been protected by the very good headpiece which I wore, I think that the outcome would have been bad for me." He suffered many small wounds and an arrow through the foot, and was hauled insensate from the field by two of his lieutenants.

But the Zuni, as bravely as they had fought, were no match for the well-armed Spanish. The Spanish had two insurmountable advantages. First, they had the advantage of technology. But even more important, they had the advantage of strategy. The Spanish had just concluded an eight-hundred-year war against the Moors, expelling them from Spain only fifty years before. Eight hundred years of fighting had honed their sense of military tactics and strategy to a keen edge.

As the soldiers battered down the Indians' defenses the Zunis sent an envoy out who explained through signs that they wanted the battle to end, and that they would yield the pueblo to the Spanish if they were allowed to leave unharmed. The Spanish agreed. The Zuni evacuated the pueblo and the Spanish entered the first of the Seven Cities of Gold.

"There," one of the soldiers wrote, "we found something we prized more than gold or silver, namely, such maize, beans and chickens* larger than those here in New Spain, and salt better and whiter than I have ever seen in my whole life." They gorged themselves until sick.

The expedition had attained its objective. Gold or no gold, the Spanish had come to conquer and Christianize. The Seven Cities of Gold had been made to submit to the alien will of his Holy Caesarean Catholic Majesty, the Emperor Charles V, a forty-year-old man with a pendulous lip and a passion for anchovies and beer, sitting on a throne in Germany eight thousand miles away.

---

*These would actually have been turkeys.

.   .   .

On July 8, 1540, the Plain of Hawikuh was empty and quiet. The Zuni had fled to the safety of Dowa Yalanne, a mesa fifteen miles distant and their traditional refuge in times of trouble. As they departed, they had likely removed their dead from the field of battle. The only sign of conquest would have been a scattering of arrows, a few dead horses, and occasional patches of earth blackened with Zuni blood.

In one great blow, the way of life of the Zuni Indians had been changed forever. While this was the first major conflict between whites and Indians in what would become America, never again would the Zunis fight the white man. No matter: a much vaster, but quieter, death for the tribe would come soon enough, as alien microbes brought from Europe began their secret, terrible work.

What the Zuni's discussions and thoughts were as they held council on their sacred mesa, what oracles their priests consulted and what was prophesied, we will probably never know, and we could surely never comprehend.

● ☰ ●

The morning of May 25, 1989, I woke up with sore lips. With no mirror I could only feel what had happened; when my fingers came away they were wet with bloody pus. Going hatless the day before had been a serious mistake; I had severely burned my lips in the hot sun.

"With those lips," Walter said laughing, "and that dirty black face, if the Zuni don't shoot you on sight you'll be damn lucky."

We both looked monstrous. Walter, small and thin to begin with, had lost so much weight that he actually appeared to have shrunk in height. I myself had lost about twenty or twenty-five pounds and had punched so many new holes in my belt that the loose end dangled a good eight inches to the ground. Both of our faces were nearly black; whether this was from sun or dirt would have to wait until we'd had a bath.

We packed up and examined our maps. That day we hoped to reach the ruins of Hawikuh, the first of the Seven Cities of Gold. We had only one small problem: Hawikuh was not marked on any of our maps. We felt confident that we could easily locate a ruin of such historical importance; it would at the least be a tourist site of some prominence, perhaps even with a visitors' center selling burritos and cold Dr. Pepper. We could hardly wait.

We began searching for a way up the volcanic mesa. I came across an astonishing sight while pushing through some brush along the edge of the canyon.

Hammered into the rock face was an extraordinary prehistoric petroglyph: a large butterfly with a smiling human face and an intricate, interlocking design on its wings. Nearby was a star within a moon within a rising sun, a crooked arrow, a serpent, the figures of two chiefs, and several spirals and double-spirals—the *sipapu* again. We gazed at them in silence, these human marks predating Coronado by many centuries. Once again I had an indescribable feeling of the sad, irresistible weight of time and the sequence of losses that created the American West.

From the top of the mesa, we had a tremendous, uninterrupted view ahead. Many miles away stood two blunt teeth of sandstone sticking over the horizon—the Twin Buttes of Zuni. In the near distance rose the piñon and juniper hills where Fray Marcos had erected his slender cross, and where Coronado had made his final camp before the assault on Hawikuh. Slightly below us was a sagebrush flat, the edge of which dropped off into blue space.

We climbed down, tied the horses to some sage, and walked over to the edge. The flat ended as if it had been cleaved with a knife. Below us, in a deep canyon, was the Zuni River, winding in tight S-curves through sculptured masses of sandstone. To our great surprise in the creek bed ran a blue thread of water.

There could be no doubt: we were looking down into the "bad passage" described by Coronado.

In this rocky defile the first skirmish between Europeans and Indians had occurred in the Southwest. And yet, 449 years later, not a trace of any kind of human life could be seen; the canyon looked just as it had for thousands of years, as if it cared nothing for the great events which had played themselves out upon it.

With great difficulty we worked our way down into the canyon, where we watered the horses in the stream and turned them out to graze. We found a small cave in which to eat our miserable lunch, a few dry crackers. We boiled water on Walter's stove and made a pot of strong coffee, hoping to kill our hunger with caffeine.

The cave—a small eroded cove in the lowest layer of sandstone— looked out over a brushy flat. The spot was cozy and well protected from the wind. The bottom of the cave had a foot of white powdery dust, and as I swept aside a spot to sit down on I turned up a potsherd—prehistoric black-on-white ware.

I handed it to Walter.

"Indians must've lived here," he said. "Look at the ceiling."

A long smudge of ancient soot streaked the stone roof. Across the river were other shallow caves in the sandstone walls.

Not only Indians had camped in these caves. Coronado's army, following the advance party in the fall of 1540, had sheltered here. "When the army was already a day's journey from Cíbola," Castañeda recalled, "there arose in the afternoon a bitter cold whirlwind, followed by a heavy snowfall. . . . The army marched until it came to some rocky caves, which were reached well in the night." There they huddled in the shelter of the sandstone, and entered Cíbola the following day.

Toward sunset we crossed the Zuni River again, which had swung north. It was bone dry, a bed of hot sand. To our right was a long plain, surrounded by low mesas; if Hawikuh was out there somewhere, all trace of it had vanished. The country was so breathtakingly remote that it was hard to comprehend the world-making events that had happened here. This was a landscape of immense historical importance, the meeting place of Europe and America. All around us a vast, teeming country of 250 million people had reared up, while this place, where it all began, had been entirely forgotten.

We rode along the arroyo until we happened on a murky pool with cattails. A little tarpaper shack stood about a hundred yards off.

We heard a door slam and a Zuni woman was standing in the door of the cabin.

Walter and I looked at each other. This was our first encounter with the Zuni—with any native Americans, in fact—and we had no idea of what to expect.

"What if she tells us to leave?" I said.

"We can't leave," Walter said. "This is the only water around here."

We held a hurried discussion. We already knew our maps did not indicate any water whatsoever between here and Zuni Pueblo, fifteen miles away.

"We've got the permission of the governor," I said.

"That don't mean shit out here. What if she's got a gun?"

"Let's unpack right away so she'll be less likely to tell us to move on."

While we had been arguing and fretting, the woman had slowly raised her hand in greeting.

"Hey, she's waving to us," Walter said.

We waved and hollered back. She came walking down toward us.

"Come on over," she called out.

We came around and I started explaining, at a mile a minute, what we were doing there, on Indian land with packhorses. She cut me off with a wave of her hand. "I know all about you boys," she said. "I'm on the Zuni Tribal Council."

We were enormously relieved. We shook hands all around. Her name was Rita Lorenzo. She owned the sheep camp, where she kept a flock of a hundred sheep tended by a shepherd. She was a plump, confident woman with a cheerful, dignified carriage. She was also well dressed, and, if I remember correctly, wore a beautiful French scarf looped around her neck. While we were talking the shepherd came to the cabin door.

"Go on up and visit with him," she said. "He's got a radio and a pot of something on the stove that he might share with you. It isn't the Marriott but you're welcome to it." She laughed and drove away in a brand-new Chevy pickup.

The shepherd was wearing a white T-shirt and jeans, and his skin was sunburned to a dark mahogany. We dismounted and shook hands, gravely and in silence.

His name was Lincoln Harker. He was a man of few words. We asked if we could hobble the horses on the grassy bank alongside the river and he nodded.

"Got some wieners in a pot," he said. "Coffee too."

We took this to be an invitation.

We unpacked the horses and hauled out the very last of our food—a handful of rice and about two tablespoons of yellow lentils. While dinner cooked, we sat outside the cabin on plastic chairs, in the gathering dusk, drinking coffee by the glow of a kerosene lantern. Harker had snapped on the transistor radio, our arrival being a kind of festive occasion, and we were listening to the Doors. The music crackled faintly, as if coming from a vast distance. The song stopped and a voice began speaking a language I had never heard before. Then more music began: "Yesterday," by the Beatles.

We were facing east, looking out over an empty plain rimmed by mesas. The sharp cooling of the air brought a gunpowdery odor of dust into our nostrils, and the sky had lost all its color, like a pool of water suddenly in shadow.

Walter told Harker about our journey, while the Zuni shepherd listened, head sunk on chest, cupping his coffee mug in both hands. When Walter had finished, Harker tilted his chair against the cabin with a thump and pointed into the darkness.

"That is Hawikuh," he said simply.

We strained to see across the dark plain.

"About three miles off," he said. We sighted down his pointing arm.

Then we saw it: a faint patch of barren ground on the shoulder of a hill. The plain in front of us, then, was the battlefield of Hawikuh. I felt my skin crawl.

We sat in silence, in the lantern glow, and watched darkness cover the land. The stars came out, trembling and strong. The radio wavered and then lost its signal entirely, the electronic hiss rising and falling like groundswell. No pinpoint of light broke that smooth field of blackness in front of us; there was nothing out there, no sign of human life at all on the Plain of Hawikuh or the ruins beyond.

And then, as the darkness became total, the faintest coloring appeared on the northeastern horizon: a scattering of light in the high desert air—the glow of man-made photons ejected from hot tungsten and charged mercury plasma, the electric halo of late-twentieth-century Zuni Pueblo itself.

21

We ate a late dinner. The cabin had no refrigerator and as a result the wieners were smelly and as soggy as paste, and the Zuni bread was moldy, but we ate with all the gusto and appreciation of starving men.

"When I first saw you coming from the west," Lincoln Harker said, with the precise, singing inflection of Zuni speech, "I was surprised. I never saw anybody come from that direction before."

"That's because there's nothing out there for a hundred miles but sand and rock," Walter said.

Harker nodded. He had a square, solid face, and framed his words with slow deliberation.

Harker made jewelry in his spare time. When I asked what kind of jewelry he did, without a word he tore a piece of cardboard off a box and drew a beautiful Zuni eagle dancer. When I said I wanted to keep it he took it back and signed his name.

"Do you make a living from this?" I asked.

"Back when the Arabs were buying," he said, becoming animated for the first time, "they used to buy all my stuff. Everything I could make. I had *two* pickup trucks then. Everybody had money."

"The *Arabs* were buying Zuni jewelry?" I asked.*

He shrugged his shoulders. "But then they got real cheap. I don't sell much to them. That's why I'm out here."

"How'd you learn to do this?" I asked.

"My uncle taught me. He was real good. He'd get mad if something wasn't perfect, if the inlay didn't fit close."

Lincoln smiled and fell silent. The smile was like a sudden gust riffling the surface of a pond; his whole appearance changed in a most startling manner.

"How do you herd sheep?"

The chair wobbled and creaked as Lincoln shifted his weight.

"They go where they want, mostly. They follow that old blackface, the one with the bell. That blackface, sometimes he'll take the herd along all the damn day without letting them graze. He's a pain." He smiled again, with affection.

We talked some more. Lincoln had also been a firefighter, working with a "hot-shot" crew for the Forest Service, crews that are dropped at critical places during the spread of massive forest fires. It is an extremely dangerous business.

"How'd you get into that?" Walter asked.

"It's not so unusual," he said. "Lot of Zunis go into firefighting."

"Why?" I asked.

He shrugged. "Don't mind the danger, I guess," he said.

"Did you fight any big fires?" I asked.

"Sure," he said.

"Did you ever see anyone killed?"

He shook his head. "If you see it, you're probably not going to live yourself."

I would learn later that the Forest Service considers the Zunis to be among its best firefighters.

Walter and I slept outside the cabin. The next morning I cooked a mess of eggs on the stove while Walter chopped wood. Lincoln insisted we take two gallons of precious water from his milk can, a very generous gift, since he had to haul his drinking water fifteen miles from the

---

*The Arabs, I have learned since, became interested in Indian jewelry because many Indian designs are of Arabic origin, coming to the Southwest through the Spaniards, who brought with them Moorish designs. One of the largest trading posts at Zuni is owned by Arabs.

pueblo. We gave Lincoln the remains of our food supply: a few ounces of chile powder and some salt and pepper. We would eat well when we got to Zuni.

Lincoln ushered the sheep out of their corral. They jostled and tumbled down to the spring, the blackface at the fore, sending up clouds of dust, rising in the dawn like golden smoke. He waved farewell to us and, stick in hand, followed the bleating flock across the Zuni River and into some low hills. Soon he had vanished and all was quiet again.

Walter and I rode off across the Plain of Hawikuh. The sunlight was so brilliant that it rendered the landscape flat and unfamiliar, and we were unsure which hill Lincoln had showed us the evening before.

We continued in silence and suddenly there it was: several large mounds of rubble.

Nestled into the base of the hill was another sheep camp: a few weatherbeaten corrals and a shed. A wizened man in a dusty cowboy hat was standing by an open gate, muttering in Zuni to a ragged flock as they squeezed through. He came wobbling over on bow legs to greet us. Since the ruin appeared to be on his grazing land, we dismounted and asked if we could wander around a bit.

He grinned, revealing two teeth, and said, "Yes! Hawikuh!" while poking a long finger toward the ruin. He nodded again, his face a mask of wrinkled delight. "Okay! Go ahead! Hawikuh! You go there, fine!"

We tied our horses to some junipers near the camp and climbed up the ancient grassy pile of stone.

At the top we shook hands. Walter took my picture and I took his, and then we both sat down. For a while, neither of us spoke; there didn't seem to be anything to say.

"Hey, we're here," Walter said. "This is it. The Seven Cities of Gold."

"Yeah," I said.

The wind gusted across the ruin.

"Goddamn, Doug. This is an important moment," Walter said. "We actually made it."

I grunted in agreement.

I continued to sit, cross-legged, at my perch on top of the ruined city. There were no tourists, no souvenir stand, no sign of human life at all. Just a landscape of buttes and mesas, layered one against the other, sharp clean terraces of light. Below me, in the Plain of Hawikuh, the old shepherd was driving his flock. He walked slowly with a long stick, a black-and-white dog trotting at his heels. Spirals of red dust blossomed away from the small group as it inched its way across the plain.

I became sleepy and lay down, resting my head on a chiseled block of stone. I kept thinking that some profound thought, some great revelation, should come to me, but all I could feel was a vague sadness. I could hear the distant tinkling of a sheep bell and the bleating of sheep. A tuft of grama grass, growing between two hand-chiseled stones, stirred in the wind, its seed head dancing like a sturdy flag. I could feel the wind, a ghostly presence, gently prodding and brushing my face, rustling across the stones, carrying with it the scent of sun-heated juniper.

Then I heard a new sound, a low-frequency rumble, and a tiny jet deposited a snowy contrail across a field of blue. The sun turned once off its aluminum skin as it vanished over the horizon. I felt strange, as if I were hovering between two worlds, and then I fell into a deep, dreamless sleep.

⚊ ⧖ ⚊

The Zuni remember the overturning of their world. Curiously, what they remember most was not the appearance of Coronado, or the battle for Hawikuh. For 450 years they remembered something else: the coming of Esteban, the Barbary Coast African.

An anthropologist named Frank Hamilton Cushing, who lived with the Zuni from 1879 to 1884, recorded a startling account. He recounted the story in a lecture to the Geographic Society of Boston:

> One evening as I sat reading an old work of travel by the firelight in the little room they had assigned me, one by one four old men came in, rolled their corn husk cigarettes, and fell to watching me. . . . Finally one of them, acting as a spokesman for the rest, punched my little foot with his outstretched fingers and exclaimed,
> "Little Brother!"
> "What?" I asked.
> "Look here. What do the marks in that paper-fold say to you?"
> "Old things," said I.
> "How old?"
> "Maybe three hundred years; maybe three hundred and fifty," I chanced to reply.
> "Three hundred and fifty years," he repeated. "Three hundred and fifty! How long is that? . . . Hold little brother, lay out three hundred

and fifty corn-grains on the floor in a straight line, then we can tell how long three hundred and fifty years is."

The corn was brought in a twinkling and curious to see the result, I began placing it, kernel by kernel, in a straight line across the floor. Meanwhile, the old men bent eagerly over my back, wrinkling their foreheads, counting up their long-nailed fingers, conferring together, and sliding the corn grains here and there with little slivers. When I had nearly completed the number, they began, wholly after their own fashion, to reckon.

"Now that's one father," said they, "and his son growing up; *one! two!*"

So they went on until they reached nearly the end of the row, when suddenly the elder jumped up, his face beaming with inner light, and exclaimed,

"Why *here*, brothers, ten men's ages, *eleven!* That must have been when our ancients killed the Black Mexican at Kia-ki-me. Hold, little brother, does your old book tell anything about that?"

"No," said I to him most eagerly, "but you must."

"Why, yes, of course," he replied, while the others settled back to their cigarettes. And he began:

"It is to be believed," said he, "that a long time ago, when roofs lay over the walls of Kia-ki-me, when smoke hung over the house-tops, and the ladder-rounds were still unbroken—It was then that the Black Mexicans came from their abodes in Everlasting Summerland. One day, unexpected, out of 'Hemlock Canyon,' they came, and descended to Kia-ki-me. But when they said they would enter the covered way, it seems that our ancients looked not gently on them, but with these Black Mexicans came many Indians of Sóno-li, as they call it now, who carried war feathers and long bows and cane arrows like the Apaches . . .therefore these our ancients, being always bad tempered and quick to anger, made fools of themselves after their fashion, rushed into their town and out of their town, shouting, skipping and shooting with sling-stones and arrows and war clubs. Then the Indians of Sóno-li set up a great howl, and then they and our ancients did much ill to one another. Then and thus, was killed by our ancients, right where the stone stands down by the arroyo of Kia-ki-me, one of the Black Mexicans. . . . Then the rest ran away, chased by our grandfathers, and went back toward their own country in the Land of Everlasting Summer. But after they had steadied themselves and stopped talking, our ancients felt sorry; for they thought, 'Now we have made bad business, for after a while, these people, being angered, will come again.' So they felt always in danger and went about watching the bushes. By and by they did come back, those Black Mexicans, and with them many men of Sóno-li. They wore coats of iron and even bonnets of metal and carried for weapons short canes that spit fire and made thunder. Thus it was in the days of Kia-ki-me."

The story differs in some respects from the historical record: there was only one 'Black Mexican,' and the death of Esteban is generally, though not universally, thought to have occurred at Hawikuh, not the pueblo of Kyaki:ma about fifteen miles away. It must surely have been one of the most important events in Zuni history for it to have been passed down orally in such remarkable detail across 350 years.

The death of Esteban not only had a profound effect on the Zuni: it was possibly the biggest event in the American West in the summer of 1539. The news quickly spread among Indian tribes nearly to the Pacific Ocean.

Esteban died as he had lived, in a spectacular fashion. Many accounts of his death have surfaced. Taken together these stories create a powerful portrait of this African explorer, who ranks as one of the most extraordinary men in the history of the European discovery of America. This is not to say he was an altogether admirable person; but few great men are. That his achievements have been ignored by most historians and popularizers can only be due to the fact that he was neither European nor white; it is perhaps a little disquieting to Americans to realize that the original "discovery" of the Southwest belongs to an African.

This brings us to another question. Was Esteban truly a black African? Or was he a lighter-skinned Moor? Most scholars have assumed that Esteban was a Moor but not phenotypically black. However, one ethno-historian who has carefully researched the question, Professor Carroll Riley, concluded that Esteban was, in fact, a black African. In the original Spanish, Riley points out, he is mostly called a *negro* (black); sometimes he is referred to as a *Moro negro* (a black Moor); but almost never is he referred to as simply a *Moro*. According to Riley, the usage *negro* and *Moro negro* in sixteenth-century Spain specifically referred to blacks, as opposed to the light-skinned people of Moorish origin.

In 1540, a year after Esteban's death, a Spanish explorer sailed up the Sea of Cortez to the lower Colorado River. Here he heard about Esteban's death from Indians hundreds of miles from Cíbola. He reported back to New Spain:

"I asked him [an Indian] about Cíbola and whether he knew if the people there had ever seen people like us. He answered no, except a negro who wore on his feet and arms some things that tinkled. Your Lordship must remember how this negro who went with Fray Marcos wore bells, and feathers on his ankles and arms, and carried plates of various colors. He arrived there a little more than a year ago. I asked him why they killed him. He replied that the chieftain of Cíbola asked the negro if he had any brothers, and he answered that he had an infinite number, and that they had numerous arms, and that they were not very far from there. Upon hearing this, many chieftains assembled and decided to kill him so that he would not reveal their location to his brothers. For this reason they killed him and tore him into many pieces, which were distributed among the chieftains so that they should know that he was dead. He had a dog like mine [a hunting greyhound], which the chieftain had killed a long time afterward."

Another Spaniard heard that the Zuni kept the bones of Esteban for a long time, as proof that he and his brothers were mortal men who could be killed in battle.

Coronado himself heard an account of Esteban's death at Zuni, which he reported to the viceroy:

"The death of the negro is perfectly certain," Coronado wrote, "because many of the things which he wore have been found, and the Indians say they killed him here because the Indians of Chichilticale said that he was a bad man, and not like the Christians who never kill women,* and he killed them, and because he assaulted their women, whom the Indians love better than themselves. Therefore they determined to kill him, but they did not do it in the way that was reported [that is, the way Fray Marcos reported it in his narrative], because they did not kill any of the others who came with him."

Castañeda also made inquiries about Esteban's death. His account, while differing in some details, is perhaps the most revealing of all:

"It seems that the negro fell from the good graces of the friars [he means Fray Marcos] because he took along the women that were given to him, and collected turquoises, and accumulated everything. . . .

"When Esteban got away from the said friars, he craved to gain honor and fame in everything and be credited with the boldness and daring of discovering, all by himself, those terraced pueblos, so famed throughout the land. . . . He had traveled so far ahead of the friars that

---

*Was Esteban a pagan?

when they reached Chichilticale, which is the beginning of the *despoblado,* he was already at Cíbola. . . .

"I say then, when the negro Esteban reached Cíbola, he arrived there laden with a large number of turquoises and with some pretty women, which the natives [along the way] had given him. . . . But as the people of that land [Cíbola] were more intelligent than those who followed Esteban, they lodged him at a lodging house which they had outside of the pueblo, and the oldest and those in authority listened to his words and tried to learn the reason for his coming to that land.

"When they were well informed, they held councils for three days. As the negro had told them that farther back two white men, sent by a great lord, were coming, that they were learned in the things of heaven, and that they were coming to instruct them in divine matters, the Indians thought he must have been a spy or guide of some nations that wanted to come and conquer them. They thought it was nonsense for him to say that the people in the land whence he came were white, when he was black, and that he had been sent by them. So they went to him, and because, after some talk, he asked them for turquoises and women, they considered this an affront and determined to kill him. So they did, without killing any one of those who came with him."

One other point may have damned him: his sacred gourd. Esteban, it will be remembered from Fray Marcos's account, sent the gourd ahead to the governor of Hawikuh. When the Hawikuh chief "took it in his hands and saw the jingle bells, he at once hurled the gourd to the ground with much anger and wrath. He told the messengers to leave immediately, for he knew what sort of people that they represented." There seems to be only one explanation for this reaction: the Plains Indians who had (probably) made the gourd were enemies of the Zuni. (The Zuni have periodically warred with various Plains Indian tribes.)

When we were at Zuni Pueblo, we heard yet another story about Esteban. The Zuni who told me the story said he had heard as a child that Esteban had not been killed because he assaulted Zuni women, but because he was so exotic the Zuni women became excessively interested in *him.* The Zuni men who killed him were merely getting rid of a potential rival.

Thus by his death we have an extraordinary picture of Esteban in life: proud, arrogant, fearless, brash, charming, attractive to women, and with a weakness for sartorial elegance. Scholars have fretted, I think needlessly, over these differing accounts of his death. Each story tells part of the truth, and taken together they add up to a convincing motivation for the normally peaceful and hospitable Zuni to get rid of this troublesome man.

"This is why," one Zuni told me, "even today, the Zuni dislike blacks. You will find this is true all across the reservation. Sometimes you will hear Zuni saying nasty things about black tourists who come to watch the Shalako ceremonies. I know it's wrong to feel like this but that's just the way it is. We've never forgotten Esteban. He was the beginning of the end."

22

Following the battle for Hawikuh, Fray Marcos was immediately sent back to Mexico for his own safety. Coronado and his men settled in at Hawikuh, using it as a base for further explorations. Three weeks following the battle, on August 3, 1540, in a small room at Hawikuh, Coronado penned a report to Don Antonio de Mendoza, viceroy of New Spain.

It was a painful report to write. Mendoza was not just Coronado's political superior; he had been Coronado's great patron and perhaps even a sort of father figure to him. It was Mendoza who, in 1535, invited the twenty-five-year-old Coronado to come with him to the New World, where he was sailing to take up the appointment as first viceroy of New Spain. Coronado had been with Mendoza on his triumphal procession into Mexico City that November. Mendoza had elevated Coronado to a string of important posts, including making him a member of the city council, a position normally requiring royal sanction. Under Mendoza's patronage Coronado's fortunes rose quickly, and he became involved in all the activities of a gentleman of rank, military expeditions as well as charitable work. He married a wealthy heiress, Beatriz de Estrada (thought to be the illegitimate granddaughter of King Ferdinand of Spain). Doña Beatriz's mother gave Coronado a wedding gift of a huge country estate. In 1538 Mendoza made Coronado acting governor of New Galicia, New Spain's northern-frontier province, and the next year elevated him to full governorship. In just four years, due to Mendoza, Coronado had become one of the most prominent gentlemen in the entire New World.

Mendoza's selection of Coronado to lead the conquest of the Seven Cities of Gold was the final confirmation of the viceroy's confidence in his young protégé. Mendoza himself had invested perhaps more than was wise in the enterprise and had high expectations of a big return.

And now, less than five years since his arrival in the New World, Coronado found himself in the position of telling his great patron of the absolute failure of his hopes and the ruination of his investment. That the expedition's failure was not Coronado's fault was but small comfort. Coronado was a pragmatic man and may have realized, even at this early date, that his splendid career in the New World was at an end.

First, Coronado shifted blame. *"Not to be too verbose,"* Coronado wrote to Mendoza, *"I can assure you that he [Fray Marcos] has not told the truth in a single thing that he said, but everything is the opposite of what he related."*

Then a plea for understanding. *"God knows that I wish I had better news to write to your Lordship, but I must tell you the truth, and, as I wrote you from Culiacán, I must inform you of the good as well as the bad. But you may be assured that if all the riches and treasures of the world had been here, I could not have done more in his Majesty's service and in that of your Lordship than I have done in coming here where you commanded me, carrying, both my companions and myself, our provisions on our back for 300 leagues, and traveling on foot many days, making our way over hills and rough mountains, besides other hardships which I refrain from mentioning. Nor shall I think of stopping until my death, if it serves his Majesty or your Lordship to have it so."*

Then he got to the heart of the matter. *"As far as I can judge, it does not appear to me that there is any hope of getting gold or silver, but I trust in God that, if there is any, we shall get our share of it, and it shall not escape us through any lack of diligence in the search."*

But all, perhaps, was not lost; there still was a glimmer of hope. *"I have determined,"* Coronado continued, *"to send men throughout all the surrounding regions in order to find out whether there is anything, and to suffer every extremity rather than give up this enterprise, if I can find any way in which to do it, and not to be lacking in diligence until your Lordship directs me as to what I ought to do."*

Coronado had but one small gift for Mendoza: he named Hawikuh "Granada," *"in honor of your Lordship"*—the Spanish city was Mendoza's hometown.

He then told the viceroy about the people of Cíbola:

"The Seven Cities are seven little villages. . .all within a radius of four leagues. . .they are very good houses, three and four and five stories high, where there are very good homes and good rooms with corridors, and some quite good rooms underground and paved, which are built for winter, and which are something like estufas."

"Estufa," the Spanish word for stove, was how the Spanish described the underground ceremonial chamber known as the kiva.

"The people of these towns seem to me to be fairly large, and intelligent. . . . I think they have a quantity of turquoises, which they had removed with the rest of their goods. . . . The climate of this country," Coronado continued, *"and the temperature of the air are almost like those of Mexico, because now it is hot and now it rains. I have not yet seen it rain, however, except once when there fell a little shower with wind, such as often falls in Spain."*

No doubt Coronado was thinking quite a great deal about Spain these days.

"The snow and cold are unusually great, according to what the natives of the country say. . . . There are no fruits or fruit trees. The country is all level and nowhere shut in by high mountains, although there are some hills and rough passages. . . . Very good grass was found a quarter of a league away, both for pasturage for our horses and for mowing for making hay, of which we had great need, because our horses were so weak and feeble when they arrived."

This grass was no doubt the fine meadows that still exist south of Hawikuh, in the vicinity of a series of natural springs along Plumasano Wash and Ojo Caliente.

"The food which they eat in this country consists of maize, of which they have great abundance, beans and game. . . . They make the best tortillas that I have ever seen anywhere, and this is what everybody ordinarily eats. They have the very best arrangement and method for grinding that was ever seen. One of these Indian women here will grind as much as four of the Mexicans do. . . .

"Your Lordship may see thus how extensive this country is. There are many animals, bears, tigers [bobcats?], lions [mountain lions], porcupines, and some sheep as big as horses, with very large horns and little tails."

This latter was not as much of an exaggeration as one might think; the Spanish had small horses.

"I have seen some of their horns, the size of which was something amazing. There are wild goats, whose head I have also seen, and the paws of the bears and the skins of the wild boars [javelinas]. For game they have deer, leopards, and very large roebucks [elk?]."

Then Coronado made mention of the buffalo and alluded to trade with the Plains Indians. *"The natives here have some very well-dressed skins, and they prepare and paint them where they kill the cattle [buffalo], according to what they tell me."*

Coronado had also made inquiries about other villages, which he now described to Mendoza.

"The Kingdom of Totonteac, which the father provincial [he refers to Fray Marcos] praised so much, saying that it was something marvelous, and of much richness, and that cloth was made there, is, according to the Indians, a hot lake, on the edge of which there are five or six houses."

Scholars have never been able satisfactorily to identify Totonteac, but it may have been a settlement near Zuni Salt Lake.

"The Kingdom of Acus [described by Fray Marcos in glowing terms] is a single small city."

This was Acoma Pueblo, between Zuni and the Río Grande.

"They tell me that there are some other small kingdoms not far from this settlement, which are situated on a river."

This was the first mention of the Río Grande and the pueblos along its banks—an area that would figure large in the events of the coming winter.

"Three days after I captured this city," Coronado continued, *"some of the Indians who lived here came to make peace. They brought me some turquoises and poor blankets, and I welcomed them in his Majesty's name with the kindest words I could say, making them understand the purpose of my coming to this country, which is, in the name of his Majesty and by the command of your Lordship, that they and all others in this province should become Christians and should accept the true God as their Lord and his Majesty as their king and earthly master."*

What happened next puzzled and hurt Coronado, but today what is most puzzling is Coronado's naïveté. The Zuni understood all too well the gist of Coronado's "kindest words" and reacted appropriately: *"After this,"* Coronado continued, *"they returned to their houses, and suddenly, the next day, they packed up their goods and property, their women and children, and fled to the hills, leaving their towns deserted."*

The "hills" were undoubtedly the sacred mesa of Dowa Yalanne, Corn Mountain, the traditional place of refuge for the Zuni.

"Seeing this. . .I went to the town which I said was larger than this." This would be Mats'a:kya, one of the other Seven Cities, today also in ruins. *"I found only a few natives there, and I told them that they need not have any fear, and I asked them to summon their lord to me."*

But Coronado was also mystified by the differences between his own stratified, monarchical society and the egalitarian, consensual society of the Zuni.

"Although, by what I can find out or observe, none of these towns has any [lord], since I have not seen any principal house by which any superiority over others could be shown."

Finally, Coronado tells us, an old man did visit him, saying he was their chief, and said that he and other chiefs would come back to "arrange the relations which should exist between us." The chiefs did come and, in response to Coronado's demands, told him they would indeed come down from their stronghold and become Christians and accept his Majesty as king. But, Coronado then complained, *"they still remain in their strongholds, with their wives and all their property."*

The Zuni told Coronado that *"it was foretold them more than fifty years ago that a people such as we are would come, and from the direction we have come, and that the whole country would be conquered."*

Coronado asked the Indians to paint a cloth for him, showing all the animals of the area, which they did, and which Coronado wrapped up and sent back to the viceroy. He also sent back a map showing his route, twelve blankets showing Zuni weaving, a garment "of very good workmanship," a "cattle skin" (buffalo hide), turquoises, earrings, fifteen Indian combs, two wicker baskets, head rolls with which the women balanced jugs of water, a shield, a mallet, and a bow and some arrows.

None of these items or the map—much to the frustration of scholars—has ever come to light.

Coronado concluded his report: *"From the province of Cíbola and this city of Granada, the 3rd of August, 1540.*

"Francisco Vázquez de Coronado kisses the hand of your most illustrious Lordship."

Coronado's main army, which had been lumbering behind Coronado, arrived at Cíbola in the fall, and with it the common foot soldier Pedro de Castañeda, who made his own very shrewd observations of the Zuni.

By this time Castañeda was undergoing something of a personal revelation in his views of the Indians. This remarkable and mysterious soldier had already expressed much puzzlement over the Spaniards of Culiacán, his hometown, and compared them unfavorably with the Indians of Cíbola. Why, he asked at one point, was it that "the Spaniards [of Culiacán] are Christians; for in the Cíbola country there is the intelligence of men, while in the other the barbarism of animals dominates, even surpassing that of beasts." (Later on we shall see just how far Castañeda's rethinking took him, when he writes with deep disapproval about what the Spanish did to the pueblos along the Río Grande.)

"The natives here are intelligent people," Castañeda wrote of the Zuni. "They have no rulers as in New Spain, but are governed by the counsel of their oldest men. They have their priests, whom they call papas, who preach to them. These priests are the old men, who mount the high terrace of the pueblo in the morning as the sun rises, and from there, like town criers, preach to the people, who all listen in silence, seated along the corridors. The priests tell the people how they should live. I believe they give them some commandments to observe, because there is no drunkenness, sodomy, or human sacrifice among them, nor do they eat human flesh, or steal."

Castañeda continued his description of the Zuni—a fascinating, well-observed, and extremely rare document of native life before it was changed forever by the Europeans.

"A man has only one wife. . . . When someone wishes to marry he must have the permission of the rulers. The man must spin and weave a blanket and place it before the woman. She covers herself with it and becomes his wife. The houses are for the women, the estufas [kivas] for the men. . . . The men spin and weave; the women take care of the children and prepare the food. The land is so fertile that. . .in one year they harvest enough for seven years. . . . The towns are free from filth. . . . Their houses are well separated and extremely clean in the places where they cook and where they grind flour. They do this in a separate place. . .with three stones set in mortar. Three women come in, each going to her stone. One crushes the maize, the next grinds it, and the third grinds it finer. . . . While they are grinding, a man sits at the door playing a flageolet, and the women move their stones, keeping time with the music, and all three sing together.

"Throughout these provinces one finds pottery glazed with alcohol,* and jugs of such elaborate designs and shapes that it was surprising."

---

*Glazes using lead.

The Pueblo women, he noted at another point, went about naked until they took a husband and had sexual intercourse, when they covered themselves. By going naked, Castañeda explained, "they say if they do anything wrong it will soon be noticed and so they will not do it." He adds, approvingly: "They need not feel ashamed, either, that they go about as they were born."

Thus the Spanish themselves, not disposed to think kindly of native people, give us a picture of aboriginal Zuni life: peaceful, cooperative, spiritual, prosperous, and happy; indeed, a far better world than the one the Spanish themselves had left behind in Europe—and a better world than the Europeans would create for Zuni.

But fifty years before, an oracle had prophesied the coming of the white men, the broken wall, the destruction and conquest. Now it had come to pass.

Did this same prophecy predict the 1598 expedition of Oñate to require formal submission of the Zuni; the building of the great mission church at Hawikuh; the baptism of the Zuni in 1629; the killing of Father Letrado in 1632; the final abandonment of Hawikuh; the Mexican Revolution; the American conquest; the arrival of Indian agents and anthropologists, of pickup trucks and HUD housing, of art collectors, of running water and propane gas, telephones, schools, television, and tour buses bringing people to watch sacred dances? Did it predict the lawyers with calfskin briefcases and topographical maps delineating the legal and absolute extent of the Zuni world, now a patch of desert ground within the most powerful country the earth has ever seen, the United States of America?

⊲ ⤭ ⊳

I woke up on the stones of Hawikuh with the sudden cool feeling of shadow on my face. Walter was standing over me.

"We better get going," he said, "if we're going to reach Zuni by nightfall."

I scrambled to my feet, hungry and disoriented. We mounted our horses and set off down the dirt road that connected Hawikuh and Zuni.

We were subdued. Something about Hawikuh had depressed us. Now we were driven by our hunger, trotting and loping toward town. The horses picked up our rising anticipation and, tired as they were, became nearly impossible to rein back. They wanted to run.

The road skirted a hill and the pueblo of Zuni came into view.

It lay in the hollow of the river valley, an indistinct speckling of houses, distorted by mirages. A haze from the outdoor *horno* ovens hovered over the town. A pickup truck crawled along, trailing a corkscrew of dust.

North of the village rose the two blunt teeth of the Twin Buttes, glowing in the afternoon sun. To the southeast lay a crowd of sand hills, sprinkled with broken rock. Farther to the south, the plain rose gradually to the foot of a solitary mesa, a thousand feet high and two miles broad. This, we knew, had to be Dowa Yalanne, the sacred Corn Mountain. Its soaring cliffs, striped in layers of pale green and red sandstone, had been chiseled by wind and rain into fantastic spires, buttresses, and arches. Even farther to the south rose other mesas, seamed with canyons opening into ever more distant canyons, like successive doorways, all finally dissolving into a blue infinity of light.

We trotted down to the village, and in a few miles passed the first houses, a HUD subdivision of fake, boxy adobes. People watched us from open doors and kids waved from yards, while dogs raced about, barking. The road turned to asphalt and we arrived at the center of town, in front of a store called "Halona."

Our arrival created a stir. Zuni children came streaming from all directions, shouting, laughing, skipping, whooping, and speaking a confusing mixture of Zuni and English. We tied the horses and bought a mass of burritos and Dr. Peppers, which we proceeded to devour like madmen, to the great delight of the children. A rich smell of juniper smoke, fragrant and musky, hung over the town.

In the midst of this pandemonium a young man stopped and introduced himself. He was Edward Wemytewa, a teacher and horseman. He invited us to turn our horses out in a pasture he owned at the edge of the pueblo.

We headed off toward Wemytewa's place, with an older boy named Delbert Kallestewa leading the boisterous crowd of children. We wound through the crooked dirt streets of Zuni, our long days of silence and emptiness at an end. The sudden crowds and excitement induced in us a state of pleasant, confused euphoria. We had not been in any town since Young, and certainly no town anywhere near the size of Zuni in a month.

The children argued loudly in their mixture of languages who was going to lead which horses. This was a tricky question, since there were more than a dozen children and only four animals. We finally resolved it by giving each horse to four or five kids, who collectively seized the lead rope and hauled it along. Every time a horse stopped to nibble a clump of grass, the children leading him would start hollering in Zuni and English and heaving on the rope. It was a comical sight.

Wemytewa's house was the very last house at the southeastern edge of the pueblo. Behind it, two miles distant, rose up the monumental form of Dowa Yalanne, a tremendous presence, a massive living thing parked on the desert floor like some slumbering creature.

That evening, Delbert took us to a little restaurant called My Place, a little shack along the main road with three tables inside. With my burned lips, I found I could eat the hot chile burrito only by holding my lower lip down with one hand, while keeping my upper lip drawn back, thus exposing the masticatory process for all to see. The process caused a great deal of half-chewed food to drop out of my mouth and all over the table.

After watching for a few minutes with great fascination, Delbert pronounced: "Wow, man, that is *gross.*"

After dinner Delbert took us to the plaza. It was pitch-dark. We scurried through a warren of back streets and climbed up on some roofs and began walking from rooftop to rooftop.

"Who lives underneath?" I asked.

"People," said Delbert.

"Aren't they going to mind us walking all over their roofs?" I asked.

"Nah. Everybody does it," he said.

To the west, Dowa Yalanne stood out black and solid against a faintly phosphorescent sky. Outdoor cooking fires—uncertain yellow points of light—flecked the darkened landscape of the pueblo, and a murmur of voices came up on the wind. The old mission church of Zuni sat across from us, a black shape, its graveyard a pond of darkness. Below us was a small courtyard.

"Down there," Delbert said, "that's where the Shalako dancers come through. It's really cool." And he shuffled on the roof, imitating them.

A head stuck out of a window and yelled at us in Zuni.

"What'd she say?" I asked.

"Nothin'," said Delbert, and stomped on the roof a few times before leading us down.

We slept in the pasture with our horses, listening to the rattle of the wind and the snorting and sighing of the magnificent animals who had carried us to the Seven Cities of Gold.

23

Despite a century of intensive archeological excavations, we still have only the vaguest idea of the history of the Southwest before 1540. We do not really know, for example, why the great, classic phase of Anasazi civilization declined in the early thirteenth century, leading to the abandonment of Chaco Canyon.

Three and a half centuries passed between the quiet collapse of Chaco culture and the coming of the Europeans. During that time, a kind of diaspora took place, with the inhabitants of Chaco breaking into smaller bands and migrating along river drainages in various directions. When the Europeans arrived in 1540, the descendants of the Anasazi lived in dozens of independent (and often mutually hostile) pueblos scattered across the Southwest, from Hopi to Pecos, speaking a half-dozen unrelated languages.

What happened in between? Nobody really knows.

One theory, which can probably never be proved, has it that some of these wandering Anasazi left Chaco and eventually settled along the Zuni River. There, perhaps seven hundred years ago, these descendants of Chaco encountered a different people altogether: the Mogollon Indians. The Mogollon, makers of intricate and beautiful pots, had been living in the area for centuries.

No one knows what happened when these two cultures met. There may have been a peaceful mingling at the boundaries, with intermarriage, an exchange of culture and technology, and a fusion of language; or there might have been a violent struggle, with the Mogollon people expelling the Anasazi—but not before appropriating many aspects of Anasazi culture.

Whatever happened, a new people sprang from this mixing of cultures: the Zuni Indians.

Originally the Zuni were more widespread. The great ruins of the prehistoric Zuni dot the countryside far beyond the bounds of the present-day reservation. As the fourteenth and fifteenth centuries passed, the Zuni people began to abandon their more outlying villages, settling in a more compact area along the Zuni River, and by the time Columbus landed on the shores of Hispaniola, the Zuni were living in six large, prosperous towns within a twelve-mile radius.

The Zuni excelled at farming, trade, diplomacy, and craft technology, and as a consequence became extraordinarily wealthy by aboriginal standards. In 1540 they enjoyed one of the highest standards of living of any people in North America. As a result they were widely known among native tribes from the Pacific Coast to the central Great Plains. It is not hard to see how poorer Indians, in describing the wealth of Zuni to eager Spaniards, succeeded in implanting the idea of the legendary Seven Cities of Gold in the minds of the Europeans.* To a poor hunter-gatherer Indian, the wealth of the Zuni *was* staggering.

In the battle of Hawikuh the Zuni learned a great lesson: that it was futile to fight the Europeans. If and when the Spanish returned, the Zuni would deal with them using means other than warfare—specifically, diplomacy, trade, and subterfuge. The Zuni were not, however, passive; they would stubbornly and violently resist domination in the areas that mattered, most of all in their religion.

While a few Spanish expeditions touched Zuni in the intervening years, in 1598 the Europeans came back again in force, this time to colonize New Mexico under a charter granted by the king of Spain. The expedition was financed and led by Juan de Oñate, a wealthy and distinguished nobleman. Oñate, who was Basque, was the son of a

---

*Extensive research on the precise number of inhabited Zuni towns has shown that there were six, not seven, cities. The number seven was a product of the Spanish imagination.

conquistador himself. He had married Isabel de Tolosa y Cortés Moctezuma—a woman with an extraordinary lineage that included both Cortés, conqueror of Mexico, and Moctezuma (or Montezuma), last emperor of the Aztecs.

Oñate and his settlers established a colony at the confluence of the Río Chama and the Río Grande, near present-day Española, New Mexico. The names of many of the colonists who came with him— Vigil, Martínez, Salazar, Carabajal, Baca, Rodríguez, Leyba, Romero—are today common family surnames in the mountain towns of northern New Mexico.

Oñate paid his first visit to the Seven Cities of Cíbola in November of 1598 and announced that the Zuni must render obedience to the king of Spain and to God. The Zuni had learned much about the peculiarity of the Spaniards over these two items, and so, "with signs of contentment and harmony," two Zuni chiefs, Negua-homi and Atishoa, signed the "Act of Obedience and Vassalage." The Spanish departed in good humor and the Zuni no doubt breathed a collective sigh of relief.

Thirty-one years later the attempted conversion of the Zuni began. In 1629 a group of missionaries and soldiers arrived at Zuni. They were astonished to be greeted with "festive applause." The Father Custodian, Estévan de Perea, immediately took this as a sign that "God hath already disposed this vineyard." Perea set himself up in a house at Hawikuh and raised a cross, telling the Zuni that they had come to "free them from the miserable slavery of the demon and from the obscure darkness of their idolatry." A great platform was erected in the plaza of Hawikuh and the following day Mass was performed, along with the baptism of many of the Zuni leaders. (What the Indians thought of the strange rituals of the Catholic Mass is not known, but being ritualistic-minded themselves the Zuni were probably impressed and may very well have enjoyed themselves.) The ceremony was followed by "a clamorous rejoicing, with a salvo of harquebuses; and, in the afternoon, skirmishings and caracolings of the horses."

Father Perea did note, with momentary unease, that the Indians "are very observant of superstitious idolatry. . .they have their gods in the mountains, in the rivers, in the harvests, and in their houses."

Assured of the peaceful intentions of the Zuni, the soldiers returned to Santa Fe, leaving the friars to finish what would no doubt be a swift conversion. The Church of La Purísma Concepcíon was built at Hawikuh and the good father began his work.

The Spanish made one fatal assumption: because the Zuni instantly welcomed their teachings of Christ, the Spanish felt sure they would just as easily relinquish worship of their own gods. This was a great misunderstanding of Zuni religion. The Zuni had no trouble accepting the Spanish god (Christ) into their pantheon; the more gods the better. Nor did they reject Mass, which, to them, became one more ceremony in their already formidable cycle of dances and ceremonies. Their reasoning was quite simple: since the Spanish were powerful they must have powerful gods, and it would be wise to honor them. The Zuni, if anything, were more fanatically religious than the sixteenth-century Spanish. The faithful practice of their religion was a matter of life and death; all aspects of Zuni life were imbued with sacred meaning and ritual. To break the cycle of ceremonies, to neglect the thanking of the gods for rain and corn and the successful hunt—this was the surest way to drought, famine, and catastrophe.

Thus, while attending Mass and taking Communion, the Zunis continued to worship their own gods. The friars then put up a "great resistance to the sorcerers," castigating the Zuni priests, seizing and smashing "idols," and breaking up Zuni ceremonial dances.

On Sunday, February 22, 1632,* nobody showed up for Mass. The priest, Fray Francisco de Letrado, a man with more zeal than sense, went looking for them. He caught some "idolaters" (presumably in the act) and began chiding them. It seems likely the Mass coincided with a Zuni ceremonial and that the good father tried to disrupt it.

The Indians had had enough. They strung their bows; Fray Francisco saw his time was up; he fell to his knees holding a little crucifix in his hands and prayed to his god; and the Indians filled him with arrows and scalped him.

Knowing the Spanish would try to avenge Letrado's death, the Zuni took refuge on the top of Dowa Yalanne. Here, at the western edge of the mesa, an entire city—built for just such an emergency—stood waiting for them.

Standing a thousand feet above the countryside, Dowa Yalanne was virtually unconquerable. It had only three access points, two hand-and-foot trails and a very steep horse trail. Life on top of Dowa Yalanne may have been inconvenient, but it was not hard. The mesa top was nearly two miles long and three-quarters of a mile wide. At the

---

*Curiously enough, exactly one hundred years to the day before the birth of George Washington.

lower end of the mesa the Zuni had built a large catchbasin for rainwater. In the winter the Zuni would roll huge snowballs into the reservoir, awaiting the next thaw. Standing beside the reservoir was a stone-and-mud pueblo, with hundreds of rooms, many kivas, and several plazas. The Indians still farmed the bottomlands along the river and at the base of the mountain; they also kept huge stores of grain on the mountain in case of a siege.

When news of Fray Francisco's martyrdom reached Santa Fe, the governor sent out a small punitive expedition of soldiers and friars. The Spaniards apparently realized the futility of attacking the Zuni in their stronghold, so a parley took place, the Zuni promised not to kill any more priests, and the transgression was forgiven. The churches at Hawikuh and Halona were eventually rebuilt.

The Zuni continued to be unhappy with the friars. But the burden borne by the Zuni, who lived at the very edge of the Spanish empire, was light compared to the pueblos along the Río Grande and in the Galisteo Basin. Closer to the center of Spanish power in Santa Fe, these Indians were exploited and abused on a much larger scale. The Franciscan friars used coerced labor to build large mission churches, while the corrupt governors of New Mexico began to impose the *encomienda* system on the pueblos, whereby prominent colonists were granted the right to use Indian labor in return for "protecting" and Christianizing them.

In 1680, the pueblos secretly united under the leadership of a San Juan Pueblo shaman named El Popé. The overthrow of the Spanish was carefully planned, and a knotted cord, signifying the number of days to the rebellion, was circulated at Zuni and the other pueblos. At the predetermined moment—August 10, 1680—all the pueblos simultaneously rose up against the Spanish.

The Indians achieved a stunning victory. A large percentage of the Spanish in New Mexico were killed and the rest driven in a humiliating retreat down the Río Grande to El Paso. In a few weeks not a European was left alive in all of the Southwest.

The friars were the first killed in the rebellion, and El Popé then supervised the systematic destruction of the great mission churches. Those Indians who had been baptized were scrubbed with yucca suds to remove the spiritual stain, and in some pueblos the Indians defiantly excavated kivas in the rubble of churches.

At Zuni, a friar named Juan de Bal was among those killed on

August 10th, and the mission at Hawikuh was burned. Once again the Zunis packed up their goods and moved into the pueblo on top of Dowa Yalanne, knowing the Spanish would be back.

For twelve years the Southwest was free of the Spanish. During this time the pueblos began squabbling and the alliance fell apart. When Captain General Don Diego de Vargas returned with a conquering army in 1692 he retook Santa Fe without a fight. He then proceeded to visit each of the pueblos in turn, trading their obedience for forgiveness.

Vargas arrived at Zuni in November. Given promises of clemency, the Zuni permitted him and his soldiers to climb up Dowa Yalanne. Vargas paraded through the pueblo on his horse, two friars administered absolution to the Zuni, and 294 Indians were baptized on the spot.

Vargas made a strange discovery on top of the mountain: "The general went in through a door," the account went, "and found the image of Christ, our crucified lord, a painting of the most glorious Saint John the Baptist. . .and some missals, on a fairly well constructed altar where two tallow candles were burning, and the whole was covered with little remnants of ornaments."

They "all marveled" at the discovery: the Zuni were the only tribe to have preserved any trace of Christianity.* Why was this?

The Zuni themselves have an interesting explanation. Their traditions tell of another friar in the pueblo during the rebellion. (This would make sense, since there were two churches, one at Hawikuh and another at Halona.) This friar was much loved by the Zuni and was affectionately called Juan-gray-robed-father-of-us. During the rebellion he abjured his faith and his life was thus spared, and he fled with the Zuni to the top of Dowa Yalanne carrying with him some things from the mission. After living with the Indians for years on the mesa top, Juan had been inducted into the tribe and had become a Zuni himself. When Vargas arrived, the mysterious Juan, presented with the opportunity to rejoin the Spanish, chose to remain Zuni.

The Pueblo Revolt had an immediate and beneficial effect on Spanish rule over the pueblos. The Spanish realized that exploiting the

---

*It was only an outward shred of Christianity; none of the Zuni were actual Christians. The Zuni had merely incorporated Christian ritual into their own animist religion.

Pueblo Indians for labor and forcing Catholicism down their throats were counterproductive. Spanish (and later Mexican) rule of New Mexico, from 1692 to 1846, was perhaps the most enlightened and benign of any European rule of native American tribes, at least until the late twentieth century.* Without question the Spanish in general treated the Indians far better than did the English, belying the "Black Spanish" legend invented and perpetuated by Anglo-American historians. Benevolent Spanish and Mexican rule is the primary reason why the tribes of the Southwest are the least changed of all native Americans—whereas brutal Anglo-American rule is the reason why the Indian cultures east of the Mississippi are now virtually extinct.

After the Reconquest, the Zunis remained on top of Dowa Yalanne. Not only were they taking no chances with the Spanish, but they were facing new enemies as well: the Apaches and Navajos. For these tribes had acquired the horse, which transformed them from poor itinerants, scratching out an existence through hunting, farming, and thievery, to a terrifying mobile force. With horses they could cross hundreds of miles of desert; they could strike anywhere, at any time, and disappear in a whirlwind of dust. The prosperous Zunis, with their herds of livestock, waffle gardens thick with produce, and vast stores of dried corn and beans, became a prime target.

The Zuni spent nineteen years on Dowa Yalanne before descending from their mountain stronghold. But rather than move back into their six towns, to protect themselves from the Apaches and Navajos they banded together at the site of Halona. Hawikuh and its ruined mission, vacant since 1680, became a summer camping ground for Zuni shepherds until the roofs finally caved in and the walls collapsed. The four other cities gradually tumbled into the earth, the final end of the Seven (or rather six) Cities of Gold.

For the next century and a half, the Zunis, living at the crumbling edge of the Spanish empire, found themselves almost untouched by political tides. In 1821, when Mexico threw off Spanish rule, the Zunis barely noticed. The only change was a positive one: the Mexican government expelled the Franciscan Order from New Mexico and all the friars at Zuni left. The great mission church of Nuestra Señora de Guadalupe at Halona was abandoned and the Catholic presence at Zuni disappeared, not to return until well after World War I.

---

*This benevolence did not extend to the governance of the Navajo and Apache, as we shall see.

The Christian faith had never taken firm root among the Zuni, and what little the Zunis had was mostly forgotten. A gradual syncretism took place. From the beginning the Zunis had been incorporating bits of Christianity into their own religious ceremonies. Once the friars left they decorated the decaying mission walls with pagan symbols and continued to bury their dead, with Zuni rituals, in the consecrated ground of the churchyard. The friars had not Christianized the Zunis; rather, the Zunis had paganized Christianity.

During Mexican rule (1821–1848) what little authority the government had exerted at Zuni ceased entirely. But other forces were at work. In the 1820s a new people appeared at Zuni: American mountain men. The Zunis had always encouraged trade, and the pueblo became a jumping-off point for trappers going to and from California and Arizona. The mountain men found the Zunis to be extraordinarily hospitable. On more than one occasion the Zunis saved the lives of starving trappers. George Yount, a fur trader whose own life was saved by the Zuni, called them a "kind and humane" people.

When the United States annexed New Mexico in the Treaty of Guadalupe Hidalgo in 1848, the isolation of the Zunis came to an end. Several military expeditions passed through Zuni, and the Americans were deeply impressed.

"They have the reputation," a private in the first troop to visit Zuni wrote in his diary, "of being the most hospitable people in the world, which I believe they merit in every respect." Not only was the soldier "fed the best dinner I ever sat down to," but later, when he and his friends explored the pueblo, they were invited again and again into Zuni houses and fed to the bursting point. The private was amazed that nothing was stolen during their visit; where else, he wrote, "can such a mass of honest people be found?"* The official chronicler of the expedition marveled at the "honesty and hospitality" of the Zuni, and called Halona "one of the most extraordinary cities in the world."

Three years later another military expedition passed through Zuni. A young lieutenant, James H. Simpson of the Topographical Engi-

---

*Certainly not among the American soldiers, who were described by various people as "a military mob. . .the most open violators of law and order. . . . About one-fifth of the whole command have died from the effects of dissipation." "Nearly the whole territory has been the scene of violence, outrage, and oppression by the volunteer soldiery. . . . All is hubbub and confusion here; discharged volunteers leaving drunk, and volunteers not discharged remaining, drunk."

neers, kept a journal of the expedition which was published and widely read, for the first time bringing the Zuni to the attention of the American public. Simpson also noted that he had heard from some trappers hanging around Santa Fe that west of Zuni lay a route to California, along which wood, water, and grass could be found. (As late as 1850 nearly the entire country between Zuni and California remained unexplored.)

This seemingly innocuous observation would have a profound impact on the Zuni in later years. Acting on Simpson's advice, the Army Corps of Engineers launched an expedition, led by Captain Lorenzo Sitgreaves, to scout a route to California. (His orders included the ludicrous suggestion that particular attention be devoted to the "navigable properties" of the Zuni River!) Sitgreaves left Zuni in the fall of 1851 and became one of the first Americans to cross northern Arizona. He reported that, although there was no inhabited place of any size between Zuni and Los Angeles, he had located a splendid route, not merely for a wagon road, but for a railroad as well.

Only thirty-two years later, the Atlantic & Pacific Railroad would connect Albuquerque and Needles, California, following much of Sitgreaves's route but bypassing Zuni Pueblo for slightly more favorable terrain some miles north. But the damage would be done; the infamous checkerboarded railroad grant, the same one that caused so much trouble in Pleasant Valley, would extend deep into traditional Zuni lands, bringing with it rapacious cattle companies, booming railroad towns, lumber and mining operations—all bent on taking Zuni land. (Later this route would become a section of U.S. Route 66 and eventually Interstate 40.)

The Zunis at first welcomed the routing of roads through their lands, as this opened up opportunities for trade. The Zunis were brilliant traders. In one incident, two members of the team surveying for the railroad bought a sackful of junk jewelry and cheap trinkets in Santa Fe, fully expecting to make a killing at Zuni, acquiring robes, weapons, and splendid Zuni handicrafts. The traders spread out their "sham bijouterie" (as one witness recalled) and loudly extolled the rarity and value of the items until the pueblo fairly rang with their peroration. The Zunis listened with stolid faces. When the men were finished, redfaced from the effort, the Zunis began bargaining. The bargaining went on "infinitely." In the end, the sweating traders departed the pueblo with two sickly sheep, "fully persuaded that the Zuni were the 'smartest' traders west of the Mississippi." The Zunis also traded with the army on a much larger scale, supplying, for example, the feed corn to Fort Defiance, which by 1856 brought them $4,000 a year.

The Americans brought something else with them: smallpox. Epidemics periodically raged through the pueblo, until, at the close of the century, there were fewer Zunis alive than there had been at any other time in at least the past thousand years. The continual raids of the Navajos and Apaches also hit the pueblo hard, although the Zuni fought back with craft and ingenuity. Many a Navajo was caught and killed in Zuni "horse-traps"—ten-foot-deep pits carpeted with sharpened stakes and covered with brush and dirt, strategically placed on trails leading into the pueblo. Zuni warriors often accompanied American troops on punitive expeditions against the Navajos.

The Americans did not reciprocate the Zunis' loyalty and hospitality. The Zunis were treated shamefully. During the nineteenth and early twentieth centuries, there occurred a wholesale theft of Zuni lands by Americans. In 1848, the year of the American takeover, the Zuni more or less controlled a piece of land stretching from the San Francisco Peaks near present-day Flagstaff in the west to Mount Taylor in the east and the Mogollon Rim in the south. These were not the ill-defined boundaries common to nomadic, Plains tribes: these were mutually understood common boundaries.

Within the area of Zuni sovereignty, the Zuni hunted, collected medicinal plants and minerals, established sacred shrines, grazed livestock, maintained and patrolled trade routes, and worked outlying farms. There was no mystery or ambiguity about what the Zuni had established as their land. When asked, the Zunis could easily draw a map showing their boundaries.

The first invaders were the Mormons, who began settling on Zuni lands along the tributaries of the Little Colorado River and the lower reaches of the Zuni River. The checkerboard lands of the Atlantic & Pacific Railroad then chopped up much of the Zunis' territory; investors from New York City and Europe bought the checkerboard lands and stocked the range with tens of thousands of cattle. Towns such as Gallup sprang up alongside the railroads. Vast sections of the Zuni mountains were clear-cut and overgrazed. Hispanic and Anglo stockmen homesteaded Zuni springs and rivers, pushing the Zuni into poorer rangelands and blocking access to sacred sites. Even the area around Zuni Salt Lake was taken.

Meanwhile, the American government did absolutely nothing.

The Zunis protested again and again to their putative American allies. Finally, in 1877 the U.S. government set aside land for a reservation. But this turned out to be the biggest land theft of all—the boundaries included only the immediate area around Zuni Pueblo itself, less than 10 percent of the Zunis' traditional area of sovereignty. While the reservation was allegedly designed to protect the Zunis, it had the opposite effect: it made Zuni occupation of lands *outside* the reservation illegal. As the century waned, the Zuni were forced closer and closer into the artificial boundaries of their minuscule reservation. Adjusting to the occupation of their best lands and outlying water sources, the Zunis turned from farming to grazing sheep. But even these poor grazing lands were tempting. Between 1900 and 1934, Anglo and Hispanic ranches expanded and the Zuni continued to be squeezed into the reservation.

In 1934, the U.S. government fenced the artificially small reservation and ordered the Zuni to keep their flocks of sheep inside. The sudden concentration of tens of thousands of sheep in a greatly reduced area caused tremendous overgrazing and all but destroyed what had once been valuable dry-farming country, causing arroyos to form all over the reservation. This led to a final insult: a government-sponsored, forced livestock reduction program that left many Zuni destitute.

Meanwhile, U.S. government agricultural "experts" came on the reservation to teach the Zunis "modern" farming methods. These men had no comprehension of traditional Zuni dry-farming technology, developed over centuries and adapted to desert conditions. The Zunis made clever use of baffles and diversion dikes to check heavy runoff and flash floods, and spread the water gently through dryland crops. The boneheaded government experts considered the irregular and widely scattered plots a product of disorganization and perverse Indian logic, and persuaded the Zuni to farm in rectangular fields using Anglo methods. As a result many good fields were left gutted with arroyos and forever unplantable. Today, much of the area behind Dowa Yalanne, once thick with cornfields and orchards, is now dotted with dead fruit trees and fit only for grazing sheep and cattle.

The Zunis had always been close allies of the Americans. They had helped American trappers, supplied food to American military bases, guided American expeditions, fought alongside American troops, and obeyed American laws. In return, the American government robbed them of their lands just as thoroughly as it robbed the Indian tribes who resisted American domination. As several Zunis pointed out to me, the Spanish and Mexicans never treated them so shamefully. And still, when Anglos* (such as us) come to Zuni Pueblo, they are welcomed with a genuine warmth and kindness that is nothing short of astonishing. Someday, perhaps, our government will atone for its dishonorable treatment of the Zunis.

◦ ⚎ ◦

In 1879, a rather unhealthy, sallow-faced white man arrived at Zuni Pueblo. His visit would amount to one of the most significant events in the history of the Zunis, and would change their relationship to the outside world.

The man was Frank Hamilton Cushing, an assistant ethnologist with a Smithsonian expedition to the Southwest. Nineteenth-century anthropology was obsessed with material culture (one reason why our older museums are so full of artifacts), and the expedition leader, Colonel James Stevenson, and his associates set up shop outside the pueblo and began buying thousands of examples of Zuni handicrafts, weapons, tools, household utensils, pottery, and the like. In the end, several wagonloads of artifacts were crated up and sent back east.

Cushing had different ideas. He wanted to learn who the Zuni were as a *people*. He hung about the pueblo, sketching in his notebook, asking questions, and making a general nuisance of himself.

He almost immediately ran into trouble when he began sketching a religious dance.

"When I took my station on a house-top," Cushing recalled later, "sketch-books and colors in hand, I was surprised to see frowns and hear explosive, angry expostulations in every direction. As the day wore on this indignation increased, until at last an old, bush-headed hag approached me, and scowling into my face made a grab at my book and pantomimically tore it to pieces. . . . I was exercised by this state of feeling, which became, as time went on—especially with those conservators of the ancient regime the world over, old women—more and more virulent."

The Zunis did not want an outsider prying into their affairs, and Cushing became increasingly frustrated. Finally he took a step that astonished his scientific colleagues: he decided to give up his comfortable quarters with the expedition and move in with the Indians. Never

---

*The term "Anglo" as used in New Mexico refers to any American who is not Indian or Hispanic—not merely those of English descent. Jews, blacks, Asian-Americans—all would be considered "Anglos" by the Zunis.

before had an anthropologist voluntarily gone to live with his subjects.
The idea was perverse.

"I moved my books, papers, and blankets to the governor's house,"
Cushing recalled. "On the dirt floor in one corner I spread the blankets,
and to the rafters slung a hammock. When the old chief came in that
evening and saw that I had made myself at home, he shrugged his
shoulders.

" 'How long will it be before you go back to Washington?' he
attempted to ask.

" 'Two months,' I signified.

" '*Tuh!*' (damn) was his only exclamation as he climbed to the roof
and disappeared through the sky-hole."

When the expedition got ready to move on to Hopi, Cushing informed them he intended to stay at Zuni. They were so disgusted that
they left without bidding him goodbye and even took with them his
share of food and supplies.

Leaving Cushing destitute turned out to have interesting results.
When Cushing explained the situation to the Zuni governor, Palowahtiwa, the man replied: " 'Little brother, you may be a Washington
man, but it appears you are very poor. Now, if you do as we tell you,
and will only make up your mind to be Zuni, you shall be rich, for you
shall have fathers and mothers, brothers and sisters, and the best food
in the world. But if you do not do as we tell you, you will be very, very
poor indeed.'

" 'Why should I not be a Zuni?' I replied in despair; and the old man
quickly answered,

" 'Why not?' "

Although Cushing was the first to live with his subjects for an
extended period, very few anthropologists since have so thoroughly
entered into the life of their people as did Cushing. The Zuni, for their
part, took on the challenge of transforming this slope-shouldered, hypochondriac of a white man into an Indian. They took away his hammock and his eastern clothes, and subjected him to hunger, cold, and
privation, a process they explained as "hardening his meat."

His first communal meal at Zuni gives only a small idea of what he
had to undergo (and provides us with an amusing look at Cushing's
fastidiousness). Cushing had burned his fingers trying to fish his food
out of the communal pot, so his thoughtful hostess "quietly rose" and
began hunting around for something for him to eat with. "Presently

she found that something," Cushing wrote, "on the floor where the baby had been playing with it. It was an old, broken-handled pewter spoon. She caught it up, and seeing that it was—not very clean—put it into her own mouth, good woman, licked it off thoroughly, then went to the waterjar and rinsed out that organ; but it never seemed to occur to her to rinse off the spoon. At any rate, without doing so, she approached me and was about to hand it to me when the old man gave her dress-skirt a surreptitious jerk and whispered something. She gave me a quick, scared look, then reached down for a brown, very old cotton mantle which was lying on the floor (the one she had on was too clean) and wiped the spoon off with it. Then with an air which seemed to say, 'Could a *Melik** woman have done better than that?' she handed me the spoon."

As time went on Cushing began to see glimpses of a "mysterious life by which I had little dreamed I was surrounded." His work at Zuni became a struggle: on one side the anthropologist relentlessly poking and prying into things he was not supposed to see, and on the other the Zunis trying equally hard to keep him out. The Zunis took this intrusion into their spiritual life seriously, and at one point Cushing overreached and was accused of sorcery, the most heinous of crimes. Cushing knew what his fate would be if he were convicted; he had already seen witches being tortured and put to death.

Cushing was brought in for trial, and the accusing priest laid out the charges. "He told the others how I had. . .stolen with brilliant colors the shadows of the sacred dance, and thereby disturbed the souls of the gods;. . .how I had brought strange medicines into the tribe, and predicted the deaths of children whom I could not cure, which predictions had invariably come true." The priest went on to say that he had heard that the Mexicans, the Mormons, and even some Americans were speaking against Cushing, claiming he was a witch. The latter accusation hurt Cushing deeply: the reason the non-Zuni of the area hated Cushing was because of his powerful support for the Zunis in land disputes.

When the charges were finished, Cushing was angry, and attacked his accusers with sarcasm.

"Why," he said in part, "did I counsel that the Mormons should not share your land? Why did I lead your parties of young men to drive away the Mexicans from your pastures? No man who loved you would

---

Melik, Zuni pronunciation of "American."

do such things as these. For the Mormons, who wear stems of red canvas for breeches (the Zuni description for the poorest and most worthless of Americans), are, as you all know, the wisest and greatest of Americans. They never lie. They love you so much that they long to live with you, and build their homes on your lands. . . . As for the Mexicans, you ought to have known that I was a sorcerer when I tried to drive them away; for they loved you so much that they came here to your pasture-grounds and brought thousands of their sheep."

By the time Cushing was finished, the Zunis, even the accusing priest, were trembling. "Enough!" they said. "Shame is soiling the blankets that cover us."

Eventually, Cushing would become fully inducted into the tribe, fluent in Zuni, a member of the Tribal Council, a Priest of the Bow, and First War Chief.

Cushing was an unlikely person to have undertaken such an adventure. A photograph of him taken just before leaving on the expedition shows a skinny, pale, mild-looking fellow with a thin mustache and a smug look on his face. He appears far younger than his twenty-two years of age. He suffered from digestive problems and ill health, and was something of a hypochondriac. The great anthropologist A. L. Kroeber, a friend of Cushing's, described him as "intensive, intuitional, mystic, neurotic and in chronic ill-health, with a streak of exhibitionism."

Cushing spent five years at Zuni. When he returned he had undergone a complete transformation. The Thomas Eakins portrait of Cushing, painted in Boston after his return, is a striking illustration of this transformation. Cushing is dressed in his own version of Zuni regalia, with buckskins and moccasins, hoop earrings through pierced ears, flowing hair, a great mustache, a quiver of arrows slung over his back, a Zuni war club in his hand, a knife in his belt, necklaces of shells and beads, and what looks suspiciously like a human scalp dangling on his hip. He once signed an official letter "1st War Chief of Zuni, U.S. Ass't. Ethnologist."

This was no play-acting on Cushing's part. The Zunis were serious about turning him into an Indian. For his part, in order to gain membership in secret societies, Cushing often found himself in extreme situations. In one incident, he and several Zunis, many miles from the pueblo, encountered the trail of an Apache band that had stolen some Zuni sheep. They lay in wait and ambushed the Apaches. Cushing ended up with an Apache scalp, and there is little doubt that he shot and scalped the man himself. Cushing had apparently committed a grave mistake, however, in taking the scalp: he used a steel, rather than a flint, knife. Before the scalp could be carried into the pueblo, the Zunis had to perform a ceremony purifying it of the taint of metal.

Acquiring an enemy scalp was the last step before he could be initiated as a Priest of the Bow, the ruling religious council of Zuni.* Becoming a Bow Priest would give Cushing access to a wealth of secret information. (He had earlier tried to satisfy the scalp requirement by sending for two scalps from the Smithsonian!)

Later, as First War Chief, Cushing was obliged to lead war parties against cattle rustlers and thieves, one of which resulted in the deaths of an American and a Mexican.

Cushing made other interesting discoveries at Zuni. In a letter to Spencer Fullerton Baird, secretary of the Smithsonian, he reported:

"It is my good fortune to have here one of the R.R. Route Exploration volumes containing occasional extracts in quotation from the journals of early Spanish Adventurers. . . . By this means I have already *definitely* located the celebrated City or Kingdom of 'Civola'. . .the ruins of which stand within rifle range of the present pueblo of Zuni. . . . many of the native names to be found throughout the first Spanish accounts must have been derived from the Civolatese—or Zunis. . . . For example, the principle 'Citie of Cibola'. . .Muzaque. . .finds a correspondence in the Zuni name of a ruined pueblo called *Ma-tsa-ki*. Also the largest city of the 'Kingdome of Civola'. . .Ahacus (Spanish pron. aspirated *Ha-ha-kus*) cannot but be represented by the splendid ruins ten miles west of here—called by the Indians *Ha-wi-kuh*."

Cushing had rediscovered the Seven Cities of Gold.

Through Cushing, the Zunis discovered America. In the spring of 1882, Cushing traveled east with five Zuni and one Hopi. The trip came about at the Zunis' request, as they were anxious to obtain water from the Atlantic Ocean, the "Ocean of Sunrise," for use in rain ceremonies.†

The party visited Washington, were received by President Chester

---

*As late as the Korean War (and possibly even during the Vietnam War) Zunis returned to the pueblo with enemy scalps for ceremonial purposes.

†Even today, when a Zuni goes east, he will usually bring back Atlantic Ocean water for ceremonial uses.

A. Arthur, and went on to Boston where they were feted at the usual round of social functions, teas, receptions, and ladies societies (Indians from the West proved a hot social item in fashionable Victorian society). They even visited my hometown, Wellesley, where the young ladies of Wellesley College had the *frisson* of meeting bare-chested savages in buckskins. At a reception in Salem, Massachusetts, the Zunis stated their approval of the Salem witch trials, and one of the Bow Priests delivered a lecture on the evils of witchcraft that, one reporter noted, "would have pleased old Cotton Mather himself."

Cushing's stay at Zuni was cut short in 1884, when he was recalled to Washington. His involvement in various disputes between the Zunis and local ranchers, and what was perceived at the time as an unhealthy identification with his subjects, made him too controversial. The director of the Bureau of Ethnology, Major John Wesley Powell, was also irritated that Cushing hadn't published his great *oeuvre* on the Zuni. (Although he was an unusually literate writer, Cushing had pathological difficulties producing scholarly work. His great work on the Zunis was never written.)

After Cushing was recalled from Zuni, he became seriously ill and was invited by a Boston socialite, Mrs. Augustus Hemenway, to recuperate at her estate on the seacoast near Boston. In 1886, while still convalescent, Cushing arranged for three Zuni to come east again, among them his old friend Palowahtiwa, the Zuni governor.

The Zuni visited Cushing at his retreat. While they were there, sitting overlooking the sea, the Zunis began questioning Cushing about the size of the oceans, and the discussion eventually led to a fascinating Zuni disquisition on the nature of the Americans, a kind of reverse ethnography. The discussion had turned to American exploration of the polar regions, and how many expeditions had failed to penetrate the ice of the North Pole.

" 'No one [Cushing told the Zunis] has ever passed into that region.'

" 'Not even the Americans?' asked Waihusiwa.

" 'Not even the Americans,' said I. . . .

" 'I see,' said Palowahtiwa, 'neither by heat, nor by danger, nor by any difficulty whatever, can the wandering of the Americans be restrained, but by cold and snow and ice individually put to them.'

" 'Yes,' said I, 'that is true, and yet again and again have they tried to pass over the ends of the worlds. For instance, during the last year I spent in Zuni, an expedition of many Americans was fitted out to penetrate into the great ice country of the north. They sailed away under a captain of the Army named Greeley. [This was Adolphus Greely, who led the ill-fated 1881 Lady Franklin Bay expedition to northwestern Greenland.] They sailed in the middle of summer, and at last entered the region of eternal ice and snow which lay upon those waters, and through a wide track broken in them proceeded further than ever before any American had done. But at last the ice closed in upon them, and broke some of their vessels, and cast others high in the air, as it were, so that some of the men died, and those who remained hastened to make houses of the wrecks of their sailing chests, and remained there month after month, consuming their substance until it was all gone. Some of them died of cold, others of starvation. They became like corpse demons in appearance, and like corpse demons at last began to consume one another.'

"Here the attention of the three was absolutely rigid. [Cannibalism was considered a most dreadful crime by the Zunis.]

" 'Yes, they consumed one another, and not long after I returned, vessel after vessel having sailed to rescue them, they were at last found, those remaining alive, five or seven of them, and were brought to their country. I saw some of them, and they were fearful to look upon; their flesh had wasted away, and their eyes were sunken deep in their sockets. For this reason it is rare that Americans attempt to pass into the regions beyond; yet they sometimes so attempt it, and will until they either perish or find their way through.'

" 'Strange people, strange people, these Americans!' said they.

" 'And beyond these mountains of ice and snow is the home of the beloved gods,' said Palowahtiwa.

" 'True, no doubt,' said the others; and Heluta added,. . .'Ah, the gods know full well the passions of the Americans, and they girdle their world about with barriers impassable by the eaters of food [that is, mortals].'

" 'Such indeed are the Americans,' remarked one of them. 'Though we Indians live in a poor and dried-up country, though we may love them not, and treat them despitefully, yet they gather around us and come into our country continually, and even strive to get our land from us. Is it possible for any man to say what they want? Where is there a country more beautiful than this we are sitting in now? Is there any water needed here? Without irrigation, on the very tops of the mountains and hills, things grow green, and there is water to drink.' . . .

" 'Yes, the Americans have all this; they have enough to eat and to spare; though their houses and villages lie scattered over the land as thickly as the pine woods and sage brush in Zuni land, still they have enough to eat and enough to wear, and what they eat and what they wear are also of the best.'

" 'Well, it is not only that,' said Heluta, 'but the sentiment of home affects them not; the little bits of land they may own, or the house they may have been bred in, are as nothing to them; and, more than all, their thoughts do not seem to dwell contentedly on their own wives and children, for they wander incessantly, wander through all difficulties and dangers, to seek new places and better things. Why is it they are so unceasingly unsatisfied?'

" 'I think why,' said Palowahtiwa; 'above every people they are a people of emulation; above every kind of man or being a people of fierce jealousies. Is not this an explanation?'

" 'Why, even so,' exclaimed the others.

" 'Most certainly so,' said Palowahtiwa. 'And if one American goes one day's journey in the direction of a difficult trail, it is not long ere another American will go two days' journey in the direction of a more difficult one. One American cannot bear that another shall surpass him! Ho! were it possible, no American would be taller than another one. Is it extraordinary, then, that the gods begirt their dwelling places with barriers of ice and snow, and fatal unceasing cold, or that they dwell in the lands above the skies or the regions under the world?' "

Palowahtiwa was greatly disturbed at what he saw in Cushing during his visit to the anthropologist in Boston. After he had been there six days he took Cushing aside.

"When you were in Zuni," he said, "you established an allegiance with the beloved of Zuni [that is, the gods]; you became their child, as we are their children. . . . It occurs to me that you have not kept this in mind, and that you have neglected to sacrifice and pray to the gods."

Cushing lamely protested that his prayer meal had been used up, and that he had been attending his own church.

"Even so," Palowahtiwa said, "I would not have you fail to pray according to the faith of our ancestors. You will and you must pray and sacrifice thrice daily hereafter. Why deceive yourself? You are still a Zuni." Palowahtiwa went on to explain that Cushing's sickness was a direct result of his neglect of his religious duties. He told Cushing he would never be well until he returned to the Zuni faith.*

---

*Cushing's spiritual investment in the Zuni religion was apparently much deeper than he had originally thought. After leaving Zuni he was plagued with disturbing

We do not know whether Cushing took the old governor's advice. He did recover enough to lead an 1887 archeological expedition to Arizona (where he spent some time excavating the old pueblo of Halona at Zuni), but he suffered a relapse and had to return east. He never did live with the Zunis again, and he died in 1900 at the age of forty-three.

No one, apparently, bothered to inform the Zunis of his death. Thirty-eight years after his death—and over half a century after he had left Zuni—a writer visiting the pueblo found the Zunis still mourning the fact that Cushing had not returned from Washington.

Cushing's stay at Zuni altered the course of Zuni history. He transformed them from an obscure group to one of the most famous Indian tribes in America. The small pueblo became a magnet for anthropologists, archeologists, and writers. Among those anthropologists who followed Cushing were such luminaries as Matilda Coxe Stevenson, Leslie Spier, Elsie Clews Parsons, Ruth Benedict, Ruth Bunzel, A. L. Kroeber, and John Adair, among many others. The nearly continual presence at Zuni of whites studying their culture and religion would try the patience of even the Zuni themselves.* Despite this massive attention, very little of real substance or understanding has been written about the Zuni since Cushing. Anthropologists and writers tended to get so hung up in the staggeringly complex religious beliefs and cosmography of the Zuni that they failed to comprehend them as a *people*.

Shortly after Cushing's departure from the pueblo, the missionaries began arriving: Mormon, Lutheran, Presbyterian, and, eventually, Catholic. But the missionaries never had the kind of success with the Zunis that they would have elsewhere. "We never," Cushing wrote, "in a lifetime, with the utmost effort and labor, can blot out of their minds what their fathers and mothers have taught them, when young, of reverence for these [religious] traditions, and replace it with equally influential reverence for our own."

Zuni religion, which is still faithfully practiced by the great majority of the Zunis, has as its central principle the notion of balance and thankfulness. Humanity and nature exist in harmony; the ultimate goal of religious practice is to maintain this balance. Drought, war, disease,

---

hallucinations, in which a man appeared to him and told him he was not—and never had been—American, but that he was a Zuni.

*And at other pueblos as well. Taos Pueblo used to have a large sign at its entrance: "NO ANTHROPOLOGISTS."

and disaster are the result of a disequilibrium between nature and humankind, often brought about by a failure to observe the proper rituals and to give thanks for one's blessings.

Each person carries within him a "life road," or "breathway," watched over by spirit beings; correct personal conduct—that is, observing all the proper religious ceremonies to supplicate these spirit beings, as well as being kind and loving to one another—assures a long and healthy life road.

The Zunis believe that their rituals are important for the entire world—not just for the tribe. This may seem like a startling and even presumptuous notion to one steeped in the Christian idea of personal salvation,* but the Zunis take this aspect of their religion seriously. For example, some of the older, more conservative Zuni believe that the terrible problems the world has experienced in this sorry century of ours—the two world wars, the nuclear threat, the cold war—were a direct result of the theft of dozens of Ahayuda, or Twin War Gods, from shrines around Zuni. The War Gods, created during Bow Priest ceremonies, are placed in open-air shrines on the reservation, where they are left to "eat themselves up" and decay into the earth. "The War Gods," one anthropologist wrote, "embody an eternal spirit which protects the tribe and all the peoples of the earth if attended to by proper ritual. If a War God is out of its place. . .all its mischievous and potentially malevolent powers are released on the world, creating disasters such as floods, wars, and earthquakes."

In the 1970s the Zunis began a quiet but determined campaign to get their War Gods back. Since the War Gods were communal Zuni property, they could not legally be sold by any individual; thus any War God out of its shrine was, by definition, "hot." In the late 1970s a War God came up for auction at Sotheby's, and with the help of the FBI the Zuni were able to get it back. In the following years the tribe successfully pressured the Denver Art Museum and the Smithsonian, among others, to return War Gods. When Andy Warhol's estate came up for auction at Sotheby's in 1987, one of the items found in this inveterate collector's Manhattan townhouse was a War God. It was returned with alacrity when the Zunis got wind of the auction. Many Zunis believe Warhol's sudden and unexpected death was a direct result of his possession of the War God.

· · ·

---

*This Zuni idea is certainly not as presumptuous as the Christian idea that one must believe in Christ in order to be "saved" and go to Heaven.

The Catholic Church finally returned to Zuni in the 1920s. The old adobe mission was restored and a school opened in 1923. The Church had learned something that the Protestant missionaries hadn't (and still haven't): trying to stamp out the native religion was all but impossible. Instead, the Catholics opted for a benevolent kind of coexistence. A stunning illustration of this is the mission church at Zuni today; its walls are covered with murals of absolutely pagan Zuni religious symbols and kachinas. The murals were done by Alex Seowtewa, son of a famous Zuni Rain Priest.

"We may drive pickup trucks," one Zuni said to me. "We may live in HUD houses with electric lights. We may wear American clothes and watch TV. But we still have the three things that make us Zuni: our language, our land, and our religion. Inside," he said with intense conviction, "we are still totally, one hundred percent, *Zuni.*"

24

⏠

On the afternoon of the day following our arrival at Zuni, we visited the governor of the pueblo, Robert Lewis. The tribal offices were located in a slightly seedy modern building along the main paved highway through the pueblo, down the street from the gas station, next to the United New Mexico Bank at Zuni.

The tribal building had obviously been designed in a government office somewhere; it could as easily have been found in an office park on the outskirts of Omaha. The wind was still blowing ferociously, and tumbleweeds skidded across the parking lot in front.

The governor's office itself was a modern, wood-paneled room, with a large conference table where the Tribal Council met. On the wall were a series of photographs of earlier Zuni governors, many with long hair, wearing headbands, necklaces, and cotton mantles.

We found the governor, wearing a modest brown suit, sitting behind his desk. He was a solid man with graying hair and sharp, handsome features. He was seventy-four years old and had been governor, off and on, for eighteen years. He had thirty-two grandchildren.

He rose as we came in and offered his hand, and gave us his card, showing the pueblo's symbol, a rainbow kachina. I set up my tape recorder.

In the confines of the office we suddenly felt self-conscious about our ragged, dirty condition. My lips were still covered with running sores. I began to apologize.

He dismissed my apologies with a motion of his hand. "Looking at you," he said with amusement, "who could doubt you'd ridden from Mexico?"

His speech was low and sibilant, with many silences, and as he spoke a hush fell over the office.

We talked about our horses. "I lived on a horse," he said. "That kind of living, back then, was so different than sitting right here today. There used to be fields out there beside the sacred mountain, beautiful fields planted in melons and wheat and alfalfa. My old uncle had a field out there. He used to put me on the cross bar of the plow and I'd ride while he was plowing. Now everyone has a *pickup truck.*" He smiled and loosened his tie.

"When you were younger," I asked, "did you know you were going to become a leader of the Zuni people? How did it happen that you ended up governor?"

"I never thought about those things. Even after I got elected I didn't know a damn thing about doing government or how things got done. I had thrown my hat in the ring because there were only two guys running and people were asking me. I was working for the government up here as a maintenance man. I told the superintendent, 'The Monday after the election I'll come here to work or I'll come up here to resign.' "

"So what happened after you were elected?" I asked.

"I walked the floors through the night and didn't know what the hell I got myself into. Wife got up and made coffee and said, 'What's bothering you?'

" 'I don't know what to do,' I said.

"She said: '*You* asked for it, *you* figure it out.'

"So I decided we should go ask our people what they wanted. We made a house-to-house survey. That's how we started."

I asked him about his family and what it was like growing up at Zuni.

"My mother, who is a Cherokee, came here in 1899 as a teacher and married my dad, who was a full-blood Zuni. When my father was governor, the Tribal Council appointed her to be the official tribal interpreter. To have a non-Zuni appointed to that very important position was a high honor. She was the first non-Zuni given that honor."

He cleared his throat and withdrew a cigarette from a crumpled pack. "The people called her 'mother.' During the tragic times when the epidemics came she and the old trader's wife, Mrs. VanderWagon, would go and visit homes where sick people were."

"When were the epidemics?" I asked.

"At different times. There were so many. A lot of our people mark their date of birth by one epidemic or another. They say, 'I was born just after the measles epidemic.' A lot of these diseases were brought here by immigrants who came through in their travels west. Our population at one time went down to fourteen hundred. Finally we had a country doctor out here, horses and buggy furnished to him by the Tribal Council."

I asked Governor Lewis a question I had been thinking about for some time.

"Do you think that the tribe is better off now than it was 450 years ago, before the coming of Coronado? If history could replay itself, do you think the coming of the Europeans was in general a bad thing or a good thing?"

Lewis became very still. The silence stretched out so long I became uncomfortable.

"This is a good question," he finally said. "A tough question." He looked down at his desk, his eyes still unfocused, a wisp of smoke curling from the lengthening ash. Then he looked directly into my face.

"Europeans came over here essentially because they wanted freedoms they never had over there. We also cherished our freedoms and our ways of life. But we *respected* the rights of others. Here, our people enjoyed the things that the Creator made. We lived with the land and we respected each other's boundaries. When the newcomers came, they invented ways to be as mean as the landlords they were trying to get away from."

He paused again, and spoke slowly.

"My people, sometimes I think we've been too kind to others, but that is our nature. When we go to our ceremonies, we pray for *all* people, not just ourselves."

Again he paused with the difficulty of what he was trying to say.

"I think there have been some good things derived from people who, supposedly, were civilized. But these newcomers did not try to understand the ways of the Indians. How *we* looked at things. We gave honor to the Creator, not only in a building—a church—but in *all* the places that He created, the religious and sacred areas. We lived with the land and treated it with respect. These things we had. They were *good* things.

"What did the newcomers bring? At one time among them a horse was worth more than a human life. You would hang somebody for stealing a horse. To be caught rustling somebody's cattle, you were hung or shot down. And the only good Indian was a dead one.

"And then, of course, like my mother's people, they moved them from Georgia to Oklahoma because they thought they found gold over there. In the Trail of Tears. Four thousand of them died on the march. These things, relocating people just to get what they had. . ."

Another awkward silence filled the room.

"Sometimes they invented systems that were even worse than what came before, because nobody tried to see what would be a better way. Lines were put up when states were created, and within the states they'd put up these counties. People were sold land under the Homestead Act and would settle, and put up barbed wire. The Indians could not roam where they pleased. The Indian people were cut off from their lands and sacred areas.

"There have been many other changes too. Telephones, TVs, iceboxes."

"Do you consider those things improvements?" I asked.

"Well, for the present day I would say they are improvements. People are getting used to them. But folks managed to do very well without those things back then. It used to be an easygoing life, a *good* life. People worked hard at their little farms. Folks had all they needed to eat from their own efforts. During the thirties, my people didn't even know there was a depression out there."

"When did things start to change?" I asked.

"After World War II. Now it's so different. We're now operating under a constitutional government, which we never had in those days. But our own traditional government was good. We are a people who always had a government and a close community. The traditional court that we had, everything was settled in a good way. We had our own method. Our regulations were not written down, but they were good. People like mine have been inured to their own way of life for hundreds of years, and they look on the traditional way as a good way.

"There was a closeness among families in those back years that we don't have now. The old customs of appreciation and thankfulness were everything in those days. There was no such thing as envying one another. Like in this day, neighbor watches neighbor to see how much they can outdo each other in material things. It wasn't like that in those days. The essentials were always worked hard for. The social life was there, the sacred kachina dances and the other dances were there. The fellowship within the kiva groups was there, the fraternities, the medicine lodges were there, the closeness in clan relations was there. Everybody looked after one another. Sometimes the government says, 'We're going to fix things to make you a better life,' but I haven't seen very much evidence of them contributing to a better way, except constitutional government, and supermarkets, things like that. But there are bad things that came too, like drugs and alcohol.

"We were under three governments at different times. The Spanish and Mexican governments never messed around with our sovereignty, but when the United States government took over we lost a lot of things, including land. Land that belonged to us aboriginally was given to others."

He pointed to a map on his wall. It was a curious map, showing a vast section of Arizona and New Mexico. Concentric bands of color illustrated the shrinking area of Zuni sovereignty, ending up with a tiny postage stamp of white, the present reservation.

"That map up there," he said softly, "shows in different colors the taking of land away from us."

"It seems to me," I said, "that Zuni is a very strong community. How is it that the Zuni have retained this very strong sense of cultural identity and community where many other Indian tribes have experienced such problems, particularly the Plains Indians? How do you account for the difference?"

Lewis answered immediately.

"I think the fact that the religious side of our people is very intricate and deep. The spiritual was always part of our government. You could not separate the two. In the days of the Seven Cities, when the Spaniards came, the high priesthood had responsibility of selecting the head man, the one who would guide the people. Then the other villages would nominate a person to be on the Tribal Council representing them.

"We are a religious people. You have to have a belief in something, and faith, and above all be *thankful*. Enjoy the blessings in a *good* way, and be kind to your neighbors. Respect, I think, is very, very important. When you think about all the people, there's a mixture of bad and good. There's a give-and-take sometimes, but all in all people are not that bad. It's a *good* world. When you're thankful, that covers a whole gamut of things. The old folks here used to say if you're not thankful your blessings can be taken away from you and given to somebody else. My dad taught me that you don't envy your neighbor. He used to joke,

'If he's not thankful maybe his blessings will be given to you some day.' "

Lewis chuckled. "About those people who were better off, my dad said, 'You be thankful for them too!'

"And our clans.* Our clans help keep us together, just like family. I have aunts from my clan and we look on each other as real relatives. When anything comes up they're the ones that give you a hand. I think too the isolation has a lot to do with what you are asking. When people are close together, close to cities, like those other [Pueblo] villages around Santa Fe and Albuquerque, they are closer to the changes that have taken place."

Lewis stubbed the cigarette out, slid his hand across the polished surface of the desk, and gently turned it palm-upward.

"Still, we have lost some good things, and we will lose others yet if the parents of younger generations do not keep on telling them about the things they should know."

"The Zuni," I said, "seem to have retained something that we, I mean Anglo culture, have lost, where kids move three thousand miles away from their parents, where everything seems so rootless."

Lewis nodded. "In the cities, where all the houses are close together in rows—well, when you're closed in you get upset. We're doing that a little with these subdivisions here. So the kids form gangs. And they're starting that here. They want to get into mischief, because attention is not given to them. Parental attention is always focused on work-work-work, get-the-money, get-the-money, and not enough on being together as a family. A lot of times they don't even teach the children their religious beliefs. So these kids grope for something. Maybe I'm wrong, but maybe the hippie movement was indicative of this. They *wanted* something. They even wanted"—Lewis's face broke

---

*A child is born into his mother's clan, and becomes a "child of" his father's clan. His clan will determine, to a certain extent, what position he will hold in the Zuni religious system. His fellow clan members are considered to be like blood relatives, while his father's clan's members also have certain responsibilities to him. While a person cannot choose his clan, every Zuni male does choose his kiva group—a kind of men's society. Each kiva group has certain religious responsibilities as well. Thus, every Zuni is enmeshed in a very tight web of family, clan, and (for the men) kiva society relationships. The social fabric at Zuni is far more complex than anything those of us of European descent can even comprehend. The downside of this closeness is rather surprising: rumormongering and gossip are rampant and considered by the Zunis to be one of their worst social ills—on par with drug and alcohol abuse.

into a gentle but ironic smile—"to learn about Indian ways. You can't blame those people. They're wandering around, looking for something to hold on to.

"In some ways here at Zuni we are no better off than cities. We've gotten some kids selling marijuana cigarettes right in the schools. Sometimes they combine this with drink. We're not unique from any other community any more."

"Not as bad as many others," I said. "You should see what New York City is like these days."

"Although I never touched dope, I never try to whitewash myself and make out I'm an angel. It's easier for me to talk to an alcoholic than somebody who never had the experience. When you have been down that road you can talk to them much easier."

Lewis stood up and shoved his hands in his pockets. He walked around his desk. "I tell my grandkids: 'Go out there in the hills and *be* what you can see. Go up in the mesas there and look around. Wonderful!' When you teach your young these things at a very early age, they can get off track and join the rest of the world in the bad things, but they never forget what they've been told while they were young. Sometimes it all comes back around to where a fellow says, 'I been foolish as hell, I've been told that these things would hurt me, I've been stung.' Then he has to admit that his mom and dad were right. And the grandmothers too!" He chuckled.

"I was like that," I said.

He said, "Yes, many of us were."

I said, "People are very interested in Zuni culture and religion. Why do you feel there is this intense interest among outsiders? Not just the anthropologists, but in general. Is there something the Zuni can offer to the rest of the world?"

"When people come to see our winter doings [the Shalako dances], they see a oneness in the whole community. This is an *impressive* thing to them. If I was a total stranger I would look at it that way, thinking: All these people have one thought in mind. This is their ceremonial time and they're going through their rituals with their hearts in it. It is this dedication to belief that my people have kept for ages, when outsiders tried to disrupt and change things. I think this has a *meaning* for the outside world. No matter what you believe, everything comes from the same source."

"The Zuni are very small in numbers," I said. "I guess there's, what, ten thousand Zuni? And think how large the world is. I come from

Wellesley, Massachusetts, a town with twenty-five thousand people, and I don't think any one of them has done anything that anybody knows about, and yet the whole world knows the Zuni. They have made a mark in the world far beyond their numbers. I'm curious what your reaction is to that."

Lewis cleared his throat and thought for a moment. "The twenty-five thousand people you mention where you come from are all different denominations. Although they have their belief—whether Jewish or Catholic or whatever—they don't get together to show that they are one unity in thought and worship. A lot of them are looking at how the other guy dresses, ladies poke fun at one another. Or if somebody has the same hat as somebody else, they say, 'Why does she have to wear the same hat that I wear?' That type of thing. It's not centered in worship. They're not listening to the Word, they're looking at one another, comparing what they have. And so *true* worship is not there.

"It's said the Creator is not the author of confusion. Here, among our people, the missionaries come and say, 'Don't go to that church. Come to mine, it's better than his.' They talk to my people that way! The confusion that exists in the outside churches makes a person feel like, 'Well, I don't know, where should I go? If that one's no good and this one says he's better. . .Well, how do *I* stand?' "

Another silence filled the room.

"A person," he continued, "usually asks this question when he wants to get back on track with his life. Jesus said, 'I am the Way and the Truth.' But nobody really helps him with the *truth*. The clergy tell him, 'This is what the Good Book says—but *we* interpret it *this* way.' And they mix him up again!"

Lewis chuckled. "When my people are met this way, they feel, 'Maybe there's *none* of them good, so I'll just stay with my own belief.' "

His voice dropped nearly to a whisper. I slid the tape recorder a little closer.

"There was a story about four chaplains on a troop ship, a Jew, a Catholic, two other denominations, I forget which. When that ship was sunk they gave their own life jackets away to save other people. They encouraged the sailors, prayed with them, kept them from getting panicky. That was *good*. That was a true thing. That sacrifice came from the same source. Because we're all in the same boat should anything happen. I don't care how big the boat is that we live on. We've got to look out for each other."

⟜ ⨉ ⟝

During the summer of 1540, Coronado remained at Hawikuh, send-ing small exploring parties to investigate the surrounding area. Their first exploration was of a province the Zunis told them about, called Tusayán, in the northwest.

Coronado sent one of his captains, Pedro de Tovar, with a group of soldiers, to investigate. Along with them was Fray Juan de Padilla, who had been bitterly disappointed in the Seven Cities of Cíbola. Might Tusayán, Fray Juan thought, be the seven lost cities of Antillia?

After a short journey Tovar and his men arrived at a series of low, fingerlike mesas, topped with little villages much like Hawikuh. These were the mesas of the Hopi Indians.

As the sun rose, the Hopis and the Spaniards faced off. The Indians stormed out of the pueblo in "wing formation," armed with arrows, shields, and war clubs, and "drew lines" on the ground, telling the Spaniards not to cross. (These lines were probably made from sprin-kled cornmeal, which are still used at Hopi to signify a line not to be crossed.)

The Hopi were terrified of the horses, having heard that the Zuni had been conquered by "very fierce men who rode animals that ate people." Even so, they stood their ground. A parley ensued. As the Hopi listened with disbelief to the Spaniards' usual demands, one Indian became angry and struck a horse on the jaw with his mace.

"Fray Juan," Castañeda recounted, "angry at the time being wasted on them, said to the captain: 'Indeed, I do not know what we have come here for.' "

Thus goaded on by the bitter man of God, the Spaniards gave the *Santiago!* and surged across the line, attacking so suddenly that they knocked down and trampled many Indians. As the horsemen pursued the fleeing Hopis, others came running out of the pueblo "offering peace and presents," and the fight was called off almost as soon as it had begun.

"On that day," Castañeda continued, "the natives of the land as-sembled and came to offer their obedience." At Hopi the Spaniards heard about "a large river" to the northwest.

Tovar returned to Hawikuh and gave Coronado his report. Coronado immediately sent another exploring party under García López de Cárdenas back to explore the large river. When he reached Hopi the Indians provided him with guides, and they continued west-ward across harsh, waterless desert.

Coming through a sparse piñon forest, they abruptly found themselves on the rim of an immense gorge, "from the edge of which," Castañeda wrote, "it looked as if the opposite side must have been three or four leagues away by air."

They were the first Europeans to gaze into the Grand Canyon.

Far more important than the view was the water at the bottom. For three days the Spaniards desperately sought a path to the cool, green river tumbling in faint rapids a mile below. At one point a small party managed to get a third of the way down the canyon before being stopped by impassable rimrock; when they got back they pointed out to the rest that some boulders which looked from the rim of the canyon to be about as high as a man were actually "taller than the great tower of Seville." Unable to reach the water, they made a mad dash back to Hopi, almost expiring from thirst.*

While these and other parties explored the country around Zuni, an event occurred that would have tremendous importance for the eventual fate of Coronado's expedition.

A delegation of Indians arrived at Hawikuh from the east, bearing gifts. "Among them came a chieftain," Castañeda recalled, "whom our men called 'Bigotes' [Whiskers], because he had long mustaches. He was a young man, tall, well built, and robust in appearance."

Bigotes told Coronado that he had come from a city called Cicuyé,† several hundred miles to the east. Word of the "strange people, bold men" who had conquered the Zuni had spread across the Southwest. And so, Bigotes said, he had come to "make their acquaintance and be their friends."

Bigotes did not appear to be perturbed by the defeat Coronado had inflicted on the Zuni. On the contrary, the Cicuyéans respected the power the Europeans represented and wanted to meet them as equals. Bigotes told Coronado that, "if the Spanish wished to visit their land, they should consider them as their friends." Bigotes gave Coronado presents of fine buckskins, shields, buffalo hides, and headdresses.

"All this was accepted with much affection," Castañeda reported, and Coronado, in turn, gave the Indians glassware, pearl beads, and jingle bells, "which they prized very highly as something they had never seen before."

---

*The Hopi guides had probably deliberately been leading the Spaniards away from water sources.

†Today called Pecos Pueblo.

Coronado was particularly intrigued by the buffalo skin brought by Bigotes to Zuni. "The hair was so woolly and tangled that one could not tell what the animals were," Castañeda wrote. A Plains Indian captive of the Cicuyéans showed the Spaniards a picture of a buffalo painted on his body, and said the plains east of Cicuyé were filled with them.

Coronado immediately ordered one of his captains, Hernando de Alvarado, to take twenty men and accompany Bigotes back to Cicuyé. The ubiquitous Fray Juan de Padilla also joined this expedition. They departed Zuni on Sunday, August 29, 1540, heading east over an ancient trade route that linked Zuni with Acoma Pueblo, the Río Grande pueblos, and Cicuyé. This three-hundred-mile trail, the Zuni-Acoma-Pecos trail, was one of the most important trade routes in prehistoric New Mexico.

For the last part of our trip, we would be retracing the historic journey of Alvarado, Padilla, and Bigotes to Cicuyé, today a ruin known as Pecos Pueblo. We chose this route for several reasons. Alvarado's and Padilla's journey was the more historic journey, the first penetration by Europeans into the heartland of New Mexico. (Coronado would follow much later, going by a somewhat different route.) In addition, this three-hundred-mile stretch of country was then—as it is today—heavily populated by Indians. We would be crossing no fewer than nine Indian reservations and meeting the direct descendants of the people the Spanish encountered 450 years ago. I wanted to know what the Indian people thought of Coronado and the arrival of the Europeans.

Our journey would end at Pecos Pueblo, the easternmost pueblo in North America. It was here that the most significant events of Coronado's expedition took place, and here where the fate of Coronado's expedition was sealed.

Our last morning at Zuni we rose in the dark. Edward Wemytewa, the Zuni who had befriended us and put up our horses, came by our camp and we all climbed a hill beyond the pueblo. Dowa Yalanne covered the horizon, a shadow printed against the brightening sky. As the unseen sun rose, the spires and buttresses of the sacred mountain divided the dawn light into a fan of probing rays, which played silently above our heads. Walter set up his 8 × 10 camera and Edward photographed us standing with our horses. There is something odd about that photograph, a look in our faces that is strange, almost alien.

It was a sad, beautiful morning. After six weeks and 650 miles, we had reached the Seven Cities of Cíbola. The first part of our trip was over.

Later that day Wicks arrived in front of the Halona store with pickup truck, stock trailer, and wife. As usual the front seat was filled with crushed beer cans, and his cheek bulged with tobacco chaw. We loaded the horses and climbed in.

"Damn," Wicks said unexpectedly.

We looked at him.

"When I got your phone call from Zuni, well, I never would have believed it."

"Believed what?" Walter asked.

"Believed that two greenhorn assholes like you could do what you just did."

Wicks laughed loudly and squirted a stream of tobacco into the coffee can and started the truck. He was actually angry.

We hummed along the Interstate back to Santa Fe, covering in five hours what it would have taken us a month to ride.

BOOK
TWO

25

Returning to the late twentieth century was a bit strange. The most marvelous thing was being able to turn a tap and get unlimited, fresh-tasting, *cold* water. It seemed like a miracle. It took twenty-four hours for my intractable thirst to slake itself. I slept twelve hours a day, was constantly hungry, ate massive amounts of meat with every meal, and threw my digestive system into a paroxysm of gastric disturbances.

During the journey, our lives had been stripped down to the barest essentials: finding water, finding grass, and keeping to our route. It was a minimalist existence. And now, like a tidal bore, all the complications of life came flooding back: I was suddenly faced with earning a living and spending the money therefrom; driving a car; writing and telephoning dozens of people; dealing with a stack of letters marked "personal and confidential" from God knows how many angry billing computers.

I made the mistake of buying a *New York Times*. I could barely wrestle the damn thing open (reading a newspaper takes dexterity), but when I finally succeeded I was thrust into a world both bizarre and unreal. How, I thought, does one suddenly start thinking about a massacre in Tiananmen Square, a vicious gang-rape in New York City, stalled nuclear arms negotiations, or a completely unintelligible speech by the president of the United States? How is one to comprehend a headline announcing one more tick in the endless Brownian motion of the Dow-Jones Industrial Average? How is one to feel when learning that Norman F. Taylor, industrialist, is dead?

For a brief window of lucidity—less than a week—I clearly understood what all this amounted to: absolutely nothing.

My first night back, I went out with a friend to have a drink at a restaurant on the Santa Fe plaza. Sitting at the table next to us was a man wearing a two-hundred-dollar cowboy hat, gray ostrich-skin cowboy boots with raked heels, tight, pressed jeans, a plaid Wrangler shirt with pearl snap buttons, and a black bandanna looped and knotted around his doughy neck. He had on a belt buckle loaded with enough chunky turquoise to split the skull of a mule. He was sucking on a margarita and talking loudly, with a heavy Oklahoma accent, about real estate and oil. He said, "Hell, my baby girl paid over fifty thousand in income taxes last year. So the IRS man calls me up and asks, 'How come this Emma Sue didn't file a return the year before?' and I says, ' 'Cause she wasn't born yet, asshole!' "

I watched in fascinated horror while the man roared with laughter, his bulging neck vibrating like a toad in heat.

God, I thought, *this* is what the West has become.

We planned to resume our trip in early August, close to the time Alvarado and Padilla made their historic journey to Pecos. By August, the summer rains would have brought back the grass, and the springs would be running and the water pans full (or so we hoped).

This final leg of the journey would be quite different from the first. We would be riding almost entirely through Indian country, leaving the ranches and cowboys behind.

The goal of our journey would change, just as it had for the Spaniards. The Spaniards' three-hundred-mile journey from Zuni to Pecos signified the first sustained contact between Europeans and native Americans within the borders of the present-day United States. We wanted to experience, if possible, who these people were today, and what had changed in the 449 years since.

Walter and I had a falling out with Wicks, and the two horses I had rented from him were no longer available. In addition, by the end of June we realized that Robin wasn't regaining her weight fast enough to go on the second part of the trip. We would need three new horses.

Walter and I bought our first horse, an Appaloosa, from a horse trader named Charlie Myers, who ran the Cattlemen's Livestock and Auction Company in Belen, New Mexico. Technically a "red-roan" Appaloosa, Wilbur was actually a mottled, dirty white color—one of those old-time Apps, a pig-eyed, rat-tailed, goose-rumped, Roman-nosed animal. In other words, he was an exceptionally ugly horse.* His habit of looking at you out of the corner of his eye made him appear smarter than he actually was. He had no papers, no brand, and no name. He cost me $475, a shade over his dog-food price, and even at that price everyone told me I had been robbed. But he was gentle, sound, friendly, and very tough, and if not exactly intelligent, at least he wasn't a complete mental defective.

We found our second animal, a quarter horse, at a dude riding stable in Albuquerque. He was one of those long, lean, bony horses with sunken cheeks and a dolorous face that you see in Remington's paintings—a real old-time cow horse. His coloring was unusual, a kind of deep, polished rosewood color which Westerners call variously red, dark sorrel, brown, or chestnut, and which the English call a blood bay.

His name was Redman, but I renamed him Redbone Moohow, in memory of the hound dog back on the San Pedro River, which he reminded me of in a vague way. The two animals seemed to share a kind of fatalistic attitude toward life.

Redbone was highly intelligent, and he had learned some interesting tricks at the dude ranch. As a result only the guides could ride him. His favorite trick with an inexperienced rider was to back up very fast as soon as he was mounted. This is highly disconcerting, and the unprepared rider's automatic reaction is to haul in on the reins. This, to a backing horse, is akin to stamping on the accelerator of a car while in reverse—which is of course exactly what Redbone counted on.

It was an excellent trick, and at the dude ranch Redbone did it to me, to the great amusement of one of the guides. He was a loud, porcine fellow who knew just enough about horses to stay out of trouble on a one-hour flat ride, and he was delighted to witness the public humiliation of a Yankee.

I bought Redbone anyway; I couldn't help liking a horse with such

---

*When I brought him home my girlfriend, who had a rather macabre sense of humor, suggested the name Elmer, after the brand of glue he had just escaped from becoming, but I thought that a little extreme. We compromised with Wilbur. Walter, who had given his horses names that would ring down in history, was upset. "Wilbur?" he said. "What the hell kind of name is *Wilbur*? It ain't dignified."

a wicked command of human psychology. I vowed, however, that next time I would be ready for him. (Which I was; the next time he tried it I gave him a resounding whack on the ass. He looked perfectly astonished and never pulled the trick again.) Redbone would turn out to be a magnificent horse.

We still needed a third horse. While shopping around I heard about an exotic breed called the Spanish barb, which many believe was the "horse of the Conquest"—the original horse the Spanish brought to the Americas, the horse of Coronado and his men.

There is some disagreement about exactly what the original Spanish horse looked like. The best scholarship indicates that it was a small, tough horse that had been brought to Spain from the Barbary coast of Africa (hence the term "barb") during the Moorish invasion.

Since the Conquest, there had been so much outbreeding in both Spain and the United States that the original Spanish horse had mostly vanished. But in the last decades some horse fanciers believed they had discovered a few isolated herds of pure Spanish stock, untouched for centuries, belonging to several Indian tribes and one or two old Spanish land-grant families in the West. These horses (technically mustangs) had peculiar genetic characteristics shared with the barb horses of the Berbers—very different from the breeds existing in the United States and Europe today.*

Horses that best matched the original barb were selected from these herds to become the foundation animals of the breed, and the Spanish barb registry was established in 1972. There is no absolute proof that the breed is identical to the horse of the Conquest. But not many years ago, the Albuquerque Museum wanted to mount a suit of sixteenth-century horse armor; the only breed the suit fit was the Spanish barb.

The typical Spanish barb today is a stout, smallish horse, very sure-footed, with a quick, smooth gait, large head, and shaggy mane and tail. It is just now becoming known for its common sense, endurance, and survival ability. It is a generalist horse, as opposed to many of today's breeds, which have been selected over many generations to emphasize a few traits at the expense of everything else.

---

*The early Berber horse is thought to have had only five lumbar vertebrae and prismatic-shaped metatarsal bones. It also had some characteristics that today are considered conformational faults—such as a low tail set—and have been assiduously bred out of American horses. The Spanish barbs of today all bear these characteristics.

. . .

I decided that our journey would not be complete without a Spanish barb. The only trouble with getting one was that there were fewer than 350 in existence, and they were expensive. It turned out that one of the top breeders of Spanish barbs in the United States—Oñate Spanish Barbs Ltd.—was located just outside Santa Fe.

I called up Roeliff Annon, one of Oñate's owners, and shocked him with a suggestion that he loan us, free of charge, one of his best horses. But he finally agreed, and gave me a dun-colored mare worth $10,000. Her name was Engwahela (the "Chosen One" in an African language), and she was the last breeding mare in a famous barb bloodline. Engwahela's grandsire was Scarface, who came from a mustang herd running on a huge ranch not far from where we would be riding. The land had originally been granted to a Spanish settler by the king of Spain, and the original horses had never, supposedly, been bred outside the herd. One of the land-grant descendants, D. D. Romero, had told Annon: "We always shot any Goddamn gringo horses that came around our herds."

"We're working to restore the horse of the Conquest," Annon said later. "That's kind of hard to prove with paperwork. We've made a lot of claims for what this breed could do. This seemed like a perfect opportunity to put these claims to the test."

There was one potential problem. I pointed out that we would be riding through areas populated with wild horse herds; there was a good chance we might bring her back in a family way, so to speak.

So be it, he said.

26

◀▣▶

We returned to Zuni on August 3rd. The next day, Edward Wemytewa brought us to the ruins of Kyaki:ma, one of the original Seven Cities—and the place where the Zuni believe Esteban was killed.

Kyaki:ma had been deserted in 1680, the same year as Hawikuh. It was now a large pile of rubble on the flank of Dowa Yalanne about three or four miles from Zuni. We picked our way up through the tumbled stones, and at the top had a sweeping panorama of the surrounding valleys and mesas. The sky was rapidly filling with clouds and a black mass of rain dropped down from a thunderhead a few miles away. A sudden press of cool air washed over the ruin, redolent of juniper and wet stone.

Kyaki:ma was a sacred place to the Zuni, and shrines and offerings were scattered about the ruins—bundles of feathers and corn husks; a cactus draped with string, turquoise, and beads; planted prayer sticks made from cholla husks. A row of upright stones along the top of the ruin commemorated (we heard) a distant and forgotten victory against the Spanish.

Walter began setting up for a photograph while I rested against one of the stone slabs, feeling the stored warmth of the sun pressing into my back. I wrote for a while in my journal, and then noticed that some of the upright stones had graffiti on them. I walked through them, copying down the inscriptions. There was the name "ERIC" carved in the rounded, Peter Max-style letters that were so common in the sixties. Below that was chiseled "Danny 1918." Another stone read "PND March 9, 1939," followed by a list of names: "Millie Soott, Ken Yazzie, Jerry Charley, Gallup."

Near this was a longer message, hoary with age and barely readable: "I Fuck Helen A Lopez [illegible] Times in a Row in Zuni under this bridge." Time, the great leveler, had obliterated the precise achievement.

It was a statement of the profane amidst the sacred, an earthy biological shout among the whisperings of spirit.

We set out on horseback from Zuni on August 7th, heading for the ruins of Pecos (Cicuyé) Pueblo, over three hundred miles away. Edward had told us about a very old trail up behind Dowa Yalanne, the only way through that area going east. At the top of the trail, he remembered, there had once been a windmill where we might find water.

We came into a broad valley, the eastern end of which was walled in by thousand-foot cliffs decorated with curious needles and chimneys of sandstone. We rode along the cliffs, and reluctantly concluded that a nasty-looking scree slope with the faintest suggestion of a trail was our route. By this time it was late. Although we had found no water, we felt it would be too dangerous to attempt the ascent this late in the day.

We camped in a little meadow amidst gullied badlands behind the sacred mountain, at a place named *Shundek'yay'a-dahna*, which means "Rivers of Grass Where Water Once Flowed." I hobbled Wilbur and staked out Redbone and Pedernal, and I was starting to hobble Engwahela when Walter protested.

"She ain't going anywhere," he said. "She'll stick with the geldings."

So we let her graze free.

The next morning she was gone.

"She can't be far," Walter said. "Make me a good breakfast."

He disappeared into first light.

The sun rose into a clear sky. By eight o'clock the temperature exceeded 100 degrees, and Walter was still gone. I moved the horses around to fresh grass and waited.

By ten o'clock the sun was white hot and the entire landscape shimmied and danced with mirages. A lone white cloud hovered over the top of a distant mesa, like a puff of steam. Desperate for shade, I wedged myself under a low juniper bush. The shady ground was covered with tiny ants that proceeded to swarm over me; but the ants were far more tolerable than the heat. It was an inferno beyond anything I thought possible.

By eleven there was still no sign of Walter, and I realized I better get the horses to water. The closest water I knew about was the spring at Kyaki:ma, three or four miles distant.

After saddling Redbone, I hung my last canteen of water around the saddlehorn and undid Wilbur's hobbles. I put up Redbone's reins for a second to untie Pedernal, and in a twinkling Redbone was walking away with Wilbur at his heels. He was only fifteen feet from me, but fifteen feet is a long distance between a man and a free horse. I had committed the grievous sin of leaving two horses unguarded, even for a moment. Now I was going to pay for it.

Leading Pedernal by his rope, I walked after the two horses, cooing and whispering about oats and grain and all the wonderful things they would have if they would only stop. Redbone was not impressed. He glanced back with a wicked smirk and broke into a gallop, with Wilbur at his heels. In horror, I watched them thunder off into the brush.

There was only one way to catch them. I threw myself on Pedernal bareback, and with only the halter and lead rope to control him jabbed my heels into his flanks.

Pedernal took off in an explosion of horseflesh. I instantly knew I had made a terrible mistake. Pedernal was an exceptionally powerful quarter horse, who, in preparation for the trip, had been eating high-protein sweet feed and the best leafy alfalfa money could buy, and he was bursting with excess energy. The quarter horse, named after the quarter-mile race, is the fastest horse ever bred, and I was about to discover just how fast one could go.

He thundered after the departing horses, leaping arroyos, plunging down banks, dodging piñon trees. With the air roaring in my ears, I hollered and tried to pull his head around with the lead rope, to no avail: without a bit, I had no way to steer him or check his headlong plunge.

I quickly found myself sailing through the air, slamming into a bank of dirt. By the time I had figured out I wasn't dead, the horses were long gone—carrying away the last of my water. In the direction they were headed I knew there were no fences until the Arizona border. What was worse, during the short ride both my hat and glasses had blown off.

I can hardly begin to describe my state of mind. I sat in the blazing sand, hatless, horseless, waterless, half-blind, and enraged. I ran through the piñon trees, yelling, whistling, and cursing, until I stumbled with exhaustion. Then I started to think.

First of all, I would never find the horses without my glasses. Second, with the heat pressing down on my head like an anvil, I had better find my hat right away. Third, I had to get water. Only then could I start searching for the horses.

I began backtracking, my thirst becoming nearly intolerable. I soon found the hat but it took a good half-hour of hunting on hands and knees to find the glasses. I then set off straight for Kyakima Spring, almost crazy with thirst.

Following the base of Dowa Yalanne, I passed through a sparse country of grasslands and junipers. Coming over a hill, in the middle of nowhere, I suddenly found myself face-to-face with a gleaming 1989 Ford Taurus automobile, two-toned white and maroon. It was a sight so shocking I momentarily thought it must be a hallucination. Then I saw a Zuni shepherd's cabin behind it, made of mud-mortared stone.

Next to the car, in the shade of a lone tree, sat a green plastic water tank. I knocked on the door, but no one answered. I tried the spigot in the tank. A stream of delicious water came spinning out, which I caught in my hat. Then I sank my face into it and sucked down water until I felt sick, the water sloshing and gurgling in my belly. I didn't know how long the bellyful of water was going to have to last.

As I stood in the front yard, wondering where I might pick up their trail, I glimpsed a speck of white moving between some trees a mile distant. It had to be Wilbur. I jogged toward it. As I approached I was able to pick out Redbone and Pedernal some distance ahead. They were moving off at a moderate pace, stopping now and then to snatch a mouthful of grass.

I managed to get within several hundred yards of them. I then filled my hands with dirt and stepped out, whistling and calling as if I had a handful of oats. Redbone jerked his head up and flew off at a gallop, with the other horses following. They were not to be fooled. With a curse I threw the dirt after them.

For hours I followed them in the blinding heat, but the brutes wouldn't let me get closer than a hundred yards. I remembered a story that a cowboy had told us in Arizona. A friend of his had gone hunting in Rim country with his favorite horse. Deep in the Rim forest he spied an elk, so he dismounted, removed his rifle from the scabbard, tucked the reins in his back pocket, and shot the elk. When he turned around his horse had pulled the reins out and had wandered off twenty feet. The man went to catch him but the horse jogged ahead. No matter what the man did the horse would always keep a dozen yards ahead of him. The man followed his horse for days, trying all manner of stratagems to catch him, all the time getting madder and madder. Finally, the morning of the third day, he leveled his rifle and shot his horse through the heart.

The story had sounded unlikely—a man shooting his favorite horse—but as the hours stretched on it became more and more believable. I began wishing that I, too, had a gun.

After miles of trotting and walking, the horses dropped down into an arroyo and I noticed that they had stopped and were huddled together. I wondered for a moment what they were doing, and then it dawned on me that they had found water and were drinking. If so, then I had a brief opportunity to catch them—if I could reach them before they slaked their thirst.

I ran like hell. They jerked their heads up, and I thought they might break for it, but their thirst won and they resumed drinking. I jumped off the lip of the arroyo and landed in a wallow of mud, grabbing as many lead ropes as I could. They danced around a bit and belatedly tried to escape, but it was too late. I had them. I cackled with glee and heaped insults upon them while they stood around looking foolish.

When I arrived back at camp, Walter was still gone.

An hour later I heard his whoop, and he appeared, coated with red dust, leading Engwahela.

"How'd you find her?" I asked.

Her trail, he said, went in a straight line west. She was moving at a good trot, not stopping for anything—wherever she thought she was going, she meant business. So rather than run her down on foot he walked back to Zuni Pueblo and enlisted Edward's help and a four-wheel-drive pickup in tracking her. For hours they drove around, "cutting for sign," finally picking up her trail some sixteen miles from camp.

Walter got out and began following the tracks, whistling and shaking a bucket of oats. Just when he reached the point of despair, he felt something nuzzle his back, and there she was. She'd been following *him*.

We had enough daylight left to move our camp to the top of the mesa, where we hoped there would be water. Edward's trail was barely discernible, very steep and covered with loose traprock.

Riding Wilbur, I got halfway up when I decided to lead him the rest of the way. I reined him to a stop and was about to dismount when he took a step backward and went off the edge of the trail.

I felt the sickening horror of a sudden drop into space. As I was already halfway off I managed to throw myself to the ground. I could hear below me a terrific clatter as Wilbur thrashed about on the steep slope. Through a miracle he managed to arrest his fall and find an unstable purchase among the rolling and sliding rocks.

I crept down to him, whispering soothing words, fearing at any moment he would take a step and roll into the canyon below. But he didn't, and I managed to collect his reins, build a little trail by shifting around some rocks, and coax him back up.

We topped out on a vast, sweeping sagebrush plain, with a red-rock mesa in the distance. The windmill and tank that Edward had described were in ruins. There was no water; we would have to continue until we found some.

At sunset we came across a muddy spring in an arroyo. A small cabin lay in the distance, and as we were watering the horses we heard the tinkling of a sheep bell and an old Zuni shepherd appeared at the edge, leading his flock to water. He was a small man with sharp features and a khaki-colored cowboy hat.

He greeted us. "You don't want to drink that," he said, pointing to the sheep wallow. "I got some good water at the house."

He took us back to his two-room stone cabin. Inside, it was cool and immaculately clean. He had three milk cans full of water, and he generously insisted we fill all our canteens.

His name was Leslie. He said he'd been living in the cabin since he was sixteen. He said he liked living alone in the country, except sometimes kids, drunk, would drive out and hassle him, thinking him strange for living so far from the pueblo. He said he'd bought his first and last vehicle in 1955, a Chevy pickup. It sat behind the cabin, a magical thing that looked as if it had taken shape in the desert itself. Once a bright turquoise, it had faded to the glaucous hues of sky and dry grass, the callipygian swell of its contours scoured by sand.

We camped a mile from the cabin, at the base of a smooth white rock nearly a hundred feet high and a quarter mile broad. The setting sun died against the rock, turning its surface the airy color of beaten electrum.

Our trail took us into a high-altitude forest seamed with grassy canyons. It rained briefly that afternoon, a quick, warm, welcome shower, while we rode through fields of thistles.

Pedernal stopped at one fat, thorny thistle flower and sniffed it. Then, his ugly lips plucked it with infinite care from its stem. He took it into his mouth and delicately rolled it about. When the thorns had softened and flattened out, he proceeded to eat it with his eyes half closed and the most exquisite expression of delight on his face. A gourmand with a tablespoon of Caspian Sea sevruga caviar in his mouth could not have looked more satisfied.

We continued into a deep ponderosa forest, and in a glade discovered a ruined cinder-block cabin surrounded by grass, where we pitched camp.

It dawned clear. As we rode east the trees thinned out and we came across a ruined ranch, with a herd of range horses hanging around a barn slumped into rabbitbrush. A stallion charged our horses and tried to start a fight, but we drove him off. There had been no water in our camp and we were now down to our last pint. We had had no luck at all finding water.

We came to the edge of a vast treeless plain. We swept the horizon with our binoculars and spied a lone house.

As we approached, a cheap HUD house materialized, a flimsy rectangle of painted chipboard with a fake adobe finish. Next to the house stood an old Navajo split-cedar hogan, chinked with mud, obviously the owner's former residence. Between us and the house was a tightly strung barbed-wire fence, the border between the Zuni and Ramah Navajo reservations, stretching gateless as far as the eye could see.

Walter began laying down the fence while I went to the house to ask about water.

I came around to the front. The door was open and a small shape was moving about in the dark interior. I halloed and a wizened Navajo woman came out. She was wearing a tattered orange velvet blouse, laden with squash-blossom necklaces, and a faded red velvet dress. Around her waist were two concho belts, and her wrinkled hands were heavy with turquoise-and-silver rings. Her iron-gray hair was tied back in a bun. Behind the open door I could see a bare house, broomswept clean, without so much as a stick of furniture. When she saw me she looked a little frightened and scowled.

I greeted her again.

She shrugged her shoulders.

"May we have some water?" I asked.

She continued to look at me, and then shrugged again.

"Do you speak English?" I asked.

She shrugged a third time.

"*Ya te'eh,*" I greeted her, thus utilizing my entire Navajo vocabulary.

This brought a faint softening to her features.

She replied in Navajo. Now it was my turn to shake my head. I tilted my head back and made a drinking motion.

She nodded.

I went back to the horses and untied our empty canteens.

When she saw me returning with the four one-gallon canteens the expression on her face suddenly changed. She shook her head vigorously.

I held up three.

She shook her head again.

I held up two.

Again she shook her head.

I held up one.

She stared at me with a stony expression.

I didn't know what to do. We desperately needed the water. I made a drinking motion again and she backed into her house. I followed, unsure as to whether this was an invitation or not.

The water was next to the front door in a brimming galvanized washtub, open to the air to keep the water cool through evaporation. With a black expression on her face, she handed me a ladle. I began filling the one canteen, while she hovered behind me, muttering in Navajo; I could feel the intensity of her stare drilling into the back of my neck.

When the canteen was three-quarters full she spoke angrily.

I felt bad about taking her water, but my feelings of guilt were overcome by my fear of dying of thirst. As it was, we had not camped at water since leaving Zuni. Only once had we even had enough water to wash our dishes, which had become truly disgusting. The only effective method for cleaning our pot was to let it dry out and savagely hammer it with a rock, knocking the old food out in one solid piece.

I thanked her profusely, while backing out of the house with my canteen. She said nothing but looked unhappy—one more white man come to take something away. As we rode off, the woman stood in her doorway, watching us.

In late afternoon we came up on the backside of El Morro National Monument, also called Inscription Rock, and camped in a broad field just outside the monument boundary.

As we were hobbling the horses a car came lurching over the prairie toward us. A tall man got out and came forward with great looping strides. He introduced himself as Dr. Robert Currier and pumped our hands with enthusiasm. A descendant of the Currier of Currier & Ives, he was director of the Zuni-Ramah community health service. He had heard about our journey and had been driving the reservation looking for us. Coronado's trail, he explained, was a hobby of his, and he spent much of his spare time mapping out ancient trade routes in the Ramah area. He had identified portions of what he felt was probably the old Zuni-Acoma trail, the route Alvarado, Padilla, and Bigotes would have been following. Part of it went right in front of his hogan, and he invited us out to have a look.

Robert lived at his father-in-law's sheep camp, in a brand-new hogan he had just finished building. It was the traditional Navajo eight-sided structure, but much larger than the usual hogan. We arrived at dusk and Robert showed us some faint parallel marks in the prairie that were obviously the remains of an old trail. He had mapped the marks for a number of miles, finding that they connected ancient watering holes. There was little doubt in my mind that he had discovered the actual Zuni-Acoma trail. My route, mapped out on U.S.G.S. maps, had missed it slightly, going a mile or two south.

At the hogan we met Robert's wife, a beautiful Navajo woman with a brilliant smile named Nada, and their child, Christopher. Behind the new hogan was an older one, where Nada's father, the shepherd, lived.

Currier bounced around the hogan with a manic energy, speaking to us and his wife, switching rapidly in mid-sentence from Navajo to English and back again. It was a completely bilingual household. (Currier, we found out later, was also fluent in Zuni and Japanese.) After hearing about some of our disasters, he hauled out a heavy basket and said: "I think you need some help for the rest of your trip." He closed his eyes and dipped his hand in, rummaged around like the Wizard of Oz, and extracted a tiny stone carving of a red fox with a turquoise arrowhead tied to its back. He gave it to me. He then extracted another little carving for Walter. These, he said, were Zuni fetishes, through which the Zuni tapped the power of a particular animal for good luck, to help in the hunt, and to help the person follow the right path in life.

He selected buckskin medicine bags for each of us. Into these he dropped our respective fetishes, sprinkled in some sacred cornmeal, and intoned a prayer in Zuni.

"And now!" he cried out, "something for your horses!"

Once again he stirred the basket and came up with a flat piece of turquoise, drilled, tied to a string with some beads on it. This, he said, was a traveling fetish; if we tied this onto the bridle of the lead horse all our horse problems would be over.

Walter and I had an argument back at our camp, and despite a damp evening he dragged his sleeping bag into the darkness, saying he was not going to share a tent with a Yankee son-of-a-bitch like me.

In the middle of the night I started awake, the sound of snoring booming across the night like a wheezing bellows.

I was enraged. The Texas bastard, after all that talk about how obnoxious my presence was, had gone and pitched his bedroll not three feet from the tent. I shouted and clapped my hands, I hollered and beat on the side of the tent, I hurled murderous threats into the darkness—but the snoring continued unabated. And then I realized what this was *really* about: Walter, knowing I detested snoring, was deliberately tormenting me.

In a rage I burst from the tent, ready to pound the scumbag into the dirt. Instead, I nearly fell over a great white mound, the supine form of Wilbur, happily snoring away. I was so furious that I gave Wilbur a kick with my bare foot, nearly spraining it. The poor innocent horse jumped up in a panic, and I chased him halfway across the field, screeching obscenities.

The next morning Walter asked, "Jesus, Doug, what was all that noise last night?"

"I didn't hear a thing," I said.

"Funny," he said. "I could've sworn I heard you yelling bloody murder."

"You must have been dreaming," I said.

27

◁ ▭ ▷

The Navajo Indians are relative newcomers to the Southwest, having arrived only a few centuries before the Spanish. They were Athabascans, a hunter-gatherer people from Alaska and northern Canada. When these poor Athabascan bands migrated into the Four Corners area and encountered the Anasazi, there can be little doubt the Athabascans were impressed. Here was wealth beyond all imagining: granaries heaped with beans and corn, permanent houses of stone, kitchens filled with elaborate pottery, people wrapped in gorgeous woven blankets, priests directing complex and powerful religious ceremonies with great fervency of belief.

The Athabascans who saw these things wanted them, and had shortly absorbed so much of Pueblo culture that they became a people quite distinct from their Athabascan cousins living in the west and east.

Those Athabascans who adopted Pueblo ways became the Navajo; those who did not became the Apache. When Coronado arrived this differentiation was still in process; it wouldn't be complete until the nineteenth century.

While borrowing from their Pueblo enemies, the Navajos retained many aspects of their own culture. Like their nomadic ancestors, they disliked living together and spread out as much as possible. Basically a secular people, the Navajo adaptation of Pueblo religion became a practical way to control nature, ward off evil, and heal sickness—in contrast to the complex, integrated theology of the Pueblos. Around the same time the Navajos acquired corn from the Pueblos and learned how to farm.*

When Juan de Oñate and his settlers arrived in the Southwest in 1598 with three thousand *churro* sheep, one thousand head of cattle, and three hundred horses, the Navajos promptly relieved him of some of each. A second transformation of Navajo culture took place: the horse quickly became the basis of their plunder economy and the sheep the basis of their household economy. They acquired fruit trees from the Spanish, turning these into a cornerstone of their agrarian economy. They learned weaving from the Pueblos and, with wool from their Spanish sheep, created one of the finest weaving traditions the world has ever seen. Later, they would pick up silversmithing from the Europeans and transform that into an extraordinary, and completely original, art form.

The Navajos were, if anything, adaptable.

To the earliest Spanish, the Navajo were the *Apaché de Nabahu*, which as an amalgam of a Zuni, a Spanish, and a Tanoan word roughly translates as "The Enemy of the Planted Fields." The Navajo, like the Apache, simply called themselves *Diné*, the People.

While Alvarado and Padilla did not mention Navajos living in the Ramah area, archeologists examining timbers from old Ramah Navajo hogans have found logs that were cut as far back as 1543. Forty years later, a Spanish explorer mentioned encountering "Querechos"—the early Spanish term for Apaches—in this area, a people who were probably the ancestors of the present-day Ramah Navajos.

The Spanish had three things the Navajos wanted—horses, sheep, and cattle—and as soon as the Spanish began settling the Navajos started raiding them. At the same time, the Navajos would have nothing to do with the friars or Christianity.

The Spanish reaction to the truculent *Apaché de Nabahu* was one of brutality. A succession of corrupt Spanish governors saw great profit in slavery, and sent expeditions into Navajo country which swooped down on small settlements, killing the men and seizing the women and children. The slaving was justified on religious grounds: those captured children would be raised as Christians. Thus, slavery

---

*The linguistic root of the Navajo word for corn means "the food of strangers."

would save at least some of the heathens from damnation. "No Hispano of New Mexico," the historian John Kessell wrote, "however
lowly his station, felt that he had made good until he had one or
more of these children to train as servants in his home and to give his
name. . . . They were as sure a symbol of status as a fine horse." So
numerous were these Navajo slaves (along with Utes, Comanches,
Wichitas, and Pawnees) that they created a new class in New Mexico: *genízaros,* that is, Hispanicized, Christianized Indians. Today
there are thousands of *genízaros* still living in remote towns in northern New Mexico.*

The slave trade started a deadly cycle that had terrible consequences
not only for the Navajos, but also for the poor Hispanics who suffered
the brunt of Navajo retaliation.

Pecos, and later Taos, became the center of the booming slave trade.
There Spanish and Indian slave traders, one witness noted, "gathered
to trade and barter. . .for Indian slaves, men and women, small and
large. . .the richest treasure for the governors who gorge themselves
first with the largest mouthfuls. . . . When these barbarians bring in a
certain number of Indian women to sell, among them many young
maidens and girls, before delivering them to the Christians who buy
them, they deflower and corrupt them in the sight of innumerable
assemblies of barbarians and Catholics. . .and saying to those who buy
them, with heathen impudence: 'Now you can take her—now she is
good.' "

The Navajos were also guilty of slaving against enemy tribes—
slaving between Indians was an old custom—and the Navajos could be
just as brutal as the Spanish. At one point a group of Navajos came into
Taos with some Pawnee boys captured on the plains; when they found
the boys couldn't be sold they decapitated them and left.

When the Americans annexed New Mexico in 1848, they stepped
into this two-century-old cycle of slaving, retaliation, and plunder
between the Hispanics and Navajos. Required by the Treaty of Guadalupe Hidalgo to protect the property rights of Hispanic† citizens of

---

*Abiquiu is one such town, and Benito, Walter's friend, was a *genízaro.*

†There has been a long debate about what to call those people of Spanish-Mexican
descent living in the Southwest. Some object to the word "Hispanic," because it lumps
them with other groups, like Puerto Ricans and Cubans, with whom they have almost
no historical connection. The term Spanish-American is unsatisfactory because it
implies a pure Spanish heritage, which is not often the case with southwestern Hispanics, most of whom have Mexican-Indian or American-Indian blood. The term "Mexican" is incorrect for obvious reasons: many never even lived in Mexico. The term

New Mexico, the Americans sent punitive expeditions against the Navajos. But these attacks were doomed to fail, because they did nothing to root out the basic cause of Navajo unrest.

True to form, the Americans not only failed to solve the problem, they made things worse. As with the Apaches, all it took was one grossly incompetent officer, of which the American military had a surfeit. That officer appeared in 1849, in the person of one Colonel John Washington, who led the first military expedition against the Navajos. The expedition left Santa Fe on August 16th, blazing a new trail to Navajo land. They encountered the first Navajo settlement on August 30th in the valley of the Río Tunicha. In retaliation for several minor raids the troops seized the Navajos' winter corn, trampled their fields, and demanded to meet with the Navajo leaders.

In response a group of Navajo headmen with a force of three hundred warriors arrived at the soldiers' camp, among them a much-beloved leader named Narbona. No blood had yet been spilled between the Americans and Navajos, and the headmen were anxious to talk peace.

A Hispanic officer in Washington's command claimed to have seen one of the Navajos riding a horse that had been stolen from him. Washington ordered the Indian and horse seized; when the company charged forward to carry out the order the mounted Navajos, thinking they were being attacked, wheeled about to escape. Like a dog instinctively biting a fleeing man, Washington ordered his troops to fire, and they blasted indiscriminately into the ranks of the retreating Indians, killing Narbona and six warriors. "Major Peck," an officer named James H. Simpson wrote, "also threw among them, very handsomely—much to their terror—a couple of round of [artillery] shot." Narbona was scalped by a trooper, and two American cartographers lamented that they hadn't gotten to the corpse in time to "secure Narbona's head for their scientist friend and associate at the Philadelphia Academy of Natural Sciences." Washington then went on to the Navajo stronghold of Canyon de Chelly,* where he burned a large number of hogans.

Chicano is too political for some and also applies to recent Mexican immigrants. The term New Mexican has been used, but it is unsatisfactory because, technically, any resident of New Mexico is a New Mexican. Some historians have even coined a new term, Hispano, to answer the difficulty. I don't take all that much stock in labels, and I have used more than one of these terms in this book, without, I trust, confusing the reader.

*Pronounced "Canyon de Shay." This is not French, but a corruption of the Navajo word *tsegi*, meaning Rock.

To stop the military rampage the Navajos quickly signed a treaty. But in one way the Navajos were like the Americans: they considered treaties to be worthless and disregarded them when they proved inconvenient. (It is also true that because the Navajo had no centralized power structure, a treaty signed by one headman meant nothing to the rest.)

Before Washington's troops had even returned to Santa Fe, the Navajos, retaliating for Narbona's killing, launched furious attacks against Pueblo Indian and Hispanic villages across northern New Mexico, kidnapping children and killing scores of men. More troops were sent against the Indians, and a whole new cycle began, this time between the Americans and the Navajos. Thus began the chain of events that would culminate in the Long March—the most disastrous episode in Navajo history.

In 1855 a peace parley between the Navajos and the Americans was convened to discuss setting aside a reservation for the Navajos. Stockmen and settlers had begun moving onto Navajo lands, and the Indians were worried. The Navajos were represented by Hastiin Chilajin, Man of Blackweed, also known as Manuelito, and the Americans by David Meriwether, territorial governor of New Mexico.* Man of Blackweed cut an impressive figure at the conference. His broad chest was scored by a bullet wound, acquired in fighting the Mexicans, and he wore a beautiful Navajo chieftain's blanket that was worth $100, an astonishing sum at the time. "He was the finest looking Indian man I ever saw," one army officer wrote. "He was over six feet in height and of the most symmetrical figure, combining ease, grace and power and activity in a wonderful degree." (Man of Blackweed would end up, like so many other Navajos, a victim of *todithit*—white man's whiskey.)

When Meriwether announced the boundaries of the proposed reservation, Man of Blackweed objected. The Navajos, he pointed out, occupied a much larger area. The new reservation even excluded three of the four sacred peaks defining the boundaries of the Navajo world.

Meriwether replied rather dryly that "one sacred mountain would be sufficient" and told the Navajos this was the best they were going to get. Urged by their agent, the Navajos signed anyway. In return for giving up raiding and agreeing to live within the reservation, the Navajos were promised foodstuffs, farming implements, and supplies until they could become self-sufficient.

---

*New Mexico, it should be remembered, at this time also included all of Arizona.

Congress failed to ratify the treaty. As a result, none of the goods promised by the treaty arrived, and encroachments on Navajo lands continued unchecked. And yet the government fully expected the Navajo to comply with all their obligations under the unratified treaty.

Meanwhile, Hispanics continued taking Navajo slaves. The Ute Indians, seeing the Navajos relatively pacified, stepped up their raids against their bitter enemy. The winter of 1856 was dreadfully severe and killed a large percentage of the Navajos' sheep and horses.

Meanwhile, the War Department, which could usually be counted to make the wrong move, cut back the number of troops stationed at Fort Defiance, the major outpost in Navajo country. The Navajos quickly exploited the resulting military weakness. Man of Blackweed took the lead, moving his sheep onto lands set aside for the military. When the commanding officer protested, Man of Blackweed sarcastically replied, "Drive me off if you think your force is sufficient." The Navajos also began helping themselves to army cattle and stealing cattle from the Hispanic herds that had moved into their territory and were eating their grass.

The situation had reached a critical point; it would take very little to start a war. The very little thing which started the war was an argument between a Navajo and his wife. Bested by his wife, the enraged Navajo went to Fort Defiance and shot the first man he saw, a black slave belonging to the commanding officer, a man named Brooks. Brooks sent for the Navajo headman and demanded that the murderer be turned over for punishment.

The headman refused, pointing out all the injustices the Navajo had suffered, in particular one recent incident not long before, when Brooks's soldiers had shot sixty head of Navajo cattle.

Brooks, concerned not about the life of a black man but rather that he had been deprived of a valuable piece of chattel, organized a punitive expedition. Both Utes and Hispanic New Mexicans were recruited. Not surprisingly, the Zunis also turned out in large numbers against their ancient enemy.

The American military forces were commanded by a particularly loathsome man named Colonel Benjamin Louis Eulalie de Bonneville. He was roundly despised by his fellow officers, and one historian would later characterize him as "a *bon vivant* and voluptuary" who "preferred lording it in the forest with a troop of red and white savages at his heels. . . . [For Bonneville], to shoot buffalo were rare fun; but men were the nobler game, whom to search out in their retreat and slaughter and scalp were glorious." Columns of troops crisscrossed Navajo country, shooting, killing, and burning wherever possible.

Several peace discussions ensued. The Navajos made it quite clear that they would not cease fighting until the government promised to protect them from the plundering of the Utes and the slaving of the Hispanics. There would be no peace until the Hispanics returned their abducted children.

Bonneville would have none of it, and presented, in a take-it-or-leave-it fashion, an outrageously inflammatory "peace treaty" that was roundly condemned as being unfair even by his own officers, one of whom wrote that it "cannot be endorsed by any enlightened mind."

The Navajo signed the worthless treaty only to gain a few weeks of respite; between themselves they had concluded that nothing of value could come from talking with the *Bilagáanas;* they would fight to the end.

By 1860, bands of Navajos were sweeping the territory, destroying settlements and driving off herds of livestock. A thousand Navajos attacked Fort Defiance and nearly took it.

Then the Civil War broke out. In a few months, one historian noted, "it could not be said that an American army existed in New Mexico."

The Utes and New Mexicans used the withdrawal of the army to step up their slaving and plunder raids against the Navajos. One knowledgeable resident of Santa Fe at the time estimated that Hispanic (and some Anglo) New Mexicans had enslaved between five thousand and six thousand Navajos, and he wrote that the trade in Navajo slaves was "as regular as trade in pigs and sheep."

The Navajos, on their end, were no longer fighting for plunder and booty. They were now fighting for their lives.

In 1862, a bungler named General James Carleton took over command of New Mexico Territory. Soon Carleton had hatched plans for the Navajos which would bring disaster to the tribe.

General Carleton figured the way to solve the Navajo problem was to move them out of their rugged homeland and concentrate them in a tiny camp in eastern New Mexico, at a bend in the Pecos River called Bosque Redondo. Although a board of army officers vigorously disagreed with Carleton's choice of site, saying it was "unhealthy," Carleton overruled them and launched construction of a new fort at the site, to be called Fort Sumner. The Navajos would be given until July 20, 1863, to surrender; after that "every Navajo seen will be considered as hostile and treated accordingly."

Under the cover of the decree, hordes of slave traders poured into Navajo country, trying to capture as many slaves as possible before the market lost its supply.

Few Navajos surrendered by the deadline. In late July troops invaded the Navajo strongholds. Carleton engaged the help of Kit Carson, who organized and commanded a volunteer force. Carson had been Indian agent to the Utes, and his sympathies did not lie with the Navajos; he even rewarded his Ute scouts with the right to keep as slaves any Navajos they captured.

Wherever the troops went, the Navajos melted away into the canyons and deserts. But Carson knew exactly how to defeat an enemy that couldn't be engaged: he employed a scorched-earth policy, systematically destroying all Navajo property he could find—hogans, crops, and livestock. In Bonito Canyon alone Carson destroyed two million pounds of grain, and in Canyon de Chelly he chopped down beautiful, ancient groves of fruit trees. As winter closed in, the Navajo began to surrender, and by March 1, 1864, more than three thousand were being held. Many of the Navajo bands scattered northward, southward, and westward: Man of Blackweed and his band fled into the Grand Canyon itself.

General Carleton gleefully concluded: "This formidable band of robbers and murderers has at last been made to succumb."

But the general had not thought to provide adequate food or shelter for the surrendering Indians. Hundreds began to sicken and die at the forts, and in a panic Carleton started them on a long walk to Bosque Redondo, three hundred miles away.

The Navajos were given rations of flour and coffee beans, but they had no idea what to do with this white powder, and could only mix it with water and eat the paste. Thinking the coffee beans were true beans, they boiled them for hours and hours, repeatedly dumping out the dirty water, and then chewed on the worthless husks.

The Long Walk was one of the most shameful episodes in American history, and Bosque Redondo was possibly the closest America has come to creating a genuine concentration camp. Most of the Indians were forced to walk, as the few army vehicles that were supplied overflowed with the aged and crippled. Those Navajo men, women, and children who couldn't keep up were left by the trail to die a lingering death—until the soldiers began to take pity on them by putting them out of their misery with a bullet.

Hispanic slaving parties attacked columns of poorly guarded Navajos on the Long Walk, overpowering the soldiers and taking the Indians captive. Slaving parties also rampaged through Navajo lands, seizing hundreds of prisoners. The army stood by, doing nothing.

The reservation Carleton planned for the Navajos was less than one-thousandth the size of their original homeland. There was nothing at Bosque Redondo: no tents or housing or even wood to build with, no animals for clothing, no seeds for crops or tools to work them with. The Navajo could only live in holes dug in the ground with their hands, and cover themselves with brush and rotten canvas. The water from the Pecos River was alkaline and nearly undrinkable. The War Department and the Bureau of Indian Affairs blamed each other for the situation and insisted that it was each other's responsibility to correct it. As a result nothing was done.

Meanwhile, the Indians began to sicken and die of starvation and disease.

Seeds finally arrived for the spring planting in 1865, but there were no implements to break the tough virgin sod. Using sharp stones, small sticks, and their hands, the Navajo chipped away at the earth, dug irrigation ditches, and planted crops. By early summer three thousand acres of corn, wheat, beans, melons, and pumpkins were under cultivation—a tremendous achievement. But before the crops could bear fruit, cutworms destroyed the corn, strong winds flattened the wheat, and heavy rains washed away everything else.

The usual theft, kickbacks, and cheating occurred at Bosque Redondo, but on such a massive scale that one reliable report estimated that Indian Bureau agents stole, on the average, approximately 70 percent of everything appropriated for the Navajo.

By 1866 the Navajo were *in extremis;* and yet Carleton forged ahead with one misguided plan after another. He tried, among other things, to put the Navajo in large barracks, despite being warned that the Navajos would abandon any structure in which a person had died.

Carleton was unable to cover up the abuses at Bosque Redondo indefinitely. Two reports came out in 1866 exposing conditions there. One report also documented that peonage and slavery were still going strong in New Mexico, with many legislators, prominent citizens, judges, and military officers owning Navajo slaves. Many other scandals were revealed: the War Department was deliberately sending food unfit for human consumption; vast quantities of supplies destined for the Navajos had been stolen; Comanches and Hispanics were driving off large quantities of Navajo stock and murdering Navajos with impunity; more than a thousand Navajos had escaped; hundreds, if not thousands, had died or were dying from starvation, dysentery, and syphilis introduced by the soldiers; both soil and water were unsuitable for agriculture; the horrors went on and on. The reports roundly condemned both the War Department and Carleton.

A furor ensued and Carleton was relieved of duty. But the War Department and the civilian agencies continued to argue about the fate of the Navajos, while the Navajos continued to die. Two more years passed. Finally, on May 29, 1868, General William Tecumseh Sherman, commander of the Department of Missouri (which had control over the territory), arrived at Bosque Redondo to hold a council with the Navajos to decide the future of the tribe. Present at the council were the important Navajo headmen, including Barboncito (Little Beard) and Ganado Mucho (Many Sheep), as well as Kit Carson.

The Navajo spoke first and at length, telling Sherman that Bosque Redondo was a living hell for them, and that if allowed to return they would cease stealing and live in peace forever.

Sherman spread out a map for Barboncito and the other headmen, showing them where the Navajos lived, and also showing them the lower Arkansas country where he hoped the Indians would agree to go, "where corn can be raised without irrigation and the land and grass are good. . ."

Barboncito was horrified by the suggestion and pled with Sherman: "I hope to God you will not ask us to go to any other country except our own."

Ganado Mucho spoke eloquently: "Let us go home to our mountains. Let us see our flocks feeding in the valleys, and let us ride again where we can smell the sage and know of the hidden hogans by the smell of piñon smoke. Let us go where we can build our homes in solitude and privacy and live again as men, not animals. Let us be free to build a better way of life and learn to live in peace where the red buttes rise from the desert sands, and eagles sweep across the sky. Let us go home. We have learned not to kill and not to steal from the flocks of others. Here we have nothing. Our children grow up in ugliness and death. Let us go home."

Kit Carson then spoke up for the Navajo. Despite his implacable war against the Indians, there is little doubt he now regretted the role he played in bringing the Navajo to Bosque Redondo.

"General," he said, "I'm not sure the Great Spirit means for us whites to take over Indian lands. I brought this proud people to this

place because they would not listen to Washington. Now they have
heard, and three thousand died here while they were hearing. Let me
lead them back [to their original lands] while they still have the will to
live."

Sherman heard the passion in all these statements, and he was
moved. He laid aside the Arkansas proposition and said, "One has pity
on you. . .I will help you."

On June 1, 1868, the final treaty document was signed establishing
the reservation. Although the new reservation was large, containing 3.5
million acres, it covered only a small fraction of the Navajos' original
territory.

Almost immediately after the signing, bands of ragged Navajos, with
their bony horses and hollow dogs, departed Bosque Redondo. When
some of the tough old Navajo men first glimpsed the blue line of the
sacred Mount Taylor rising over the horizon, they fell to their knees
and wept.

"On they pushed," the historian John Terrell wrote, "north beyond
Shiprock, by Teec Nos Pos, beyond Red Rock Valley and Shelagaidesa
Canyon. And they went west far beyond Canyon de Chelly and Beautiful Valley, past Ganada Mesa and Black Mountain, on beyond the
Hopi country to Moenkopi. Some of them moved on as if they never
intended to stop, northwestward toward Kayenta and Monument Valley and Navajo Mountain to the San Juan River. Or south to Klagetoh
and the Painted Desert and on to Red Lake. Into a thousand canyons,
big and little, into a thousand valleys, hidden and open, they moved,
determined to survive somehow, preferring to suffer hunger and defy
death than live under the domination of the white men."

There were many traditional Navajo areas left out of the treaty
reservation. One of these was the area we were now in, between the
Zuni Indians and the El Malpaís lava beds. The Navajo band living
there called this area Tl'ohchini, "Onions," after a spring in the center
of a valley surrounded by wild onions. (The name "Ramah" comes
from the Book of Mormon and wasn't given to the area until Mormons
arrived in the 1870s.) Although the treaty stipulated that any Navajo
not living within the reservation would forfeit his rights, two family
groups who had probably lived at Tl'ohchini before the Long March
returned.

These two families were headed by Old Man Cojo and Many Beads.
By 1870 there were about twenty-five Navajos at Ramah, coexisting

peacefully with the other inhabitants of the area, who were mostly Hispanics from the nearby town of Tinaja. In the 1870s Mormons came to Ramah and began homesteading. Since the Navajos at Ramah had no legal rights to the land and did not understand the homestead process, the Mormons were able to homestead the choicest lands. The Navajos found themselves pushed south, away from water, into arid desert.*

Eventually, in the 1920s, the Ramah Navajos were able to take title to their now reduced lands, and the result was a checkerboard reservation, with Navajo, private, and public lands all mixed up. For centuries the Ramah Navajos had lived separately from the main body of the Navajo tribe and today they remain fiercely independent, almost a distinct people.

Curiously, however, much of what we know about the Navajo people in general comes from Ramah. Here is where many of the great ethnographic studies of the Navajo took place, such as Clyde Kluckhohn's famous work, *Navajo Witchcraft*, as well as the Ramah Project and the Harvard Values Project (in which Ramah was pseudonymously called "Rimrock"). So many anthropologists have studied the Ramah band of Navajos that the local Navajos tell a joke: What does a typical Ramah Navajo family consist of? A father, mother, three children, and an anthropologist.

---

*The Ramah Mormons later hired the Navajos to build a new church. The Navajos worked for months, all the while singing Yeibechei songs. When a friend of mine asked them why the Mormons couldn't build their own church, one Navajo replied, "That's okay, we're getting all our spirits in here."

28

⬤⟩ ⟨⊠⟩ ⟨⬤

Robert came by our camp early and invited us to breakfast at his hogan. Shortly after we arrived his father-in-law came in.
Robert greeted him.

"Ya te'eh, hastiin."

"Ya te'eh," he said, and sat down slowly, scraping the chair. Nada
slid a mug of coffee to him. He cupped it in his hands, hunched over,
and sipped.

Nada introduced us to her father, Cheppie Natan. He was a quiet,
dignified man with a face so wrinkled and sunburnt that it was hard to
tell how old he was. He had iron gray hair, with a headband fashioned
from a red bandanna, and he wore old boots and a checked shirt. When
he spoke, his breath whistled through gaps in his teeth. His movements
were slow and deliberate. He did not speak English.

I asked Nada if I could interview him. She spoke to him in Navajo
and he nodded his head.

"My dad speaks Spanish," Nada said, "but he says that was so hard
to learn that when the Anglos came he just wasn't going to learn
English too. One language was enough!"

She laughed delightedly.

I set up my tape recorder and asked Natan about the history of his family. Had they been interred at Fort Sumner with the rest of the tribe?

Nada translated the question into Navajo, and he replied at length. Navajo is a tonal, singing language, full of sibilant sounds, clicks of the tongue, and glottal stops. It is spoken in a measured, dignified way. There are very few languages as beautiful to listen to as Navajo. When he stopped, Nada began to translate.

"He said that these Navajos were so foolish, so silly and so ignorant, they didn't know right from wrong. They were stealing horses, and stealing livestock, constantly stealing. That was the main reason they were sent to Fort Sumner. It wasn't the Ramah Navajos doing the stealing, it was the Big Navajos* way up there by Chinle Navajo area. But it just covered the whole Navajo, we were *all* labeled as stealers. He said that's why the *Bilagáanas* sent us out there. He says his father told him his great-grandpa and -grandma said it was the most painful thing that they ever went through.

"There wasn't hardly anybody living here then. They weren't doing the stealing. They didn't know why they were going to Fort Sumner. His great-grandpa, he got away and stayed behind, with a couple of babies. He doesn't know what happened to them. They were never seen again."

"What was Fort Sumner like?" I asked. "Have you heard any stories about the life there?"

Nada translated her father's reply.

"They hardly ever talk about it," she said. "They thought it was a. . ." She paused, searching for the right English word. "A spell. . .a *curse* put on them, so they never talk about it. They would get one handful of corn, that was their meal. It was hard. It was during winter-time that they went down there. Many of them died on the way, especially the older folks. They didn't have any funeral service. They were put between rocks and left there. That was the reason why they don't really want to talk about it.† In the end most of them died anyway.

"He said the walls were made out of bricks.‡ And it was so thick, and the door was real thick, made out of boards with two or three locks

---

*"Big Navajos" refers to the Navajos living on the big reservation in the Four Corners area, whom the Ramah Navajos heartily dislike.

†The Navajo have a great aversion to speaking about or referring to death.

‡Carleton's barracks?

on it. They were cold, and they had sheep skins, that was about all they had for the cold. If they froze, they froze.

"So, he says, most of the medicine men would get together and try to plan out a way they could escape. One of the men had a vision that they should drill a hole in the wall, which was thick and it took them almost six or seven months to drill a hole in it. A lot of them escaped through there. That's how Grandma escaped, she came back. This was about two years before they were released."

"She came back here?" I asked.

"She settled on Ramah Lake down there. It took her almost three months to get back. They think there was this spell put on them and they don't want their kids to have that same spell, so they never really talk about it. But up in Big Navajo, up in Chinle, they have the strength to talk about it. I guess they got books out about it. But the books never really tell the full story. Some of the ladies came back with white kids, and with black kids, but they never told that story. My mom was saying that her grandma, she was about eighty or ninety years old, she had a big old scar on the side of her ribs that never healed."

"What was it from?" I asked.

"I don't know what it was. She said there was a lot of torture that went on there. She really didn't talk about it. She finally died from that scar.

"My grandpa, he always warned, 'Never think of the Anglos as an enemy.' He would always say, 'Even though you went through all that hardship don't ever have anything wrong on them, always think of them as yourself.' "

Nada giggled. "But while *we* were growing up we didn't like Anglos because they would make us go to school, and we hated them, *hated* them so much for that." She laughed and tossed back her black hair.

"Can you ask your father," I said, "if there are any stories about what it was like when the white people first came? Are there any stories or memories about what life was like before, and how the coming of the Spaniards and the Anglos affected their way of life?"

Nada asked Natan the question. While he replied Nada made many expressions of surprise and interest.

"His great-great-*great*-grandfather said you could see that early morning flash up there, the flash of their armor. They could see them but they didn't know what it was. He says his grandpa used to talk about it.

"The way they described Coronado in the books is not the way my grandfather described him. The books say he was a stocky-looking man, but he was a skinny, *very* skinny man. They say he was a Mexican, but his grandpa says he didn't look like a Mexican at all. There was white-faced people, and blacks that came through here with him. It wasn't all Spaniards.* The Jemez were the ones that guided them. It wasn't the Zunis.†

"He was a very old man, but he could see them coming through here. They didn't know then what a month was. They didn't have a calendar. It was in the fall 'cause the leaves were starting to turn different colors and it was cooling down.‡

"A group of Ramah Navajos got together because they didn't want the Spanish going through here, and completely shut that water from a spring over on the other side.

"When they came back from Fort Sumner they were afraid they would be taken away again, so they chose the mountains and the canyons and caves to live in. There was one real big canyon, where his grandpa and grandma settled and some other people. He says that in that canyon there was too many people, over a hundred people. They brought a little corn and squash. When they were at Fort Sumner they had pumpkins. Some of them tried planting it but it dried out. There wasn't enough water. It was really hard for them to be in that canyon.

"They decided they needed to spread out so they just started walking one morning, took whatever they had. And they were so happy when they came to Ramah Lake. They heard about it but they never seen it. He says you could hear the Zunis at night singing. They spent a couple of months there, and went on down to Five Cents Hill. They call it that because it is a *small-l-l-l* hill," and she held up two fingers to show how small.

"And you can see it from miles away. He says they used to gamble there. Two or three Mexicans were living here already, and they had

---

*All these statements are true. The Spaniards were white-faced Europeans, not like Mexicans who are dark because of a large proportion of Indian blood. There were blacks with Coronado's army. And, of course, the man leading the group was not Coronado but Hernando de Alvarado, who came from northern Spain and was reportedly light-skinned with sandy hair. He would have been skinny, having nearly starved to death with the rest of the army on the trip to Zuni.

†This is an extremely interesting observation. The Jemez Indians are the only people left that speak Towa, the language spoken by the now extinct Pecos Indians who were leading Alvarado.

‡Alvarado came through in September.

thousands and thousands of sheep. His great-grandpa used to work for them, the Mexicans, herd sheep for them. Their kids and their kids all worked for one Mexican. They learned how to speak Spanish from there.

"When the Navajo came out, they figured this whole land was theirs because there were no landmarks and they would say that from that sunset to sunrise is our land, all the forest you can see. And my dad says back then grass was plenty and the sunflower was *big* like this one right here, thousands of them *everywhere* so you could make trails in them. And the rabbits were huge, compared to the rabbits we have now. And the porcupines, he said there were just fat, *fat* porcupines. They were delicious back then, and now you can't even eat it. And the prairie dogs were like *dogs*, they were that big, and there was tall green grass everywhere.

"Now you hardly ever see animals, and he says this is not what you would call grass"—she gestured outside the window to the burnt plains beyond—"compared to what they had back then. His life was much easier back then than now. *Now* it is hardship, because there is hardly any grass and you have to drive the sheep way out there and try to find water. Back then water was everywhere. He had an easy life back then, because everything was there for him.

"My grandma didn't really like him," Nada continued. "He was a cowboy. He could stay on a bronc horse for almost twenty minutes. The Mexicans had a dance hall under a brush arbor. They used to stand underneath and these Mexicans used to wear *big* hats with all fancy stuff. So that's how some of the Ramah Navajos started to dress with all that stuff on their clothes. They admired that and got the idea from the Mexicans. They put conchos around their hat. Him and his parents, his great-grandparents, used to really mix with the Mexicans. That's how he learned how to speak Mexican."

"How did your dad meet your mother?" I asked.

"My mom always talks about it. But anyway. . ." She laughed and covered her mouth.

"You don't want to ask him?" I said.

"Hmmmm," Nada said, shaking her head. Natan said something and she translated.

"They didn't need to have treats back then. Gum was made out of sap. There was this plant, and you could pop it just like bubble gum. They had teas, I used to go out there and gather tea and bring it back. And coffee, they found it, but it wasn't the coffee we drinking now. And in the wintertime there was these bugs on a tree. You put a can under a whole bunch of these bugs, and in the morning you could have syrup, like they get maple syrup. That was their sugar. You boiled it and set it out in the sun and it would crack.

"He said everything was out in nature. You could find *anything* out in nature. But now you can't. You have to go to the store to find whatever you're looking for.

"He said he was a good bronc rider and he won a lot of money and he won horses and chickens. He said he was offered ladies here and there but he wasn't really interested, he was just trying to show off."

Nada pealed with laughter and swept back her long hair.

"Yeah, he said he was real good. I heard that when I was in high school my dad and his brother, they were real good bronc riders."

"How did he learn?" I asked.

"He says it's easy. The trick about it is that you started when you were a small kid. I don't know where his great-grandpa learned this trick, but there is a particular tree sap that you get and you boil it and there's things you put in. And you plaster the child with it, put thick layers of sap all the way around his thighs. That keeps him on a horse. You can wash it but it doesn't come off. I guess"—she giggled—"it was the nastiest thing you could do to a child. You just *stick* on the horse. If you try to fall off you can't fall off. You have to jump off or somebody has to catch the horse. That's the way they did it, how they got him started. Him and his brothers were real great and he was well known. The Mexicans said they were going to take him somewhere, join him in some rodeo. But he was scared, he thought he might have been left behind and not know how to get back here, so he didn't go.

"The Mormons, down here, used to have rodeos in the canyon. So he joined them and he would get cans of coffee that would last him for two or three years, and he'd get flour and food for the whole family. After they had won, people would come to the house. It wasn't a hogan, it was just a little shack, made out of pine and bushes and whatever, and they had one that looked like a sweat lodge and you would fit in about fifteen people. We used to have a lot of people up there at that event and people would come take their share of whatever. He was kind of like the *president* he said. Yeah."

"This is kind of a tough question," I said, "but ask if he thinks the life of the Navajo people is better since the coming of the Europeans or is worse."

Nada quickly answered herself, not even putting the question to her father.

"He talks about that *all* the time. When he comes over in the morning, he often says that the world would have been much, *much* better if the Anglos, the Mormons, and the Mexicans didn't come. The grass would still be *that* high, the river would still be *flowing* if they didn't come. He says, you don't want to blame them. It's not *them* that did it. It's the modern life. Now that we have cars, and electricity, modern stuff, the whole modern life and everything, he says, *the earth just finally gave up.*"

There was a brief, electric silence.

"The earth doesn't want to give us nourishment like it did back then. Back then the earth was happy, the sun was happy, everything was happy that all the Navajos were there, happy with these people being Navajos. He says the grass was real *big*, the water was *everywhere*. But then after the *Bilagáanas* showed up, the earth started going down and was pretty unhappy. He talks about it a lot. If they didn't come, the earth still would have been happy with us. We wouldn't be in this mess we're in. We wouldn't be into what we call the sorrow. We call this mess the *sorrow.* . ."

She paused. Walter and Robert were very quiet, listening.

"At one time we had a lot of sheep. My great-grandmother had almost a thousand sheep. Now he has about thirty. Down through the years we lost a lot of sheep. My mom said they used to have six hundred horses. And they *all* died over there. They had a big snowstorm, the snow was real big and it covered most of the horses, and the other animals. For years we could see tons of bones there."

She laughed again, perhaps to take the sting out of what she was saying. "When that happened, they said, *blame* it on the Anglos. *They're* the ones that brought evil spirits to the Navajos."

29

⬬ ⧗ ⬬

As we headed east, the rock of El Morro thrust out of the plain, white in the sun, like a giant scapula bone. Great leaves of rock had split off the cliff, leaving smooth, cleaved faces. At the very base of the rock was a natural catchbasin of water, holding up to two hundred thousand gallons of rainwater, an important source of water in this area since time immemorial. It was now a national monument and nobody was allowed to bring livestock into the monument or allow them to drink from the catchbasin. We watered our horses with a hose at the visitor's center.

Because of this natural water hole, El Morro had been a major camping place along the Zuni-Acoma trail for a thousand years or more. As people stopped, they gradually covered the rock faces with the scrawlings of ten centuries.

The earliest marks were petroglyphs of mountain goats, the sacred corn plant, hands, broken arrows, and lizards. When the Zuni-Acoma trail became the major Spanish trade route from Santa Fe westward, passing Spaniards covered the rock with names and messages, as did the Americans after them.

We tied our horses up near the visitor's center and took a new asphalt trail along the base of the rock, looking at inscriptions, layered, like some mysterious palimpsest, one over the other, on the smooth face. The oldest ones were higher on the rock, the younger ones farther down, as erosion had gradually lowered the level of the ground. Almost the entire history of New Mexico was carved, one way or another, on the rock of El Morro.

We read one inscription after another.

"Paso por aqi el adelantado don ju de oñate o daescubrimiento de la mar del sur a 16 de Abril de 1605"

"Passed by here the Governor Don Juan de Oñate, from the discovery of the South Sea [the Sea of Cortez] on the 16th of April, 1605." (Oñate's inscription was, strangely, carved over an Anasazi petroglyph, although there was plenty of empty space nearby. The inscription is one of the oldest European artifacts in the United States.)

There were others:

"Here was the General Don Diego de Vargas, who conquered for our Holy Faith, and for the Royal Crown, all of New Mexico at his own expense, year of 1692."

And another:

"I am the captain General of the Provinces of New Mexico for the King our Lord, passed by here on the return from the pueblos of Zuni on the 29th of July the year 1620, and put them at peace at their humble petition, they asking favor as vassals of his Majesty, and promising anew their obedience, all of which he did, with clemency, zeal, and prudence, as a most Christian-like [obliterated] extraordinary and gallant soldier of enduring and praised memory." (This inscription speaks much about the personality of its writer, the notorious governor Juan de Eulate, exploiter of Indians, whom one historian called "a petulant, tactless, irreverent soldier whose actions were inspired by open contempt for the Church . . .and by an exaggerated conception of his own authority"; Eulate was hated by the friars, and in this inscription the missing word—evidently "gentleman"—was deliberately scratched out.)

"They passed on March 23, 1632, to the avenging of the death of Father Letrado. Luján." (As we know, there would be no "avenging"; the Zuni had fled to the inaccessible Dowa Yalanne.)

. . .

*"The 14th of July of 1736 passed by here the General Juan Paez
Hurtado, Inspector."* (Below this was added, hastily, in a different
hand, no doubt when the general's back was turned: *"and in his company the Corporal, Joseph Truxillo!"*)

*"Year of 1716 on the 26th of August passed by here Don Feliz Mar-
tinez, Governor and Captain General of this realm to the reduction and
conquest of the Hopi. . ."* (Martínez found the Hopis irreducible and
after two months of fist-shaking and threats returned empty-handed to
Santa Fe.)

Then the Americans came. *"Lt. J.H. Simpson U.S.A. & R.H. Kern,
Artist, visited and copied these inscriptions, September 17th 18th 1849."*
(The first American inscription; this is the same Simpson who chroni-
cled the disastrous Washington expedition against the Navajos; Simpson later accompanied Sitgreaves's expedition across Arizona and was
eventually killed by Indians in Utah in 1853.)

"N H HuTTon Nov 1853." (Hutton was a topographical engineer on
an expedition following up on Sitgreaves's effort to locate a trail to
California; soon a wagon road was established through El Morro.)

"John. Udell. AGE 63. July 8 1858. FIRST EMIGRAVT." (Udell,
a Baptist preacher, and his wife, was with the first emigrant pack train
to California along the wagon road. They were going to visit their
children in Sacramento. Udell was born in New York City; with his
wife, Emily, he would move thirty times in fifteen years, ever westward, working as a farmer, peddler, book agent, and preacher. The
train was attacked by Indians at the Colorado River, the stock driven
off and many killed; Udell and his wife, along with the survivors,
walked the six hundred miles back to Albuquerque. His wife was so
weak that the starving sixty-four-year-old carried her on his back much
of the way; the next year Udell and his wife tried again and made it to
Sacramento, where Udell found his children and lived to be a very old
man.)

"P. GILMER BRECKINRIDGE VA. 1859" ("Peachy" Breckinridge stopped at El Morro in 1859 with a train of twenty-five camels,
part of an army experiment to see how camels would do in the South-

west. Peachy was an aristocratic graduate of the Virginia Military Institute; his commanding officer wrote in his journal that "that man Breckinridge" was one of those "trifling lazy boys whose friends have influence enough to get them on parties of this kind where they invariably become a burden to themselves and everybody connected with them, the result is they go home disgusted and humiliated to see how badly they compare with men infinitely beneath them in birth and fortune." Peachy would grow up soon enough; fighting for the Confederacy he would be killed in Virginia in 1863.)

"A.v.d.W.—Zuni—1898." (Andrew VanderWagon, whose wife and Governor Robert Lewis's mother took care of the sick during the terrible epidemic of 1899 at Zuni.)

By the turn of the century the inscriptions disappear. This is not, of course, because people stopped carving on the face of the rock; indeed, there are countless polished, blank spots on El Morro where names once stood. Back in the 1930s, Park Service bureaucrats decided to purge the rock of unimportant people. In an act of grotesque official vandalism, a WPA crew burnished off hundreds of inscriptions, simply because the supervisors did not recognize the name, or thought the person too insignificant, or thought the date too recent, to be of importance. The ignorance of the people who directed this effort was appalling: among the names thought to have been removed were "C. Carson" (that is, Kit Carson) and "William Bonney" (a.k.a. Billy the Kid). Today the rock stands cleaned and sanitized, the inscriptions fenced off, numbered, and forever frozen in time. A small stone stands in front of the visitor's center, with a sign inviting the tourist to leave his mark there. The stone is rapidly being whittled into nothing by eager teenagers. The effect is absurd and bathetic—in short, a typically American answer to history.

We set off across a valley toward the Zuni Mountains. They lay heavily across the plain, like some lumpy, sleeping creature, covered with a furry layer of pines and spruces. Due to an oversight in my navigational planning we had no maps of the Zuni Mountains; our idea was simply to ride east through the mountains until we popped out the other side.

We struck the mountains and rode directly into them, climbing a steep ridge. There was no trail. We topped another ridge and the trees parted; there, below us, lay a grassy valley with a spring bubbling up in the middle, a little Eden. It even came with a picturesque ruin, next to a lightning-split ponderosa. A dirt track wound through the bottom of the valley.

As we were tightening down the packs next morning a pickup truck came lurching down the road, and a man in high-water polyester bell-bottom pants got out. He hiked his pants up to his chest and strode over as fast as his stumpy legs would carry him. The man meant business.

"This here's private property," he said, with a nervous tremble in his voice.

We feigned great surprise. Surely this was national forest?

Oh no, the man said. This prime ranch property had been subdivided into lots of 20 acres each and was now a development. The least expensive lot was pegged at $20,000 and there were financial expectations. High expectations. They couldn't have cowboys and horse packers and other such people scaring away their clientele.

We promised to leave as soon as we could, but he seemed doubtful and said he was obliged to report us to the "management."

Pretty soon the management arrived, in the form of a lean man with a ponytail and bowlegged walk named Sonny Jim. He was a cowboy turned real estate salesman, and as soon as he saw us he cracked a big grin.

"I heard there were some desperate characters around here. You seen 'em?"

He gave us a small map of the western Zuni Mountains, and showed us the best way to go. He was one of the lucky cowboys; he had survived the transition from ranch to development. I wondered what had happened to the rest of the hands when the ranch was subdivided.

We had a long beautiful ride that day, across open meadows dappled with light, past old waterpans carpeted with sunflowers, through hot, piney stands of ponderosa. We ate lunch at a mysterious little ghost town buried deep in the mountains. Around three o'clock, we struck the top of a high ridge and crossed the Continental Divide. To the east and south we could see the vast, rumpled lava fields known as El Malpaís,* which we would be crossing in a few days. To the northeast rose Mount Taylor, an eleven-thousand-foot extinct volcano and one of the four sacred peaks of the Navajo people.

We followed the divide for a few miles and plunged down a hill into

---

*Don't ask me why, but the common New Mexico pronunciation of this word is "mal-pie," or "mally-pie"—rather than the Spanish *malpaís*.

a country of rolling meadows dotted with wildflowers and pine glades. We had gone off the edge of Sonny Jim's map and were riding blind again. Black clouds tumbled through the atmosphere, the forest grew dark, and a rain began to fall. Later the sun came out and illuminated the falling raindrops, turning them into little streaks of golden fire.

We arrived at the town of Paxton Springs. It, too, was a ghost town, with only one cabin still standing. The cabin was made of peeled logs chinked with white plaster; blue curtains hung in the windows and around the front stoop grew a riot of blooming chamisa. A spring rose behind the cabin, in which was half-sunk a 1939 De Soto. The top was bashed in and a mass of plant life thrust out of the back window, like a loud green explosion. The car was so weather-beaten and oxidized that it resembled a great round fungus that had pushed up out of the soil.

Many years ago, the Navajo say, the Twin Gods fought a giant on the place where Mount Taylor stands today. During the epic battle they struck off the giant's head: it bounced and rolled eastward, becoming Cabezón Peak. The giant's blood gushed over the ground and pooled southward, coagulating into the Malpaís. From our vantage point at the head of Bonito Canyon, the Malpaís did indeed look like the ropy gore of some beast. It was a most forbidding landscape.

The black lava spread nearly to the horizon, several hundred thousand acres in extent, a rubbled, broken flat knobbed with trees. Its blackness swallowed the light of midday, making it look more like a blackwater swamp than a lava flow. Far to the south we could see a chain of cinder cones. Beyond the lava, we could see the low rimrock of Cebolleta Mesa, the beginning of the Acoma Indian reservation.

Close up, the lava took on a different look. It lay piled on the prairie as if it had been dropped there—twisted into ropes, broken into tilted rafts, heaved into jumbled piles, collapsed into great pits and caves (some so deep they are filled with perpetual ice), churned into a black froth, split and splintered—with a surface so razor sharp that it would cut skin and slice open a leather boot.

The Malpaís is actually many series of lava flows, the oldest nearly a million years old, and the youngest so young that it cannot be dated by normal geological dating methods. The Acoma Indians have legends of a river of fire inundating their planted fields, a story that is probably true, since the youngest flow—McCarty's Flow—did spread over thousands of acres of virgin prairie within the traditional Acoma domain. Some geologists believe that McCarty's Flow may have pre-dated Coronado by only a century or two, or possibly even just a few decades. It is as fresh and unweathered as the recent lava flows on the Hawaiian Islands.

The Malpaís is part of the vast Jemez Lineament, a place where the crust of the earth is being stretched apart, creating leaks of magma from the upper mantle. (These stretching forces are the same as those that created the Mogollon Rim, the basin-and-range country of southern Arizona, and the Río Grande Rift, where the Río Grande now flows.) The area has been volcanically active for nearly a billion years; at one point, the largest volcano in the world existed just east of Mount Taylor. It exploded much like Krakatoa—but with a force thousands of times more powerful—showering ash as far as Kansas. Its shattered remnants are the Jemez Mountains west of Santa Fe.

Humans have occupied the Malpaís for over a thousand years, and hundreds of ruins dot the surrounding mesas. For centuries the Indians buried their dead and hid stores of food in lava caves in the Malpaís. When Alvarado and Padilla came through, the Malpaís was probably uninhabited, abandoned by the Indians in favor of larger, fortified pueblos.

Basque shepherds were the first to settle around the Malpaís. After World War I there was a flurry of homesteading, but most could not hang on for the three-year minimum needed to acquire title, and the area today is dotted with their ruined log cabins. In the forties the U.S. government took over six thousand acres of the Malpaís for a bombing range, but abandoned it because the lava terrain was so rough their personnel could not get in to construct and repair bomb-ing targets. Even today, live ordnance lies scattered about the lava beds.

Scholars have debated just where Alvarado and Bigotes crossed the Malpaís. Some have assumed Alvarado went north and detoured the Malpaís where Grants is today. Others think he may have skirted the southern end of the Malpaís. Most claim that Alvarado's horses could not have crossed the rough, waterless lava beds.

Both routes, however, entail a long detour. It seemed to me that Indians, on foot, would not detour twenty or thirty miles to avoid some rough, waterless country. I was convinced that Alvarado's Pecos Indian guides would probably have taken him right across the lava. I wanted to prove it; I wanted to cross the Malpaís on horseback.

We camped near the head of what the Park Service had told us was the Zuni-Acoma trail. Our first problem was water. Search as we might, we could find none anywhere near us. As we were poking about near a road that runs between the Zuni Mountains and the lava, a rancher and his son stopped. They introduced themselves as Pierre and Jacques Arrossa. Jacques was a striking man with black hair and a deep, strong face. Seeing our predicament, he immediately offered to haul water from their ranch to our camp. He returned with a trough and a fifty-five-gallon barrel.

We chatted. I asked how a Spanish family had ended up with French first names. Ah, he said, but they were not Spanish at all; they were French Basques from the Pyrenees. The Arrossa family had been one of the most prominent Basque sheepherding families in the Malpaís, but when the market for wool collapsed in the twenties and thirties they had converted to cattle. Now they ran cows on thirty-three sections of land alongside the western boundary of the lava.

That evening, a virga of rain formed above the Zuni Mountains, a curtain of red fire hanging over the dark peaks.

We started into the Malpaís the next morning along the so-called Zuni-Acoma trail. There was no trail, just a line of posts marking the way. We soon struck the main flow, a heap of rubbled lava covered with pine trees. We dismounted and led the horses up.

We passed a series of yawning pits—collapsed lava caves—one scattered with the bleached bones of a hapless cow. It was fiendishly difficult, and the horses had to be coaxed and gentled along. The lava baked in the sun and radiated so much shimmering heat that the rocks about us looked unstable, as if they were evaporating. The pines, which thrived in the lava, filled the air with the scent of hot resin.

The stress was intense; the lava rocks taxed the horses to the very limits of their ability. A single fall here could cut a horse so badly as to ruin him for life. The lava was only seven miles wide at this point, but after several hours we had only gone about half a mile. We finally stopped and Walter scouted ahead on foot.

He was gone a long time. I dozed in the heat.

When he returned, his hands were cut and his boots had been scoured by the lava. His face was white.

"How does it look?" I asked.

He sat down and mopped his brow. "That's the closest I've come to seeing hell itself," he said, breathing hard.

"Worse than what we just went through?" I asked.

"A thousand times worse. That's no Goddamn Indian trail. Only a *white* man would be dumb enough to hike through that son-of-a-bitch."

We turned back.

We came back out of the lava and started riding north, having resigned ourselves to riding around the lava beds. My experiment was a failure.

Toward late afternoon we came to a ranch house baking in the heat, with some wrecked stock trailers in front. A woman came to the door as we rode up and welcomed us in. Her name was Kathy Mirabal.

We watered the horses and filled the canteens, and as we were leaving, her husband, Alfred, arrived in a pickup truck. We shook hands all around and told him about trying to get across the Zuni-Acoma trail.

Mirabal laughed heartily. "That ain't any Zuni-Acoma trail," he said. "You guys were just wasting your time over there. That's just something dreamed up by the park people. The *real* trail, the old Indian trail, starts right here on my property. They wanted to mark it once but I told 'em to get the hell out."

He smiled broadly. He had a genial face and was missing his two front teeth. We talked for a while. Alfred came from one of the most prominent families in New Mexico. His great-grandfather, Monico Mirabal, had fought against Geronimo in the Apache campaigns and had come to the Malpaís area in the late nineteenth century. One of Monico's sons, Silvestre Mirabal, built up an empire in the Malpaís based on sheep, and at one time was reportedly the largest landowner in New Mexico. Don Silvestre entered the territorial legislature and was chairman of the State Constitutional Convention. Much of the state constitution of New Mexico was actually penned by him.

He was a potbellied man who mocked his wealth by dressing, one old friend remembered, in a "worn-out pair of bib overalls, an old hat someone else had thrown away, and, in the wintertime, a ragged serape." He was the last large sheepowner in the Malpaís, and when he died in 1939 the era of sheep came to an end. Alfred Mirabal's forty-thousand-acre ranch was only a small piece of Don Silvestre's original holdings, divided among many heirs.

Alfred told us how to find a hidden stock tank some miles from the ranch house, where we could camp. He then drew a map showing a place where we could cross the lava.

I asked him more about the old trail, the real Zuni-Acoma trail, while switching on my tape recorder.

"I'd been hearing about that trail all my life," he said, "but it took me twenty years to find it. I just happened to go after a cow one day, tracked it to the Malpaís, and then I found this trail. I followed it and suddenly came out there on the other side at Route 117. I said, 'Aha! I found that trail!' I even had to put a little fence across there, to keep the cows from getting across. And now I *knew* it was an old man-made trail, because all the cracks had been packed in with pieces of malpaís. I'll meet you in your camp later and take you to see it."

We set up camp in the hollow, surrounded by old lava beds. At sunset Alfred returned and the two of us drove off to look at the trail. We bumped and crawled along the prairie, not following any road, weaving among the scattered junipers. All of a sudden we came to an impenetrable wall of lava, twenty to thirty feet high. He pulled up and we got out. I couldn't possibly see how a trail could exist in that lava.

Mirabal pointed to the wall. "It's just over in there," he said.

Right at the edge of the lava the prairie dipped down, and there, to my complete astonishment, was a fissure with a narrow but unmistakable trail leading into it. It was so devilishly concealed that it could not be seen unless you were right on top of it. One could see where the cracks and holes in the trailbed had been painstakingly packed with little pieces of lava to make a smooth path.

"Back when old Fort Wingate was up there by San Rafael," Mirabal said, "the Indians would attack 'em up there in Zuni Canyon and Bonito Canyon and run into the Malpaís. Now this trail is what they used to get away from the cavalry. It was a trap. Only one horse at a time could get through there, and so the Indians would get on top with their bows and arrows and just pick 'em off, one by one. So once the Indians got into the Malpaís here, the cavalry would just let 'em go free.

"Later," Mirabal said, "when they brought cows through there, they'd have to string 'em out one cow at a time. If they had a thousand cows it would take 'em all day to get across there. But that's a lot better than going twenty miles around. Yup," he said, starting the truck. "I don't doubt but this is the old Zuni-Acoma trail. I heard talk about it all my life."

I said that some scholars doubted the Spanish crossed the Malpaís, because of the lack of water.

He snorted derisively. "Lack of *water?* Hell, there's water all over the Malpaís if you know where to find it. Shallow pools, and even some holes back up in here, five, six feet deep, just *full* of water."

We headed back to camp. It had grown dark. I couldn't know for sure whether what we'd seen was indeed the actual Zuni-Acoma trail, but it certainly was an excellent candidate. Prehistoric Indians, many laden with trade goods and provisions, would never have crossed at the park's so-called trail. This trail was as direct, and it brought the traveler to the head of what the Acoma Indians themselves said was the Zuni-Acoma trail leading across their reservation.

The truck lurched and rattled over the prairie.

"There's supposed to be a lost church made out of gold in there," Mirabal said. "I've looked for it, never found it. But I knew some old-timers who found that church. One lady told me she knew where it was, been there herself. She was about eighty years old. She wouldn't give me any directions. She said that it was underground. A great big rock covered the opening, and you have to move the rock to get into it. She said all the walls were made of pure gold, and there was a lot of Spanish people and a lot of Indians in there. They were having a secret kind of service, out there in the Malpaís.

"The thing about this Malpaís, you get in there and the first thing you know you can't find your way back. You can be stuck there for a week. Lot of people get lost back there. One time when I was real small I chased a cow into the Malpaís, and I couldn't find my way out. Finally I fell asleep on the horse. Next morning I woke up and there I was in front of the gate there by the house. That's what I tell my wife and kids: If you get lost you let the horse take you back. He knows the way home."

We got back to the camp. Walter had dinner going, and Alfred and Kathy joined us for a big pot of beans and rice.

We crossed the Malpaís the next day. Halfway across we passed a diamondback rattlesnake. It had a head the size of a spade and a body as fat as a man's thigh, and when it sensed us coming it drew into an S-curve striking posture and buzzed so loudly we could hear it a good hundred yards away. On seeing it, Walter suddenly lost his enthusiasm for roasted snake and we gave it a wide berth.

We struck Route 117 on the far side of the Malpaís. While I was riding inside the fence, someone stopped his pickup ahead of me and got out with a shotgun.

"God *damn*, cowboy, you ain't packing out a side a my beef on that horse, are ya?" he asked.

I assured him I wasn't, and that he could look under the tarp if he had any doubt.

"You cuttin' any a my fences?"

I swore up and down that I had not.

"Well, then," he said, getting back into his truck. "All I can say is that damn pack shore lookit like a side a beef."

30

⊲▷ ⊠ ⊲▷

We had arrived at the border of the Acoma Indian reservation. Of all the Pueblo Indians, the Acoma are probably the least willing to go the white man's way or bend to Anglo rules, and the most resentful of intrusive questioning. It took Walter and me several months of discussions with the Acomas before they would allow us to cross the reservation by the ancient Zuni-Acoma trail. It would be, they said, the first time in living memory that a non-Acoma had been allowed across the western section of the reservation.

The Tribal Council provided us with a guide. We arranged to meet our guide that afternoon at an abandoned ranch on the eastern side of the Malpaís. His name was Harold Lowden, and he arrived with his brother Albert.

We camped next to a corral at the old ranch. Albert built a roaring fire. He said that, in general, the Acoma Indians disapprove of the Zuni. Why, he said, they let *tourists* watch their sacred dances! They let Anglos go anywhere, all over the reservation. And, he added, lowering his voice, I hear they do a lot of drinking during their rain dances.*
He shook his head sadly.

---

*I've been to many Zuni rain dances and have never seen any sign of drinking. Stereotypes between different Indian peoples in the Southwest are just as common as

. . .

We rode up Cebolleta Mesa into a wild country of shallow canyons and broken hills, little twisted trees, grassy flats, and knobs of wind-sculpted sandstone. It was as if a great landscape had been miniaturized. Each little canyon had a stream flowing in the bottom and was devilishly hard to cross. If there had once been a trail through here it had long since vanished. Mount Taylor—which Harold said was sacred to the Acoma—rose like a dark pyramid to the north. (When I remarked that it was also a sacred peak to the Navajo, he said, rather briskly, that he'd never heard such a thing and whoever told me that was probably a liar. The Acomas, like most other Pueblo Indians, do not like the Navajos.)

Toward afternoon we suddenly came to the brink of a great escarpment, looking down on a landscape of overpowering grandeur. A plain swept away into the blue distance, here and there punctuated with soaring sandstone mesas, their sides so clean and shear they looked as if they had been cleaved.

This is the landscape that Willa Cather, in *Death Comes for the Archbishop*, described so perfectly.

"This plain," she wrote, "might once have been an enormous city, all the smaller quarters destroyed by time, only the public buildings left,—piles of architecture that were like mountains. . . . Every mesa was duplicated by a cloud mesa, like a reflection, which lay motionless above it or moved slowly up from behind it. These cloud formations seemed to be always there, however hot and blue the sky. Sometimes they were flat terraces, ledges of vapour; sometimes they were dome-shaped, or fantastic, like the tops of silvery pagodas, rising one above the other, as if an oriental city lay directly behind the rock. The great tables of granite set down in an empty plain were inconceivable without their attendant clouds, which were a part of them."

In the middle distance rose up the Rock of Acoma itself, an orange bluff with a precise, geometric line of gray on top—the skyline of the oldest inhabited city in America.*

⟐ ▤ ⟐

---

stereotypes between ethnic groups within our own culture. I've heard some Hopis talk about Navajos in the identical way I've heard prejudiced whites talk about blacks.

*Some say that Old Oraibi Pueblo in Hopi country has this distinction; one can, however, make a very good case for Old Acoma.

Acoma made a deep impression on Alvarado and Padilla. One soldier wrote that it was "the greatest stronghold ever seen in the world. . . . The natives came out to meet us peacefully, although they could have spared themselves the trouble and stayed on their rock and we would not have been able to trouble them in the least." Another soldier marveled at the ability of the Acomas to ascend by the difficult and dangerous trail: they "go up and down so freely that they carry loads of provisions, and the women carry water, and they do not seem to touch the walls with their hands."

Alvarado himself had much to say about Acoma. It was one of "the strongest [cities] ever seen." The Indians were friendly and allowed him up the rock. "The ascent," Alvarado added, "is so difficult that we repented climbing to the top."* Where the trail came out on top, the Acomas had piled up quantities of stones, ready to be rolled onto the heads of any enemy foolish enough to ascend.

When the Spanish first saw Acoma, it was already a city of great antiquity, being at least three and possibly four centuries old. In 1540 there was probably only one trail up the Rock of Acoma, although other trails—and a road—would eventually be built.

Two natural catchbasins on top, holding thousands of gallons of rainwater, gave the Acomas their apparent invincibility. The Peñol de Acoma—the Spanish term for it—had never been conquered and appeared to be siege-proof. Perhaps this is the reason that Acoma, of all the pueblos, would resist most fiercely the Spanish occupation of the Southwest, and for this they would pay a terrible price.

When Juan de Oñate, colonizer of New Mexico, visited Acoma in 1598, he had apparently no trouble in gaining the usual submission of the governor of the pueblo, Zutucapán, and his people. He went away satisfied, leaving the Acomas resentful and insulted.

Toward the end of 1598, Oñate's nephew, Don Juan de Zaldívar, stopped at Acoma for provisions while traveling to Zuni to meet his uncle. Here he was met by a smiling Zutucapán, who invited him and sixteen of his companions up the Peñol de Acoma for a tour of the

---

*Castañeda, who did not accompany Alvarado, gives us a very contradictory picture of Acoma: he tells us that the Acomas came storming off their rock in a warlike mood, and drew lines in the sand; when Alvarado made as if to attack they quickly changed their minds and offered peace. It is likely in this instance that Castañeda confused Acoma with Hopi.

ancient city. They were gradually separated from one another and suddenly set upon by warriors. All were killed except for five soldiers who leapt off the cliffs. Incredibly enough, four of the soldiers survived their fall by landing in soft windblown sand that had accumulated at the base. They fled and brought the news to Oñate.

Oñate was enraged by the death of his nephew. He gave Juan's vengeful brother, Don Vincente de Zaldívar, the formidable task of punishing the Acomas. If Acoma weren't taken and the Indians punished, the Spaniards reasoned, it would encourage insurrections throughout the area. Oñate realized correctly that this was not a battle for one pueblo; it was a battle for New Mexico itself.

Zaldívar arrived at the base of Acoma on January 21, 1599. He and his soldiers listened, throughout the night, to the sounds of the Indians dancing, beating drums, and hurling insults and rocks down on them from the edges of the Peñol. When Zaldívar called on them to surrender, they answered with a shower of stones and arrows. They would not capitulate: the Peñol de Acoma was impregnable.

The next morning a Spanish force of sixty soldiers feigned an attack up the trail. The Acomas massed at the top and kept the Spanish at bay. During the night, however, a small Spanish force had climbed up another way, to a point just below the south mesa, taking, of all things, a small cannon, which they hoisted up with ropes. During the feint at the trail the men scaled the remaining cliffs and fell on the Indians from the rear.

For two days the Spaniards and Indians fought on top of the rock in fierce hand-to-hand combat. The Spanish eventually drove the Acomas into the city itself. Then they set up their cannon and proceeded to blast down the walls at point-blank range. Once the walls were breached they set fire to the pueblo and moved from roomblock to roomblock, kiva to kiva, rooting out the warriors.

The Acomas fought with tremendous bravery, but they could not repel an invader who had the advantage of muskets, armor, and artillery. When it became clear they were losing, the official Spanish account says that many Indians threw themselves into the burning houses or off the cliffs, and that some warriors rushed about murdering their wives and children rather than surrender. What is more likely, however, is that the Spanish themselves did most of the killing and burning. One Spanish soldier in the battle declared three years later that after the Acomas had surrendered, Don Vincente ordered many of them murdered and pitched over the cliffs. Some five hundred Acomas were taken prisoner—men, women, and children—and brought to Santo Domingo Pueblo for trial.

Oñate himself presided over the trial and pronounced sentence. All Acoma males over the age of twenty-five, he decreed, were to have one foot cut off and serve twenty years in slavery; all males between twelve and twenty-five and all females were sentenced to twenty years in slavery. All the girls under twelve were distributed to convents in Mexico, and all the boys were given to Zaldívar to be made into "Christians." Two Hopi found on the Peñol after the battle were sent back to their tribe with their right hands cut off, as a warning. Beginning on February 12, at Santo Domingo Pueblo, the sentences were carried out on a chopping block.

The defeat of Acoma was a great shock to all the pueblos, which had hitherto thought the Peñol invincible, and it did much to quash any incipient thoughts of revolt.

Oñate would not get away with such brutality. When a new governor of New Mexico was installed in 1609, Oñate was sent back to Mexico where he was tried and convicted for (among other things) his treatment of the Acomas. He was fined and banished forever from New Mexico. Zaldívar, for his part in the slaughter, was also punished.

It is a tribute to the spirit of the Acoma people that they survived their ordeal. Survive it they did, withdrawing to their rock and having as little to do with the Spanish as possible. Since the pueblo lay in an extremely remote section of New Mexico, they were relatively successful in drawing a curtain of isolation about them. In many ways, the intense privacy of the Acoma tribe today can be traced back to their terrible ordeal at the hands of Oñate four hundred years ago.

Acoma could not, however, avoid the Christian missionaries. It received its first permanent friar, a man named Fray Juan Ramírez, in 1629. Fray Juan helped them rebuild the Sky City, which was still mostly in ruins from the battle. Fray Juan was, by Indian and Spanish accounts alike, a remarkable man. Even today the Acomas regard him practically as a saint.

When the city was rebuilt Fray Juan supervised the construction of the great church of San Estévan del Ray on the Rock of Acoma. Every particle of dirt for the church, every timber, every stone, had to be carried up from below on the backs of the Indians. The timbers were carried from Mount Taylor, forty miles distant. Water to mix the adobe bricks had to be carried up the trail, since the ancient cisterns at the top held enough only for drinking. Even dirt for a consecrated burial ground was hauled up, potful by potful. It is a testament to Fray Juan that he was able to motivate the Acomas to perform such heroic labor using only kindness and gentle persuasion.

During the Pueblo Revolt of 1680 Acoma was almost the only pueblo to refrain from destroying its church.

In the early eighteenth century a schism developed in the pueblo and some Acomas, along with other Keresan-speaking Indians who had sought refuge on Acoma, moved off the Rock and founded a pueblo to the east, near the shores of a small lake. The new pueblo called itself Laguna, "Lake."

In the years that followed, the two pueblos, Acoma and Laguna, became embroiled in various disputes. The worst dispute, which almost resulted in war, was caused by a battered and almost indiscernible painting of San José that hung (and still hangs) in the mission church at Acoma. The image had allegedly been presented to the Acomas by Charles II of Spain, and they came to believe the picture brought prosperity to the pueblo.

The Lagunas, on their side, began to believe that their own misfortunes could be alleviated by the miraculous picture. The Laguna Tribal Council asked Acoma for a one-month loan of San José. The Acomas agreed, and the Lagunas hung the picture in their church. Immediately (or so it seemed to them) their fortunes began to improve. During Holy Week it was paraded about the pueblo by throngs of worshippers.

Several months passed, and finally the Acomas sent runners to Laguna to find out what was holding up the return of the picture. They were sent back with the message that the painting now belonged to Laguna. The Acomas were furious and began planning an attack on Laguna, which was narrowly averted by their priest. He insisted that the two tribes meet and draw lots to determine which tribe should have the painting. There was a conference between the two councils, a High Mass was observed, and then two little girls, one from each pueblo, drew paper lots. The Acoma girl drew the San José lot, and the priest declared that "God has decided in favor of Acoma." Reluctantly, the Lagunas returned the painting.

The picture did not hang long in the Acoma church. One night, Lagunas snuck up the Rock and spirited it back to Laguna. This time the Acomas took their sister pueblo to court.

In 1857, the Honorable Judge Kirby Benedict of the territorial supreme court ruled in favor of Acoma: "The history of this painting," he said in his opinion, "its obscure origin, its age, and the fierce contest with which these two Indian pueblos have carried on, bespeak the inappreciable value which is placed upon it. The intrinsic value of the oil, paint, and cloth of which San José is represented to the senses, it has been admitted in argument, probably would not exceed twenty-five cents; but this seemingly worthless painting has well-nigh cost these two pueblos a bloody and cruel struggle."

The Acoma triumphantly set out on the trail to Laguna to fetch the painting. Legend has it that they found the painting under a tree halfway there; San José, so the Acomas believe, had already started for home.

The return of the painting did not prevent other lawsuits and bitterness between the two pueblos over water rights and land claims, many of which were not settled until the late 1960s.

Acoma was the first and only pueblo to elect a non-Indian governor, a man named Solomon Bibo. Bibo had come to Santa Fe from Germany when he was sixteen years old, traveling west via the Santa Fe Trail. Bibo was a remarkable man: an observant Jew who spoke Yiddish, along with two dialects of Keresan, Navajo, Zuni, German, Spanish, and English. In 1882, at the age of thirty-two, he struck out on his own and founded the first trading post at Acoma, on top of the Rock itself. He married Juana Valle, the granddaughter of a prominent Acoma governor.

Bibo branched out into stock raising and persuaded the governor of Acoma to lease him an empty part of the reservation for running livestock—the same section we crossed on the Zuni-Acoma trail. The Indian agent in charge of Acoma protested, and a confused hearing was held, in which it appeared that Bibo had acted to protect the Acomas against two other people in league with the agent who had been trying to cheat the Indians. Nevertheless, the Indian agent took steps to revoke Bibo's license to trade at the pueblo. In 1885, just when it looked as if the agent were going to prevail, Bibo was elected governor of the pueblo.

Bibo became the center of a struggle at Acoma between progressive and conservative factions. Such schisms were (and still are) very common among Pueblo Indians, but Acoma had a particularly deep streak of conservatism. Bibo was leader of the progressive faction, and among other things brought the first schoolteacher to Acoma. Bibo's successor was a conservative, and tried to undo Bibo's educational program by tying up and horsewhipping any Acoma boy who went to school. Bibo complained to federal officials, who arrested and imprisoned the governor, leaving many bitter feelings on both sides.

The conservative and progressive factions of the pueblo traded governorships for a while. Around the turn of the century Bibo left his sheep in care of relatives and took his Acoma wife and children to San Francisco, where they became leading members of the congregation of the famed Temple Emanu-El. The reasons for their leaving are not entirely known, but it was likely Bibo wished to raise his children in the Jewish faith. During his absence the conservative faction gradually gained control and in 1920 the governor of Acoma more or less kicked Bibo and his family out of the tribe. Bibo protested, pointing out that he still owned a farm at Acoma, that his wife was Acoma, and that his children half-Acoma, but the dispute was never resolved.

Juana Valle Bibo was interred in the Temple Emanu-El cemetery with her husband, the only Acoma to be buried in that illustrious burial ground. Relations between the Bibo family and the tribe have been bitter and confused ever since.

The railroad and later Interstate 40 were built across the Acoma reservation, and today most Acomas live in towns along the Interstate. But the Sky City remains inhabited, and it is the center of Acoma religious life—both pagan and Catholic. The great church of San Estévan del Ray still stands above the mud and stone houses of the pueblo, a hoary, scarred edifice, one of the oldest churches in America.

We reined our horses up at the edge of the cliffs, looking out over the fantastic landscape in silence. It was our first glimpse of Acoma. Walter rode off to photograph while Harold and I went to search for the old trail down the escarpment.

Harold's horse was a striking animal, a sorrel-colored gelding with a lean, muscular body, a massive neck, roached mane, and alert brown eyes. It was more than just his looks: the animal radiated an unusual kind of intelligence and strength.

"Where did you get that horse?" I asked him.

"Caught him when he was a colt seventeen years ago," he said. "Right up here in these hills."

"You trained him yourself?" I asked.

"Yes."

"He's unshod," I said.

"Don't need shoes," Harold said. "He knows where to put his feet."

The horse's name was Oats.

Oats was beautifully trained. When Harold dismounted, Oats would stand until he gave him the signal to graze. When Harold approached to fetch him, with a soft greeting, the horse would immediately stop grazing and stand still so that he could be mounted. In the rocks he walked like a cat, probing ahead with his feet, testing each rock before putting his weight on it. Harold and his horse moved lightly and silently down through the rimrock while our horses clattered and scrambled, the ring of iron on stone mingling with our passionate imprecations.

"This is his country," Harold said proudly. "This is where he was born."

We rode into the plain, thick with grass, while storm clouds reared up behind the Peñol de Acoma. The ancient city, blazing topaz in the setting sun, stood starkly against a black sky. The great edifice of San Estévan del Ray rose heavily above the low line of stone houses, looking as old and imperturbable as the rock-face itself.

Rocks poked up out of the plain like the ribbed, knobby bones of half-buried monsters. The rocks had scooped-out coves and channels in their sides, which Acoma shepherds had fenced off to make corrals. Some of the coves had small overhangs in the back, in a few of which we could see the remains of prehistoric cliff dwellings.

A quarter mile from the base of the Rock we found an old corral built into one of these coves, with a partly collapsed coyote fence across it. Water draining off the rock had left rich green grass in the little corral, so we propped up the fence and turned our horses loose.

As we were setting up camp, I found a fetish on the ground, a flint arrowhead lashed to a pewter Christian cross. It was a perfect symbol of Acoma, where the traditional and Catholic are so intertwined as to be inseparable. The Acomas will often go directly from Mass into their nearby kivas and then spend the rest of the day in pagan dances and religious ceremonies.

That evening, a hungry little fawn-colored puppy came by and hung around the edges of the camp, with a wildly optimistic look in its face. When we got up the next morning we found it had eaten our leftover beans and was sleeping contentedly by the remains of the fire.

In the early afternoon an out-of-breath tribal official came down and said a religious ceremony was unexpectedly going to take place that evening and we would have to leave the reservation immediately. He was apologetic but firm. He was vague about the ceremony, but we gathered it was connected with an eclipse of the moon happening that night.

We packed up and rode east toward Laguna, past the great mesa known to the Acoma as Katzima, called by the Spanish Mesa Encantada. The word *katzima*, however, in the Keresan language means "accursed" rather than "enchanted." Acoma legend has it that Katzima once had a small pueblo on top, accessible by a narrow hand-and-foot trail. One evening, when most of the inhabitants of the village were working the fields, a storm came with a flash flood which undermined part of the mesa. A great pinnacle of rock peeled off, carrying with it the trail, leaving the mesa-top inaccessible. Those few trapped on the rock then died of starvation.

We crossed into the Laguna reservation around six. The wind gusted, the sky grew dark, and a few heavy raindrops fell, landing in little puffs of dust.

"Looks like we got a friend," Walter said.

"What?" I said.

"That dog is following us."

I looked back in time to see the puppy trotting from one cholla cactus to another. It was following us just like a cartoon spy, dodging from bush to bush.

"Oh, hell," I said.

"Now look here, Doug," Walter said, "the trip's just not gonna be complete without a dog."

We camped at the base of a rock pinnacle sticking out of the desert floor. The rock had some convenient overhangs, where we stowed our gear, expecting rain. We hobbled the horses, belled Redbone, pitched the tent, and lit a fire.

The little dog came creeping into camp with that same ridiculous look of expectancy on her face. She was a skinny little puppy with great big ears, like a coyote.

"Jesus," I said.

"It's too far to send her back to Acoma," Walter said. "She'll share our beans tonight." He laughed. "She knows a good thing when she sees it."

The rock was covered with cowboy graffiti, scratched into the soft sandstone with the points of knives. On one face I read:

J.S. Poncho
7–14–30
D.R.
L.L.D.
From R head quarters

Round Up at Allamo
Every Sun Clays
Every Body Welcome

There were other names and dates, from 1913 to 1952, and several crude pictures, one of an Indian with a feather in his headband and a cowboy in a cowboy hat. We called the pinnacle Cowboy Rock, and the next morning I added our names to the rock, carving "DP + WN Foll Coronado 1989." I have never scratched my name into anything before, but I figured that we were not casual tourists, that we had ridden eight hundred miles, and, by God, we deserved to add our names to the people who had left their mark on the rock.

The little puppy greedily wolfed down the remainder of our beans and lapped up an alarmingly large quantity of water. We named her Acomita, "Little Acoma."

The next morning the hobbled horses were gone. I climbed Cowboy Rock and in the intense pre-dawn stillness could hear the faint ringing of Redbone's bell. I set off toward the sound.

After a mile of hiking the ringing hardly seemed to be getting closer. I climbed a hillock and saw the problem: our horses had fallen in with a herd of wild horses. The mustangs were keeping a good third of a mile between me and them, and our horses were moving along with them. Then I noticed with an electric shock that Engwahela's expensive, commercial hobbles were dragging behind one leg; she was free. Oh God, I thought, was she going to vanish with the wild herd? If so, it would be virtually impossible to capture her. I hoped that Robert Currier's traveling fetish, which she had been wearing, would save us.

I got back into the trees and started jogging. I could hear Redbone's bell ringing furiously and I knew the herd was moving off quickly. Soon I came across Wilbur, unable to keep up in his hobbles, covered with sweat, whinnying piteously after his vanished friends. I started running.

The ground suddenly shook with the thundering of hooves, and a great cloud of dust rose above the junipers as the mustang herd stampeded. A few moments later I burst out of the trees into the open and there, several hundred yards ahead, were Pedernal and Redbone, running away from me in their hobbles for all they were worth. They had had a taste of wild freedom, and they were damned if they were going to get caught. Engwahela stood some distance in front of them, looking with pricked ears at the departing herd. I called to her and she turned back toward Redbone and Pedernal. Her herd attachment to our horses had grown strong enough to keep her from bolting.

Pedernal and Redbone continued to run away in great leaps, their front legs still tied together, with Engwahela trotting after them. No matter how fast I ran I couldn't catch up with them. I began circling around, hoping eventually to drive them up against the Acoma-Laguna boundary fence. I had been told that a hobbled horse could outrun a man, but I had never quite believed it until now.

Pedernal finally gave up. He dropped to his knees and rolled in an attractive patch of dirt, kicking and flailing about happily, while the other horses stopped. I came up and clipped lead ropes on them. I was very unhappy to see that Redbone's pasterns were raw and bloody from running in the hobbles. I would have to start hobbling him above the knee.

31

The sky had cleared during the night and as soon as the sun rose we were drowned in heat. Toward midday we came to the edge of a low badland cliff. The badlands fell away to a flat desert stretching to the horizon, a sandy waste littered with chunks of volcanic rock and sprinkled with clumps of snakeweed and cholla cactus. The only landmark was a lumpy volcanic hill, called Dough Mountain, on the distant horizon. At the base of this is where Laguna Indian tradition says Coronado camped. There appeared to be no end to this desert, nor could we see any trace of water. We had found no water since leaving Acoma Pueblo, and we were worried.

Miles away, we saw a cloud of dust rotating into the air, attenuated in the heat. A distant herd of wild horses emerged from it. They were running away from *us*, I realized with a start. God knows but we were probably the first human beings they had seen in months.

"Where there's horses, there's got to be water," Walter said. We rode into the desert.

The heat was awful. There was no shade anywhere, and no one suffered more than Acomita. For a while she trotted from cactus to cactus, keeping to the shade as much as possible. When the cactus thinned out she tried walking in the shadow under Redbone's belly. I yelled at her and tried to get her out, but she paid no attention. The expected soon happened: I heard a shrill yelp and the poor puppy streaked off and buried herself under a cholla, squeaking in pain. The horse, for his part, jumped like he had been shot.

Walter rode up.

"Redbone stepped on your Goddamn dog," I said. "She's under that cactus."

Walter hopped off his horse and I heard him murmuring words of comfort to the little dog, coaxing her out of the cactus. We continued on, the dog limping after us, looking shocked at the turn of events; perhaps, she seemed to be thinking, following these white boys wasn't such a great idea after all. She began to fall behind and soon we could barely see her little form weaving through the hot sand.

"Shit," Walter said, "that dog's not gonna make it." He whistled and we waited for her to catch up.

We saw a lone horse standing in the distance, watching us. He soon came running up. He was a chestnut gelding with a lonely look on his face; he pranced around, greeting our horses like long-lost friends. He had a brand on his left hip and was covered with old scabby horse-bites, indicating he was probably a domesticated horse run out of a wild herd by a stallion. He started trotting after us. Walter waved his hat at him and tried to shoo him off. The horse ducked his head and ran in a short circle, but refused to clear out.

"We're starting to look like a traveling circus," I said.

We stopped for lunch. We were now down to about two quarts of water. Walter unscrewed his canteen and started filling his hat to water the dog.

I protested. This was, I said, a damned dangerous thing to do when we had so little water. Any fool could see what kind of desert we were in. Let her take care of herself. If she's such a great Indian dog, I said, let her find her own water.

We argued and finally Walter said: "This dog threw her lot in with us, and for better or worse we got a responsibility for her. If we don't give this dog water now, she's gonna die. It's as simple as that."

I gave in. Walter was right. We were all in this thing together.

The puppy lapped up a pint of water and ate a big greasy piece of hard salami, while I watched, feeling very unhappy, half convinced that we were all going to die in that terrible desert. The scabby horse disappeared while we were eating and came galloping back forty minutes later, looking fresh and well watered.

"That Goddamn horse," I said, "knows exactly where water is." We scoured the horizon with our binoculars, but could not see even so much as a bush.

We rode and rode, horse and dog following. All sense of scale vanished, and with it all feeling of time or forward motion. It felt like we were stationary in a vast silent bowl of sand and sky, the endless wind slapping our packs.

Quite abruptly, we found ourselves on the edge of a skimming of water, a large rainwater puddle, as viscous and opaque as tomato soup. Acomita jumped in gleefully, swimming and splashing about, lapping it up. The horses drank deeply and I filled up a canteen.

As we rode past Dough Mountain, the horse following us got bored and ran off, his dark form flying against the horizon, mane whipping in the wind. As we watched him get smaller and smaller, we had a brief glimpse of the immense scale of this place, but as soon as he vanished the disorientation came back.

At the base of Dough Mountain our maps indicated a small permanent pond, but all we found was a hard pan covered with alkali weed. There was no sign of Coronado's camp or anything else.

We crossed the dry Arroyo Colorado, pushing our way through a line of salt cedar brush, and a mile later hit an old Laguna sheep camp, a hut built of volcanic rubble. We hunted around looking for water and found nothing. The wind gusted mercilessly through the camp, rattling a discarded pile of corrugated tin.

Toward evening we found another deserted sheep camp. We unrolled our bedrolls in an open-sided tin shed. Nearby was a corral littered with oat hay, bleached white by the sun, which the horses nosed through rather unhappily. We could still find no water. There was nothing to burn either—not even cow chips—forcing us to dip into our precious supply of white gas and cook on the backpacking stove. We boiled the canteen of puddle water to settle out the sediment.

The water was surprisingly delicious, with a faint but not unpleasant taste of sandstone. We realized we had made a serious mistake in filling only one canteen.

"Hell," Walter said. "It's just rainwater. We should've known it would taste good."

As it grew dark we could see what looked like a thin pencil-line of light on the northeastern horizon. Walter fished out the binoculars.

"Cars!" he said. "A whole bunch of 'em."

We examined our larger-scale map and discovered it was Interstate

40, far enough away that neither the headlights nor the motion of individual cars could be resolved by the naked eye. It appeared as a thin streak of phosphorescence, slowly dimming and brightening, like a glowworm plowing through humus.

As it became pitch-black, we could see a bright radiance on the eastern horizon.

"What the hell town is that?" Walter asked.

"That's Albuquerque," I said, still looking at the maps.

"No way," Walter said. "Albuquerque is forty miles away."

"It's got to be," I said. "There's absolutely nothing else between here and there."

Walter sipped his coffee. Heat lightning played silently to the south.

The next morning a more careful search of the sheep camp's corrals disclosed a small galvanized box on stilts, in which had collected about twenty or thirty gallons of rainwater. The water was choked with algae and completely covered with a layer of large, dead, swollen insects—bees, big black beetles with bloated abdomens and spread wings, stink bugs, and ants. We filled up one canteen and gave the rest to the horses, who drank it with a distinct lack of enthusiasm. The water tasted like slime.

As we rode along the endless plain, Acomita often dropped behind, and we had to whistle and call to encourage her to keep up. When we stopped to give her a drink, she would be shaking and exhausted. There was no shade anywhere and her little rib cage was sticking out. The bright, hopeful look in her eye had all but vanished.

We rode for hours and hours. Even Walter, who often sang or recited poetry, had fallen silent since leaving Acoma. The boredom became nearly intolerable. I had drifted a quarter-mile behind Walter, and on a sudden impulse I whipped Redbone and Wilbur into a furious gallop. I tossed Wilbur's lead over his pack, turning him free, and went flying on toward Walter, whooping and yipping and waving my hat over my head with Wilbur pounding alongside. Naturally my antics spooked both Pedernal and Engwahela, who charged forward and began running. While Walter hollered at me we all went running along together, four runaway horses tearing across the prairie. We finally managed to rein them in.

Walter bore his horse around on a short rein. "You idiot," he cried out, "you nearly caused a four-way wreck. What the hell's the matter with you?"

"I know," I said. "I'm sorry. I was bored. I couldn't help myself."

Walter shook his head. "You looked like a Goddamn red Indian on the warpath," he said. "How'd you learn to ride like that?"

Search as we might, we found no water, and the water from the sheep tank had been so disgusting that we had only filled up one canteen and were now out of water again. We were still twenty-five miles from Albuquerque, and since leaving Acoma we had not had enough camp water to wash our dishes.

Toward evening we saw, in the distance, the telltale flash of light from the blade of a windmill. As we approached it became a true vision of beauty, with a tank brimming with water, a lone cottonwood, and some green grass.

Whooping and cheering, we kicked our horses into a lope. I reached the windmill first and rode Redbone around to the other side of the tank. All of a sudden the horse spooked, jumping sideways and spinning around. Lying two-thirds submerged in the water was a cow. Bright, fresh blood was spattered all over the sides of the tank and gore and brains floated in the water. A calf stood nearby, bawling.

Walter came around and looked at the scene.

"Jesus," I said. "We can't drink this water."

Walter dismounted and went to look at the cow. Her head was partly blown away with a very recent shotgun blast. Her eyes rolled around to look at us and her legs trembled. A snoring sound issued from her throat.

Walter looked at me. "I don't know why not, the cow ain't dead yet. Water can't be poisoned."

"You have a point there," I said.

We proceeded to fill up our canteens.

A more immediate problem was the threat of the cow's owner coming back and blaming us for the killing. We were still on Indian land, near the border of the Laguna and Isleta reservations, and if we were discovered the stockman might very well blast us to kingdom come. What else would he think, coming across two dirty Anglos at his cattle tank, with one of his cows freshly murdered? He might not notice what we now saw: faint, but distinct, tire tracks that circled the tank and led off into the distance.

We decided in the end to camp. We figured it like this: we could ride only another few miles before dark anyway. If the owner discovered his cow he would naturally follow our tracks to our camp. If we camped right there, we hoped, it would look less suspicious than if we moved on. Besides, we needed the water.

The water tasted dreadful. In addition to being polluted by the dying cow, it was carbonated, salty, with a malignant sulfurous reek, which bubbled out of the tank and hung over the camp like a fog. But water was water. We washed ourselves in the tank; we washed our clothes in it; and we washed our dishes in it. And we drank that water all the way to Albuquerque.

"From the look of things," Walter said, "I'd say the devil himself had paid this place a visit."

We decided to call it Devil's Camp.

Acomita was in bad shape. She was shaking uncontrollably and threw up her dinner. She finally sank into the dirt in front of our campfire, whimpering.

Walter took a close look at her. "I hate to say this," he said, "but I think she's dying. All this heat and walking for fifty or sixty miles, it just plain did her in."

I felt a sudden pang. It didn't seem fair, really. In the end we'd failed her.

Walter insisted that we let her sleep in the tent, and I didn't have the heart to refuse.

The dying cow moaned and wheezed all night long.

The next morning we got up in the pitch-dark, to get away as fast as possible from a potentially murderous rancher. I heard Walter stirring and grunting, and then I heard:

"Uh-oh."

"What?" I said.

"Doug," he said, "now don't you get mad, but Acomita did something in the tent."

"Oh God," I said, "what'd she do, throw up?"

"Worse," Walter said.

I was outraged and came over to examine the damage. There, in the dark, I could barely see the outline of a large and dreadful accident, right next to Walter's sleeping bag.

"Damn lucky I didn't roll in it," Walter said feebly.

Acomita was up, wagging her tail, with a big grin on her face. She had not died after all; in fact, she had never looked better. I cursed and booted her out of the tent and told Walter that I knew this was going to happen, that it was all his fault, and that he better get something to clean it up with.

Walter exited the tent and I rolled up my sleeping bag. The sky began brightening. I could hear him going through the gear, looking for something, grunting unhappily to himself. I knew he wasn't going to find anything disposable; we had already jettisoned all but the most essential supplies.

"Face it," I called out. "It's either your bandanna or your extra shirt."

"Yeah, yeah," he said, rattling through the gear.

I looked at the accident. In the increased light there was something funny about it. It was kind of big for a small puppy. I looked closer.

"Hey, Walter!" I called out. "Come here quick!"

I heard another grunt and he stuck his head in the tent.

"What?"

I picked up the accident and flipped it into his face. He let out a roar and tried to duck, but it bounced off his forehead with a hollow thud.

It hadn't been Acomita at all. The night before, one of us had kicked a hard, dried-up little cow chip into the tent.

A mile from our camp we rode across a small Anasazi ruin: a mound of rubble with four roomblocks barely outlined in the dirt. A small rattler occupied the exact center of the ruin, coiled and buzzing away. Several perfect metates—Indian grinding stones—littered the ground, along with hundreds of painted potsherds. Walter found a beautiful flaked spearpoint.

Just beyond the ruin we struck the Río Puerco ("Dirty River"), at the bottom of a deep, broad arroyo. We found an old cow path to the bottom and hacked our way through a dense mass of brush. The river was a malevolent gray trickle winding through a greasy layer of silt. So evil-looking was the water that no amount of persuasion, however firm, would induce the horses to cross, and in the end we had to resort to violence. While Walter hauled Pedernal by the reins I whipped his ass from behind, and we finally got him across. (Ped was the lead horse; the others followed with little fuss.) Emerging on the far side, we could see two ruined houses down the Valley of the Puerco; next to them stood the trunk of a dead cottonwood, with its branches, having rotted and fallen off, lying in a heap around it.

◦▩◦

The life and death of the Río Puerco Valley is a cautionary tale, an ecological nightmare repeated on smaller scales all across the Southwest. One hundred and fifty miles long, the Río Puerco drains an area of six thousand square miles. The Spanish had originally settled the Valley of the Puerco in the eighteenth century, but were quickly driven out by the Navajos; in the 1870s, when the Navajo raids ceased, the Spanish settlers returned and built new villages in the ruins of the old.

The Puerco found by the Spanish wound through a broad flat valley ringed by stony hills, low mesas, and jutting volcanic plugs. The early settlers irrigated the bottomlands along the river by throwing brush across the stream, diverting the flow, and sheeting, or "warping," the water through their fields. They also built *acequias* (irrigation ditches) to carry water to more distant fields. The farmers stocked the valley and its surrounding hills with cattle. Soon a string of small but relatively prosperous towns had sprung up in the Valley of the Puerco: Cabezón, Guadalupe, Casa Salazar, San Luis, Los Quelites, and Los Cerros, among others.

The cattle herds quickly increased. By 1900, the number of cows grazing the land exceeded the natural carrying capacity by 500 percent. The productive grasses were cropped to the roots and died, to be replaced by snakeweed, saltbush, and tumbleweed. When heavy rains came in the summer, the desert could no longer hold the water and it roared down the hills and across the fields, rutting off the topsoil. Clear-cutting of timber at the source of the Puerco, the San Pedro Mountains, exacerbated the heavy summer runoff.

The Río Puerco began cutting into its bed. At each rainstorm, the Puerco would flash-flood with increasing energy, the water busting through diversion dams and irrigation canals and scouring out the river bottom, carrying the sediments to the Gulf of Mexico. As it deepened and widened its channel, the towns in the Puerco Valley had an ever-increasing task in bringing the water in the river to the level of their fields for irrigation. The diversion dams, which started out as simple brush and log barriers, soon had to be constructed of dirt, and then of stone and cement. As flash floods destroyed one dam after another and cut deeper into the riverbed, the replacement dams had to be constructed that much higher. In 1922 the very best dam Cabezón could build was washed out. Irrigation was suddenly impossible; the farmers in the town were forced to leave. More dams washed out until 1936, when, at San Luis, the very last dam on the river was swept away. Farming in the valley ceased forever.

Old photographs show the spectacular changes that took place between the 1860s and 1939. The river channel widened from an average of 75 feet in 1881 to 790 feet in 1939. In many places, the depth of the riverbed went from almost nothing in the 1860s to eight feet in the 1870s, to fifty feet in the late 1950s. The water was still there—it was just inaccessible, fifty feet below the level of the now extinct fields. Meanwhile, severe gullying and sheet erosion assailed the valley and its surrounding hills, until nothing was left but sterile sand.

In a little over fifty years the Río Puerco had become the largest man-made arroyo in New Mexico.

The people living along the Puerco could do nothing except walk away from their homes and gutted fields. One by one the towns were left to the elements and the land itself was abandoned. In 1939, a government survey found that, of forty-four families still living in San Luis—the last town to die—forty-one were receiving some form of government welfare. In a final insult, tailing piles from mining in the 1940s and 1950s began leaching uranium into the river, rendering the Puerco measurably radioactive.

Today, an area of six thousand square miles—significantly larger than the state of Connecticut—has been reduced to uninhabitable desert. The short happy life of the Valley of the Puerco came and went with scarcely a whimper.

A mile beyond the river we came up against a scarp known as the Ceja del Río Puerco (the "Eyebrow of the Dirty River"). We worked our way to the top, where we found ourselves among surreal crescent sand dunes, some fifty or sixty feet high, crisp arcs of sand against an electric blue sky. Sandia Crest had grown enormously until it now loomed above us, an eleven-thousand-foot cuesta with pyramids of rock on its steep western face, intensely violet in the midday sun. Ahead stretched the Llano de Albuquerque, ten miles across, an emptiness broken only by looping high-tension wires. The city of Albuquerque, we knew, began just below the far end of the plain, spread along the broad hollow formed by the Río Grande.

The city came upon us without warning. One moment we were singing and laughing our way through a windswept emptiness; and the next we found ourselves on the edge of a low bluff, suddenly silent, staring down on a vast city. The entire metropolis was laid out before us: houses, lawns, streets, highways, skyscrapers, parking lots glittering with cars, cloverleaf interchanges, all sunken in a pool of brown smog. Curving through the middle was the muddy somnolent mass of the Río Grande itself.

And suddenly the faint sounds of the city were drifting upward: a honking horn, a distant screech of brakes, the sound of a gunning, backfiring engine, the rhythm of white noise from the interstates. It was not the sound of humanity: it was the sound of the *car*. And there was also the *smell* of the car, a tang of photochemical ozone and nitrogen dioxide that assailed our nostrils. From our lookout, human beings were not in evidence.

The city began abruptly: here was desert and there was city. There were no suburbs, no outlying farms, no thinning of houses at the edges. Where the city's water system ended was where dense human habitation stopped. Between us and the beginning of the city lay a warren of crisscrossing dirt roads amidst a sea of garbage stretching north-south as far as the eye could see. It was as if the city were some great nest from which the insects periodically removed their excrement and their dead, dumping them at the periphery.

Never in my life had I been so repelled by the ugliness, the bizarre grotesqueness, of the city. It wasn't Albuquerque itself. Rather, it was the shock of arriving so unprepared at the city's stinking underbelly; it was the shock of coming upon three hundred thousand people after having seen not one single human being since leaving Acoma Pueblo; but most of all it was the shock of seeing the city in a completely different context. It was a classic case of *jamais vu;* here I had spent ten years in Manhattan, but never had I seen so clearly the hideous, repulsive, depraved, malefic character of the city. I had thought that a "revelation" would come on the silent stones of Hawikuh, but never had I anticipated *this* revelation, while staring at a city that my own culture had created.

There was something profoundly anti-human about the modern city: and that anti-humanness was generated almost entirely by the totalitarian exigencies of the car. I could hardly believe, looking down on Albuquerque, how much the car had dictated the shape and character of the city; how much it filled the city with loud mechanical sound, poison gas, and mephitic stink; and how much hot shining vulgarity was generated by asphalt, traffic, gas stations, parking lots, and the like. In one great moment of clarity I realized that this invention, the car, more than anything else across history, has forced humankind to remake itself in a new, ugly, machine-like image.

Walter and I hardly exchanged a word. We were sickened beyond speech. We were also afraid: how in God's name were we going to get our horses and ourselves through that mess?

We started down the bluff and threaded our way through the piles of garbage: used diapers, burned-out mattresses, old refrigerators, washing machines, heaps of drywall and broken cinder block, two dead dogs, the rib cage of a horse, and everywhere the rotting carcasses of gold-toned, crushed-velvet sofas. It was as if half the city had been furnished from the same tasteless showroom.

The garbage terrified the horses. They shied at every sofa, jumped at every flapping newspaper, bolted from every white refrigerator. They trembled and blew when the smell of decomposition washed over them. Even Redbone, our calmest horse, tried to flee when we encountered a busted hair dryer.

We struck the edge of the city and rode into a poverty-stricken barrio. Neither one of us knew Albuquerque, and we had no idea where we were. People stared at us and cars roared by, filling our eyes with exhaust and dust. The chain-link fences had pieces of trash and toilet paper pressed into them by the wind.

Acomita had never seen a car before in her life, and she trotted out into the middle of speeding traffic, wagging her tail, cars braking around her. Walter dismounted and hauled her up into his saddle.

The street eventually struck a major thoroughfare, which a sign identified as Coors Road, and there, on the corner, was an Allsups gas station and convenience store. We tied up our horses and went in. When the cashier saw us her eyes widened in fear, and she silently shook her head when we asked where we might find a corral for our horses. She knew nothing and no one else in the store knew anything. We were clearly demented and they wanted us out of there as fast as possible.

We bought a six-pack of beer and sat down in the dirt of a vacant lot next door, and in twenty minutes had drunk the entire thing. After three weeks without a drink, the beer hit us like a bomb, and we sat amidst the omnipresent garbage, holding our heads in our hands, with rush-hour traffic roaring by, wondering just what the hell we were going to do.

32

After climbing the Peñol de Acoma, Hernando de Alvarado, Fray Juan de Padilla, and Bigotes continued east. The Zuni-Acoma-Pecos trail they were following struck the Río Grande somewhere in the vicinity of modern-day Albuquerque, not far from the spot where we first saw the Great River.

There, standing on the edge of the same escarpment, Alvarado found a more welcoming sight than we did: a "mighty river" flowing between deep groves of cottonwoods, with emerald fields of corn and beans unfurling along the irrigated bottomlands. Twelve or more large pueblos, built from the reddish earth of the valley, stood on the high ground above the floodplain. Behind the river rose a "snow-covered sierra, very high and rough."

The province, Alvarado learned, was called Tiguex.* The group felt it prudent to camp before entering Tiguex. "We sent the cross," Alvarado wrote, "by a guide to the pueblos ahead. On the following day, from twelve pueblos, there came chieftains and people in proper

---

*"Tiguex" in sixteenth-century Spanish was probably pronounced "TEE-waysh"; today this group of Indians are called the Tiwa Indians. Some Tiwa-speaking pueblos that still exist today are Sandía, Taos, and Isleta.

order, those of one pueblo after another. They marched around the tent, playing a flute, and presented me with the food, blankets, and skins they had. I gave them some small articles, whereupon they went away."

Alvarado noted with satisfaction that "the people seem good, more given to farming than to war."

Fray Juan de Padilla, the religious who went with Alvarado, immediately began the work of conversion. "In the places where we erected crosses," Alvarado noted, "we taught the natives to worship them, and they offered them their powders* and feathers. . . . They did it with such eagerness that some climbed on the backs of others in order to reach the arms of the crosses to put plumes and roses on them."†

Alvarado made himself comfortable for a few days and received visitors from more distant pueblos up and down the river—of which there were eighty.

Alvarado immediately sent word back to Coronado that this fine, rich valley would be an ideal place for the main army to overwinter. Coronado was "highly pleased to learn that the country was improving." He dispatched one of his captains, García López de Cárdenas, to Tiguex with some soldiers to set up winter quarters, while Alvarado went on to Cicuyé with Bigotes and Padilla.

Alvarado's route to Cicuyé probably took him upriver to a small province the Spanish called Quirix.‡ Here he left the river, going east, until he arrived at a verdant river valley, shut in by mountains to the north and a high mesa to the south. Dominating the center of the valley, built on a ridge of rock, was Bigotes's home, the great city of Cicuyé (later called Pecos).** Here, no less than two thousand people occupied one large, multi-storied building.

In 1540, Cicuyé was probably the largest and most powerful city in all of America.

"It is feared throughout that land," Castañeda wrote. "It is square,

---

*Sacred cornmeal.

†This was not done to appease the Spaniards. As noted earlier, Pueblo Indian religion was all embracing, and its adherents saw nothing strange or sacrilegious in worshipping other people's gods as well as their own.

‡This word in sixteenth-century Spanish would have been pronounced KEE-reesh. Today it is spelled Keres or Queres. These Indians spoke the Keresan language, spoken today by Acoma and Laguna, as well as Santo Domingo, San Felipe, and Santa Ana.

**Cicuyé was the name the pueblo gave itself; but many of the other pueblos called it "Pecos," which was soon adopted by the later Spanish and the name it is called today.

perched on a rock in the center of a vast patio or plaza, with its *estufas* [kivas]. The houses are all alike, four stories high. One can walk on the roofs over the whole pueblo, there being no streets to prevent this.

"The people of this town," Castañeda also noted, "pride themselves because no one has been able to subjugate them, while they dominate the pueblos they wish." One of the secrets of Cicuyé's invincibility was a spring, bubbling out of the rock within the fortified perimeter of the pueblo. With sufficient stores of food, Cicuyé, like Acoma, could survive a siege indefinitely.

The Cicuyéans at the time were able to muster a crack fighting force of five hundred warriors, an army of some reckoning at a time when the entire population of most pueblos was less than two hundred. Furthermore, they were highly skilled at warfare, not only through fighting with other pueblos, but also by defending themselves against massed attacks from the Plains Indian tribes living east of them. And they were very, very wealthy.

Cicuyé was the easternmost pueblo in North America. By occupying the strategic Pecos River Valley, gateway to the Great Plains, the Cicuyéans were able to control most of the trade flowing between the Pueblo Indians and the southern Plains Indians. They acted as brokers for buffalo hides, dried meat, turquoise, feathers, cotton blankets, buckskins, flint knives, and slaves. Bigotes's boast that they had never been defeated in battle is a claim that archeology has verified. With good reason, the Cicuyé Indians felt themselves well-nigh invincible.

As Alvarado and Bigotes approached the pueblo, "the people came out to meet him and their captain," Castañeda wrote, "with demonstrations of joy and took him into the pueblo with drums and flageolets, similar to fifes, of which they had many. They presented the Spaniards with quantities of clothing and turquoises, which are found in abundance." The Spaniards met the governor of Cicuyé, whom they nicknamed Cacique, or "Chief."

The Cicuyéans were less insular and more sophisticated than the other pueblos when it came to trade and diplomacy, and they no doubt realized the importance of forging an alliance with these peculiar and powerful invaders. In turn, all that the invaders wanted of them was to agree to a set of incomprehensible and no doubt unenforceable requirements that they call some distant king their lord and some strange god their savior. Cicuyé was powerful; Cicuyé had never been defeated in battle. What did these bizarre demands signify? Nothing.

Alvarado, Padilla, and their men rested at Cicuyé for a few days. The friar had been profoundly disappointed on reaching Cíbola; had been angry and disappointed by Hopi; and now he was disappointed once again. The Seven Cities of Antillia, Padilla thought, must lie farther east.

During their stay, the Spaniards spent much of their time inquiring after gold, passing around samples, and pumping the Indians for information on other kingdoms and provinces. They also wanted to hear more about the "cattle"—the great buffalo herds that roamed the plains to the east.

In response to this questioning the Cicuyé Indians brought out a slave of theirs, "a native of the farthest interior of the land." He called his province "Quivira."

Alvarado and Padilla were greatly taken with this Indian. He had the lean, handsome physique and high-cheekboned face typical of Plains tribes—very different from the rounder faces of the Pueblo Indians. Alvarado and Padilla thought he looked like a Turk, and they nicknamed him El Turco for that reason.

The Turk was probably a Caddoan-speaking Wichita Indian from what is now central Kansas. We know nothing about the Turk except what the Spanish told us later, but even seen through this lens of anger and bitterness he emerges as a kind of hero. He was a remarkable man, a genius in his own way, with a deep understanding of human nature. He also possessed amazing nerve (as we shall see), was an eloquent talker, and was very adept at sign language. Alvarado hired him as an interpreter and guide to go see the buffalo, about which the Spanish were very curious.

It was probably late September when they set off from Pecos going eastward into the Great Plains. The Turk—who had quickly sized up the Spanish—began telling stories about the riches of his land. As Padilla and Alvarado got more and more excited, the Turk's stories got more and more outrageous.

"The Turk," Castañeda writes, "told so many and such great tales about the riches of gold and silver found in his land that the Spaniards did not care to look for the cattle, and as soon as they saw a few they turned back." They departed Cicuyé in a great rush to meet Coronado at Tiguex and tell him "the rich news."

At the same time Alvarado, Padilla, and the Turk were exploring the Great Plains, Cárdenas and his small force of men arrived at Tiguex to prepare winter quarters for the army. Cárdenas immediately demanded the Indians give up a pueblo for the Spanish army. The Indians turned over a pueblo called Alcanfor to Cárdenas, but he did not even allow them time to remove "any belongings but their persons and clothing."

While the Indians submitted to this first indignity, the beginnings of disaster were taking shape.

Just after Alvarado and Padilla returned to Tiguex from Cicuyé, Coronado arrived with a force of thirty men. There, Alvarado and Padilla informed Coronado of the astonishing news about Quivira. The Turk was pushed forward to tell the story himself.

The Turk, with an inventiveness that was quite extraordinary, spun a tale of riches so stupendous, and yet so convincing, that Coronado and his captains were driven into a virtual frenzy of excitement. "The Turk claimed," Castañeda recalled, "that in this land there was a river, flowing through plains, which was two leagues wide, with fish as large as horses and a great number of very large canoes with sails, carrying more than twenty oarsmen on each side. The nobles, he said, traveled in the stern, seated under canopies, and at the prow there was a large golden eagle. He stated further that the lord of that land took his siesta under a large tree from which hung numerous golden jingle bells, and he was pleased as they played in the wind. He added that the common table service of all was generally of wrought silver, and that the pitchers, dishes, and bowls were made of gold."

The Turk even had a name for that most precious of metals: "He called gold *acochis.*"

If the Turk were telling the truth, Coronado realized, this was wealth beyond anything even *imagined* at the Seven Cities of Gold, wealth greater than the Aztec empire itself. Not even Moctezuma at the height of his glory had such riches at his command.

It would be nothing less than the greatest prize in all the Indies.

It was almost too good to be true. If there was really so much gold in the land where the Turk came from, Coronado demanded to know, why did the Turk have none?

Simple, replied the Turk. He had some gold bracelets, but Bigotes and the Cicuyé Indians had taken them away when he was captured.

Coronado had one final test of the Turk's story. He ordered that some trinkets made of brass be brought up and shown to the Turk. Then he asked the Turk whether this was the gold he was talking about.

The Turk made a great show of smelling the brasswork and turning it over in his hands. Then he informed Coronado disdainfully that it was *not* gold, "that he knew gold and silver very well, and that he cared little for other metals."

That last test clinched it. With that demonstration, how could the Turk possibly be lying? Coronado at once ordered Alvarado back to Cicuyé to get the gold bracelets.

The Cicuyé Indians received Alvarado warmly, but Alvarado was all business. He wanted the gold bracelets. The Indians "denied in all possible ways that they had them, saying that the Turk was lying and deceiving them."

Alvarado was furious; surely it was the Cicuyé Indians who were lying. But the pueblo was too powerful even for the Spaniards to attack. Instead, Alvarado used treachery: he invited Bigotes and Cacique into his tent outside the pueblo, where he had them seized, collared, and chained.

"The men in the pueblo," Castañeda recalled, "came out to fight, shooting arrows and berating Hernando de Alvarado, saying that he had broken his word and friendship."

Alvarado beat a hasty retreat to Tiguex with his prisoners. Here they continued to deny knowledge of any gold bracelets. Coronado flew into a rage and ordered dogs set on Bigotes, trying to extract the nonexistent information. When that failed he threw them into a makeshift prison, saying they would not be released until he had the gold.

One soldier at least disapproved of the behavior of his superiors. "This was the beginning," Castañeda wrote, "of the distrust the Indians had from then on for the word of peace which was given them, as will be seen by what happened next. . .[for] when the army arrived [at Tiguex] we found that land or province up in arms, for causes that were sufficient and not at all slight, as will be told."

When the people of Tiguex learned that Coronado had brought Cacique and Bigotes back in chains, they were disturbed. While they may have had their own differences with Cicuyé, this kind of treachery went far beyond what any pueblo would consider fair dealing.

"This ill feeling," Castañeda wrote, "was aggravated by the general's desire to gather some clothing to distribute among the soldiers." Winter was descending on the Río Grande, and the extreme cold had been an unpleasant surprise for the Spanish. Average wintertime temperatures in the Río Grande Valley of northern New Mexico are about the same as those on the New England coast, and the Spaniards and their Indian allies had no warm clothing.

Coronado sent for one of the pueblo governors, a man the Spanish had nicknamed Juan Alemán, "John German," because he looked like a prominent man of that name in Mexico. He demanded that Juan furnish him with three hundred or more pieces of clothing from the twelve pueblos.

Juan explained to Coronado that "it was not in his power to do this." Rather, he said, all the pueblos would have to discuss the matter and, at any rate, the Spaniards would have to make the request of each individual governor.

Coronado brushed off Juan's objections and gathered a group of soldiers. They split up and visited each of the twelve pueblos demanding blankets. "As all this was unexpected," Castañeda remembers acidly, "the natives were not given time to discuss or consult about the matter. As soon as a Spaniard came to the pueblo, he demanded the supplies at once. . . . With all this there was nothing the natives could do except take off their own cloaks and hand them over. . . . When the [Indians] gave them some blankets or skins that they did not consider good enough, if they saw an Indian with a better one, they exchanged it with him without any consideration or respect, and without inquiring about the importance of the person they despoiled. The Indians resented this very much."

If this weren't enough provocation, Castañeda wrote, "an outstanding person, whose name I shall omit to spare his honor, left the pueblo where the camp was and went to another one a league distant [called Arenal], and on seeing a beautiful woman in the pueblo, he called her husband down below and asked him to hold his horse. . . . While the native was detained there, some commotion took place, the man came back, took his horse, and rode away. When the Indian [went home], he learned that [the Spaniard] had ravished or attempted to ravish his wife."

The Indian and other prominent people from Arenal Pueblo came to Coronado and demanded punishment of the offender. Coronado assembled all his soldiers so the Indian could identify the rapist, but the Indian was unable to do so. He was able, however, to positively identify the horse, which belonged to a man named Juan de Villegas. Villegas denied everything, saying that because the Indian had not identified him "perhaps he was mistaken also in the horse."

"In the end," Castañeda wrote, the Indian "went away without getting any redress for what he had demanded." This enraged the inhabitants of Arenal.

. . .

Not long after this incident, an Aztec wrangler with the Spaniards limped into camp, bleeding and wounded, saying the Arenal Indians had revolted, killing another wrangler and driving part of the horse herd toward their pueblo. Among the stolen livestock were seven mules belonging to Coronado.

Coronado sent Cárdenas out to recover the horses. Cárdenas found some two dozen lying dead in the fields. Approaching Arenal Pueblo Cárdenas heard a great noise and discovered that the Arenal Indians had constructed a palisade around their pueblo and were stampeding the horses in circles, shooting arrows into them.

Coronado ordered an attack. Cárdenas assembled a large force and stormed the pueblo. The Arenals held them off until a force of mounted men and Aztecs stormed the walls and punched holes in the basement rooms of the pueblo (the pueblos had no ground-floor doors). There they built heavy smudge fires. The Indians in the upper stories were quickly overcome with smoke and requested peace in return for mercy. Two captains "answered their signs for peace by similar ones, which consisted of making a cross."

Thus assured, the Indians laid down their arms and were taken to Cárdenas's tent. But Cárdenas, Castañeda tells us, apparently did not know (or didn't care) about the promise of clemency made by the other captains. Coronado had ordered a punishment "that would intimidate the others": none of the Arenal Indians should live. Cárdenas therefore commanded that stakes be driven in the ground and the Indians burned alive. "Those [captains] who had arranged the terms of the peace," Castañeda recalled with anger, "kept silent, believing it was none of their business."

When Cárdenas began burning the first thirty Indians, their horrible shrieks and moans alerted those still imprisoned in the tent, and they attempted to escape. Many were cut down immediately by swordsmen, and the rest were pursued by mounted men across the plains. "As the ground was level," Castañeda wrote, "none escaped alive."

A few Indians who were hiding in the pueblo, however, had escaped, and "spread the news throughout the land, telling how the peace that was granted them had not been kept. This resulted in great harm later."

The main army finally arrived at Tiguex late that fall. The entire Spanish expedition was now reunited for the first time in nearly eight months. News of Quivira raced through the ranks of the soldiers and generated tremendous excitement. But there were more pressing matters to be taken care of. The entire province of Tiguex was now in general revolt. The Spaniards had broken their word twice, first at Cicuyé and then at Arenal. The Indians concluded that the Spaniards were violent and treacherous liars. The Pueblo Indians, steeped in a culture that valued hospitality, honesty, and peace, were deeply shaken by the behavior of the Spanish. At all costs they must be driven from the land.

Around the same time the army arrived, snowstorms swept down on the valley, and sections of the river froze so solid that laden pack animals could be driven across it. "It snowed so much," Castañeda remembered, "that the Spaniards could do nothing except go over the trails and tell the natives. . .that they would be pardoned, giving them all sorts of assurances. To this the Indians replied that they would not trust those who did not know how to keep the word they had pledged and reminded them that they were still holding Bigotes a prisoner and that, at the burned pueblo, they had not kept the peace."

At one point Cárdenas himself went to ask a truce from Juan Alemán. Juan decided to give Cárdenas a taste of his own treachery, and demanded that Cárdenas drop all his weapons before discussing peace. When Cárdenas had done this Juan seized him while two other Indians drew hidden clubs and bashed him over the helmet; the Spaniards quickly wrested the stunned Cárdenas from their grasp and fled.

In retaliation, Coronado ordered the attack of a pueblo called Moho. The Moho Indians resisted with tremendous valor, and the attack became a siege lasting weeks. For the first time the Spanish and their Aztec allies suffered significant casualties: over a hundred were wounded and a half dozen killed. The Moho Indians themselves suffered two hundred killed, a good percentage of the entire population.

What finally defeated Moho was that greatest of enemies in the desert, lack of water. The Spanish had surrounded the pueblo, cutting it off from their sources of water. The Indians tried to dig a well in the center of the pueblo, but it collapsed, killing thirty men.

No matter what assurances were given, the Moho Indians refused to surrender on any terms, fully convinced the Spaniards would kill them anyway. "They insisted that we would not keep our word. . .they did not want to trust people who did not keep their friendship or the word they gave."

One night fifty days into the siege, the Moho Indians attempted to flee to the hills. A group of mounted guards discovered them and attacked, killing dozens and driving the rest into the Río Grande, which was "high and extremely cold." Most of those Indians not killed outright were found the next morning frozen to death on the opposite bank. Those women and children still alive were brought back to the Spanish camp, revived, and taken as slaves.

During the battle the other Tiguex Indians had abandoned their pueblos, and by spring the green and fertile valley of the Río Grande was uninhabited and laid waste by the conquerors.

Coronado was anxious to journey to Quivira as soon as the weather warmed up. So convinced was he about the riches of Quivira that, against the advice of his officers, he declined to send an advance party to verify the Turk's stories. The entire army would march to Quivira.

They decamped from the Río Grande Valley on April 23rd, 1541,* the Turk leading the way.

There was another native of Quivira, also from Pecos, who accompanied the expedition. His name was Isopete, and he became something of a problem to the Spanish: he insisted that the Turk was lying. Nobody believed him, but a rumor circulated the camp that one of the Turk's guards had seen him "talk to the devil in an *olla* filled with water." This created a wave of anxiety among the common soldiers, but not enough to dampen their enthusiasm about Quivira.

The Turk, for his part, claimed that the presence of Isopete was so obnoxious to him that he required the Spaniards to keep him in the rear, well back from any Indians they might encounter on their travels. The Turk's plan required that he travel in front, to prime any Indians they might encounter along the way. He could not have Isopete spoiling his plot.

A week of travel brought them to Cicuyé, where they camped in the meadows outside the pueblo. At this time Coronado returned Bigotes to the pueblo (Cacique having been freed earlier). The army departed from Cicuyé, Castañeda wrote, "leaving the pueblo at peace and to all appearances pleased. . ."

"To all appearances" was the impression. A thousand miles later the Turk would implicate Cicuyé in a devious plot to destroy the Spanish invaders for good.

---

*Castañeda says the date was May 5; it may be that the copyist in the 1590s changed the date to the Gregorian system.

33

It was getting on toward evening and we had absolutely no idea what we were going to do with ourselves or the horses. Our mere presence with horses in Albuquerque city limits was illegal. As we argued over our options, a truck towing a stock trailer full of cattle pulled in for gas, and Walter sprinted over. The driver said he was delivering the cows to a roping arena down the road.

To get there we had to ride for a half-mile down Coors Road, on a narrow sidewalk, with honking cars roaring past. It was neither a pleasant, nor a safe, ride. The horses were upset and constantly on the verge of panic.

The roping arena lay at the very edge of town. We found a crowd of Hispanic cowboys there, standing around drinking beer and watching two men team-rope their way through a chuteful of Mexican cattle.

"Hey Leonard!" a cowboy called out to one of the ropers. "You got a couple dirty gringos here want to talk to you." He laughed and slapped Walter on the back.

Leonard trotted his horse into a corral, flipped the reins over a fence, and walked over. He scooped up some beers on the way, opened one with a spray of foam, and sunk his face into it. He was a tall, skinny fellow with an impatient look.

"What the fuck's this?" he said, peering at us. "Who the fuck are you?" He handed us each a beer.

We told him about our situation and he jerked his head toward some pens. "You can turn your horses loose in there, with the burro." He looked us and our horses up and down.

"Jesus," he said, walking away.

Leonard and his family bred racehorses for a living. He also trained jockeys, taking poor boys in the neighborhood and teaching them how to race. Some of them had gone on to fame and big money. Later we met a jockey whom Leonard had found as a little boy, under a bush, starving and abandoned.

We quickly finished our beers and opened two more. The sun had set and someone turned on the lights in the arena. A fellow named Steve Kelly showed up with his fourteen-year-old daughter and a horse. He was a beefy man with a mustache, who said he was an electrician who liked to rope in his spare time.

"Don't mind these guys," he said. "They may talk a little rough, but they got hearts of gold."

We talked about roping. He had only been roping for a while but he had already won a saddle and a number of belt buckles. He was a heeler, the one who ropes the hind legs, the more difficult of the two skills. (The man who ropes the horns is called the "header.") Roping a galloping cow's hind legs is not easy. Some heelers, Steve said, try to lay the loop on the ground the instant before the cow steps in it and then pull up, but the true heeler slaps a vertical loop against the inside back legs, so the cow's forward movement just naturally puts its legs into it.

"Yeah," Steve said, "these cowboys would like to make you think it's hard. I wanted to rope all my life, but I thought, Hell, I'm just an *electrician*. But then I started with a good teacher. See, these guys know how to do it, but they can't tell you what they're doing. I could teach you in five minutes. Lemme show you."

He found a dummy calf head with a spike on the end, which he stabbed into a bale of hay. He was an excellent teacher and in five minutes I could drop a loop over the horns on two tosses out of three.

"What I tell ya? Even *you* could rope." He coiled his rope and went into the arena with his horse.

By ten o'clock everyone was staggering around drunk. Roping and drinking seemed like a dangerous combination, but when a cowboy who could barely walk got on a horse, he became a new man.

Steve invited us back to his house for the night, where he cooked up a huge mess of bacon and eggs and biscuits.

It turned out Steve was no simple electrician, but a millionaire electrical contractor who lived in a modest house in the barrio because he liked it. "These Mexicans," he said, "their kids'll rob you blind, but you know what? They're the best people in the world. When a Spanish guy says he's your friend, he's your *friend*. Everyone helps each other out. I could live in the Heights with all the rich people, but you know, I wouldn't have anything to say to them and they wouldn't have anything to say to me."

We waited around the stables that morning for rush hour to clear before leaving. There we met an old man who had once been attacked by an angry stallion. The horse had knocked him down, planted a foot on his chest, and bit off his nose.

"Why doesn't he get that nose fixed?" I asked Leonard.

"Are you kidding?" he said, laughing. "He's fucking *proud* of that missing nose."

We rode down toward the Río Grande, where there was a trail northward along the levees. At Isleta Boulevard we passed a drive-through Lotaburger. I pulled up in the parking lot and tried to calm my horse enough to approach the talking menu-board. We danced around a bit.

"What the hell you doing?" Walter called out.

"I'm gonna ride through here and buy me a burger," I said.

Walter roared with laughter, doubling over on his horse.

"Hey, good idea," he said.

With great difficulty we managed to get our horses to ride up to the little speaker. We waited there, knocking on the device and shouting into it, with no response. The horse, not being a car, hadn't tripped the speaker. We tried riding to the takeout window, but something about it scared the hell out of both horses and no amount of persuasion would make them approach. The horses pranced about the parking lot, we began cursing, and people started to stare and point. We were creating a scene.

"Let's get the hell out of here," Walter said.

We finally struck the Río Grande, a sluggish moving sheet of water banked by cottonwoods. Enormous steel tank traps wired and chained together for erosion control were scattered through the trees. The riverbed itself looked dangerously boggy. We had been able to figure out where to cross other rivers by finding the place where cows forded, but in downtown Albuquerque there were no cows. We would have to use a bridge.

We crossed the river at Central Avenue, along a three-foot-wide sidewalk. Inches from the curb cars were whizzing past at fifty miles an hour. There was railing low enough for a horse to step over and a long drop to the river.

It took us quite a bit of time to work up the courage to cross. Walter said, "I'd rather ride out of the Salt River Canyon again."

Crossing the Río Grande on the Central Avenue bridge was, without a doubt, the most dangerous part of our whole trip.

One by one we coaxed the horses across. They were badly frightened by the drop and the hollow sound their hooves made on the pavement. As usual, people honked at us and flashed their lights. Whether they were trying to be friendly, or thinking they were warning us of their presence (as if we didn't know), it did not have a calming effect on the horses.

We picked up the trail along the top of the eastern bank of the river. Toward evening, near the northern boundary of Albuquerque, we came to a gate with a series of parallel logs laid down over the trail. The purpose of this was to discourage motor vehicles from entering while allowing horses to step across. Even though we had crossed several of these barriers before without incident, Wilbur balked. He was *not* going to step over those logs. I worked with him a while and then Walter lost his temper.

"Lemme take care of that son-of-a-bitch," he announced, and dallied Wilbur's lead rope around his saddlehorn.

Professional packers have a name for tying the lead rope of a pack-horse to your saddlehorn. They call it "suicide packing." We were about to find out why.

Walter urged Pedernal forward and started pulling Wilbur across the barrier. At the last minute Wilbur panicked and heaved back violently on the rope. This, in turn, tightened down the knot on the saddlehorn and jerked hard on Ped's saddle. Ped himself panicked and began to pull forward with all the power he had.

In the blink of an eye we had two half-ton horses engaged in a frightened tug-of-war.

The rope had become as tight as a steel cable, pressing against Walter's left leg and trapping him in the saddle. With Walter shouting hysterically, the horses strained and lunged against each other. Then

Pedernal skidded sideways into Engwahela, who had been tied up too close. The taut rope slid up under her pack and heaved it upside down.

This drove Engwahela into a choking frenzy. With the 175-pound pack hanging under her belly she began rearing, bucking, flailing, and kicking.

We now had three terrified, out-of-control horses in one big wreck. Utter pandemonium reigned.

Walter finally cut Wilbur's lead rope loose from the saddlehorn and the two horses sprang apart. Freed from the saddle, Walter jumped off Pedernal and grabbed Engwahela's lead rope, while I unsheathed my knife and tried to get under her twisting belly to cut her pack off without gutting her in the process. I waited for a lull, ducked under her, flashed the knife through rope, and jumped back. The pack dropped to the ground. Engwahela was so excited that she continued to buck and kick, treading and stamping all over the pack and Walter's $8,000 Deardorff camera. With each stomp I could hear things crunching and cracking.

We finally got her calmed down and off the destroyed pack. The actual Deardorff itself was, miraculously, intact, but three or four hundred dollars' worth of film holders had been shattered. Our pots and pans had been mangled; our small steel frying pan was folded like a taco; and a jug of neat's-foot oil had exploded. As far as the horses went, Engwahela was a little skinned up, Wilbur had thrown a shoe, and Ped was upset—but otherwise they were fine.

At the very moment the wreck occurred a man had appeared next to the trail. When it was all over he shook our hands and introduced himself as Gene Crabtree. He had heard about our trip, and then he had seen us from his house just across the river.

"I think I was about one minute too late," he said, fishing a key out of his pocket and unlocking the gate for Wilbur.

"You got here in time to see the worst wreck of the whole trip," I said.

"That wasn't so bad," he said.

"Whaddaya mean?" Walter said. "That was terrible."

"A *bad* wreck," Crabtree said cheerfully, "is where someone gets killed."

He was a soft-spoken man with the nimble gestures and vocabulary of a college professor. We were astonished to learn he had broken mules for a living.

"Mules are highly intelligent," he said, "much harder to break than a horse. Training an animal is partly a process of psychological domination, and the more intelligent the animal the more he resists that domination. A lot of tricks you can use on a horse don't even work with a mule. And you know, mules *remember*. If you strike a mule unfairly, he'll wait a day or two, and then when you least expect it he'll haul back and whale you to kingdom come."

"Why'd you give it up?" I asked.

He smiled. "You can only break mules so long before you start to feel the onset of a nervous breakdown."

Some miles north we entered the boundary of Sandia Pueblo, one of the northerly Tiwa (Tiguex) pueblos. We rode through endless cool groves of cottonwoods alongside the river. The understory had been swept clean by periodic floods, creating the look of an exquisitely maintained English park.

At the little town of Bernalillo, Walter rode into town to buy film while I swam in the Río Grande, my baptism in those historic waters. They looked cloudy and I wondered what kind of poisons were now flowing downstream from Española and Los Alamos.

I swam nearly opposite the ruins of Kuaua Pueblo, known since the 1940s as the Coronado State Monument. The state excavated this ruin in the late 1930s, believing it was the pueblo where Coronado had wintered. The excavation failed to find any evidence that Coronado had even slept there, but it did uncover spectacular religious murals from a great kiva. State bureaucrats named it after Coronado anyway.

In 1986, a grading crew widening a right of way about two miles south of Coronado State Monument uncovered some charcoal-stained earth with a scattering of pottery. As required by New Mexico law, the crew stopped work and an archeological team from the University of New Mexico, headed by Bradley Vierra, came out to investigate. The site was discovered about four hundred yards west of the ruins of Santiago Pueblo, one of the pueblos occupied by the Tiwa when Coronado came through.

The archeologists were at first mystified by what they found. In the excavated area fifteen shallow depressions had been dug into the desert floor and trampled down, each with hearths and postholes. The dugouts appeared to represent tent bases.

A very puzzling array of artifacts were discovered at the site. First, they found iron fragments, including what was probably a horseshoe nail, as well as a piece of armor. They also discovered sheep bones.

Both these finds proved a post-1540 date, since neither sheep nor iron were known in the Southwest before Coronado. On the other hand, there was no colonial-era Spanish pottery, only prehistoric Indian pottery, which indicated a temporary, very early site. Radiocarbon dating of various organic remains gave a mean date of 1527, with a margin of error of about plus or minus eighty years.

There were other clues. One of the stone artifacts, a broken stone blade, was determined to be made of a kind of obsidian found only near Mexico City. Because the fires were lit inside the tent bases, and never outside, the archeologists concluded the camp had been occupied only during the winter. Furthermore, the 1930s excavation of the nearby Santiago ruin had recovered six crossbow tips, including one imbedded in the chest of an individual who had obviously died as a result. The large amount of broken pottery would indicate that the camp had been occupied for at least several months.

All this evidence, carefully analyzed, pointed to only one conclusion: the campsite must have been occupied by Coronado. The carbon date, along with the lack of colonial pottery, indicated a pre-1598 occupation of the site. Yet the sheep bones and pieces of iron proved that the Spanish had lived there. Of the several pre-1598 Spanish expeditions to New Mexico, Coronado's was the only one that had crossbows; Coronado's was the only one that camped in the wintertime in the Río Grande Valley; and Coronado's was the only one that spent more than a few days in the area. Only Coronado's and Oñate's expeditions brought sheep, and Oñate spent less than a week here, in June, before moving north. Finally, Coronado's expedition, unlike the others, had recruited large numbers of Aztec Indians from the Valley of Mexico, thus explaining the obsidian blade.

The general consensus now is that Santiago Pueblo was Alcanfor Pueblo, where Coronado spent the winter. As the army was too large to fit in the pueblo, the scholars reasoned, there would have been a spillover camp nearby.

I'm not sure I agree with this theory. Alcanfor was requisitioned without a fight, making the crossbow tip in the skeleton difficult to explain. Rather, I believe that Santiago Pueblo was Moho, the pueblo besieged for fifty days during February and March of 1541. The camp would therefore have belonged not to the main army, but to the Spanish and Aztec besiegers. Over two hundred Indians at Moho died during the siege, including many by crossbow fire.

The camp was a quarter-mile from the pueblo—a little far for soldiers with Coronado, who, it seems to me, would have camped just outside the walls. Four hundred yards would have been a good *strategic* distance—well out of arrow range, not too close to be hit with a surprise attack, but close enough to keep the Indians from escaping. The main Spanish campsite was occupied until late April; surely the soldiers would have been cooking outside by that time (cooking inside a tent is a nasty, smoky affair). On the other hand, the besiegers' camp was abandoned in early March, when it still would have been very cold.

Either way, the discovery of one of Coronado's camps is one of the most important archeological discoveries in New Mexico in a decade. It is one of only two sixteenth-century Spanish camps known in all of the United States, the other being in Tallahassee, Florida.

Unfortunately, we may never know any more about the site. The part that was in the highway right of way was destroyed after being excavated, and much of the rest of it—still unexcavated—lies on land belonging to AMREP Southwest, Inc., a subsidiary of the huge New York City–based real estate developer. The site is temporarily protected by an agreement with the Environmental Protection Agency, but AMREP is in court trying to overturn the restriction. AMREP plans to build a subdivision around (and over) the site, called River's Edge. Meanwhile, heavy equipment has been run through the site, trenching it and destroying about 10 percent of the unexcavated portion. AMREP claims someone else must have done these things. The Historic Preservation Division staff archeologist working on the site, Jim O'Hara, says he believes it must have been AMREP, as nobody else has been in there with heavy equipment. AMREP's lawyer told O'Hara that, hey, the people who buy these houses don't care about archeological sites: the primary goal of the company is to earn money for the *shareholders*. When I talked to an AMREP representative about the site, he said words to the effect: "It's on our private property, okay? You understand that, don't you?"

Half of Santiago Pueblo itself was destroyed in the 1970s, being mined for gravel. The part that remained was acquired and saved by the Sandia Indians who live across the river from Santiago; they were able to show, in a lawsuit, that they were likely the direct descendants of the people who once occupied Santiago.

If this had been an early English site occupied, say, by those overblown religious bigots known as the Pilgrims, you can bet the outcry would have been loud enough to halt the destruction. But such is how America treats its Hispanic heritage.

. . .

We camped that night in a thick grove of cottonwoods on the San Felipe Reservation. The river swept past us in a broad turn over a cobbled bed, the water blazing with reflected sunlight. As we set up camp a wild stallion trotted out of the trees on the far side of the river and drank. Suddenly sensing our presence, he raised his head, wheeled about, and galloped off through the shallows in a chandelier-like explosion of water.

In the middle of the night Acomita began barking and we heard a bloodcurdling scream of equine sexual excitement. I ran out of the tent to discover the stallion trying to mount Engwahela. He bolted into the darkness and we tied Engwahela closer to our tent, but we could hear him hanging around in the brush, snorting and moving about. Acomita barked and chased him off whenever he got too close.

On Thursday, August 24th we rode into Santo Domingo Pueblo. It stood at the confluence of Galisteo Creek and the Río Grande, a cluster of adobe houses smelling of dust and cedar smoke. The governor of the pueblo, Ernie Lovato, had asked us to drop in when we rode through, so we tied up our horses in the main plaza and went into the tribal building.

Governor Lovato was a small, barrel-chested man with a staccato, intense way of talking. He invited us to join him and other tribal officers for a magnificent feast of corn, mutton, and green chile stew, with heaps of traditional Santo Domingo bread—a flat, soft loaf and the best Indian bread I had ever eaten. As we were leaving, Governor Lovato, Lieutenant Governor Moquino, and several tribal elders saw us off. Lovato pressed our hands.

"The Santo Domingo people," he said, "have a great tradition of hospitality, which you have seen today. Many centuries ago we greeted Coronado the same way. I hope," he continued with a smile, "that you do not return our hospitality the way Coronado did."

We left the Río Grande at Santo Domingo, going east up Galisteo Creek. We stopped briefly at the Santo Domingo Trading Post, a lonely old stucco building in a dusty flat near the railroad tracks. An enormous multicolored sign announced that John F. Kennedy had been there. While we were inside we heard a terrific commotion, and I rushed out to find an ugly Shetland pony stallion, no bigger than a large dog, with an erection far out of proportion to his size, trying to climb up on Engwahela. I shouted and chased him away, hoping that we didn't bring her back to Roeliff impregnated by that awful thing.

Another day of riding up the creek brought us to the ghost town of Waldo, a rubble-covered hill above some railroad tracks. There was still a sign at the tracks announcing "WALDO," but the trains no longer stopped. Waldo's main industry had been fifteen coke ovens, which processed high-quality smelting coke from coal mined in Madrid, just up the road. When the mines in Madrid closed in 1954, Waldo and Madrid both became ghost towns.

In the late sixties a commune sprang up in Waldo, and squatters from New York and San Francisco moved into the old stone buildings. The commune lasted for a few years, but as the seventies rolled in people started to argue and drift away. Then, one day, all the buildings in Waldo were dynamited to the ground. A hippie who was squatting nearby had started a large marijuana plantation in the hills behind Waldo. The man became suspicious that the people in the Waldo commune were stealing his plants, so, like any good capitalist, he took steps to protect his investment.

Six months before the trip I had visited Waldo and had met the town's only resident, a fellow with a beard and wild black hair named Kelly. He lived in a tiny stone hut perched against the side of a hill. He had been one of the original commune members. The reason he had moved back to Waldo, he said, was to avoid being served papers by his ex-wife.

He had given me a tour of the place. On top of the hill he pointed out the mound of rubble that was once the biggest house in Waldo. This was the heart of the commune, where he and his wife had been married back in the sixties. With pride he showed me where his bride had stood and where he had stood. He told me about the beautiful ceremony they had worked out together. They were all barefoot and had desert flowers in their hair, and a salt cedar fire burned merrily in the fireplace; everybody hugged each other and danced all night and took a lot of really great drugs. It had been a beautiful time back then, he said, with a tremble in his voice, but the sixties had turned into the seventies, they'd blown up the town, and now the fucking bitch was suing him for child support.

We tied up at the creek and I hiked up the hill to see if Kelly was still there; but his stone hut was deserted, the door blowing open and shut in the wind. Eddies of sand had collected on the floor and the fireplace was full of desiccated chicken bones. I could hear the door whacking maniacally against a rock as I walked back down.

34

Four miles down the creek we hit the town of Cerrillos (Little Hills), a collection of wood and adobe buildings lining a dirt street. The only precious mineral Coronado would find in the Southwest was turquoise, almost all of it coming from a cluster of cone-shaped hills just outside of Cerrillos, called (rather redundantly) the Cerrillos Hills. It is ironic that Coronado passed within several miles of this mine without realizing it. His Pecos Indian guides wisely neglected to mention its existence. When Esteban arrived at Zuni, he was loaded down with Cerrillos turquoise, and the turquoise that the Cicuyé Indians gave Alvarado came from the Cerrillos Hills.

In 1540, turquoise was, truly, the hard currency of the Southwest, being the most important medium of exchange. Expeditions to Chaco Canyon have recovered staggering caches of turquoise—at Pueblo Bonito alone some 65,000 pieces were discovered, much of it thought to be from Cerrillos. Prehistoric Cerrillos turquoise has been found deep in Mexico; some claim it has been found as far north as Ontario, Canada, as far west as California, and as far east as Arkansas. The turquoises in the crown jewels of Spain are allegedly from Cerrillos. Some of the treasures Moctezuma gave Cortés had Cerrillos turquoise inlay.

When the first Americans came into New Mexico, they were astonished at the extent of the prehistoric workings at Cerrillos. In 1540, Mount Chalchihuitl at Cerrillos may have been the site of the largest prehistoric mine in all of America. One person, stumbling on the old workings at Chalchihuitl in 1858, wrote that he was "struck with astonishment at the extent of the excavations. . .it appears to be 200 feet in depth and 300 feet or more in width. . . . This great excavation is made in the solid rock, and tens of thousands of tons have been broken out." Inside the mine were found many stone hammers, along with prehistoric pots and other primitive mining paraphernalia.

The surrounding Pueblo Indians had a monopoly on Cerrillos turquoise, which greatly enhanced their wealth. Turquoise was far more valuable back then; small quantities were traded for cotton mantas, horses (when they became available), pottery, corn, Navajo blankets, salt, and even healing ceremonies. Further afield, they traded turquoise with Mexico and California for macaw and parrot feathers and shells.

Turquoise wasn't the only mineral found in Cerrillos. In 1879, two prospectors found silver-bearing ore in the area, and overnight a tent city sprang up. Gold, copper, lead, and coal were also discovered and soon there was a proliferation of mines with names like the Sulky, the Little Emma, the Piñon, the Cash Entry, the Silver Chief, the Last Lode, and the Lucky Dutchman Lode. A boom followed, with the population soaring to 2,500 people; twenty-eight saloons kept the population well lubricated and even water cost twenty-five cents a barrel. For one hysterical moment someone suggested making Cerrillos the new state capital. But the boom was based mostly on rumor and hype, and the bust came shortly. Cerrillos ore was "refractory"—hard to process—it was deep, and it was not very good. Thomas Edison stopped briefly in Cerrillos to experiment with a static electricity method of recovering fine placer gold, but the process was a failure. The population dwindled almost to nothing.

Aside from coal, turquoise continued to be about the only paying mineral at Cerrillos, and a small population managed to scratch out a living. It never quite became a ghost town, although it got close enough to be listed in most of the popular ghost-town guides. Its poverty and declining population created a town frozen in time, so authentic that since the 1950s it has been used as a movie set for many well-known films.*

---

*Young Guns was the last that I know of.

. . .

Cerrillos was a perfect little Western town, and as we arrived a tumbleweed rolled by, obligingly completing the picture. At Cerrillos we had arranged to meet Anthony Flynn, a friend of mine from New York City who wanted to ride with us for a few days. Anthony was Irish (educated on the continent and speaking with a British accent), multi-lingual, urbane, lettered, impeccably dressed. I had only known him in the city, and as we rode toward town I was having a little difficulty imagining what he was going to look like in this setting.

We found Anthony and his rented horse waiting in a vacant lot across from Cerrillos's only saloon. He had taken my suggestion that he buy Western clothing, but when I saw him the effect could only be described as farcical. Everything was brand-new and he smelled like a menswear shop. He wore a bandanna carefully folded and tied around his neck, a Stetson hat so white it could be seen twenty miles away, a starched pair of jeans as stiff as a board, and spit-polished cowboy boots. When he moved you could hear the rustle of stiff cotton and the creak of leather. Had he been wearing robes and a kaffiyeh he wouldn't have looked more out of place.

We found him in a singularly foul mood. The seventy-five-year-old woman who ran Cerrillos's last saloon had apparently taken a dim view of his sartorial getup and his British accent, and she had refused him service.

"That *dreadful* woman in there," Anthony said, "wouldn't even give me the time. I say, have you ever heard of a tavern-keeper without a clock?"

"She better not refuse us service," Walter said, belligerently pushing his way into the saloon. "I'm thirsty as hell."

We piled into the interior, as dim as a cave. As soon as the proprietress saw us a broad smile lit up her features.

"Come in, boys, and get yourselves a beer," she said, pointing to an old Coca-Cola ice trunk shoved up against the bar. She was greatly taken with us. We looked just like the other cowboys in the saloon, only more so. She took quite a bit of persuading, however, before she would believe Anthony was a friend of ours. In the end even he got a drink.

"You know," she said to me later in a loud whisper, "we sometimes have to be careful what *kind* we serve around here." As she said this her eye swiveled malevolently toward Anthony, who was sitting at his stool, sipping his beer from a glass, pinkie extended. He looked as innocent as a nun.

I asked her exactly what "kind" she had to watch out for. *"Tourists,"* she hissed.

Upstream from Cerrillos we rode into the Galisteo Basin. When Alvarado and Padilla passed through here in the fall of 1540, on their way to Cicuyé, they found scenes of considerable destruction.

"Between Cicuyé," Castañeda wrote in one of his most intriguing passages, "and the province of Quirix [that is, between Pecos and Santo Domingo], there is a small strong pueblo, which the Spaniards named Ximena, and another pueblo, almost deserted, for only one of its sections is inhabited. This pueblo must have been large, to judge by its site, and it seemed to have been destroyed recently. This was called the town of the silos, because big maize silos were found there.

"Farther on there was another large pueblo completely destroyed and leveled. The patios were covered with numerous stone balls as large as the jugs of one arroba.* It looked as if the stones had been hurled from catapults or guns with which an enemy had destroyed the pueblo. All that we could find out about it was that some sixteen years before some people called Teyas† had come in large numbers to that land and had destroyed those pueblos. They besieged Cicuyé but could not take it. . . . They must have been powerful people who must have had war machines to batter down the pueblos."

The prehistoric inhabitants of the Galisteo Basin were Tano Indians, and the Basin contains some of the largest Indian ruins in the country, but no one has satisfactorily identified which ones were Ximena, the Pueblo of the Silos, and the destroyed pueblo.‡

As we rode into the middle of the basin, we came upon a strange sight. A church steeple rose from the plains, and gradually an entire town came into view. As we approached it began to take on a bizarre look: half built, half in ruins, partly burned, the windward side of its fences piled with tumbleweeds. It was an odd place for a town, out in

---

*Weight equivalent of about twenty-five pounds.

†The Teyas Indians—also spelled "Tejas" or "Texas"—were probably Wichitas or Pawnees from eastern New Mexico or west Texas. The word *teyas* probably meant "friend," being the word called out by the Indians when they first approached the Spaniards. The word gave the state of Texas its name.

‡There is one ruin in the Galisteo Basin, called San Lázaro, which has a number of natural, round sandstone concretions scattered about it; it seems safe to say that this pueblo is probably the "leveled" one described by Castañeda.

the open like this, built on a treeless, waterless rise, scoured by winds day and night. Strangest of all, there was no road to the town. Then we realized that most of the buildings were false fronts propped up by two-by-six scaffolding. It wasn't a town at all, but a movie set— Hollywood's version of the Western town. It looked both eerie and ridiculous, this ersatz town, this Southern California vision of the Old West.*

We soon came to a real town, the village of Galisteo, several dozen adobe houses shoveled in amongst a grove of cottonwoods along the creek. As we were looking for a gate in the fence at the road, a fellow hauling some horses pulled up. He looked very much the picture of a rugged, masculine cowboy, only he was a shade too well-dressed, his mustaches a trifle too carefully waxed and curled, his face a little too well-scrubbed, and his boots suspiciously free of mud and manure. He pressed a business card on us that identified his name as "Boots" and indicated he was a wrangler/cowboy for the movies. Walter started telling Boots about how we had ridden nine hundred miles across the Southwest. Boots listened for a few minutes with a cocked eyebrow and then denied such a thing was possible, said that we were pretty good liars, and roared with laughter at the joke. Just as Walter was sputtering and swearing that it was, in fact, the truth, Anthony came trotting up on his horse—posting away, elbows out, hat bobbing—with his horse's breast collar dangling around the animal's knees.

Boots pointed at Anthony, guffawing louder, and said, "I sure hope you didn't ride all nine hundred miles looking like *that*." He swaggered off in his pointy-toed cowboy boots, shaking his head, his masculinity intact, relieved that we weren't the real thing after all.

"God dammit to hell." Walter said to Anthony, "I *told* you five miles back to fix that damn thing."

"Oh dear," Anthony said feebly, "I'd been meaning to correct it."

Later Walter pulled me aside. "That damn hat of his is ruining my pictures," he said. "It's so. . .so *white*."

We camped that night in the immense ruins of San Cristóbal Pueblo, the easternmost of the Galisteo Basin pueblos. San Cristóbal lay several miles east of Galisteo Creek on a large ranch.

The ruins, rocky mounds covered with cholla and prickly pear, extended for several hundred yards on both sides of San Cristóbal

---

*I learned later it had been built for the movie *Silverado*.

Creek. Across the creek a lonely, ragged wall stood above the mounds, all that was left of an old mission church, destroyed in the Pueblo Revolt and never rebuilt. As we lit our fire, a small herd of cows wandered through the ruins and watered at the creek, lowing in the dusk.

San Cristóbal had been the largest of the Tano pueblos, but its location was poorly defensible and it came under heavy Apache attacks in the late seventeenth century. Sometime in the 1680s the San Cristóbal Indians relocated fifty miles to the north, and their old pueblo fell into ruins, never to be occupied again.

The San Cristóbals joined a minor Indian revolt in 1696, killed their two priests and arranged the half-stripped bodies in a macabre cross. When the revolt failed, the San Cristóbal Indians, knowing full well the consequences of this action, abandoned their new pueblo and fled deep into the west, finding safe refuge with the Hopis.* There they were gradually assimilated into Hopi society and have ceased to exist as a separate people.

San Cristóbal Pueblo will always hold a hallowed place in the annals of archeology. Shortly after the turn of the century, a young archeologist from the American Museum of Natural History in New York City, Nels C. Nelson, surveyed and excavated portions of the major Galisteo Basin pueblos. While digging at San Cristóbal he tried an experiment: he painstakingly excavated the pueblo's trash heap in systematic layers—to see if potsherds and other artifacts showed evolution over time. It was the first time an archeologist had tried this kind of systematic stratigraphic analysis, and American archeology was forever transformed. Two decades later, at nearby Pecos Pueblo, the archeologist A. V. Kidder would use Nelson's method in the "greatest rubbish heap" in the Southwest, and would thereby establish the entire, thousand-year cultural sequence of the Pueblo Indians.

That morning, Walter discovered that Pedernal's withers were slightly swollen. As we had eaten most of our food, we were able to pack everything on Engwahela. Then came a decision: which of my horses would Walter ride?

"I'll tell you one thing: I ain't riding Wilbur," Walter declared.

*After 1680 the Spanish never did reoccupy Hopiland. The Hopis celebrate August 10, the date of the 1680 revolt, as their Independence Day.

I asked him what he thought was wrong with Wilbur; Walter ejected a word of coarse vulgarity; I expressed my opinion of Robin; Walter expressed his opinion of Redbone; I cursed and damned Walter's packing ability; Walter ridiculed my riding ability; I told Walter the sight of his ugly face had become offensive to me in the extreme; Walter informed me that my Yankee ass was finally going to get the drubbing it so richly deserved; and before we knew it we were shoving, pushing and pounding each other, each cuff sending up a cloud of dust, while Anthony looked on in scandalized horror.

The fight quickly ended in a tearful embrace, and we continued on toward Pecos.

Leaving San Cristóbal the morning of August 28th, I spread out the maps and took a compass bearing toward Pecos—the old Cicuyé pueblo of Coronado—our final destination, twenty-five miles distant. As we proceeded through the piñon-juniper forest east of San Cristóbal, we noticed a light scattering of potsherds, both prehistoric and Spanish colonial, extending for several miles from the pueblo, along with some old, parallel marks in the prairie. We explored a bit and found that the sherds extended in a narrow swath along the precise compass alignment between the two ruins.

There could be little doubt; we had discovered the ancient trail between San Cristóbal Pueblo and Pecos Pueblo.

It was now late August, and the nights had begun sharply cooling off; autumn comes early in the high desert. We spent our last night in a grassy meadow filled with wildflowers.

It had rained on us several times and Anthony had slept on his hat, and as a result he was starting to look a little more broken in. Still, whenever Walter wanted to take a picture of us he would make Anthony remove his hat.

"That thing's so damn bright it'll throw off my light meter," he would say.

We gradually climbed the western slope of Rowe Mesa. After rising almost imperceptibly from the Galisteo Basin, Rowe Mesa suddenly drops off in thousand-foot bluffs to the Pecos River Valley.

We struck the edge of the mesa around noon on the last day.

Compressed in this little space between the Rowe bluffs and the Sangre de Cristo Mountains lay one of the great thoroughfares of the American continent. It was the only easy route to Pueblo Indian country, and for thousands of years it had been a main trade route between the Great Plains and the Río Grande. Later the Santa Fe Trail was routed through here, followed by the Atchison, Topeka, and Santa Fe Railway, and finally by Interstate 25.*

We looked down to the Interstate cutting across the valley, a broad double-stripe of gray across green meadows. The railroad lay closer to the bluffs, winding in gentle curves. In the east, where the valley opened up, we could see the beginnings of the Great Plains fading into blue haze. The little Hispanic towns of Rowe, Pecos, and East Pecos were all visible; but the ruins of Pecos Pueblo were either too small or too far away to be seen.

---

*In this peculiar little valley, I-25 North runs south and I-25 South runs north.

35

Ⅎⅎ ⊠ ⅎⅎ

In the spring of 1541, Coronado and his army rode through this river valley eastward on their way to the great kingdom of Quivira. After a few days, "I came to some plains," Coronado wrote to King Charles, "so vast that in my travels I did not reach their end, although I had marched over them for more than three hundred leagues [930 miles]."

The Spaniards struggled to comprehend the vastness of the Great Plains. It was, Coronado wrote, as if "we were surrounded by the sea. Here the guides lost their bearings because there is nowhere a stone, hill, tree, bush, or anything of the sort. . .we wandered aimlessly."

The buffalo herd—in 1541 there was only one herd and it covered over a million square miles—also astonished Coronado and his men.* "I found so many cattle," he wrote, "that it would be impossible to estimate their number. For in traveling over the plains, there was not a single day, until my return, that I lost sight of them."

Another soldier wrote that the buffalo "were the most monstrous beasts ever seen or read about. . . . There are such quantities of them

---

*In the late nineteenth century the transcontinental railroad tracks would split the herd into two, which became known as the Northern and Southern Herds.

I do not know what to compare them with, unless it be with the fish in the sea. . . . Traveling these plains is like traveling at sea. . . . Since the land is so level, without a mountain or a hill, it was dangerous to travel alone or become separated from the army, for, on losing it, one was lost."

The men who went off hunting every day to supply the army with meat often would get lost, wandering in circles for days. "Every night," Castañeda wrote, "the soldiers fired their artillery, blew their horns, beat their drums, and lit great bonfires," to help the lost find their way to camp. Even so, one man on horseback got separated from the army and was never seen again.

Compounding the difficulty was the short, tough buffalo grass. "Who would believe," Castañeda wrote, "that although one thousand horses, five hundred of our cattle, more than five thousand rams and sheep, and more than 1500 persons, including allies and servants,* marched over these plains, they left no more traces when they got through than if no one had passed over, so it became necessary to stack up piles of bones and dung of the cattle."

There was, at least, no shortage of bones: they littered the ground as far as the eye could see. Once the army came to a salt lake with bones washed up along the shores by strong winds—a bone pile hundreds of feet long, ten feet high, and twenty feet wide.

They encountered bands of wandering Indians, whom they called Teyas and Querechos. "They go about like nomads," Castañeda recalled, "with their tents and with packs of dogs harnessed with little pads, pack-saddles, and girths. When the dogs' loads slip to the side they howl for some one to come and straighten them. . . . These people eat raw meat and drink blood, but do not eat human flesh. They are gentle people, not cruel, and are faithful in their friendship." So skillful were they in the use of sign language that the Spaniards found they could understand them almost as clearly as if they were speaking Spanish.

From these Indians the Spanish eventually learned a new method of navigation. Just as the sun rose in the east, an Indian would take his bearing and fire an arrow in the correct direction. They would march toward the arrow, but just before they came to it they would stop and shoot another arrow directly over it, repeating the process the entire

---

*Some of these numbers seem a little exaggerated.

day. It was a method of travel with pinpoint accuracy, enabling the Indians to journey between water sources many miles apart.

As they traveled eastward, the Turk urged them ever forward, spinning marvelous tales of Quivira. The Turk was always at the fore, meeting the Indians and interpreting, and the Indians corroborated the Turk's story. At the same time, the Turk's compatriot, Isopete, became more and more insistent that the Turk was lying. There were no great cities of gold and silver in Quivira, he said, and besides, the Turk was leading them into nowhere, where they would all die. "For this reason," Castañeda noted dryly, "no one paid any attention to [Isopete]."

As the army continued deeper into present-day Texas, much of what Isopete said bore out, while the Turk's fabulous descriptions never seemed to materialize. Isopete claimed the Turk was coaching the Indian groups they met, so Coronado, as an experiment, had the Turk moved to the rear. The next group of Indians, thus uncoached, gave the Spaniards a real shock: they contradicted everything the Turk had said about Quivira. The houses were not made of stone, they signed, they were made of straw and hides. Of gold and silver they knew nothing. And finally, Quivira was north, not east.

"This information caused me considerable worry," Coronado wrote to the king. Conditions had become difficult: they had nothing to eat but buffalo meat, which was starting to make the men sick; their water sources were mostly buffalo wallows that, Coronado wrote, "tasted more like slime than water." They had to cook with buffalo dung, which they considered disgusting. One day the army was caught in a vicious hailstorm, with hail "as large as bowls and even larger." The storm stampeded and bruised their horses, tore their tents to pieces, broke all their crockery, and dented many headpieces.

Somewhere in the middle of the Texas Panhandle Coronado called his captains together to discuss the worsening situation. They concluded that maybe the Turk really was a liar and that Isopete should be given a chance to guide. Coronado decided to send the army back to Tiguex while he proceeded with thirty handpicked horsemen to Quivira.

Isopete immediately turned the truncated expedition 90 degrees, heading due north. For forty-two days the Spaniards rode across the plains, at one point encountering an old blind Indian who, long ago in the south, had met Cabeza de Vaca and Esteban.

And then, in midsummer, somewhere near the Great Bend of the Arkansas River in central Kansas, they spied a group of Indians in the distance. The Indians started to run, but Isopete called out to them in his language.

They had reached Quivira.

If Cíbola had been a disappointment, this was worse. There were no multi-storied stone houses, no gold or silver: only a sad little village of straw huts alongside the river. One soldier wrote angrily: "At Quivira there is a bestial people without any organization in their houses or anything else." Coronado himself wrote to the king: "The people are savage like all I have seen and passed up to this place. . . . All they have is the tanned skins of the cattle they kill."

The Spaniards asked about for gold or any other metals, and a native handed over a piece of copper that a chief had been wearing around his neck, which the Indians considered of great value. Another Quiviran gave Coronado a piece of something that looked like gold, but Coronado realized with annoyance that it was a sample that one of his own servants had brought along.

Coronado had the Turk brought forward and asked him "why he had lied to them and guided them so perversely."

His plot having failed, the Turk freely admitted that he and the Indians of Cicuyé had plotted to "take the Spaniards out there and lead them astray on the plains. Thus, through lack of provisions, their horses would die and they themselves would become so feeble that, upon their return, the people of Cicuyé could kill them easily and so obtain revenge for what the Spaniards had done to them."

Coronado was humiliated and furious at having been so thoroughly duped. He ordered the Turk secretly brought to a tent in the dark of night, where a Spaniard threw a rope around his neck and twisted it with a garrote until he was dead.

Coronado spent twenty-five days wandering around central Kansas. All the local Indians agreed, uncomprehending, to the Spaniards' requirement of obedience and vassalage. Back at Quivira Coronado erected a cross, "at the foot of which some letters were cut with a chisel, saying that Francisco Vázquez de Coronado, general of the army, had reached this place."

There was nothing else to be done. They turned their horses southwest, back to Tiguex, a thousand miles distant.

On their return, the Spaniards found Cicuyé unfriendly, the ladders withdrawn to the rooftops. The Indians would not respond to any of the Spaniards' demands for provisions. They swarmed out once and engaged the Spanish in a quick battle, but the firing of a cannon sent them back inside. The Galisteo Basin pueblos, likewise, refused the Spaniards help. When the army marched into the Río Grande Valley, the Tiguex Indians again fled to the hills.

That winter of 1541–1542 was a dispiriting one. Through long discussions, Coronado and his captains convinced themselves that perhaps, after all, they had not made a diligent enough search of the lands beyond Quivira. Maybe the Turk had been partly right: after all (they reasoned), the Turk had a name for gold—*acochis*.

When the snows melted, they decided the entire army would journey back to Quivira and push even farther eastward, beyond the eastern edge of the Great Plains.

These plans would come to nothing. One fine spring day,* Coronado rode out with a friend, Don Rodrigo Maldonado, to race. In the middle of the race Coronado's saddle cinch broke and he fell in front of Maldonado's horse. The horse struck him on the head with a hoof, causing a severe injury. Coronado was in a coma and "on the point of death" for many days.

When he finally recovered, something in him had changed forever.† All thoughts of gold and conquest were gone, for Coronado had remembered a prophecy made for him by an astrologer in Salamanca once, many years ago. In the prophecy, Coronado had been told that he would "find himself in strange lands, that he would become mighty and powerful, and that he was to suffer a fall from which he would be unable to recover." During his long convalescence Coronado had turned this prophecy over and over in his head. It became an obsession that drove out all other thoughts, and the young conquistador finally came to believe he was dying. "This thought of death," Castañeda wrote, "made him desire to go back to die near his wife and children."

Another soldier remembered: "He longed for this more than anything else."

Most of Coronado's captains, however, wanted to explore and per-

---

*Castañeda may be mistaken here; the accident might have occurred in the winter.
†There is little doubt Coronado suffered brain damage; everyone who knew him said his personality changed after the accident, that he behaved in a strange, suspicious fashion.

haps even settle Quivira. They had noticed how rich the black soil was and how fine the grass. Having been there in the heat and humidity of summer, they erroneously concluded that Quivira was a much warmer land than Tiguex.

Coronado knew that if he were to return to Mexico City, he'd better have a good reason. His reason would be that the soil was so barren, the Indians so hostile, and the winters so cold that the lands were virtually uninhabitable. Against many of his captains' and soldiers' wishes he ordered the return of the army to Mexico. No one would be allowed to settle; that would belie Coronado's excuse for returning.

As soon as the snow melted the army left, filthy with lice, their clothes in rags, their horses dying by the score. Coronado's captains, disgruntled at being forced to return, began openly disobeying him, and when the army reached Culiacán, the northernmost outpost of New Spain, the soldiers and captains began deserting. When Coronado rode into Mexico City to present himself to Viceroy Antonio de Mendoza, his once beloved patron, the thousand-plus army consisted of fewer than a hundred men.

Mendoza, Castañeda noted dryly, "did not rejoice" at Coronado's return. According to Castañeda, the general was so poorly received, in fact, that "from then on Francisco Vázquez lost reputation." Coronado remained as governor of New Galicia for a little while longer, but during his *residencia* (the traditional hearing following an official's tenure) he was accused of many acts of corruption; that same year he was also charged with abuse and brutality to the Indians of Cíbola, Tiguex, and Cicuyé and with the murder of the Turk. (The *residencia* was often political and a person who had fallen out of official favor, like Coronado, would be roasted, whereas an equally corrupt person still in favor was likely to get off scot-free.) While Coronado was acquitted on the brutality charges,* he was convicted on *residencia* charges of corruption and fined.

He spent the rest of his short unhappy life appealing his conviction and petitioning various officials. He died in 1554 in relative obscurity in New Spain at age forty-four.

◦ ⚎ ◦

---

*His captain, Cárdenas, was not so lucky: he was convicted of brutality, including the burning at the stake of the Indians of Arenal Pueblo at Tiguex, and suffered banishment to Africa and very heavy fines.

In the end, not all the Spaniards would go back to New Spain. Coronado did not have the authority to order the return of the friars.

Fray Juan de Padilla still believed passionately in the Seven Cities of Antillia, and he was now convinced they lay somewhere beyond Quivira, beyond the end of the Great Plains. His dream of bringing the Seven Cities back into the Christian fold was stronger than ever. On the eve of their departure from Tiguex, Fray Juan packed up several mules with supplies and left for Quivira, taking with him a Portuguese assistant and several servants.

Another friar also stayed behind. He was Fray Luis, a simple, gentle old man unable to face the walk back to Mexico City. He wished to stay behind at Cicuyé, where he hoped to "baptize the children he found on the verge of death and send them to heaven."

Nothing was ever heard from Fray Luis again, and there can be little doubt the kindly old padre was killed by the Cicuyé Indians as soon as the Spanish army had left.

Two years later, Fray Juan de Padilla's Portuguese assistant would appear in Panuco, on the Caribbean coast, ragged and emaciated, carrying a bundle of bloody robes. The good friar, he related, had been martyred—murdered shortly after his arrival in Quivira. The story was confused and the murderers might have been his Pueblo Indian guides or the Quivirans themselves, but whatever the cause, his bones were now bleaching in the grass somewhere on the Great Plains.

"And this," Castañeda wrote, "was the end of these discoveries and of the expedition that was made to the new land."

⚬ ☰ ⚬

In 1540, Cicuyé—Pecos—was probably the greatest city within the present-day boundaries of America. For over three centuries the Pecos Indians had held sway over the Pecos River Valley, and they had grown wealthy and proud. In 1540, they were at the apex of their power.

The coming of Coronado marked the beginning of the end for Pecos Pueblo. In the decline and fall of this city, which took place across three centuries, the history of the Southwest would be reflected in microcosm.

In 1590, a Spanish adventurer and erstwhile colonizer, Gaspar Castaño de Sosa, entered New Mexico on an unauthorized expedition. The Pecos remembered and hated the Spanish, and they humiliated one of Castaño's advance guards. Castaño ordered the pueblo punished. A fierce battle took place; once again, armor, horses, artillery, and firearms prevailed against arrows and rocks. On New Year's Day, 1591, Castaño paraded through the pueblo and was amazed at the number of kivas, the fine plastered and whitewashed houses, the intricate and costly dress of the men and women, the "very elegant" pottery, and the supply of maize so great that "everyone marveled."

It was a picture of Pecos in its prime, poised at the abyss.

Castaño was soon arrested for his illegal *entrada* into New Mexico, and his defeat of Pecos was a wasted effort. The defeat, however, came as a deep psychological shock to the Pecos Indians: never before had anyone been able to conquer them. Thus, when Juan de Oñate arrived at Pecos on July 25, 1598, the Pecos Indians chose not to fight. They allowed him entrance and submitted to the usual bombastic recitation of the *requiermiento*, swearing their obedience without complaint.

A friar was left at Pecos in the fall of that year to begin the conversion at this, the greatest pueblo in the land. That effort was soon aborted; when the news reached Pecos of the killing of Zaldívar at Acoma, the friar quickly decamped. The Indians expressed their opinion of Christianity by wrecking the church and using the beams to build a kiva.

The friars assigned to Pecos were especially zealous. One friar, who took up residence at Pecos in 1620, launched a full assault on idolatry, invading the kivas and smashing many stone "idols." Archeological excavations of Pecos three hundred years later would uncover many of these smashed effigies, put back together and buried in specially prepared shrines and hiding places—even behind the church altar. Like the Zunis, the Pecos remained silently, but stubbornly, pagan.

Pecos required a church befitting its great size and importance. In the 1620s, the construction of a great church began, Nuestra Señora de los Angeles de los Pecos. The dimensions of the church were truly enormous: the nave was approximately 40 feet wide—the span of the longest timbers that could be obtained—and 145 feet long. The side walls were from 8 to 10 feet thick, with 15-foot-thick buttresses; and the back wall stood a staggering 22 feet thick. The church had six great towers. The job required 300,000 adobe bricks weighing 40 pounds apiece, with the final structure containing 6,000 tons of dried mud. During its lifetime it was the largest single structure in America.

Historians, reading early Spanish accounts, assumed the dimensions of the church must have been grossly exaggerated; no church in New Mexico had ever been close to that size. It wasn't until 1967 that an archeologist, working underneath the ruins of the smaller eighteenth-century church and *convento*, discovered its massive foundations.

The church may have been magnificent, but its construction—by forced labor—did more harm than good to the padre's cause. Far from being a monument to God, to most of the Pecos Indians the church was a living symbol of their humiliation and defeat. While they went through the motions, their pagan hearts remained unchanged. The governor they elected annually at the Spaniards' insistence was only a figurehead; the real head man was a pagan priest. The friars could lash the "idolaters" at the mission whipping post, but mere physical pain could not root out the centuries-old beliefs of a proud people.

The Plains Apaches continued to trade at Pecos, setting up their *tipis* in the meadows outside the walls of Pecos. Here the Apaches would trade hides, jerked and powdered meat, tallow, and sometimes captives of the "Quivira nation" (most likely Wichitas or Pawnees) for corn, squash, beans, cotton blankets, pottery, and turquoise from the Cerrillos Hills.

In 1641 an ominous trend shows up in the historical record: a census in that year counted only 1,189 Indians living in Pecos. If true, this would represent a shocking decline of 40 percent in only twenty years. Such a decline could only be the result of an epidemic disease brought to the New World by the Spanish.

The *encomienda* system imposed by the Spaniards put a great strain on the resources of Pecos. A severe drought in the mid-1650s caused crops to fail, and other epidemics swept through. The Indians naturally began to wonder: What kind of god *was* this god of the Spaniards? A god who brought nothing but starvation and disease?

When the pueblos revolted against the Spanish in 1680, the Pecos (along with the Indians of San Cristóbal, San Lázaro, and Galisteo) were at the forefront. They led the first assault against the Palace of the Governors in Santa Fe. As they approached the town, the Indians sent a message to the Spaniards holed up in the *casas reales*—a very revealing message indeed: "The rebels were saying," an Indian scout relayed to the Spanish governor, "that now God and Holy Mary, whom the Spaniards worshipped, had died, but the god they obeyed had never died, and therefore they would take possession of the kingdom, having done with all the Spaniards."

During the Pueblo Revolt, the great church at Pecos—the pride of the Franciscan fathers in New Mexico—was leveled. Destroying the largest single structure on the continent was no mean feat. Archeological excavations give a clear picture of what happened. First they piled brush on the roof and set fire to it. The roof went up in a spectacular gout of flame. The church itself turned into a furnace, with a firestorm draft sucking air in from the clerestory windows and blowing ashes out the door. As soon as the structure had cooled the Indians clambered over the walls, gouging and chiseling out thousands of adobe bricks and hurling them to the ground, until the great mission of Nuestra Señora de los Angeles de los Pecos was reduced to a mound of dirt. They defiantly built a kiva in the ruins of the *convento* using adobes from the church.

The leader of the rebellion, El Popé, made a triumphal tour of the pueblos, to make sure that all surviving images of Christ, the saints, crosses, and other Christian items were destroyed. The great bronze church bells of Pecos were broken and dumped into an arroyo. Popé's followers tore up the vestments and fouled the chalices with human excrement. Any couple married by a Christian priest was separated. He forbade the speaking of Spanish and even demanded the burning of all seeds introduced by the Spanish.* They made masks of the devil and danced around praising the Satan the Spanish so feared.

Indirect evidence from Pecos, however, indicates that not all the Indians were enthusiastic rebels. A rift appears to have developed at Pecos between pro-Spanish and anti-Spanish factions. This rift would widen in the next century, with fatal consequences; Pecos would become a house divided, eaten from within.

After Vargas retook Santa Fe in 1692 he went to Pecos to gain its submission. He found the pueblo deserted. After scouring the hills he was able to capture some Pecos Indians, who said a group of younger men in the pueblo had forced the evacuation of everyone.

Vargas knew that Pecos, as the largest and (still) most powerful pueblo in New Mexico, held the balance of power. The Pecos had to be brought back into the Spanish fold.

Vargas did something quite unexpected. Instead of torching the pueblo and imprisoning his captives (the usual response), he tried a different tack. He freed all the prisoners and left the pueblo and its fields untouched. By this "judicious and prudent resolution" (as he would later describe it) he undercut the anti-Spanish faction at the pueblo, led by the younger men, who had staked their credibility on the assumption that the Spanish were utterly treacherous.

Three weeks later he sent two runners to the Pecos Indians: Now, he said, he was returning. He had proven his good intentions. They must now prove theirs.

The strategy worked. Reassured that they would be treated fairly,

---

*This order was the only one widely disobeyed.

the Pecos Indians were waiting for him with a large cross and arches of evergreen branches. Vargas triumphantly entered the pueblo, raised the banner three times, shouting "Long live the king, our lord! God save him! Charles the Second! King of the Spains, of all this new world, and of the kingdom and provinces of New Mexico, and of these subjects newly won and conquered!" The soldiers cheered and threw their hats in the air, and the friars fell to their knees, intoning the *Te Deum Laudamus*. Then, one by one, the Pecos Indians, kneeling, were absolved of their apostasy and sins, and several hundred children were baptized.

Through all this, however, a violently anti-Spanish faction simmered at Pecos.

A new friar was installed at Pecos in 1694. He counted 736 living Indians; more had died from epidemics and many of the anti-Spanish faction had left, angered by the pueblo's docile submission. A new church was soon built on the rubble of the earlier one. While still massive, it was only about half the size of the earlier one; there were only half as many Pecos.

By 1696, Pecos stood on the verge of a civil war. The leaders of the anti-Spanish faction had been murdered by the pro-Spanish governor and his supporters. As the eighteenth century progressed, the pueblo stood deeply divided and terribly weakened, a shell of its former self.

And then came the Comanches.

Pecos's strength and a major source of its wealth had been trade. With the coming of the Spaniards, the annual fall trade fair at Pecos had become even more important; the Spanish became their best customers, particularly in the slave market. Pecos's strategic position at the gateway to the Great Plains now became a sword that cut both ways: when the pueblo was strong it was a tremendous asset; but in the pueblo's divided, weakened state, it became a terrible liability. Had the Pecos remained united, they might have been able to repel the Comanche threat that seemed to materialize out of nowhere. In their divided state they didn't have a chance.

The Comanches, who had migrated into New Mexico from the basin-and-range country west of the Rockies,* quickly put an end to the lucrative trade at Pecos. The Comanches' first victims were the Jicarilla Apaches, one of the prime trading partners of the Pecos. As Jicarillas fled from the advancing Comanches, trade shifted from Pecos northward to Taos.

---

*They probably gravitated toward New Mexico by the opportunity to acquire horses.

Much worse was to come. In 1746 a tremendous attack on Pecos occurred. A vast command of mounted Comanches appeared in the eastern opening of the valley and galloped around the pueblo, yelling and whooping. They fought in an absolute frenzy and tried to fire the church with a burning log. They came not merely to plunder but to destroy: for a mysterious reason that historians have never been able to discover, some of the Comanche leaders bore a deep and terrible grudge against Pecos.

During the attack a dozen Pecos Indians were killed and the Comanches departed with all the pueblo's horses. A Spanish force from Santa Fe pursued them into the plains and fought a pitched battle, where, to the great surprise and outrage of the Spaniards, the Comanches killed nine soldiers and a civilian—a shocking loss. To underscore their success the Comanches hit Galisteo Pueblo two weeks later.

In 1748 a second major massed attack on Pecos occurred, with the Comanches swooping down "with such an outcry and screaming" that it was terrifying to behold. They were repulsed only with the help of a large, hastily assembled Spanish force.

The Comanches continued to strike at Pecos, often in small parties that would lie in wait outside the pueblo and ambush a few unprotected Indians herding livestock or going to and from their fields. In one six-year period alone, at least 15 percent of the population of Pecos were killed "a manos de los Comanches." The Pecos Indians were forced to abandon their irrigated fields along the Pecos River and had to rely on dry-farming areas closer to the pueblo. Droughts then caused terrible famines, exacerbated by the absence of trade.

Meanwhile another terrible enemy continued to assail Pecos: European diseases. Every ten or fifteen years an epidemic would sweep through the pueblo—smallpox, measles, "fevers"—each one carrying off another 10 percent of the population.

A friar passing through Pecos in 1776 wrote: "these miserable wretches are tossed about like a ball in the hands of fortune. . . . Today these poor people are in puribus, fugitives from their homes, absent from their families, selling those trifles they once bought to make themselves decent." He counted only twelve "sorry nags" and twenty cattle belonging to the pueblo. In the two centuries since Coronado had entered the valley, the Pecos Indians had been reduced from great wealth and power to abject poverty and disease.

Various censuses at Pecos show the decline:

1540	2,000 more or less, with 500 warriors
1620s:	"More than 2,000 souls"
1641:	1,189
1694:	736
1730:	521
1750:	449
1776:	269

In 1779 things looked like they might turn around for the pueblo. A new and capable governor of New Mexico, Juan Bautista de Anza, defeated the Comanches in a battle in southern Colorado, killing the Comanches' able leader, Green Horn. Once Anza proved his ability to humble the Comanches, according to Comanche custom he became a man they could surrender to without dishonor, which they promptly did.

The triumphant peace treaty was concluded at Pecos. A great crowd of Comanche chiefs attended, splendidly dressed in feathers, beads, and buckskins. When Anza arrived, one shocked chronicler noted, the Comanches "manifest[ed] their great joy and delight" by rubbing their faces against Anza's.

The treaty called for several items: a lasting peace; permission for the Comanches to move closer to Santa Fe; access to Santa Fe through the Pecos gateway; free trade at Pecos Pueblo; and an alliance with the Spaniards against hostile Apaches.

A huge trade fair at Pecos sealed the peace, with a quantity of goods exchanging hands to the great profit of all. Things started looking up for Pecos. Trade would resume, they could return to their fields, and life would become normal once again.

But in 1794 an insignificant event occurred that would have grave consequences for Pecos. A small land grant was given to one Lorenzo Márquez, Spanish citizen of Santa Fe, at a place known as El Vado, "The Ford," about twenty miles eastward down the Pecos River. El Vado was the traditional crossing point for traders going to and from Pecos Pueblo.

El Vado, soon renamed San Miguel del Vado, quickly preempted Pecos Pueblo as the major trading site. It was closer to the plains, and, with the Comanche threat gone, more convenient than Pecos. A small but brisk trade began at El Vado.

Unbeknownst to everyone, a far more fabulous trade was about to begin, with an entirely new trading partner. With it, San Miguel del Vado would prosper greatly; for Pecos, it would be the final end.

In November of 1821, a ragged pack train appeared at San Miguel del Vado, led by an American calling himself Becknell. He had come from Missouri with goods to trade, and he was hoping that with the recent Mexican independence, trade between the United States and New Mexico would be allowed. (Spain had previously outlawed direct trade between the United States and its Mexican colony.)

Becknell passed through the astonished town and continued up through the valley of the Pecos, past Pecos Pueblo, and on to Santa Fe. There Becknell was welcomed by the governor and allowed to spread his wares in the Plaza. He made a tremendous killing. A few months later another *Americano* arrived, a fellow named Thomas James. James had been relieved of most of his goods by Comanches, but he was in good spirits and kept an account of his travels.

"We stopped," James wrote, "at the ancient Indian village of Peccas about fifteen miles from San Miguel. . . . I was informed by the Spaniards and Indians that this town [is]. . .of unknown antiquity, and stood there in considerable splendor in the time of the Conquerors. . . . The inhabitants, who were all Indians, treated us with great kindness and hospitality."

To Becknell, James, and the thousands who would follow down what became known as the Santa Fe Trail, San Miguel del Vado, as the easternmost town on the New Mexico frontier, would be the customs station and entry point to New Mexico. It would boom and prosper, while Pecos would become a mere relic, a curiosity on the trail. As the Santa Fe Trail opened, the population of Pecos stood at 58, while the population of San Miguel had soared to 735. There was nothing left for Pecos, no hope of a trade revival at all, nothing that would check the pueblo's drastic decline.

The last baptism at Pecos was recorded on June 2, 1828, and the last burial supervised by a friar on December 3. Then the great book of baptisms, marriages, and burials at the Pecos mission church closed, never to open again.

But the Pecos Indians hung on. In 1829 there were still thirty or forty, inhabiting a small cluster of rooms amidst the apocalyptic wreck of their civilization. One of the Santa Fe traders, Josiah Gregg, recalled those last days.

"Even as late as ten years ago," he wrote in 1844, "the traveller would oftimes perceive but a solitary Indian, a woman, or a child, standing here and there like so many statues upon the roofs of their houses, with their eyes fixed on the eastern horizon, or leaning against a wall or a fence, listlessly gazing at the passing stranger; while at other times not a soul was to be seen in any direction, and the sepulchral silence of the place was only disturbed by the occasional barking of a dog, or the cackling of hens."

A few years later, in 1839, a journalist passing through wrote about the town he called "Pecus": "The houses are now all unroofed, and the walls crumbling. The church alone yet stands nearly entire, and in it now resides a man bent nearly double with age, and his long silken hair, white with the snow of ninety winters. . . . The writer with a single American companion once passed a night in this old church, entertained by the old man with a supper of hot porridge made of pounded corn and goat's milk, which we drank with a shell spoon from a bowl of wood, sitting upon the ground at the foot of the ruined altar by the light of a few dimly burning sticks of pine."

Between 1834 and 1839 the Pecos Indians had vanished altogether.

It would be another century before researchers would piece together a picture of the end. Sometime in 1838, the last seventeen Pecos Indians had carefully packed up their sacred and ceremonial belongings and a few small possessions. They asked the local Hispanics to take care of the church, and walked out of the pueblo and down the Santa Fe Trail, heading west. Thirty miles past Santa Fe they sought refuge at Jemez Pueblo, the only other pueblo that spoke Towa, their language.*

As the empty city crumbled to ruin, Santa Fe Trail travelers, passing by its great walls, told and retold many fantastical tales about Pecos, about Moctezuma's eternal fire still tended there in secret, about a giant snake that lived in an underground kiva, and many others. Fortune hunters looted the ruin for relics, and many of the graves in the church were opened, the bones scattered about. Sometime around 1858 a squatter named Kozlowski, who operated a small ranch nearby, pulled down the old carved beams of the church to make corrals and stables.

Two decades later the Santa Fe Railway Company completed its tracks through the Pecos River Valley. The Santa Fe Trail went into

---

*Every year since, in August, the Jemez descendants of these Pecos survivors journey to the ruins of the pueblo and hold their annual feast day celebrations.

history. Travelers on the train could now see the ruins from the comfort of a railway car; to ensure the tourist did not miss the site, the railroad company erected a billboard proclaiming it as one of the great wonders of the Southwest.

The last Pecos Indian, Cota, also called Augustín Pecos, died in 1919. A photograph taken of him in 1902 shows him standing against a cracked adobe wall at Jemez Pueblo, with long black hair and soiled white shirt. He moved slightly when the picture was taken, but one can still see a fleeting, blurry sadness in his eyes.

36

⚫ ⧖ ⚫

As we rode the last four miles toward Pecos, a dark ledge
of cloud advanced out of the Sangre de Cristo Mountains, its shadow
moving up and down through the foothills like a stalking beast.

We rode into the asphalt parking lot of the Pecos National Monument and unloaded our packhorses in front of the visitor's center.
Anthony stayed at the trailer while Walter and I trotted up to the ruins
on a service road.

The old pueblo was now a cluster of mounds covered with grass,
looking like a body under a blanket. The approaching storm sent winds
pressing through the grass, sweeping along ripples of lighter and darker
green as the seed heads angled and turned. In front of us stood the
eroded adobe walls of the eighteenth-century church, surrounded by
the ruins of the *convento;* and there, in the middle of the ruins, the kiva
that the Pecos Indians had defiantly built following the Pueblo Revolt
of 1680.

An asphalt walking path started at the parking lot and wound among
the old walls, each point of interest marked with a numbered sign.
Behind the ruins the hills rolled away, mounting upward to the eleven-
thousand-foot peaks of the Sangre de Cristo Mountains, now black in
shadowy raincloud.

As we arrived, we surprised a group of tourists in pastel pantsuits and straw hats, who converged on us and began taking pictures. As they clustered about us, talking excitedly, I had the feeling of a sleeper awakening from a long dream; these people seemed surreal, like ghosts.

Who are you? they wanted to know.

We explained how we had ridden a thousand miles.

Did you stay in hotels? someone asked.

We rode across the desert, camping as we went, we said.

And what about water?

We drank whatever we found.

But how could that be? There's no water in the desert!

Sure there is, I said, and emptied the brown muddy water from my canteen.

The crowd backed up.

You drank *that*?

I took a sip.

Oh my God, someone said.

Shuffling about, the crowd took more pictures.

Where're you from originally? someone yelled.

Boston, I said.

Hey, I'm from Massachusetts, someone else called out.

I tipped my hat.

The wind picked up and blew a cloud of dust through the ruins, followed by a scattering of heavy drops. The crowd, clutching their hats and cameras, went running for their cars. We sat astride our horses among the ruins, in silence, with the rain drumming on our heads, trickling down on our shirts, running down the steaming flanks of our horses.

◦ ⊐⊏ ◦

The sound of the rain rose like a whisper from the eroded walls of the pueblo, and the smell of wet earth and turf root blossomed around us. It was here, at the height of Pecos's power, that Alvarado had been greeted with flutes and drums; and it was here, at the bitter end of its existence, that the first Americans had rumbled past in Murphy freighter wagons, staring in mute surprise at the silent red walls rising from the grassy ridge.

Once the very life of the Southwest revolved around Pecos; it stood at the center of the world. Now it lay at the darkening edges of history. I felt here, more than anywhere else, the silent dumb amoral weight of history. This was the endpoint of our journey, but it was an ending of another sort. There was a kind of death squatting here among the ruins of Pecos, a death worse than mere loss of life. This was the death of a people, a culture, an entire world.

Pedro de Castañeda, at the very end of his story, wrote: "This will suffice to bring our narrative to a close. In all other matters, may the Almighty Lord of all things, God Omnipotent, who knows how and when these lands are to be discovered, determine for whom this good fortune is preserved."

Four and a half centuries later, we now know for whom this good fortune was preserved. And this was *extraordinary* good fortune indeed: on the wreckage of the past we Americans have built the wealthiest and most powerful nation ever seen on the face of the earth. Let us be clear: our wealth derives from our land and our natural resources, both of which we took from the native inhabitants of this continent. We would have nothing had we not destroyed what came before.

As I watched the walls of the ancient pueblo, once the greatest city in America, slowly darken in the rain, I had to wonder again: Was the death of *this* world worth the birth of our world? Is this fabulous America of the late twentieth century truly a better world? Is it, in the end, the world we wanted to create?

Although our trip had taken place within the borders of America, we had seen the ghosts of the alien worlds that preceded this one. We had seen worlds glimpsed behind rubbled walls, worlds chiseled in petroglyphs and lying scattered among broken potsherds; worlds blowing across vast deserts; worlds buried in memories of cattle, dust, and grass; worlds laughing in dry saltbushes, muttering and whispering to us from a thousand dry arroyos; worlds flying up into the night sky at that moment between sleeping and waking.

In peeling back these layers of history, what had we found? Surely not the culmination of Manifest Destiny, the triumph of American history. We had uncovered instead layer after layer of loss. The great myth of the West is that there had been a winning of it. No, there had been no winning here, not here at Pecos, or Hawikuh, or in the Sulphur Spring Valley: we had heard no triumph in the words of Cheppie Natan, or Dee Wear, or Robert Lewis, or Rod of the Salt River. The Indians, the cowboys, the wilderness, the great cattle drives, the unfenced range, the homestead families, all these things have been lost, not won. In 950 miles of hard travel, Walter and I had witnessed the last dying glimmer of that peculiar, eccentric, ugly, violent, free, and beautiful place known as the American West. As the Old West had died a new one was born; and Pecos along with everything else had been incinerated in the great *nuée ardente* of the modern world.

We Americans believe, just as the Spanish believed before us, that in the conquering of this country we would have the freedom to make it anew—the freedom to create whatever world we wished. Now I understood that the process was, in truth, an inexorable one, in which many individual choices summed up to a stochastic inevitability. The Indian had to be contained, shunted to reservations. The trails had to be replaced by wagon roads, which in turn had to be buried under the coke beds of railroads and the asphalt of interstates. The mountains had to be mined and the forests cut. The beefmasters and brangus cattle had to replace the Texas longhorn, and the range had to be fenced. The prairies had to be busted and planted and the rivers diverted. The Power brothers and their ilk had to go. It could not have happened any other way; it was as deterministic a process as the earth orbiting the sun. The West had to be lost.

I remembered what the old Navajo shepherd, Cheppie Natan, had said: that the earth finally gave up. For him and his people the earth *had* given up. But our earth—the earth of the Anglo-American—was just being born. This was the earth of highways and automobiles and great cities of reinforced concrete; the earth of massive integrated economies involving the movement of ten-digit wealth at the speed of light through copper wire; the earth of the Doors and *E.T.* and the New York Philharmonic Orchestra; the earth of plastic and plutonium, of LSD and Vietnam and the fearful sudden light on the sands of Alamogordo. It is an earth where one can fly from one end to the other in less time than it once took to travel from Pecos Pueblo to San Cristóbal Pueblo.

This is not a bad world we have created, at least for most of us Americans. In the course of history there are few societies that have provided so much freedom and prosperity to so many people. And yet the very creation of late-twentieth-century America required the obliteration of almost all that came before it, nineteenth-century America included. Like the cities of Troy, each world was built on the tumbled and burned walls of its predecessor. We built our great new world on top of the ruins of the worlds of Cheppie Natan and Coronado and Cota and the Power brothers and a million others, swept away by the chill winds of history, vanishing unloved and forgotten into a darkness that will have no end.

In the spring of 1540 the people of Pecos stood at the very apex of power. As they looked about their domain, they could see no one who could possibly challenge them, no one as strong or wealthy as they. Their trading network must have seemed as if it embraced the farthest corners of the world: the great rubbish heap at Pecos tells us that they traded goods with tribes thousands of miles distant—spanning an area as extensive as the Roman Empire. The Pecos Indians lived in one of the largest and most beautiful structures in the Southwest; they wore splendid clothing and ate from elegant pottery; their pueblo was filled with the sounds of flutes, drums, and singing; their storehouses overflowed with food; and their gods were benevolent. They and their pueblo cousins possessed technology as advanced as any on the continent. They were feared throughout the land. Nor had they grown soft with their success: they had been tested sixteen years before, when they withstood a massive assault by the Teyas Indians. These Indians had laid waste the large Galisteo Basin pueblos; and yet they could not take Pecos.

What more powerful enemy could they face? Who could possibly touch them?

And then, in the summer of 1540, rumors from the west brought news of a strange people, bold men, whose bodies glittered like the sun, men who rode on the backs of monstrous creatures and carried sticks that spat fire and thunder. So the Pecos Indians held a council and sent a delegation, led by Bigotes, to investigate, to make peace, to forge an alliance.

The rest, as they say, is history.

Today Pecos lies across the landscape like an autopsied corpse, excavated, tagged, macadamed over, each point of interest marked with a numbered sign. It has parking lots and a modern visitor's center and an audiovisual presentation narrated by a famous actress, replete with thunderous drumbeats, Indians silhouetted against the setting sun, and portents of doom. Pecos is a place now populated with pink-cheeked ladies pressing cameras to their faces and men in tasseled loafers flipping through the brochure looking for the correct number.

Pecos was a victim not of some epic convulsion in war and fire, but of the creeping smolder of history. It ended its life without even a whimper, passing away as imperceptibly as a coal losing its internal heat. When the last seventeen Pecos Indians packed up and left, there was no one to see them go, no one to record the event.

This is the way other civilizations have died—Egypt, ancient Greece, the Roman Empire—and it may be our end yet.

Sixteen years after the death of Pecos, another Indian in another land, a chief of the Dwamish tribe, spoke the following to the governor of Washington Territory: "It matters little where we pass the remnant of our days. They will not be many. A few more moons; a few more winters—and not one of the descendants of the mighty hosts that once moved over this broad land or lived in happy homes, protected by the Great Spirit, will remain to mourn over the graves of a people once more powerful and hopeful than yours. But why should I mourn at the untimely fate of my people? Tribe follows tribe, and nation follows nation, like the waves of the sea. It is the order of nature, and regret is useless. Your time of decay may be distant, but it will surely come, for even the White Man whose God walked and talked with him as friend with friend, cannot be exempt from the common destiny. We may be brothers after all. We will see. . . .

"When the. . .memory of my tribe shall have become a myth among the White Men, these shores will swarm with the invisible dead of my tribe, and when your children's children think themselves alone in the field, the store, the shop, upon the highway, or in the silence of the pathless woods, they will not be alone. At night when the streets of your cities and villages are silent and you think them deserted, they will throng with the returning hosts that once filled and still love this beautiful land. The White Man will never be alone.

"Let him be just and deal kindly with my people, for the dead are not powerless. Dead, did I say? There is no death, only a change of worlds."

ACKNOWLEDGMENTS

I would like to thank a number of people. First, and most important, I owe more than I can express to Christine Gibbons and Selene. My great thanks to Michael Korda, for his encouragement and his thoughtful, expert editing; thanks also to Scott Steward. I'd like to thank my brother Dick, who was supportive when I was having trouble with an ex-publisher. My very deep appreciation to my grandfather, Jerome Preston Sr., who contributed financially to this book; to my grandmother Dorothy McCann; and to my aunt and uncle, Anna and Bob Taggart, for buying us Bobby. I'd like to thank my father, Jerome Preston Jr., for instilling in me a love of the wilderness, and my mother, Dorothy Preston, for giving me a curiosity about the peculiar, the fantastic, and the bizarre.

I would like to thank Professor Carroll Riley, scholar and Coronado expert, for invaluable help and for vetting the manuscript. I certainly owe a great debt to *Smithsonian* magazine, and in particular Jack Wiley, Senior Editor, and Don Moser, Editor, who offered invaluable financial and moral support. I'd also like to express my appreciation to my agent, Marian Young; and my deep thanks to Janet Bailey for her advice and help. I would like to acknowledge here the Cottonwood Gulch Foundation and Prairie Trek, which first introduced me to the Southwest. Thanks also to Lincoln Child, who read portions of the book and gave me excellent advice; to Tim Maxwell; to Peggy Nicoll for keeping my house in order while I was gone; to Stuart Woods; to the Santa Fe Public Library (in particular the interlibrary loan department); to Firestone Library at Princeton University; to the New York Public Library; to the New Mexico State Library; to the Photographic Archives of the Museum of New Mexico; to the Arizona Historical Society; and to the Laboratory of Anthropology. I would also like to thank my English 151 students at Princeton for reading an abominable first draft of an early chapter and offering good advice. The Bureau of Land Management officials for the San Pedro Riparian Area were true professionals and helpful beyond the call of duty, as were Wendell Peacock and the other BLM officials of the Arizona State Office. I'd like to thank Olivia Tsosie of Oñate Spanish Barbs for her research on the history of the Barbary horse, and Roeliff Annon, also of Oñate, for loaning me his prize brood mare, Engwahela (sorry we brought her back pregnant). Thanks to Dick Pool; Norma Carnett; Dick Walther; Dusty Nussbaum; Jim Butler; Bill Bennet; and the other ranchers, cowboys, and rural people of Arizona and New Mexico who were so kind to us on our journey. There is still a strong ethic of hospitality in the West—particularly in rural Arizona—that I'm afraid much of the rest of America has lost.

I have not thanked here most of those who actually appear in the book, as their contributions will be obvious to the reader. I will make one exception: Walter Nelson. Walter was, simply, the best friend and traveling companion I could possibly have expected. This journey would not have been possible without Walter's extraordinary courage, skill, and fine companionship.

Finally, I would like to reserve some of my most profound thanks to the American Indian people who helped us along the way. Without exception, the Indian people of New Mexico welcomed us with great kindness and hospitality. First, I would like to thank Governor Robert Lewis of Zuni Pueblo, as well as Rita Lorenzo and the rest of the Zuni Tribal Council for giving us permission to cross Zuni lands and for their warm reception. I wish some of our national leaders had the wisdom of Governor Lewis. I would also like to thank Edward Wemytewa and Arlene Bobelu at Zuni for their tremendous kindness and help; Edmund Ladd for his interest; and Lincoln Harker for his hospitality. I would like to thank Martha Garcia, President of the Ramah Navajo Chapter of the Navajo Nation, and Michael Gross and Eric Treisman, lawyers formerly with Dinebeiina Nahiilna Be Agaditahe, Inc. My deep appreciation to Governor Ray Histia and the Tribal Council of Acoma, who gave us permission to cross Acoma lands; deep thanks also to Gilbert Ortiz and Danny Sanchez of Acoma. I am also indebted to Governor Robert Velasquez of San Felipe Pueblo, Governor Delfino Begay of Laguna Pueblo, Governor Verna J. Williamson of Isleta Pueblo, Governor Joe Lujan of Sandia Pueblo, Governor Clyde Leon of Santa Ana Pueblo, and last but certainly not least, Governor Ernie Lovato, Lieutenant Governor Moquino, and Benny Atencio, all of Santo Domingo Pueblo, who gave us a welcome and treated us to a meal that I will remember for the rest of my life.

BIBLIOGRAPHY

This is a selected bibliography of the easily accessible sources.

Adair, John, and Dorothea C. Leighton. *People of the Middle Place*. New Haven: HRAF Press, 1966.

Adams, Alexander B. *Geronimo: A Biography*. New York: Putnam, 1971.

Arizona Historical Review.

Bandelier, Adolph. *The Gilded Man*. Chicago: Rio Grande Press, 1962.

Barnes, Will C. *Arizona Place Names*. Tucson: University of Arizona Press, 1988.

Bolton, Herbert E. *Coronado: Knight of Pueblos and Plains*. Albuquerque: University of New Mexico Press, 1964.

Cather, Willa. *Death Comes for the Archbishop*. New York: Knopf, 1948.

Cooke, Philip St. George. *The Conquest of New Mexico and California: An Historical and Personal Narrative*. New York: G.P. Putnams, 1878.

Covey, Cyclone, trans. and ed. *Cabeza de Vaca's Adventures in the Unknown Interior of America*. Albuquerque: University of New Mexico Press, 1988.

Crampton, C. Gregory. *The Zunis of Cibola*. Salt Lake City: University of Utah Press, 1977.

Cushing, Frank Hamilton. *Zuni: Selected Writings of Frank Hamilton Cushing*. Edited and with an Introduction by Jesse Green. Lincoln: University of Nebraska Press, 1979.

Dary, David. *Cowboy Culture: A Saga of Five Centuries*. New York: Knopf, 1981.

Dedera, Don. *A Little War of Our Own*. Flagstaff: Northland Press, 1988.

Dobie, J. Frank. *A Vaquero of the Brush Country*. Austin: University of Texas Press, 1957.

Ellison, Glenn R. "Slim." *Cowboys Under the Mogollon Rim*. Tucson: University of Arizona Press, 1968.

El Morro National Monument. *El Morro Trails*. Tucson: Southwest Parks and Monuments Association, 1990.

Faulk, Odie P. *Tombstone: Myth and Reality*. New York: Oxford University Press, 1972.

Faulk, Odie P. *Geronimo Campaign*. New York: Oxford University Press, 1969.

Ferguson, T.J., and E. Richard Hart. *A Zuni Atlas*. Norman: University of Oklahoma Press, 1990.

Flint, Timothy, ed. *The Personal Narrative of James Ohio Pattie of Kentucky.* New York: Lippincott, 1962.

Frazier, Kendrick. *People of Chaco.* New York: W. W. Norton, 1986.

Goodman, James M. *The Navajo Atlas.* Norman: University of Oklahoma Press, 1982.

Guam, Alvina, trans. *The Zunis: Self Portrayals.* By the Zuni people.

Hammond, George P., ed. *Coronado on the Turquoise Trail.* Coronado Cuarto Centennial Publications, 1540–1940. Albuquerque: University of New Mexico Press, 1949.

Hammond, George P., and Agapito Rey, eds. *Narratives of the Coronado Expedition 1540–1542.* Albuquerque: University of New Mexico Press, 1940.

Hodge, Frederick Webb. *The Excavation of Hawikuh.* New York: Museum of the American Indian, Heye Foundation, 1966.

Hodge, Frederick Webb. *History of Hawikuh,* Vol. 1. Los Angeles: The Los Angeles Museum, 1937.

Hoig, Stan. *The Humor of the American Cowboy.* Lincoln: University of Nebraska Press, 1970.

Horgan, Paul. *Conquistadors in North American History.* New York: Farrar Straus and Co., 1963.

Horgan, Paul. *Great River: The Rio Grande in North American History.* Austin: Texas Monthly Press, 1984.

Horgan, Paul. *Lamy of Santa Fe.* Farrar, Straus and Giroux, 1975.

Kessell, John L. *Kiva, Cross, and Crown: The Pecos Indians and New Mexico 1540–1840.* Albuquerque: University of New Mexico Press, 1987.

Krutch, Joseph Wood. *The Desert Year.* New York: Viking, 1966.

Lockwood, Frank C. *Pioneer Portraits.* Tucson: University of Arizona Press, 1968.

Mangum, Neil C. *In the Land of the Frozen Fires: A History of Occupation in El Malpais Country.* Santa Fe: Southwest Cultural Resources Center, 1990.

Minge, Ward Alan. *Acoma: Pueblo in the Sky.* Albuquerque: University of New Mexico Press, 1976.

New Mexico magazine.

New Mexico Historical Review.

Ortiz, Alfonso, ed. *Handbook of North American Indians,* Vol. 10: *Southwest.* Washington, D.C.: Smithsonian, 1983.

Power, Tom, with John Whitlatch. *Shoot-out at Dawn: An Arizona Tragedy.* Phoenix: Phoenix Books, 1981.

Sedgwick, Mrs. William T. *Acoma: The Sky City: A Study in Pueblo-Indian History and Civilization.* Cambridge: Harvard University Press, 1926.

Simpson, James H. *Navajo Expedition.* Norman: University of Oklahoma Press, 1964.

Stevenson, Matilda Coxe. *The Zuni Indians.* 23rd Annual Report of the Bureau of Ethnology, 1901–1902. Washington, D.C.: Bureau of Ethnology, 1902.

Tedlock, Dennis. *Finding the Center: Narrative Poetry of the Zuni Indians.* New York: Dial Press, 1972.

Terrell, John Upton. *The Navajos.* New York: Perennial Library, 1970.

Thrapp, Dan L. *The Conquest of Apacheria.* Norman: University of Oklahoma Press, 1967.

Turner, Frederick W. III. *The Portable North American Indian Reader.* New York: Penguin, 1973.

Udall, Stewart L. *To the Inland Empire.* New York: Doubleday, 1987.

Underhill, Ruth M. *The Navajos.* Norman: University of Oklahoma Press, 1956.

Wagoner, Jay J. *Arizona Territory, 1863–1912: A Political History.* Tucson: University of Arizona Press, 1970.

Wagoner, Jay J. *Early Arizona: Prehistory to Civil War.* Tucson: University of Arizona Press, 1975.

Walker, Henry, and Don Bufkin. *Historical Atlas of Arizona.* Norman: University of Oklahoma, 1979.

Winship, George Parker, ed. and trans. *The Journey of Coronado.* New York: Allerton Book Co., 1922.

Worthington, H. M. *Prehistoric Indians of the Southwest.* Denver: The Denver Museum of Natural History, 1969.

INDEX